Preaching the Gospels without Blaming the Jews

A Lectionary Commentary

Ronald J. Allen
Clark M. Williamson

Westminster John Knox Press
LOUISVILLE • LONDON

© 2004 Ronald J. Allen and Clark M. Williamson

Book design by Sharon Adams
Cover design by designpointinc.com

First edition
Published by Westminster John Knox Press
Louisville, Kentucky

This book is printed on acid-free paper that meets the American National Standards Institute Z39.48 standard. ∞

PRINTED IN THE UNITED STATES OF AMERICA

04 05 06 07 08 09 10 11 12 13—10 9 8 7 6 5 4 3 2 1

Library of Congress Cataloging-in-Publication Data
Allen, Ronald J. (Ronald James), 1949–
    Preaching the Gospels without blaming the Jews / Ronald J. Allen, Clark M.
    Williamson.
        p. cm.
    Includes bibliographical references (p.).
    ISBN 0-664-22763-5
    1. Bible. N.T. Gospels—Homiletical use.   2. Christianity and antisemitism.
    3. Preaching.   4. Lectionary preaching.   I. Williamson, Clark M.   II. Title.

    BS2555.54.A44   2004
    251'.6—dc22   2004043034

In honor of Rabbi Dennis Sasso and Rabbi Sandy Sasso,
companions and guides in the rapprochement
of synagogue and church.

Contents

Year C

Preface

A preacher picking up this book might ask, "Do I really need another commentary on the lectionary?" This volume, however, has a specific interest—prompted by the Jewish-Christian conversations that began in the wake of the Holocaust and have intensified in the last thirty years—that is not found in the same way in other lectionary helps, or even in the formal scholarly commentaries on the Bible. These conversations, in conjunction with scholarly insights, call attention to two elements that are in tension with one another. On the one hand, the four Gospels are thoroughly steeped in Judaism. One cannot understand any one of the Gospels without a grasp of Jewish people, practices, scriptures, and institutions. Indeed, we should see these documents as part of a first-century Jewish discussion regarding what it means to be faithfully Jewish. On the other hand, the Gospels reflect tension and even animosity between the communities of the Gospel writers and other Jewish groups. Indeed, the Gospel writers often portray some Jewish people, practices, and institutions in caricature so as to justify the separation that grew in the latter years of the first century C.E. between traditional Jewish groups and the communities of Mark, Matthew, Luke, and John.

In this commentary, we explore the two poles of this tension: (1) We call attention to ways in which the lections are continuous with the theology, values, and practices of Judaism, and (2) we reflect critically on points at which the lections caricature Jewish people, practices, and institutions. We explain these polemics in terms of their first-century settings, but criticize them historically and theologically. We suggest ways that preachers can help congregations move beyond these contentious themes to a greater sense of kinship and shared mission with Judaism.

The title of this book, *Preaching the Gospels without Blaming the Jews*, deals with an issue raised long ago by Jules Isaac in his book *The Teaching of Contempt*.[1] Isaac shows that through much of its history, Christianity has taught Christians to hold Judaism and its adherents in contempt. It did this in many ways, the most important of which was in how it interpreted the Scriptures from week to week in preaching and teaching the Christian faith. The arrogance that the church developed toward Judaism is one of the great tragedies of history. Our book joins many others influenced by the growing dialogue between synagogue and church to call the church to teach respect for Judaism. Teaching Christian congregations to respect Judaism is no mere matter of political correctness. It is a theological necessity. The God of Israel is also the God of the church and loves both church and synagogue with unconditional love and wills for all people to live together in love. We pray that this book will help transform Christian contempt into respect by helping preachers and congregations discover the thoroughly Jewish character of the beginnings of our movement.

Introduction

Since the Second Vatican Council in the 1960s, scholars have been exploring the profound and diverse relationships between Jesus and Paul and their Jewish contexts, and between the Gospels and the canonical writings of Israel and the literature of Second Temple Judaism. Teams of Jewish and Christian scholars have worked on the task of translating the Scriptures, and Jewish as well as Christian scholars have written extensively on Jesus and Paul.[1] Theologians and homileticians have written books on Christian preaching and anti-Judaism, describing how eliminating anti-Judaism from biblical exegesis and Christian thinking frees up the gospel to be preached and heard.[2]

This commentary on the Gospel passages in the Revised Common Lectionary seeks to move the concern for relations between Jews and Christians directly into the sermon preparation process.[3] Doing so means that a number of things will happen in this commentary that depart from what you would typically expect to find.

Possible Anti-Jewish Ways of Misreading

First, we alert the reader to possible anti-Jewish ways of misreading the text and misinterpreting the Christian faith. The most frequent way in which anti-Judaism remains alive in the teaching and preaching of the church is through the negative images of Jews and Judaism that occur throughout the Gospels. Sociological studies suggest that the more Christians believe deprecatory things about the Jews in Jesus' time, the more they tend to project those negative images on Jews today.[4] It is the effect of the Gospels on contemporary hearers and readers with which we are primarily concerned, not the intent of the Gospel writers. The Gospel writers were engaged with other kinds of Jews in controversy over the proper course that faith in God should take following such traumatic events as the destruction of the temple. Matthew, for example, knew about the efforts at the Pharisaic academy in Javneh to recreate Jewish faith around the study of Torah, the life of the synagogue, and the figure of the rabbi—a new religion coming into being at the same time as the early church. When Matthew says that "the scribes and the Pharisees sit on Moses' seat," he shows that he respects the teaching authority of the Pharisees but is frustrated by the fact that they do not recognize God's work through Jesus, which he can attribute only to their "hypocrisy," of which he relentlessly accuses them (see Matt. 23). From this attack, Christians have often concluded that Jews or Jewish leaders are essentially hypocritical.

To take another example, Luke, in his story of the woman who anoints Jesus' feet (Luke 7:36–8:3), places the event in the house of Simon the Pharisee in the village of Nain, in Galilee, whereas the earlier version in Mark identified this same Simon as "the leper" (Mark 14:3) and placed the event in Bethany, in Judea. In Luke's Gospel, the Pharisee is the foil in the story. He denounces the woman as a "sinner," and Jesus then explains forgiveness to the Pharisee. In Mark's version, there was no Pharisee and the woman was not a sinner. Luke's version can tempt us to think that Jewish leaders obviously had nasty attitudes toward women and clearly needed to have forgiveness explained to them. We have no way to know if Pharisees held foul attitudes toward women, and we do have reason to think that they understood forgiveness quite as well as Jesus did.[5] Because the Pharisee is added to a story from which he is absent in the earlier version, the negative image of him arguably reflects later conflicts read back into the life of Jesus. Indeed, the further removed the Gospels are in time from Jesus, the more they introduce hostility into the story. We should not let the sectarian conflicts of the late first century continue to be the breeding ground for anti-Judaism in our time.

Calling Attention to Biblical and Jewish Themes

Second, we surface Jewish and biblical themes, resonances, and echoes in the text. Christian scholars for a long time used the criterion of dissimilarity to establish what the historical Jesus "really" said. This criterion means that if a saying is dissimilar to the Judaisms of Jesus' time or before and to the interests of the later church, Jesus probably said it. The problem is that no saying that the Gospels attribute to Jesus falls outside the range of the Judaisms of his time or before. The deeper problem is that it gives us a non-Jewish Jesus, a person with no history and no context, and who made no impact.

The more we know about the Judaisms of Jesus' time and before, the more we see Jesus as a Jew of his time and place. We are told that he wore fringes on his clothes (Mark 6:56), that a woman was healed when she touched the fringe of his garment (Luke 8:44//Matt. 9:20), as were men. The word *kraspedon* refers to the border of a garment, the tassels worn in accordance with the Torah (Num. 15:38–39; Deut. 22:12) to remind wearers of the commandments, to get them into the heart. Pharisees wore such fringes (Matt. 23:5). The Gospels tell us that Jesus dressed as befits a pious Jew.

They also tell us that when he taught, he sat down to do so, whether in a boat, on a hillside, or in a synagogue (Mark 4:1; 9:35; Matt. 5:1; 13:2; 26:55; Luke 4:20; 5:3; John 6:3; 8:2). What they do not say, because they assumed that their readers knew it, is that when he did so, he was characteristically Jewish. Matthew was making a point that we can easily miss— that Jewish teachers sat to teach (Matt. 23:2). In the Israel Museum in Jerusalem there is a "seat of Moses," sculpted from basalt and brought from the synagogue in Capernaum, where Luke tells us that Jesus sat to teach. The seat, from the century after Jesus, vividly reminds us that the Gospels tell us of the ministry of a first-century Galilean Jew.

Wearing fringes, sitting down to teach: these are small things. Small things add up to a big picture of Jesus as a faithful, first-century Galilean Jew. We intend to make this larger picture clear.

Roman Occupation as Social Context

Third, we point out the Roman context when it throws helpful light on a passage. What did it mean to ordinary people that they lived in the Roman Empire?[6] What was the view "from below"? To live in a land like Israel, subject to Roman domination and occupation (Judea was occupied, Galilee dominated), was to be subject to Roman taxation, exaction, and expropriation. The major goal was to protect the status and well-being of the upper classes in Rome and the upper classes (through whom Rome ruled) in the rest of the empire. The army fought wars on the border of the empire, shifting conflict away from the city of Rome for its safety.

Economically, there was "an abysmal gulf separating the upper from the lower classes."[7] The top one percent of the population—the rulers and governors—owned half the land, causing widespread homelessness and unemployment since land was the basis of the agrarian economy. Priests owned about 15 percent of the land. Generals and bureaucrats were below priests in the economy, and under them were merchants, who could develop some affluence and power. Below them were the peasant farmers, who had to hand over about two-thirds of their crops for the support of the upper classes. They eked out a level of existence that marginally allowed them to survive, to support their family and animals, and to save enough seed for next year's crop. We hear the story of the prodigal son and the dividing of the family farm differently when we know this context.

Beneath the peasant farmers, who after all still had some land, were those who practiced skilled trades—tailors and carpenters, for example. These came from those whom John Dominic Crossan terms the "unnecessary" members of the peasant class, who had no land and could not farm. The "expendables," again Crossan's term, were last on the economic pecking order.[8] Slaves, prostitutes, beggars, bandits, hustlers, and day laborers brought up the rear. Little wonder that Jesus could address himself to "you who hunger now."

The Gospels tell us that Jesus was born in the days of Herod the Great, king of Judea (Luke 1:5; Matt. 2:1). What they do not mention is that when Herod died, social and political revolution occurred all over the land. Judas in Galilee, Simon in Perea, and Athronges in Judea were the popular military leaders. They came from the impoverished classes, from which armed revolt broke out in Galilee, Judea, and Perea. It took three Roman legions and additional troops to quell the outbreak, at the end of which two thousand rebels were crucified outside Jerusalem. Note that crucifixion was a Roman punishment meted out to put down rebellion or the hint of rebellion against the empire.

Social and political turmoil were the order of the day. Roman soldiers would be quickly recalled from the frontier in Syria or from Caesarea Maritima to restore order swiftly and brutally. Taxation, exaction, and expropriation of money, land, and crops brought about unemployment, homelessness, and destitution. Social banditry flourished, as it often does in depressed economies, and local bandits could become folk heroes and even emerge as military threats to the empire. Bandits figure strikingly in the Gospels' story of Jesus; he is crucified between two of them. Tensions ran high between different classes of people. Rich and poor, Essenes and temple priests, violent rebels (Zealots) and those with other strategies for survival could be at each other's throats.

The people Israel, marginalized on the edge of the Roman Empire, did not need Jesus to tell them to love one another. They knew that. They did not need him to tutor them in how to get their sins forgiven. God had taken care of that in quite adequate ways, as anyone with a Sunday school grasp of Scripture should know. They were in captivity in their own land, in exile at home, under occupation by a series of emperors who claimed to be God. They wanted and needed bread and freedom, not hot air.

Imagine yourself at Passover walking with Jesus from Bethany to the temple in Jerusalem. Approaching the city from the east, you cross over the Mount of Olives and see the temple in all its glory. Your purpose is to celebrate Passover, to reenact God's liberation of the people from slavery in Egypt. Yet the reality in which you live makes the feast ring hollow. Standing next to the temple and overlooking it is the Fortress Antonia, where the Roman Tenth Legion was stationed. On the battlements of the fortress and atop the walls surrounding the temple courtyard stand the Roman soldiers. You are in bondage in the land of promised freedom, in exile at home, celebrating liberation under Roman auspices. Caesar is the new Pharaoh. We cannot depoliticize the meaning of Passover for Jews then (or now), nor can we depoliticize the ministry of Jesus and have any understanding at all of him, his message, and his ministry.

Would God once again redeem the people from oppression? Would someone come, some kind of messiah, announcing that only God is sovereign, thus denying that Caesar is either God or king? "It was to this people that Jesus came. It was these whispers that he heard in the lanes and backyards of his native Galilee. It was these aspirations that he found himself called to fulfill."[9]

Relations between Jesus and Other Jewish Groups

Fourth, we deal frequently with relations between Jesus and various Jewish groups at the time, notably Sadducees and Pharisees, most often with the latter. Scribes were not a distinct group. Rather, priests and Levites frequently served as scribes, carrying out a variety of activities: "copying texts, drawing up legal documents, and serving as experts on the law."[10] In the fifth century B.C.E., Ezra provides the first example of a priest who was also a "scribe skilled in the law of Moses" (Ezra 7:6). Later, Nehemiah appointed "Zadok the scribe" as a treasurer (Neh. 13:13); Zadok's name indicates that he was also priest. Scribes were scholarly writers (the word scribe derives from the Latin *scribo*, "to write") and were essential to many aspects of society. Scribes were associated with every religious movement within the multifarious Judaism of the time; the early churches had scribes who produced the Gospels (see Matt. 13:52). Paul used a scribe to write his letters (Gal. 6:11), and Qumran had a scriptorium where scribes wrote and copied the scriptures of Israel and those peculiar to the Essenes. Hence, when the Gospels refer pejoratively to "the scribes," we should be aware, at the least, that they hardly include all scribes.

Sadducees were aristocrats, comprised as well of aristocratic priests (or "chief priests"), who gave their allegiance to biblical law (*torah*, or "way" of life), that is, to the written Torah and not to the comparatively new oral Torah, the Pharisaic innovations on the written Torah. Sadducees, unlike Pharisees, denied the resurrection of the body (Mark 12:18; Matt. 22:23; Luke 20:27). Indications are that they tended to look upon cooperation with Roman rule as the most prudent and least destructive course for Israel (John 11:49–50).

Ordinary priests and Levites served in the temple on a rotational basis and were particularly needed at such times as Passover, when hordes of pilgrims from around the Mediterranean crowded into the temple. While there was only one high priest at a time, chief priests were from the priestly families that lived in Jerusalem west of the temple and had daily access to the holiest site in Israel. The high priest served at the pleasure of the Roman procurator and had to receive his vestments—without which he could not enter the Holy of Holies on the Day of Atonement— from the procurator. Whereas the Gospels depict Pilate as manipulated by Caiaphas, the high priest, the reality was otherwise.

Of the various Jewish groups mentioned in this commentary, we pay most attention to the role of the Pharisees because it is from the Pharisees that rabbinic Judaism arose in the late first century of the Common Era. Rabbinic Judaism and Christianity were new religions that developed alongside each other; they are the fraternal twins of Israelite faith. It is helpful to state early on what we do and do not know about the Pharisees. We have three sources that tell us about the Pharisees. One is Josephus, the late-first-century historian, who claimed to have been a Pharisee; he characterized them as one of the "philosophies" in Judaism at the time, alongside such others as the Essenes. Another is the later rabbinic tradition—the Mishnah, the oral Torah written down by the middle of the second century, and the Talmud, which includes the Mishnah and commentary upon it. A third, of course, is the Gospels. These three sources present different pictures, pictures that tell us as much about those who drew them as they do about the Pharisees.

The apostle Paul is the only Pharisee whose writings we have, but he tells us nothing about the Pharisees other than that he himself was one

(Phil. 3:5). In his silence lies one remarkable fact: Paul never mentions Pharisees in a negative way, nor does he ever characterize them as opponents. Aside from his one statement that he had been a Pharisee, every New Testament mention of Pharisees is in the Gospels and the book of Acts. By the time the Gospels were written, a generation or two after Paul, derogatory references to the Pharisees abounded. They are called "hypocrites," "blind guides," "blind fools," "blind men," and "whitewashed tombs." Clearly these disparaging references reflect a later situation and its conflicts. The churches were becoming more Gentile and increasingly differentiated from other forms of Judaism. Also, they were becoming more alienated from their Gentile neighbors who found their refusal of idolatry offensive. As Luke Timothy Johnson shows, vindictive, name-calling language, typical of many ancient groups, found its way into the Gospels.[11] Such name-calling is hardly coherent with an approach to life that says that we should forgive "seventy-seven" times (Matt. 18:22). Lest we allow the charge of hypocrisy to be leveled against Jesus for not practicing what he preached, we need to be suspicious of this name-calling directed at Pharisees as well as anyone else.

What we most likely know about the Pharisees is, first, that there were not many of them. Josephus claims that there were only a few Sadducees, more than four thousand Essenes, and about six thousand Pharisees (*Antiquities* 13.298; 18.20; 17.42). Josephus's numbers are hardly exact, but they do let us know that a very small percentage of the people belonged to these groups, at most a few thousand out of a total Jewish population at the time of several million people, most of whom did not live in the land of Israel but in the Dispersion. There were two groups of Pharisees in Jerusalem, followers of the more conservative Shammai and of the more liberal Hillel. Pharisees were lay people, not ordained and not religious professionals. Acts tells us that Paul made his living as a tentmaker (Acts 18:3). Whereas scribes were members of a learned profession, Pharisees were not. Their chief interests, according to the Gospels, the rabbis, and Josephus, were in making the family dinner table as holy as the altar in the temple.[12] In saying that the family table can be as holy as the temple altar, the Jew "is acting as if every Israelite were a priest."[13] This is the Pharisaic version of the priesthood of all believers.

Eating their food in ritual purity, living by the oral Torah (the Pharisaic contemporizing of the written Torah), a stress on prayer and sanctification, living life in the way that God disclosed in the commandments—this is characteristic of the Pharisees. Mark thought that all Jews followed Pharisaic practices such as the washing of hands (Mark 7:3), actually required by the Torah only of priests in the temple. In truth, centuries would pass before the heirs of the Pharisees would develop Judaism into a somewhat well-defined cohesion (although it always remained diverse). In the time of Jesus, Pharisees were in control of nothing, which is mutely testified to by their comparative absence from the passion narratives.

They were concerned about purity laws. As to the nature of these laws, there is considerable dispute among scholars. Some contend that they created a world with sharp social boundaries, separating rich from poor, pure from impure, sinners from the righteous, Jew from Gentile, and male from female.[14] They then contrast Jesus' "politics of compassion" to this segregating "politics of purity." The problem with this view is that it follows the long-established habit of making Jesus look good by making other Jews of his time look bad. For example, Hegel compared Jesus favorably with the "dung heap" of Judaism, and Harnack thought Jesus looked quite good against the background of the "rubbish" that was Pharisaism.[15] This is both inaccurate about the Pharisees and at best a left-handed compliment to Jesus. It is what Rosemary Ruether has called the "left hand of Christology": "Is it possible to say 'Jesus is Messiah' without, implicitly or explicitly, saying at the same time 'and the Jews be damned'?"[16]

Other scholars deny that the purity laws had the kind of socially divisive effect that Marcus Borg claims, that this claim is a caricature of the purity laws.[17] Claiming that every table is the Lord's table and every Israelite a priest is not necessarily bad. Leviticus makes it plain that the remedy for most impurities was to let the sun set or to take a bath (see, for example, Lev. 22:2–7). The sun sets on the pure and the impure. If I am impure, I cannot go to the temple; that is the one thing that we know being impure made it impossible to do. So I go ahead of time, take a bath, let the sun set, and enter. "Wash and wait" was the way to handle most impurities. Nor was the purity system one of social apartheid, of sharp social segregation. As Sanders puts it, "Not only did the Pharisees not achieve apartheid, they seem not to have wished it: there is not a word about social isolation in any of the ancient literature. . . . [E]arly Christians would have criticized their Pharisaic opponents for this kind of exclusivism, but Christian literature is as silent on such topics as is Josephus."[18]

It is also important to remember that purity or impurity had nothing to do with sin or morality; it was a strictly ritual category. When the Rabbis later discussed which books of Scripture were to be in the canon, they used the expression "defile the hands" to designate those books regarded as Holy Scripture, for example: "All Holy Scriptures defile the hands.

Song of Songs and Ecclesiastes defile the hands" (*m. Yadayim* 3:5).* To this day, Jews do not touch the Torah scroll because it is too holy to touch. Yet accidentally touching it would not make one a sinner or immoral, simply ritually impure.

Jews remember Antiochus IV, who called himself "Epiphanes" (God made manifest) and who killed about 80,000 Jews who revolted against his rule (2 Macc. 5:11–14). Antiochus decided to stamp out Judaism, so he had the temple polluted, banned the Sabbath and festivals, and had two mothers who brought their children to the temple for circumcision thrown over the city walls (2 Macc. 6). Following his decree, his soldiers "put to death the women who had their children circumcised, and their families and those who circumcised them; and they hung the infants from their mothers' necks" (1 Macc. 1:60–61).

Imagine that your grandparents had been killed because they had your uncles and aunts baptized as infants, or had refused to, insisting on believers' baptism. This would not lead you to think highly of the wisdom or morality of the killers. Such an imaginary scenario can lead us to sympathy for the actual victims of Antiochus and to some understanding of why there might have been a stronger emphasis on the purity laws among Pharisees in Jesus' time.

Unfortunately, the polarizing, vindictive rhetoric typical of first-century sectarian groups finds its place in the Gospels.[19] It is at odds with the teachings of love of the neighbor, love of the enemy, and forgiveness piled upon forgiveness that are found in those same Gospels. Preaching should be liberated from the inherited biases and ideologies of the tradition, including those that found their way into the Scriptures.

The good news conferred in Jesus Christ is that God freely loves each one of us, as though each of us is the apple of God's eye. God loves everybody else, even Pharisees, in precisely the same way—enough even to die for them and us. Let us allow that love to shape our preaching.

The Mutual Love of God and Israel

The typical Christian view of the "law" is a major roadblock to better understanding of Jews and Judaism. All too often Christians regard the law as incapable of justifying human beings and/or burdensome at

*Herbert Danby, *The Mishnah: Translated from the Hebrew with Introduction and Brief Explanatory Notes* (Oxford: Clarendon Press, 1933). All Mishnah quotes are from Danby unless otherwise noted.

best—external, legalistic, and arid at worst. That Jews do not think of law as justifying them—God having already taken care of that in the election of the people Israel—and that they respond with exuberant joy to Torah comes as a surprise to many Christians, particularly those who have never shared in the joy of worship in a synagogue.

Deuteronomy 10 asks of the people Israel, "What does the Lord your God require of you? Only this: to hold YHWH your God in awe, to walk in all his paths, to love him, and to serve YHWH your God with all your heart and all your soul" (v. 12). It adds, "It was only for your forebears that YHWH took a passion, loving them, so that he chose their descendants after them—you!—from among all the peoples, as it is today" (v. 15).[20]

At the heart of the covenant, as Deuteronomy makes clear, is a mutual love, an unfathomable love of YHWH for Israel and the responsive love of Israel for YHWH, who gives Israel the *mitzvoth* (commandments) for Israel's well-being (Deut. 10:13). "It is not a question of law *or* love," says Jon Levenson, "but law conceived in love, love expressed in law."[21] Divine grace takes the initiative: what YHWH has done for Israel, the indicative, precedes what Israel is to do in return—love YHWH with all its heart and soul. And it does that by loving the neighbor and the stranger in ways informed by YHWH's *mitzvoth*.

"Law" is an inadequate translation of *torah*; "way of life" is much better and reminds us also that the early church referred to itself as people "of the Way" (Acts 9:2). *Simhat Torah*, the rejoicing of the Torah, is observed annually in the synagogue when the entire Torah has been read and the cycle begins again. To experience the joy in the synagogue on *Simhat Torah*, the procession of the Torah through the congregation, people kissing their prayer books or shawls and touching the cover of the Torah is to experience Ps. 119 being acted out and set to music and, sometimes, dance. Understanding this would contribute immensely to Christian understanding of Judaism.

Two Sets of Oral Tradition

In this commentary, we will frequently point out the relationships, usually parallels, between sayings that the Gospels attribute to Jesus and sayings that such rabbinic sources as the Mishnah and Talmud attribute to the sages and rabbis of Judaism. We do not know that the sayings from Jewish sources go back to the time of Jesus or before. Neither do we know that the sayings attributed to Jesus (or which sayings attributed to Jesus) go back to the time of Jesus (which is one reason why the "historical Jesus" researchers present us with so many different reconstructions of Jesus). On the other hand, it is the case that sayings from an oral tradition obviously antedate their being written and preserved in documents. What we are concerned to show is that the same attitudes came to expression in both the early church and early Judaism, the two movements of faith that drew upon the scriptures of biblical Israel.

How to Name Early Churches

One matter continues to vex us: How do we speak in a concise and accurate way of the earliest communities to whom the four Gospels were written? It is anachronistic to call them "Christians" or "the Christian community," for to do so is to risk implying a much greater degree of separation between Judaism and this early movement than was the case in the first century. Indeed, the term "Christian" does not even occur in the Gospels, and while it is found in Acts 11:26, Luke does not typically use it to refer to the early community of people who believed that God had acted and was continuing to move toward the final manifestation of the eschatological redemption of the world through the life, death, and resurrection of Jesus. Our reservations are not as strong when it comes to using the term "church" to refer to the communities to whom the Gospels were written. While this designation does not occur in Mark or John, Matthew does use it for the evangelist's community (Matt. 16:18; 18:15, 17, 21), and Luke uses it nineteen times in the book of Acts. We find, however, that contemporary people too easily understand the first century in terms of today's almost entirely Gentile Christian communities, who have no relationship at all with Judaism. Even the slightly more satisfactory terms "Christian Judaism" and "Christian Jewish people" evoke a greater sense of institutional separation than pertained in the ancient world.

We are convinced that the communities to whom the four Gospels were written still very much considered themselves Jewish. The Gospels are concerned with how God's purpose, the bringing in of the reign of God, was unfolding in history; they are not concerned with starting an entirely new religion. They saw the Jesus movement as the right way forward for the people Israel. We might think of the relationship of Sunday school classes in a congregation today as a rough analogy. The different classes are part of the same parish, but each has its own identity and characteristics. The classes even come into conflict with one another over the use of space or how best to understand the purpose of the congregation. However, they share a common core of identity.

Each Gospel seeks to show how the divine work through Jesus Christ and the community that witnesses to that work are a part of the forward movement of Judaism. To be sure, the four communities to whom the Gospels were written manifested various degrees of tension with some Jewish people in antiquity, as well as sometimes with each other. Such tensions are perhaps best understood as a kind of sibling rivalry; family fights are sometimes quite painful, and the community to whom the Fourth Gospel was written was likely excommunicated from the synagogue. However, as the following commentary makes abundantly clear, the Gospel writers repeatedly stress that the early communities are faithful expressions of Judaism. Their distinctive mark is their belief that God was acting through Jesus Christ to signal the eschatological consummation of history and the full manifestation of the realm of God.

We confess that we do not have a fully satisfactory set of terms for the earliest communities. In this book, we experiment with calling them the Matthean community, the Markan community, the Lukan community, and the Johannine community. From time to time we use other designations, but these are the ones that are most common. We ask the reader to remember that these groups did not understand themselves to be jettisoning Judaism, but were seeking to show how their twist on Judaism was faithful to God's self-disclosure to Israel and in Jesus Christ.

Year A

First Sunday of Advent/Year A

Matthew 24:36–44

"Have you hoped for the salvation of Israel?" That is, did you believe in the coming of the Messiah? According to the *Shabbat* tractate (31a) of the Babylonian Talmud, this is one of the questions that will be asked at the final judgment. Matthew, in this parable of watchfulness, does two things. On one hand, he urges his community to hold fast to its deeply Jewish faith in the coming of the Son of Man or Messiah, identified as Jesus. On the other, he works hard to disclaim an exact time frame in which Jesus will return and to focus the community on faithful discipleship now.

Matthew inherited from Mark the saying of Jesus, "Truly I tell you, this generation will not pass away until all these things have taken place" (24:34; Mark 13:30). Mark had balanced this claim with a disclaimer: "But about that day or hour no one knows, neither the angels in heaven, nor the Son, but only the Father" (13:32). The need for the disclaimer indicates that already by the time of Mark's Gospel, some had begun to question whether "all these things" had indeed taken place before the generation that heard them had passed away.

By the late first or early second century, this question had become sharper. Second Peter comments to its readers, "First of all you must understand this, that in the last days scoffers will come, scoffing and indulging their own lusts and saying, 'Where is the promise of his coming? For ever since our ancestors died, all things continue as they were from the beginning of creation!'" (2 Pet. 3:3–4). We should not be misled by the fact that 2 Peter tries to dismiss a perfectly reasonable question by attacking the character of those who ask it.

Jewish hope in the coming of the Messiah was a hope for the days of the Messiah or for what we Christians call the reign or kingdom of God. Paul the apostle, two generations after the resurrection of Jesus, said: "I consider that the sufferings of this present time are not worth comparing with the glory about to be revealed to us," that is, in the second coming or parousia of Jesus (Rom. 8:18). Mark, Matthew, and Paul are all aware in characteristically Jewish ways that a messiah without the days of the messiah—a proclaimer of God's rule without the reality of God's rule—is meaningless. So they hold to "an already and a not yet" understanding of the advent of the Messiah/Son of Man. Swords have not yet been beaten into plowshares nor spears into pruning hooks. Poverty, oppression, and starvation stalk the world. No wonder that Paul talked of the "sufferings of this present time." No wonder that Matthew further played down the notion that the Son of Man would come during "this generation."

Characteristically, apocalyptic literature claimed to know the precise time of the end of this present age (not of the world!) of sin and oppression. The book of Daniel clearly illustrates this. Pointing up the problem raised by such detailed claims is the fact that Dan. 7–12 has to provide four timetables, each longer than the one before. Often in the news we see an apocalyptic group claiming that the end is coming soon. Shortly afterward, we see them returning to their day jobs and recalculating dates. Instead, Matthew would have us understand the relationship between eschatology and ethics differently: We are always to act as though preparing for the arrival of the rule of God, the advent of justice, peace, love, and economic sufficiency.

What it means to be ready is to affirm, with the people Israel, "I believe with perfect faith in the Messiah's coming. And even if he be delayed, I will await him."

Second Sunday of Advent/Year A

Matthew 3:1–12

Only Matthew tells us that John the Baptist preached in the wilderness "of Judea." The location is important, for this is the area in which the Qumran community lived a life of ritual purity, of copying the Scriptures, and of waiting for the days of the Messiah. This is the area through which, in the biblical story, Joshua and the people Israel entered the land of promise. John quotes Isaiah, "The voice of one crying out in the wilderness: Prepare the way of the Lord, make his paths straight" (Matt. 3:3, quoting Isa. 40:3). The Qumran community cited this same verse to justify its life of messianic expectancy by the Dead Sea.

We do not know John's relationship to the Qumran community. He and they were active in the same area, committed to the coming rule of God, and made ritual use of water. Matthew depicts John as an observant Jew who ate a diet of "locusts and wild honey," locusts were designated clean and honey was never designated unclean (Lev. 11:22). John kept kosher in the desert, modeling for Matthew's community the keeping of "the least of the commandments."

All movements in Palestinian Judaism at the time were, in part, ways of responding to Roman occupation. The land of Israel, the *eretz yisrael*, was supposed to be the place in which the Israel of God was free to worship and serve the God of Israel. For this purpose they had been liberated from oppression, and to redeem this purpose they had been brought back from slavery in exile. Yet when they went to the temple to celebrate the Passover of liberation from oppression, they were carefully monitored by the troops of the Roman Tenth Legion stationed next door in the Fortress Antonia. They celebrated freedom under the watchful eyes of an occupying army. In exile in their own land, many found the contradiction unbearable.

Qumran's response was to withdraw to the desert and await the coming of the teaching and priestly messiahs. John's response was to proclaim "the rule of heaven." (Consistent with Jewish piety, John and Jesus avoid using the name of God in Matthew.) John baptized in the river Jordan, symbolically reenacting Joshua's entry into the promised land (Josh. 3). Antiochus IV Epiphanes and the Caesars, various foreign kings ruling over Israel, claimed to be God. In the face of such a claim, to proclaim that only God is sovereign was to issue a strong denial, to make a counterclaim, and no leader of a realm of God movement had a long career. Herod Antipas had John executed because, so Josephus tells us, he feared that John might stir up sedition (Josephus, *Antiquities* 18.118–19). Pilate asks in every Gospel whether Jesus claims to be "king of the Jews."

Matthew's Gospel adds the Pharisees and scribes to this scene (they are present in it in no other Gospel) so that John can engage in name-calling: "You brood of vipers! Who warned you to flee from the wrath to come?" The name-calling, particularly with regard to Pharisees, will intensify. "Hypocrites" is Matthew's favorite epithet. Doubly unfortunate, this results in a garbled message (as in "judge not, hypocrite!") and can occasion anti-Jewish preaching, which was not Matthew's intent. We should resist engaging in his polemic and instead examine how we polemicize today.

Scribes were scholars who could write; Matthew explicitly refers to scribes in the community (13:52). Pharisees were lay people who believed that the family table was as much the table of the Lord as the altar in the temple. They developed ways for ordinary people to live by the Torah in everyday life. By Matthew's time they had emerged as leaders of synagogue Judaism after the destruction of the temple. After the Holocaust, preachers should speak against Matthew's polemic.

Third Sunday of Advent/Year A

Matthew 11:2–11

This passage deals with two topics: John the Baptist's question to Jesus (11:2–6) and Jesus' statements about John (11:7–11). Matthew repeats his earlier statement (see 4:12) that John was "in prison" when he sent disciples to Jesus to ask: "Are you the one who is to come, or are we to wait for another?" In the parallel passage, Luke does not mention that John is in prison, perhaps because he had already made this clear and expected his readers to remember it (Luke 3:18). Ever since the exodus from Egypt, redemption in biblical faith included liberating the enslaved. Jesus' first sermon in Nazareth, according to Luke, quoted Isaiah: "He has sent me to proclaim release to the captives and recovery of sight to the blind" (Luke 4:18).

Several difficulties plague the interpretation of 11:2–6. John's question strikes us as odd following Matthew's story of Jesus' baptism (3:13–17). The "one who is to come" is not a messianic title. There was no messianic "check list" against which to measure whether the deeds of any figure, including Jesus, qualified. Messiah means "anointed one." Messianic expectations were pluralistic; anointed priests, teachers, prophets, and kings were anticipated.[1] There was no single, agreed-upon idea of the Messiah in this or any other time of Jewish history. Would the Messiah, in the manner of God in Isaiah 35, open the eyes of the blind and unstop the ears of the deaf? Or would the Messiah, in the manner of the *Psalms of Solomon* (17–18), be a military leader who would renew Israel as a nation-state and free it of Roman occupation and oppression? Nor was there any one view of the Messiah among the early followers of Jesus. Yet whatever "the one who is to come" means, Jesus is that one.

Jesus' response to John's question is ambiguous. He does not say yes or no, simply "tell John what you hear and see: the blind receive their sight, the lame walk. . . ." Is he saying that in spite of the fact that these are not the deeds expected of the Messiah, nonetheless he is? Several "mighty men of deeds" were famous among Galilean Jews in those days; Honi the drawer of circles and Hanina ben Dosa were well known for exorcisms, restoring of sight, and healing of withered limbs. Yet none of them is the Messiah.

The second topic is Jesus' view of John the Baptist: "Among those born of women no one has arisen greater than John the Baptist; yet the least in the kingdom of heaven is greater than he." Such a one is the messenger sent to prepare the way before Jesus. Immediately following this reading, Jesus refers to John as Elijah (11:14). Only later in Judaism was Elijah thought of as the forerunner of the Messiah. The least in the kingdom is greater than John probably because for John the kingdom, although near (3:1–6) was still future. With Jesus the kingdom is both already here and yet future. We can live now in the power of the future because God's rule is "among us." John, in Matthew's view, pointed ahead of himself to the one who was to come. Jesus, in contrast, led a movement that was both a present actualization of God's ruling and a foretaste of its possibilities.

Those who would base faith on proof will be frustrated by this passage. Those who find the majestic love of God "hidden" by the ordinary things in, through, and under which it is present, will not. The truth of faith is not obvious in the manner of a biblical spectacular.

Fourth Sunday of Advent/Year A

Matthew 1:18–25

Unfortunately, the lectionary drops Matthew's genealogy of Jesus from its Advent readings, thus missing several major theological points that Matthew wants to register with his readers. Only in the context of the genealogies do either Matthew or Luke's stories of Jesus' virginal conception make theological sense. Matthew traces Jesus' lineage to David and Abraham to make clear that the one whom we confess to be the Messiah is also heir to David and the Davidic covenant. The point is that Jesus takes shape in the Scriptures and the people of Israel. When the later church rejected Marcion's denial of the Old Testament as Scripture, it said: If you want to understand Jesus, you have to understand the scriptures of Israel in which he took shape. Jesus would not be possible apart from the covenant between the God of Israel and the Israel of God. He is, therefore, a gift to the church from the Israel of God and from the God of Israel.

Five women are listed in Jesus' genealogy: Tamar, Rahab, Ruth, the wife of Uriah (Bathsheba), and Mary. Two, Rahab and Ruth, were Gentiles, and the wife of Uriah may have been. Three were regarded as sexually immoral, possibly preparing the reader for similar questions about Mary. Theological points here are: that God delivers blessing through and for both Jews and Gentiles; that God works through human sin and error and not with perfect people (which is fortunate, since none exist); and that women as well as men are crucial to the working out of God's providence.

The theological point about the birth of Jesus from a virgin (*parthenos*) is that Jesus Christ is a gift to us from the God of Israel (as well as from the Israel of God), that his name "Jesus" means "YHWH saves" (*Joshua* in Hebrew, *Yeshu* or *Yeshua* in Aramaic). The God who created the world for blessing also redeems it; the God who saved Israel in the Exodus is here at work again. Salvation is a gift from the God of Israel, not a human achievement; that's the theological point of the virgin birth. Yet this gift comes not from God alone, because God is "God with us," Emmanuel, as God has always been with Israel.

The relationship of Mary and Joseph has to be understood in the context of the times. Mary and Joseph had been "engaged." Engagement was the first part of the marriage process; Mary is Joseph's wife, he is her husband. The question for Joseph was whether to continue with the next step, which involved bringing Mary into Joseph's father's home. Marriages at the time were within the extended family. The discovery that Mary was pregnant—an impossible secret to keep in close-knit village life—presented Joseph with his problem. He considered divorcing her (by dismissal) "quietly," which would spare her being ostracized. An angel ("messenger") of God explains matters to Joseph: God's spirit is active here in human salvation. Another theological note: Jesus does not save us from the wrath of God. Rather, the name "Jesus" reminds us that "YHWH saves."

All this happens "to fulfill" a prophetic declaration. The fulfillment quotations in Matthew (e.g., 2:5; 3:3; 4:14; 8:17; 12:17; 13:14) stress the dialectic between the new and the old. Matthew's is a new interpretation of Jewish faith taking shape across the street from synagogue Judaism, also a new interpretation of faith that was taking shape at the same time. Neither was biblical religion. Neither one is "empty" as compared to the other, nor fulfills the other. Each stands solely on the ground of God's justifying grace.

Christmas Day/Years A, B, and C

John 1:1–14

Contemporary Christians typically hear this text (especially 1:1c: "the Word was God"; Greek: *ho logos ēn theos*) as a statement of the incarnation of God in Jesus, and even of the doctrine of the Trinity. Another impression emerges, however, when we hear the text with the ears of a first-century Johannine Jewish community, a group that shared the theological worldview of Hellenistic Judaism represented by such diverse sources as Wisdom of Solomon, Ben Sira (writer of Sirach, or Ecclesiasticus), and Philo of Alexandria.

Monotheism was a fundamental tenet of first-century Judaism. The Jewish community insisted that God alone is God. The Christology of the Fourth Gospel honors this monotheism while stressing the intimate relationship between God and Jesus.

Jesus is "the Word" (*ho logos*) who was present with God before the creation of the world ("in the beginning"). In Gen. 1, God created by the word. For many first-century Jews, the *logos* was intimately related to wisdom (*sophia*), one of God's closest agents. God worked with wisdom to make and sustain the world, to reveal the divine purposes, and to redeem (Prov. 8:22–31). Wisdom is "all-powerful . . . [pervading and penetrating] all things . . . a breath of the power of God . . . a reflection of eternal light, a spotless mirror of the working of God . . . [who] can do all things . . . she renews all things . . . against wisdom, evil does not prevail" (Wis. 7:22–30; see also Sir. 24:1–22). Some Jewish authors of John's time considered *logos* and *sophia* to be the same. The *logos*, however, is above all things except God. The *logos* serves God.

A technical point of grammar comes into play. In an expression such as "the Word was God" in which the verb (*ēn*) is from the family "to be," the Greek language ordinarily uses the article "the" (*ho*) with a noun to indicate the subject (*ho logos*) and a noun without an article for the predicate (*theos*), which would be rendered "and the Word was God." However, Philo of Alexandria points out a specialized exception to this usage. Many Hellenistic Jewish people reserve the article with the noun for God (*ho theos*) while using *theos* without the article to refer to the *logos* and to other beings who are closely related to God but are not God (Philo, *On Dreams* 1.229–30). From the perspective of Philo, 1:1c would be translated colloquially: "The word was of divine origin and force."

The Johannine Jesus clearly acknowledges that he is *sent* from God (e.g., John 3:34; 5:19–30; 7:14–18; 12:44–50; 20:21). When Jesus says,

"The Father and I are one" (10:30), he does not mean that they are the same entity but rather that they share the same purpose and mission, as when I say of my relationship with a colleague on an important issue, "She and I are one." This use of oneness is even more evident when the Johannine Jesus prays that the disciples "may be one as we [Jesus and God] are one" (17:11, 22). The congregation is one in spirit and community even while the various members are still individuals.

Jesus thus functions in the Johannine community much as wisdom and the *logos* in Judaism: as agent of creation, as revealing God, as power that redeems. These themes are evident in the description of Jesus in John 1:1–5: present in the beginning with God, all things come into being through him (creation), source and sustainer of life, light in the world. In this respect, the Christology of the Fourth Gospel is thoroughly Jewish.

For commentary on Luke 2:1–20, please see Christmas Day/Year C.

First Sunday after Christmas Day/Year A

Matthew 2:13–23

The Matthean congregation was likely comprised mainly of Jews who believed that through Jesus the God of Israel was signaling the end of the present evil age and the beginning of the final manifestation of the realm of God. Biblical scholars increasingly point to similarities between first-century synagogues and the Matthean community.[2] Although Matthew referred to his community as a "church" (16:18; 18:17), we should not read the later separation of church and synagogue into his Gospel. We should imagine his community as a synagogue in tension with the traditional synagogue (perhaps over the Gentile mission). Matthew resorted to caricature to justify the distinctiveness of his community in relation to the traditional synagogue. We need to keep both of these points in mind when interpreting today's lesson.

Matthew frequently parallels the ministries of Moses and Jesus (as in today's lesson). Just as God worked through Moses for Israel to bless the nations, so God worked through Jesus in behalf of the Matthean community to bless the wider world.

Matthew 2:13–18 reminds the reader of the harsh fact that leaders of the present evil age resist God's redemptive efforts. This passage parallels Pharaoh and Herod: Both sought to secure their own power by killing the firstborn of Israel (Exod. 2:15; Matt. 2:16). Whereas Pharaoh was a Gentile idolater, Herod was Jewish and a surrogate of the Roman Empire, thus prefiguring tension between Jesus and selected Jewish leaders in the First Gospel and pointing up Roman barbarity.

Although Christians usually associate Egypt with repression and slavery, Judaism also contains a lesser known tradition of Egypt as a place to flee for refuge and safety during famine and difficulty (e.g., 1 Kgs. 11:40; Jer. 26:21). This detail contributes to the reader's sympathy for the Gentile mission as the Gentile land becomes the place of safety for Jesus while the land of Herod is a place of danger.

In 2:15, Matthew uses Hos. 11:1 to interpret the flight of Jesus' family into Egypt. In the days of Hosea, Israel's injustice led to the collapse of the nation. Hosea 11:1–11 reminds the community that as God released the people from Egyptian bondage, so God would deliver them anew. God's presence in Jesus operates analogously.

A similar theme recurs in Matt. 2:18 with Matthew's citation of Jer. 31:15: While the people weep because they have gone into exile, the time for sorrow is ending. God will end the exile (Jer. 31:16–17). The same restoring power that God expressed in the time of Jeremiah is present in the time of Jesus.

The providence for the community that is promised through the quotations from Hosea and Jeremiah is presaged in providence for the young Jesus. After Herod died, the family returned to Israel. Archelaeus (son and successor of Herod) makes Judea unsafe.

The family finds refuge in Nazareth in Galilee, which Matthew describes as "Galilee of the Gentiles" (Matt. 4:15), that is, a Gentile setting not to be feared. Scholars note the ambiguity of Jesus growing up as a "Nazorean" (Matt. 2:23). Since this alleged quotation from Scripture does not occur in any Jewish source, its interpretation is unclear. It could play on the motif of reversal: Small Nazareth in Gentile friendly Galilee provides safety, in contrast to large and Jewish Jerusalem where Jesus is killed. The word "Nazorean" is similar to the Hebrew *netzer* (branch) in Isa. 11:1, a famous oracle (11:1–9) that anticipates God restoring the world. The word is also reminiscent of "nazirite," who were persons who cut their hair and practiced asceticism to demonstrate and strengthen their faithfulness (see, e.g., Num. 6:1–21; Judg. 13:5–7).

Second Sunday after Christmas Day/Years A, B, and C

John 1:1–18

The Fourth Gospel is indebted to Hellenistic Judaism, which brought together ideas from Judaism and Hellenistic philosophy. Those dual roots led it to understand existence to consist of two dimensions: (1) heaven, the sphere of God—for example, light, life, grace, spirit, truth; and (2) the created world (*kosmos*), the sphere of Satan—for example, darkness, death, works, flesh, falsehood. While John sometimes uses spatial language—for example, "up" (heaven) and "down"—to describe the relationship of these two dimensions, they are not two different physical levels but different force fields or spheres of influence within the same space. Heaven can exert a force field within the *kosmos*.

The preacher needs to help the congregation recognize the ambiguity in the relationship between Judaism and Jesus (and the church) in the Fourth Gospel. On the one hand, this Gospel is inherently Jewish, as it uses Hellenistic Judaism to interpret Jesus and the church. On the other, while John does not reject Judaism as such, the Gospel is bitterly critical of Jewish communities who do not recognize the validity of Christ and the mission of the Johannine community. A major purpose of the Fourth Gospel is to offer theological justification for the separation of the traditional synagogue and John's community by arguing that the church is a true heir of the synagogue. Supersessionists later used Johannine motifs (with others) to justify rejecting Judaism itself.

This ambiguity permeates today's reading. John 1:1–5 supplements Gen. 1 by presenting Jesus Christ as the word (*logos*, agent) through whom God created the world. Apart from Jesus, the *kosmos* is an arena of darkness and death. Jesus, however, infuses the *kosmos* with light and life. This paragraph presents a polemic: Jews who are not in the Jesus movement do not understand their own scriptures fully.

This polemic surfaces in 1:10–13. Although Jesus was God's agent for creating the world and was present in it, not even Jesus' kindred (the Jewish people) recognized him. Some did, of course; otherwise, he would have had no followers. Consequently, those who believe in Jesus as revelation of God are now "children of God." In Judaism, the expression "children of God" bespeaks the covenantal community.

According to 1:14, the *logos* (Jesus) became incarnate and lived among us. This idea is drawn from Judaism, which speaks of representatives of heaven, including God, as incarnate in the world (see, e.g., Gen. 2:7; 3:8; 17:1–22; Exod. 33:19–23).[3] This is underscored by the word "lived," which translates the Greek *skēnoō*, a word that is better rendered "pitch a tent," and which calls to mind the divine presence or name, *shekinah*, "tenting" with Israel in the wilderness, in the temple, in the exile, and in the new temple (see, e.g., Exod. 25:8–9; Ezek. 43:7; Joel 3:17; Zech. 2:10; Philo, *On the Preliminary Studies* 116).

In 1:17 John declares that the law (Torah) is a gift of God given through Moses. Although John later criticizes some Jewish people for not following Moses' law, John does not reject the notion of law itself. Indeed, Jesus articulates commandments that are appropriate for the Johannine community (see e.g., John 13:31–35).

This section emphasizes that the creating, redeeming, and sustaining *logos* is present in the Johannine community, and mediates divine grace and truth without reservation or end ("grace upon grace," v. 16). The preacher can affirm this reality for the church without simultaneously claiming that Judaism is now deprived of grace and truth.

Epiphany of the Lord/Years A, B, and C

Matthew 2:1–12

At the very outset of his Gospel, Matthew makes clear the hostility directed at Jesus by Herod the Great. The Roman Senate appointed Herod "King of the Jews" in 40 B.C.E. He took control of Jerusalem three years later. Known as "Herod the builder" for his construction projects—Masada, the Fortress Antonia, the Herodium, the temple, Caesarea Maritima—he was famously cruel to his family members and to the people who paid for his building projects. Revolts broke out across the land after his death.

The important point to be noted about the magi is that they are Gentiles. In leading them to Jesus, God makes good on the promise to Abraham and Sarah that their descendants would be a light and a blessing to Gentiles. And they are also a foretaste of the Great Commission at the end of Matthew: "Go therefore and make disciples of all the Gentiles" (*panta ta ethnē*).

Herod's title was "King of the Jews." The merest hint of a competitor for his title and power alarmed him. Matthew tells us that he "killed all the children in and around Bethlehem who were two years old or under" (2:16), attempting to eliminate any potential competition. Matthew makes clear that hostility toward Jesus came from those holding corrupt and oppressive political and military power. Pilate will place the title "King of the Jews" on the cross, indicating that Jesus was crucified for sedition.

We should not waste time or brain power on pseudoscientific theories about the "star" that guided the magi to Bethlehem. Many stories in the folklore of the ancient world tell of stars heralding the birth of such important people as Alexander the Great. Jewish traditions tell of stars accompanying the birth of Moses, Abraham, and Isaac. Matthew uses the star referred to in Num. 24:17 ("a star shall come out of Jacob") to witness to the importance of Jesus. The star had come to symbolize the Messiah. Rabbi Simon bar Yohai said, "My teacher Akiba would expound, 'A star rises from Jacob, Koziba (bar Kokhba) rises from Jacob'" (*y. Ta'anit* 4:9, 68d). Bar Kokhba led the second revolt against Roman occupation.

"All the chief priests and the scribes of the people" (v. 4) are a confusing bunch. There was only one high priest at any given time. "Chief priests" as a phrase occurs rarely in rabbinic sources. Perhaps Matthew has in mind those Jerusalem-based priestly families from whom the high priest was chosen or those who had served as high priests (usually a short term, except in the ten-year tenure of Caiaphas). Scribes were the scholarly class familiar with the writings (scriptures) of Israel and the ones who could write. Scribes wrote the Gospel of Matthew. Matthew is contrasting the disenfranchised with the elite. The well-to-do Herod "and all Jerusalem" are opposed to the displaced holy family and the Gentile magi who genuinely seek to worship Jesus.

This passage presents Jesus as a Moses figure and points ahead to his passion. Matthew's story of Jesus' birth recapitulates that of Moses (Exod. 1:8–2:10). As in Moses' case, so here a malevolent ruler directs the killing of Hebrew children. Jesus, like Moses before him, is saved. Whereas Moses was saved by Pharaoh's daughter and some midwives, here Joseph saves Jesus by fleeing to Egypt and then to Galilee. Joseph models righteous behavior again as he had earlier in marrying Mary. He serves his family; he does not dominate it. In Matthew, those removed from positions of power exemplify truly moral behavior, as did Tamar, Rahab, Uriah, and Ruth, who are mentioned in the genealogy.

First Sunday after the Epiphany/Year A

Baptism of the Lord

Matthew 3:13–17

This passage follows Matthew's description of the difference between the baptisms practiced by John and Jesus. John's baptism was "with water for repentance" (3:11); neither Mark nor Luke mentions that John's baptism was "for repentance." John's baptism differed also from the ritual baths of the temple and Qumran. In ritual baths, people baptized themselves. Also, such baths focused on ritual purity, not moral purity and repentance. Scholars usually say that such baths were not understood eschatologically, but against this is the fact that the Qumran community paid great attention to ritual baths and was intensely eschatological.

Those differences are clear enough. The difference between John's baptism and that of Jesus is less clear. Jesus' baptism, John says, will be "with the Holy Spirit and fire" (3:11). The contrast being drawn is between John and Jesus, not between the Matthean church and the synagogue. Jesus never baptized people with water (or at least Mark, Matthew, and Luke never mention his doing so). Jesus' baptism will gather the wheat into the granary and burn the chaff (3:12). This refers to the parable of the last judgment (Matt. 25:31–46), in which the sheep and the goats are separated according to whether they did deeds of loving-kindness to those in need, with the goats going away "into eternal punishment" (25:46). Jesus' baptism is a "winnowing fork" (3:12).

That John baptized Jesus embarrassed the early church. Mark's account alone is unadorned: Mark says plainly that Jesus came from Nazareth and was baptized by John in the Jordan (Mark 1:9–11). Luke remarks that Herod Antipas threw John in prison and then tells the story of Jesus' baptism without mentioning John (Luke 3:19–22). For all that John's Gospel says about John the Baptist testifying to Jesus, it never mentions his baptizing Jesus (John 1:19–36).

Matthew deals with this discomfiture through the conversation that occurs between the two of them. John protests against the idea of baptizing Jesus: "I need to be baptized by you, and do you come to me?" (3:14). Jesus responds that "it is proper for us in this way to fulfill all righteousness" (3:15), and John proceeds to baptize Jesus.

Was the early church embarrassed because it did not think Jesus needed to undergo a baptism of repentance, or simply because the idea seemed to make Jesus subordinate to John? Whatever the answer may be, Matthew's point is that Jesus "fulfilled all righteousness." Matthew has been concerned from the very beginning of his Gospel with celebrating those whose behavior fulfills a higher righteousness. His genealogy lifts up instances of higher righteousness: Tamar, Rahab, Uriah, Ruth. Joseph manifested the higher righteousness, married Mary, saved and served his family, and did not dominate them. Those in places of power and prestige, such as Herod, dominate and destroy. Trusting in status and rank, being full of oneself in matters of faith, counts for nothing in Matthew's eyes. What counts is morally responsible actions.

Hence, God is "well pleased" with Jesus, the beloved Son, because he fulfills all righteousness. "Beloved" was a frequently used epithet for the Messiah. The "voice from heaven," literally "the daughter of a voice" (*bat qol*), was God speaking directly to people. Matthew puts all this testimony to the identity of Jesus together from the rich language of the scriptures of Israel: "You are my son" (Ps. 2:7), "your only son Isaac, whom you love" (Gen. 22:2), "in whom my soul delights" (Isa. 42:1). Jesus Christ takes shape in the scriptures of Israel and in the people Israel.

Second Sunday after the Epiphany/Year A

John 1:29–42

John the Baptist interprets the significance of Christ: "the Lamb of God who takes away the sin of the world." The "world" (*kosmos*), for John, is not simply the creation but a negative term for the sphere of existence enslaved to the devil and characterized by darkness, falsehood, and death (John 8:34). First John describes this situation as lawlessness (*anomia*; 3:4) and injustice (*adikia*, "broken relationships"; 5:17). John summarizes distorted life in the *kosmos* with the singular "sin" and speaks of particular actions of distortion by using "sins" in the plural.

Listeners who hear Jesus described as "Lamb of God" associate him with the Passover lamb (Exod. 12:1–13) and with the Suffering Servant, who is described as a lamb, in Isa. 53:7. Passover celebrates freedom from slavery in Egypt. The song of the Suffering Servant notes that the servant suffers as a part of the community's deliverance from exile (Isa. 52:13–53:21).

The term "takes away" (*airo*) fits here. The Septuagint sometimes uses this word to refer to removing sin in the way that one removes a burden (1 Sam. 15:25; 25:28). Just as the Passover lamb and the Suffering Servant signaled deliverance from bondage, so Jesus releases people from slavery to sin and to the distortions of the *kosmos*. Jesus accomplishes this task not by complicated propitiation or expiation but by revealing God in the world and by establishing a community of love.

The Baptist is subordinate to Jesus (v. 30). Indeed, John came to baptize for only one reason: to reveal Jesus, the *logos*, to Israel (vv. 31–33). To "reveal" in this Gospel is not only to show forth but to release power. God's power to free us operates when Jesus is revealed.

While the Fourth Gospel typically uses the expression "the Jewish people" in a way that casts aspersion, it nearly always uses "Israel" positively, thus reminding us that while the Fourth Gospel is often critical of "the Jews" (i.e., persons not sympathetic to Jesus), it regards Judaism itself positively.

John the Baptist functions in this narrative to verify that the Spirit remains, abides, or, better, identifies with and operates powerfully in Jesus. Jesus not only acts and speaks in the Spirit but also can cause the Spirit to abide in the church. The Spirit continues the presence and ministry of Jesus in the *kosmos*. Through the Spirit, Jesus continues to be revealed and to free the community from sin.

The Johannine community did not separate water and Spirit baptisms. The water assures the baptisand that the Spirit continues not only to free people and cause them to be reborn within the *kosmos* but also to live in the heavenly sphere (John 3:5–8; 7:45–52).

John the Baptist's testimony is so powerful that two of the Baptist's own disciples follow Jesus (vv. 37–39). Jesus is the true rabbi (teacher) of the Johannine community. After the rabbinical model, the disciples go to Jesus' lodging not merely for a social visit but also for instruction, thus modeling a key aspect of discipleship (vv. 38–42).

The call of the first disciples also reminds the reader that the Johannine community dwells within the *kosmos*, in which Jesus' followers experience freedom, light, truth, law, justice (right relationship), and eternal life. They are in but not of the *kosmos* (John 8:23; 15:19; 17:14, 16).

Third Sunday after the Epiphany/Year A

Matthew 4:12–23

Incarnation brings geography with it, so now we pay attention to matters of place. It is somewhat confusing when Matthew says that Jesus "withdrew" (*anechōrēsen*) to Galilee when he heard that John had been arrested, for the verb indicates that Jesus left for Galilee out of apprehension for his safety. But Herod Antipas, who arrested John, ruled over Galilee. Jesus would have been safer where he was, in Judea.

Galilee was one of the three parts into which the realm of Herod the Great was split at the time of his death in 4/5 B.C.E. A small area (less than fifty miles south to north), its eastern boundary was the Sea of Galilee and the Jordan River. Samaria lay to its south and Syria to the north and west. The Way to the Sea, a major Roman highway, crossed it. Roman mile markers can be seen in Capernaum today. Religiously, Galilee was close to Judea and Jerusalem. Galileans made pilgrimages to the major festivals in Jerusalem, and Jesus himself may well have done so more times than the

Synoptics indicate. Sepphoris, about three miles up the mountain from Nazareth, was the Roman capital of Galilee. It is one of several significant Gentile towns that the Gospels never mention Jesus visiting. Perhaps he avoided them (Matt. 10:5).

Matthew tells us that Jesus "made his home in Capernaum" (*K'far Nahum*, the village of Nahum). On the northwest shore of the Sea of Galilee, in Capernaum today one can visit "Peter's house," one of a set of first-century stone houses that have been excavated. According to archaeologists, "Peter's house" was a house church, which they conclude from the symbols on the inside walls. It is but a few steps from the synagogue, a marvelous building from the second century built over the site of an earlier synagogue. The incredibly close geographical proximity of church and synagogue makes clear that without the synagogue there never would have been a church. Capernaum became the base for Jesus' ministry, which Matthew, Mark, and Luke tell us mostly took place in Galilee until the journey to Jerusalem. Jesus goes there, says Matthew, to fulfill what had been spoken by the prophet Isaiah, applying to Jesus an expression of hope originally related to an Assyrian invasion of 732 B.C.E. The theological purpose of the saying is to highlight that Jesus' movement accorded with God's purposes.

Peter and Andrew, James and John, the first disciples called by Jesus, were in the fishing business. Fishing was an important industry on the Sea of Galilee. Matthew makes clear that the first disciples had the necessary financial means to participate in it. Mark's Gospel mentions the "hired men" of Zebedee (Mark 1:20). The first followers of Jesus give up a dependable way of making a living. The two sets of brothers forsake everything—their nets, their boats, and even, for the sons of Zebedee, their father. Their action in abandoning all these securities parallels that of Jesus in turning his back on the securities of comfort, safety, and power in his temptation.

Jesus approaches these workers and says to them simply, "Follow me, and I will make you fish for people." It would have been typical in Jewish circles for disciples to look for and choose a teacher. Jesus is depicted as a teacher who searches for his disciples, as God graciously seeks out all of God's children.

The passage ends with Jesus preaching the good news "in *their* synagogues." Here is a theme running through Matthew—putting distance between followers of Jesus and other Jews. The distance has been greatly increased over the last two millennia. It is our task to reduce it, not to widen the chasm further.

Fourth Sunday after the Epiphany/Year A

Matthew 5:1–12

Matthew continues to paint Jesus as a Moses figure. Moses had lived through the persecution in Egypt and had been tested by the temptation to lose faith in God in the wilderness. Then he went up Sinai to convey the Torah to the people Israel. Jesus, having survived the persecution of Herod the Great and been tested in the wilderness, climbs a mountain by the Sea of Galilee and delivers the Sermon on the Mount. Moses presented the Torah to a bunch of homeless slaves seeking their way to the land of promise, while Jesus delivers his sermon to "the poor in spirit" (in Luke, simply "the poor").

The Greek word that Matthew (and Luke) use for "poor" is *ptōchoi.* "Destitute" or "beggars" would be a better translation, for they capture the economic situation of peasants in a Roman-occupied land. Whenever the land of Israel was occupied by a foreign power, it was the upper classes, particularly in Jerusalem, who were most ready to accommodate to the views and religion of the occupier. This was so when Antiochus IV Epiphanes was trying to stamp out Jewish faith altogether and later when under Roman rule Jerusalem became a highly hellenized city. People are sometimes shocked when viewing a model of first-century Jerusalem to see a horse-race track (hippodrome) directly south of and close to the temple.

"Rich" means more than simply "well-off." It carries the connotation, in this context, of "irreligious, unfaithful." It was the disenfranchised, those who did not benefit from the occupation, who remained faithful to the Torah and the traditions of Israel, or who were disenfranchised because they remained faithful. "Poor" meant one who was faithful, a *hasid.* Jesus addresses the disenfranchised faithful. The Essenes referred to those who gave up their possessions to join the community and await the eschaton as "the poor in spirit."

Jesus "sat down" to teach, typical of Jewish teachers at the time. He begins with nine blessings. Beatitudes are found in the wisdom tradition (Proverbs), Second Temple Jewish writings, and the rabbinic tradition. His concern for the poor and those who mourn reflects the biblical understanding of God's special concern for the poor, the weak, and the marginalized (Lev. 19:9–10, Deut. 15:7–11). The "meek" is another way to refer to the "poor in spirit"; Jesus is not referring to separate groups here.

The expression "for they will be comforted" is a roundabout way of saying that God will comfort them. "Those who mourn" reminds readers of Isaiah's mission to comfort those who mourn in Zion, that is, over the destruction of the temple (Isa. 61:23). Those who read or heard Matthew's Gospel in the late first century had another temple to mourn. The "meek . . . who will inherit the earth" calls to mind the Mishnah: "All Israelites have a share in the world-to-come, for it is written, 'Your people shall all be righteous; they shall possess the land forever'" (*m. Sanhedrin* 10:1, quoting Isa. 60:21). The "meek shall inherit the land," says the psalmist, "and delight themselves in abundant prosperity" (Ps. 37:11). This was an inspiration shared by more than one eschatological movement (i.e., movement of restoration of the Jewish people under conditions of occupation).

Blessed are people of integrity (the pure in heart) and those who make peace. Indeed! *Shalom*, peace, is a gift of God, a gift that is freely offered but has to be wanted to be received. Blessed are those who seek it.

Fifth Sunday after the Epiphany/Year A

Matthew 5:13–20

When Jesus says to his disciples, "You are the light of the world," his words tap into the deepest roots of biblical faith. Jesus now unfolds the meaning of the blessings he has announced, recalling their deep scriptural connotations. Blessing is inclusive well-being: shalom, justice, liberty, economic sufficiency, health. It is available to us from God as a gift, provided that we share it with others as a gift. God blessed Adam and Eve in their difference from and mutuality with one another and in their difference from and mutuality with all "the living things." God blessed Abraham and Sarah and their descendants in their difference from and mutuality with "all the peoples of the world" (Gen. 22:18; 26:4). The people Israel are to be a blessing to the Gentiles. Only by accepting blessing as a gift from the God of Israel and the Israel of God can the Gentiles receive it.[4]

Here Jesus taps into these roots as articulated by Isaiah: "It is too light a thing that you should be my servant to raise up the tribes of Jacob and to restore the survivors of Israel; I will give you as a light to the nations [i.e., Gentiles], that my salvation may reach to the end of the earth" (Isa. 49:6; see also 51:4). In a similar way, Jesus' disciples are the "salt of the earth." Salt was valuable as a conserving agent; it kept things from going bad. Jesus' followers are to act in the world in ways that will keep it wholesome, that will prevent it from going to rack and ruin. Preserving peace, justice, and human dignity does not sound like an exciting, revolutionary thing to do, but one of the first ethical principles is to do no harm. We are to conserve as much well-being as we can.

Jesus calls his followers "the light of the world," making it clear that as God called Israel through Abraham and Sarah to be a blessing to the Gentiles, so the God of Israel calls us to the mission to which God called Israel. We join Israel in God's service; we do not replace Israel in that role. Jesus' statement, "Let your light shine before others, so that they may see your good works and give glory to your Father in heaven," comes from the heart of Jewish faith: "God shall be gloried among the Gentiles through you, but through those who do not what is good, God shall be dishonored" (*Testament of Naphtali* 8:4). Jesus is more interested in what his followers do than what they say, an attitude that comes to conclusive expression in the parable of the last judgment.

"A city built on a hill cannot be hid" would lead hearers shaped by Scripture to think of Jerusalem. Some forms of messianic expectation envisaged the age of the Messiah as a time when all Gentiles would come to Mount Zion to learn Torah. Thus, the promise that Israel would be a "light to the Gentiles" would be actualized.

"Do not think that I have come to abolish the law or the prophets; I have come not to abolish but to fulfill. For truly I tell you, until heaven and earth pass away, not one letter, not one stroke of a letter, will pass from the law until all is accomplished." Jesus' fulfillment of the Torah affirms it; Jesus does not negate the Torah. Matthew's attitude toward the law (*torah* means "way, teaching") is that followers of Jesus are to keep all of it, including "the least of these commandments." Rabbis would frequently distinguish between "the light and the grave" commandments, as Jesus does here. Doing good works, deeds of loving-kindness, is not a matter of earning God's love, which is always graciously given. It has everything to do with living a new and transformed life, a possibility with which God graciously empowers us. It is living in such a way as to be a blessing, a light, to the world.

Sixth Sunday after the Epiphany/Year A

Matthew 5:21–37

This section begins the six "antitheses" that have, unfortunately, often been understood in an anti-Jewish manner, with Judaism representing the rejected side of each antithesis. So we need to clarify two basic matters at the outset. First, the manner of teaching here, "You have heard . . . but I say unto you . . . ," is not that different from what became the rabbinic method of interpretation (*midrash*): "You have read . . . but the meaning is . . ." The nature of midrash was to "penetrate" (*darash*) the text and get to its deeper meaning.

Second, Jesus' antitheses move from the commandment against a certain kind of behavior—murder or adultery, for example—to identifying its underlying motivation. There is nothing new about this move on Jesus' part. The Ten Commandments themselves end with a commandment dealing with motivation: "You shall not covet." *Kawwanah*, "motivation," and *lishmah*, "the love or praise of God," are profoundly important in Judaism. As the rabbis will say: "It matters not whether you do much or little, so long as your heart is directed to heaven [God]" (*b. Berakhot* 17a). Rabbi Nahman ben Isaac said, "Better is a sin which is done with the right intention than a commandment which is not done with the right intention" (*b. Horayot* 10a). Torah is grounded in love, and love is acted out in deeds of loving-kindness.

Jesus' teaching on forgiveness—"first be reconciled to your brother or sister, and then come and offer your gift" at the altar (v. 24)—is exactly what rabbis still advise Jews on the Day of Atonement. For God to forgive me my sins against my friend without my working things out with that friend would be cheap grace, and it would do nothing for putting right the relationship between us. (We have never met a biblical inerrantist who takes literally the remarks about tearing out one's right eye and cutting off one's right hand.)

Jesus' teaching about divorce in Matthew differs from Mark's absolute prohibition in that it adds an exception: "the ground of unchastity." Matthew's Gospel, written later, had more time to live with this teaching and adapted it to speak the truth in a way adequate to its experience. Much misinformation exists about Jewish teaching on divorce and what is claimed to be Jesus' liberation of women from that teaching. Let us begin by noting that the Torah and later Judaism permit divorce; they do not command it.

Some interpreters have claimed in recent years that Jesus' banning of divorce was liberating for women, because a woman sent away from her husband in those days would have been totally abandoned, outcast from society, and would starve to death or be forced into prostitution. This seems not to be true. Jewish marriages at the time were arrangements between families with complex prenuptial agreements that endowed the new couple and protected the bride's rights in case of a divorce.[5] Divorce would have been financially prohibitive for most husbands.

In Judaism, divorce became a woman's right—that is, she could go to a rabbinic court and ask that her husband be commanded to grant her a bill of divorce, a millennium before the church recognized divorce. Preachers dealing with this passage should face the issue of whether removing the possibility of divorce has been beneficial to women (or men) trapped in violent or emotionally empty marriages.

Seventh Sunday after the Epiphany/Year A

Matthew 5:38–48

Life under Roman occupation was one of order imposed by violence and the fear of violence. Jesus' first four teachings in this pericope all have to do with ratcheting down the spiral of violence, the interminable cycle of retaliation and counterretaliation. Followers of Jesus are to ratchet down the violence.[6]

The earlier law pertaining to harm inflicted by one person on another, "eye for eye, tooth for tooth, hand for hand," and so forth (Exod. 21:23–25) was intended to restrain reactions to violence. According to Lev. 24:19, "Anyone who maims another shall suffer the same injury in return." By Jesus' time, however, this law had been replaced by the payment of a fine decided by a court. "Do not resist an evildoer," reflects Jesus' consistent rejection of all violence, including retaliatory violence. He would have agreed with the rabbinic saying, "He who is yielding, who ignores a slight or a wrong, has all his sins forgiven" (*b. Yoma* 23a).

"But if anyone strikes you on the right cheek, turn the other also" (v. 39). A slap on the right cheek would normally be given with the back of the hand, an insult. It is not clear what it means to "turn the other [cheek]." Is it a defiant gesture asserting one's dignity, as if to mock a Roman soldier's assumption of superiority? Or does it mean to turn away from the aggressor? Jesus could be simply making again the same point as before: Do not respond to violence with violence. "If you are struck, you must forgive the offender, even though he does not ask for your forgiveness" (*b. Baba Qamma* 9.29).

The "coat" (*chitōn*) in verse 40 was a body-length shirt worn under the "cloak" (*himation*). Giving both away would leave a person naked. This saying conveys an attitude of nonretaliation, not an instruction to be strictly followed.

"If anyone forces [*aggareusei*] you to go one mile, go also the second mile." The verb means to compel, to impress into service. In context, we imagine a Roman soldier of the army of occupation compelling an Israelite to work as a baggage carrier, a human beast of burden. The wisdom being conveyed is that not only should you go along with the soldier's demand but you should astound him and carry the burden twice as far as he ordered.

Jesus' instructions about giving have to do with beggars and borrowers. Give to all beggars and refuse no borrowers (even if they cannot be expected to repay; hence the link with beggars). This instruction reflects exactly the sabbatical year laws about giving and lending in Deut. 15:11: "I therefore command you, 'Open your hand to the poor and needy neighbor in your land.'"

In v. 43 Jesus says to love your neighbor and your enemy; there are no limits to love. There is no biblical commandment to hate our enemies. "Pray for the wicked that they should repent," said the rabbis, "and there will be no more wicked." Some Qumranites were instructed to hate "the sons of darkness," and some apocalyptic passages (including those in the Gospels) have winners gloating over losers.

Jesus' saying in v. 45 that God "sends rain on the righteous and on the unrighteous" also reflects Jewish teaching. The Talmud records this saying as "Greater is the day of rainfall than the day of resurrection, for the latter benefits only the pious, whereas the former benefits pious and sinners alike" (*b. Ta'anith* 7a).

Eighth Sunday after the Epiphany/Year A

Matthew 6:24–34

"No one can serve two masters. . . . You cannot serve God and wealth." The idea that God and money are incompatible masters and that we cannot serve both of them was well known among Jews at the time of Jesus and afterward. The *Sayings of the Sages*, a wisdom document in the Mishnah (*Avot*, Neusner, *Torah from Our Sages*), cites Rabbi Zadok as proclaiming, "Do not make Torah a spade with which to dig. . . . Thus have you learned: Whoever derives worldly benefit from teachings of Torah takes his life out of the world" (*m. Avot* 4:5). Similarly, "You shall not say to yourself, 'I will learn Torah to become rich, or to be called Rabbi, or to receive reward'" (*Sifre Deuteronomy* 79b–80a).

The term "wealth" has traditionally been translated in scripture as "mammon." "Wealth" may well be the better translation today since about as many people know what mammon is as can identify an ebenezer. But we should not lose the awareness that some scholars derive *mammon* from a root that means "to trust or believe in." Mammon alludes to that in which we place our trust, and as Martin Luther trenchantly observed, whatever we put our ultimate trust in is, in effect, God for us. The logic is clear enough: God is the one whom we trust to do for us everything that only God can do and the one on whom we rely for the ultimate meaning of our lives. If we place that ultimate trust in something else, that something else is in effect God for us. The point is not that wealth is bad in itself; the point is that we should not trust or rely upon as God anything other than God. Money is a good servant and a poor master.

"Therefore, do not worry," or, in the King James Version, "be not anxious." Anxiety is the opposite of faith, its lack. Do not worry about "what you will eat." In the narrative flow of Matthew, Jesus has just taught his disciples how to pray (6:5–15) by giving them the example that has come to be known as the "Lord's Prayer." In this prayer, very much like the Kaddish offered in every synagogue service, we petition God, "Give us this day our daily bread." As Israel in the wilderness collected enough manna on which to live one day at a time, so Jesus teaches us to ask only for our "daily" bread. And then he says not to worry about what you will eat (or wear, or drink). A similar rabbinic remark goes, "Whoever has a morsel of bread in a basket and says, 'What shall I eat tomorrow' is one of those who has little faith" (*b. Sotah* 48b).

In one of a number of places where Gentiles serve as the negative foils for his teaching, Jesus comments, "For it is the Gentiles who strive for all these things" (6:32; see also 5:47 and 6:7). Jesus uses the word *ethnē* (ethnics), often in Second Temple Jewish literature a technical term for Gentiles.

"Today's trouble is enough for today." We do not need to borrow imaginary troubles from tomorrow just to find a way to keep our minds occupied today with matters other than spreading in the world the love of God and the love of the neighbor.

All this is wisdom teaching in the service of the reign of God: "Strive first for the kingdom of God and his righteousness, and all these things will be given to you as well." Jesus is calling for a warm, joyous, wholehearted service of God.

Jesus was talking with the "expendables" of his society, the nobodies. His words are wisdom "from below." Jesus takes the perspective of the underdog; his sympathies are with the poor and humble. He recommends to them simplicity, an unencumbered life, freedom from anxiety, and closeness to nature—"consider the lilies of the field." If God cares about them, how much more does God care about you?

Ninth Sunday after the Epiphany/Year A

Matthew 7:21–29

Only those who do the will of Jesus' Father in heaven will enter the reign of God. Luke's version is more direct: "Why do you call me 'Lord, Lord,' and do not do what I tell you?" (Luke 6:46). The difference between Luke and Matthew here is that Matthew makes entrance into God's reign conditional upon doing God's will as interpreted by Jesus. The will of God that must be done is what Jesus has been teaching since the beginning of the Sermon on the Mount—Matthew's *mitzvoth* (commandments, teachings). Jesus declares the inadequacy of impressive religious stunts—prophecy, exorcisms, and miracles. What counts is the cup of cold water given to a thirsty person.

"A wise man . . . built his house on rock." There are several similar parables in other Jewish literature. Rabbi Eleazar ben Azariah said,

> Anyone whose wisdom is greater than his deeds—to what is he to be likened? To a tree with abundant foliage but few roots. When the winds come, they will uproot it and blow it down, as it is said, *He shall be like a tamarisk in the desert.* . . . But anyone whose deeds are greater than his wisdom—to what is he likened? To a tree with little foliage but abundant roots. For, even if all the winds in the world were to come and blast at it, they will not move it from its place, as it is said, *He shall be as a tree planted by the waters.* (*m. Avot* 3.17, Neusner, *Torah from Our Sages*)

The *Sayings of Rabbi Nathan* compares a person who has studied much Torah and in whom there are many loving deeds to one "who builds first with stones and afterwards with brick; even when much water comes and collects by their side, it does not dislodge them. But one in whom there are no good works, though he studied Torah, to what may he be likened? To a person who builds first with bricks and afterwards with stones: even when a little water gathers, it overthrows them immediately" (*Sayings of Rabbi Nathan* 24).

"He taught them as one having authority, and not as their scribes." This verse sets Jesus' authority over against that of other Jewish teachers. It is not scribes who are criticized here; it is "their" scribes. "Their" scribes do not teach with authority. We are not told what this statement means or why it is true. Do their scribes lack authority simply because they are theirs and not ours? If so, that is not a good reason. Do their scribes lack authority because, instead of simply uttering their teachings, they cite biblical verses and other scholars and make a case for why they say what they do? If so, this also is not a good reason. Making a case for one's views is what enables a conversation to take place. Simply declaiming one's views (even loudly) is no reason why anyone should take them seriously. For a record of Jewish teachers who taught authoritatively and simply by asserting their views, as Jesus seems to have done, one need only consult the Mishnah, *Avot*, often cited in this commentary.

This passage makes clear that in Matthew's view the reader must accept or reject Jesus' teachings. Not to accept and live by them is to fail to enter the realm of God. People will be divided at the last judgment, rewarded or punished, depending on whether or not they accept and live by Jesus' teachings. Those who live by them will be rewarded; those who do not will not (the division is not between Jews and Christians or Jews and Gentiles).

Last Sunday after the Epiphany/Year A

Transfiguration Sunday

Matthew 17:1–9

Matthew 16 ended with Jesus telling his disciples that "there are some standing here who will not taste death before they see the Son of Man coming in his kingdom." The Son of Man, said Jesus, will come "in the glory of his Father." The story of the transfiguration is not simply concerned with the glory revealed in Jesus himself. It is a vision (see 17:9) of the glory that will be Jesus' in the future completeness of God's reign. We who are given and called by Jesus to live now in the power of the future see Jesus both as he already is and as he is not yet. He is who he is only in relation to the God of Israel ("his Father"), the Israel of God (Moses and Elijah), and the reign of God ("his dominion").

As much as the story looks forward to the completion of God's purpose with human beings, it also looks back to stories of Moses and Elijah. "Six days later," says Matthew, reminding us of Moses on Mount Sinai where, after "the glory of the Lord settled on Mount Sinai, and the cloud covered it for six days," God called Moses up the mountain (Exod. 24:15–18). So, after six days, Jesus leads Peter, James, and John "up a high mountain."

What does it mean to say that Jesus "was transfigured," that "his face shone like the sun, and his clothes became dazzling white"? The Greek for "was transfigured" is *metemorphōthē*, a term that refers to a change of form, "transformation." But what follows in the account of the transfiguration has nothing to do with the understanding of transformation in Greek culture or with the idea of an internal transformation of the sort associated with being "transformed by the renewing of your minds" (Rom. 12:2) or with our being transformed "into the image" of the glory of God (2 Cor. 3:18).

Matthew tells us, first, that it means Jesus' "face shone like the sun." Exodus says that when Moses came down from Mount Sinai, he "did not know that the skin of his face shone because he had been talking with God" (Exod. 34:29). Matthew expects us to know that the reason Jesus' face shone like the sun was because he was in communication with God, that we see God's glory reflected in the face of Jesus. In subsequent Jewish literature, this becomes a frequent motif, particularly in Second Temple Judaism (e.g., *4 Ezra* 7:97). The splendor, grandeur, and glory of God rest on Jesus, are seen in Jesus. In Hebrew this is the *ziv ha-Shekhinah*. Matthew's theological point is that Jesus is a Moses figure, that Jesus takes shape in the history and scriptures of the Israel of God.

Second, says Matthew, "his clothes became dazzling white." In rabbinic and apocryphal literature, shining clothes reflect the majesty of God and mark individuals as elected by God. This is true also in the book of Revelation: "Around the throne are twenty-four thrones, and seated on the thrones are twenty-four elders, dressed in white robes, with golden crowns on their heads" (Rev. 4:4; cf. 7:9). "A bright cloud overshadowed them," as a cloud covered Sinai for six days, also representing the *Shekhinah*.

Malachi ends with the promise "I will send you the prophet Elijah before the great and terrible day of the LORD comes" (Mal. 4:5). Matthew regards John the Baptist as Elijah to Jesus as the Son of Man (Matt. 3:4). Jesus reflects the glory of the God of Israel; the *Shekhinah* is upon him. He is at one with Moses and Elijah, the law and the prophets. The voice of God (*bat qol*) confirms what it said of Jesus at his baptism (Matt. 3:17).

Ash Wednesday/Year A

Matthew 6:1–6, 16–21

Lent turns our attention to the practices and disciplines of the Christian life and the formation of Christian character. The Gospel for Ash Wednesday focuses on three practices of faith: giving alms, praying, and fasting. Giving alms is the first topic. Jesus' instructions come from the

heart of the scriptural and Jewish traditions. In Hebrew, giving alms is
zedaqah, related to the concept of righteousness. Charity for the needy is
part of the Torah: "When you reap your harvest in your field and forget
a sheaf in the field, you shall not go back to get it; it shall be left for the
alien, the orphan, and the widow, so that the LORD your God may bless
you in all your undertakings. When you beat your olive trees, do not strip
what is left; it shall be for the alien, the orphan, and the widow" (Deut.
24:19–20; see also 14:28–29). Part of Job's "defense" was that he had given
zedaqah to the poor, the orphan, the widow, the wretched, the blind, the
lame, the needy, and the stranger (Job 29:11–16).

More pertinent to Lent is Isa. 58:6–7: "Is not this the fast that I choose:
to loose the bonds of injustice, to undo the thongs of the yoke, to let the
oppressed go free, and to break every yoke? Is it not to share your bread with
the hungry, and bring the homeless poor into your house?" The rabbinic
tradition expresses the same spirit as Jesus in Matthew: "He who gives
zedaqah in secret is greater than Moses" (*b. Bava Batra* 9b). The story is told
that Rabbi Yannai "once saw a man give money to a poor man publicly. He
said: 'It had been better that you gave him nothing than that you should have
given to him and put him to shame'" (*b. Hagigah* 5a). There was also a tradition in the temple of "the Vestry of the Secret Ones," in which people
could place alms so that those who were in need "might be helped in secret"
(*m. Sheqalim* 5.6). Matthew's use of "hypocrites" is typical ancient name-
calling; "brood of vipers" and "whited sepulchers" are other instances. We
do well to remember that each of us is to some extent a hypocrite, and that
hypocrisy does not distinguish one faith community from another.

Matthew 6:5–7 makes the same point about prayer: Do not do it to be
seen by others and do not heap up empty phrases. Jews prayed standing
up and wherever they found themselves when it was time for prayer. Jesus
does not criticize standing to pray or praying in public; he criticizes those
who love to be seen praying. Pastors stand and pray in public; they are
not necessarily hypocritical. As to empty rhetoric: "Repeat not your words
in prayer. Be not rash with your mouth and let not your heart be hasty to
utter anything before God, for God is in heaven and you are upon the
earth, therefore, let your words be few" (*b. Berakhot* 61a). "God said to
Moses: 'My children are in distress and you are making long prayers!'"
(*Mekilta* of Rabbi Ishmael on Exod. 15:25).

Matthew 6:16–21 deals with fasting, and the point is the same: Whenever you fast, do not do it in such a way that you show others you are fasting. Do not go about with a hang-dog look. We do not usually think of
Jesus' followers as fasting, yet that Matthew includes teachings on fasting

suggests that it was important to his community. The concluding verses on storing up "treasures in heaven" rather than on earth have to do with giving alms to the poor and thereby placing our ultimate trust and reliance on God ("heaven" in Matthew) and not in anything or anyone that is less than the one who is ultimate. This is the theological root of all authentic practices of faith.

First Sunday in Lent/Year A

Matthew 4:1–11

"Ten trials were inflicted upon Abraham, our father (may he rest in peace), and he withstood all of them, to show you how great is His love for Abraham, our father (may he rest in peace)" (*m. Avot* 5:3, Neusner, *Torah from Our Sages*). It was widely accepted in the ancient world that great leaders should be tested before setting out on their undertakings. Abraham is the most significant individual instance of such testing in the Jewish tradition, the people Israel in the wilderness the most significant collective example. Jesus in Matthew recapitulates the story of the Israel of God in relation to the God of Israel.

Jesus accepted John's baptism to "fulfill all righteousness." His resolve to do so is now put to the test. As it was God who tested Abraham and Israel, so it is God who tempts Jesus, in spite of the clear appearance that the devil, the tempter, does it. For "Jesus was led up by the Spirit into the wilderness to be tempted by the devil." The devil is under God's control; Matthew does not affirm a theological dualism.

Jesus is offered a life of ease (the first temptation), security (the second), and authority (the third). All he could ever want to eat, angels to protect against any misstep, and rule over "all the kingdoms of the world"—what else could a person want? But Jesus denies himself these things, turns his back on them, for the sake of the dominion of God. Later he will ask people to abandon all their securities—family, business, familiar surroundings—and follow him. He must do the same if he is to create a community founded not on grasping for one's own security but on service to others.

Jesus begins his test by fasting "forty days and forty nights." Likewise, Moses "was there [i.e., on Mount Sinai] with the LORD forty days and forty nights; he neither ate bread nor drank water" (Exod. 34:28). Also, Elijah "got up, and ate and drank; then he went in the strength of that food forty days and forty nights to Horeb the mount of God" (1 Kgs. 19:8). Matthew depicts Jesus as a Moses figure throughout his Gospel and so here. Elijah was a northern Israelite, a Galilean, and a prophet, as was his successor, Elisha. These two prophets fed the hungry in the desert, performed miracles, and had freer and more open relationships with women. Jesus is in that same tradition.

The reference to the "pinnacle of the temple," sometimes translated the "wing," is unclear. The greatest height of the temple would have been at the southeast corner of the court, overlooking the Kidron valley that drops away below. A later rabbinic tradition says that when the Messiah came, he would stand on top of the temple.

Jesus responds to and overcomes each test by quoting the Torah: "One does not live by bread alone, but by every word that comes from the mouth of God" (Deut. 8:3). "Do not put the Lord your God to the test" (Deut. 6:16). "Worship the Lord your God and serve only him" (Deut. 6:13). In each case, Jesus appeals to the written Torah: "It is written . . ." The major theme of Deuteronomy is the covenant between God and Israel, initiated by God's unfathomable love for Israel. Jesus trusts utterly in and relies utterly upon that love, as he will later teach his disciples to do. In Deut. 6–8, Moses challenges Israel to remember that God had tested them to "know what was in your heart, whether or not you would keep his commandments" (Deut. 8:2). Jesus makes clear his solidarity with the people Israel in accepting God's test and Moses' challenge. Jesus' character is shaped by this solidarity with the God of Israel and the Israel of God.

Second Sunday in Lent/Year A

John 3:1–17

The reading should be John 3:1–21; the text does not end until v. 21.

John's synagogue of Jesus' followers was in tension with the traditional synagogue. The passage speaks eloquently of God's love for the *kosmos* as pastoral encouragement for the synagogue of Jesus' followers in its painful separation from the traditional synagogue. We must, however, confront the passage's negative evaluation of Jews who do not believe in Jesus.

Nicodemus represents leaders from the traditional Jewish community. By having Nicodemus come "by night" (darkness is a symbolic time of lack of understanding), John signals the listener that Nicodemus and those he represents need instruction from Jesus.

In the first phase of the encounter, John describes how one comes to believe that Jesus is revelation from God (vv. 1–10). John invokes spatial symbolism of revelation coming down from God's sphere (heaven), and hence, a person must be "born from above." To be born from above is to believe God's revelation in Jesus.

By presenting Nicodemus as not understanding Jesus (vv. 4, 11), John warns the reader that the conventional synagogue is spiritually inadequate. People are born from above because of the action of the Spirit. John does not mean that the Spirit is arbitrary or capricious when he says that like the wind, the Spirit "blows where it chooses." Rather, the point is that only under the impulse of the Spirit do persons accept Jesus. Baptism ("born of the water") assures people that they have insight from the Spirit.

The second phase shows that Jesus' revelation is reliable (vv. 11–13) because he was in the heavenly world (John 1:1–2) and descended to bring news from God.

The third phase of the encounter, vv. 14–17, demonstrates the effect of revelation. When Jesus is lifted up, he draws persons to him. "Lifting up" refers to Jesus' crucifixion and glorification. In Num. 21:4–9, the Israelites in the wilderness were threatened with death by serpent bites. When Moses lifted a bronze serpent on a pole, the people were spared. Similarly, people live when they believe in Jesus (vv. 14–15).

John 3:16 is justly famous as a summary of Johannine theology: God graciously loves the *kosmos* (even though it manifests characteristics—e.g., falsehood, slavery, and death—that contradict the divine aims) and intends to save persons. On the fifth Sunday of Lent, we comment on eternal life and salvation in John.

The final phase of the encounter, vv. 18–21, names the consequences of not believing that Jesus reveals God. Nonbelievers are condemned, are denied eternal life and salvation, and must continue to dwell amid the corruption of the *kosmos* in the present and in the next phase of existence. Given the conflict between John's community and the traditional synagogue, John obviously has in mind Jews as the nonbelievers in the traditional synagogue; they "loved darkness rather than light" and commit "evil deeds."

Although we can sympathize with John's encouraging the church to recognize the trustworthiness of God's revelation through Jesus, the contemporary preacher must help the congregation reject the condemnation of Jews who do not accept Jesus. If God truly loves the world (3:16) and is faithful, then God truly loves the Jewish community. John uses Nicodemus to show that people can change in response to revelation. In 7:50–52, Nicodemus defends Jesus. In 19:39 Nicodemus has become a disciple, for he helps bury Jesus. If Nicodemus can change, Christians can change the attitude that God loves and saves only those who believe in Jesus.

Third Sunday in Lent/Year A

John 4:5–42

The initial interchange between the woman and Jesus (vv. 4–10) reflects the tension that existed between Jews and Samaritans. It reached a height when Samaritans spread bones in the temple and made it unclean (Josephus, *Antiquities* 18.29–30).

In vv. 11–15, Jesus offers the woman "living water," recollecting passages in Jewish literature that speak similarly of God (e.g., Jer. 2:13; 17:13), salvation (e.g., Ezek. 47:9; Zech. 14:8), and wisdom (Prov. 13:14; 18:4; cf. Sir. 24:21). Philo describes God as "the spring of living water" (*On Flight and Finding* 198) and the *logos* as "full of the stream of wisdom" (*On Dreams* 2.245). In John 7:37–39, Jesus says that the living water is the Spirit, that is, the presence of Jesus (the *logos*) with the community continuing to reveal the ways of God, including the way to eternal life.

Many scholars think that John 4:11–15 and 7:37–39 are key to understanding baptism. God uses the water of baptism to assure the members of the community that they partake of living water. In v. 15, the woman models how John wants the reader to respond to this insight: by seeking the living water of baptism and life in the Spirit.

Christians often think that Jesus' reference to the woman's five husbands (vv. 16–19) indicates that she was sexually (or otherwise) immoral, but the text does not mention immorality. Feminist commentators posit that her multiple husbands and current single status may result from a series of levirate marriages in which the last levir refused to marry her (see Deut. 25:1–10). In any event, she was subject to the social and economic marginality that was stressful for single women in antiquity. Her existence typifies broken life in the *kosmos*.

By the time of John, both the Samaritan worship center on Gerizim and the temple in Jerusalem had been destroyed (respectively, 128 B.C.E. and 70 C.E.), and Judaism was reformulating its understanding of authentic worship. According to 4:20–26, a temple is not needed for worship, for authentic worship is in spirit and truth. John gives the community the confidence that worship in the synagogue of Jesus' followers honors the God of the Jewish people, from whom salvation comes (v. 22).

However, in John, spirit and truth are associated mostly with Jesus' orb (see, e.g., 1:17; 14:6, 15–17, 26; 16:12–15) and not with traditional Jews (e.g., 8:39–46). John thus indirectly criticizes the worship of the synagogues that were not hospitable to the Jesus movement. Today's preacher, by contrast, can point out that the deepest values of spirit and truth can be embodied in both Christian worship and synagogue worship.

As the encounter with Jesus ends, the woman becomes a model disciple by witnessing to the revelation of God through Jesus (4:27–30). As a result of her testimony, Samaritans became a part of the Jesus movement and worship God truly (4:39–42). The fact that the woman witnesses indicates that she has full status as a disciple (cf. 1:35–51). She is now liberated from inhibitions in religious leadership placed on women.

Building on a strand of Judaism represented by Isa. 2:2–4, several Jewish communities contemporaneous with John anticipated a time when people from various nations and ethnicities would gather into one family under the aegis of the God of Israel (see, e.g., Philo, *On the Special Laws* 58.317–18). Some other thinkers and groups in the Hellenistic world similarly envisioned a common human community. This story uses the change in circumstance of the Samaritan woman to claim that through Jesus Christ, the peoples come together in the church (cf. John 17:20–26).

Fourth Sunday in Lent/Year A

John 9:1–41

This story offers a theological explanation in narrative form for the separation of John's community from the traditional synagogue. However, it caricatures the Pharisees and makes theologically inappropriate judgments about them and other matters.

Verses 1–12 constitute a miracle story, and preachers sometimes develop a sermon only on these verses that assures the congregation that Jesus heals our figurative blindness. This approach violates the integrity of the text, however, for vv. 1–12 are not a distinct literary unit but only set the stage for vv. 13–41. Preachers also typically celebrate the theological claim of v. 3, that the person's blindness was not caused by sin, while neglecting the horrifying and theologically inappropriate claim of the same verse that *God* made the person blind from birth so that when Jesus came along "God's works might be revealed." This claim violates the notion that God loves the blind person (and all persons) unconditionally and wills for that person (and all persons) to live in wholeness.

Verses 13–41 explain why John's community is no longer a part of traditional Pharisaism. The non-Pharisaic crowd acknowledges its respect for the Pharisees by taking the formerly blind man to the Pharisees in v. 13. The Pharisees conduct an inquisition. The inquisition manifests Johannine irony, for while the Pharisees appear to ask the questions, their questions and judgments call their religious authority into question and condemn them.

Each stage of the inquisition reveals further the depth of Pharisaic confusion. In vv. 13–22, the Pharisees cannot even agree among themselves on how to evaluate the testimony of the crowd and of the blind man, thus misunderstanding an essential tenet of Jewish life: The testimony of two persons establishes truth.

The man's parents will not testify because they "were afraid of the Jews; for the Jews had already agreed that anyone who confessed Jesus to be the Messiah would be put out of the synagogue." The narrator blames the rupture of John's community and traditional Pharisaism solely on the Pharisees.

In vv. 24–34, the Pharisees reveal the depth of their ignorance. They contend that both Jesus and the formerly blind man are sinners, whereas the reader knows that Jesus is sinless (John 1:29) and the blindness was caused not by sin but by God. The formerly blind man speaks the truth (as defined by the narrator), but the Pharisees act falsely and unjustly and excommunicate him (v. 34).

Verses 35–41 come to a devastating conclusion: Traditional Pharisees are the truly blind persons. When they do not recognize Jesus, Jesus condemns them (v. 41). The formerly blind man represents people who once did not recognize Jesus but now confess that he is not only a prophet but the Messiah, and who have become Jesus' disciples.

This story negatively caricatures the Pharisees for the purpose of showing the superiority of the Johannine community. John's Gospel systematically identifies "the Jews" and "the Pharisees" with the counterfeit principle of the world of "darkness" and "blindness." Its contrast between Jesus' followers and "the Jews" is the strongest of all the Gospels.[7] This caricature is both historically irresponsible and unjust. Furthermore, John implies that the Pharisees (and others who do not confess Jesus as Messiah) are excluded from the circle of God's love. This move is inappropriate to the gospel of God's unconditional love for all.

Repentance is a major Lenten theme. Preachers can help the congregation repent of both continuing to accept the caricature of the Pharisees and of perpetuating the exclusive claim that God loves only those who confess Jesus as Messiah.

Fifth Sunday in Lent/Year A

John 11:1–45

According to John 11:4, the purpose of this event is to demonstrate the effect of the revelation of God through Jesus and to clarify the Christian hope. That is why, after hearing that Lazarus is dying, Jesus waits two days before going to him; the sign is not merely a healing but effects eternal life (vv. 1–5).

The passage underscores the fact that Lazarus is dead (11:7–17, 32, 39, 44). Death is a preeminent characteristic of the *kosmos*. For John, death is not simply the end of physical being but is existence now and in the future apart from the life-giving purposes of God. The dead Lazarus thus represents the fatal brokenness of the *kosmos*.

Martha has faith that Jesus can raise Lazarus. However, in 11:24 she voices an apocalyptic viewpoint that John seeks to correct. For apocalyptists, the dualism of life was chronological: God shows love for the universe by destroying the old (present) age, replacing it with a new (coming) one. The human being is not made up of two parts (body and soul) but is a single unit. At death the self becomes like dirt: lifeless and unconscious. As part of the apocalypse ("the last day" of v. 24) God brings bodies to life.

In articulating the Johannine understanding of eternal life (vv. 24–25), John, in contrast, draws on a strand of Hellenistic Judaism that is an amalgam from the Hebrew tradition and Greek philosophical movements, especially middle Platonism. In this worldview, time continues indefinitely. The dualism of life is of qualities of existence rather than chronology. Some Hellenistic Jewish writers thought that an aspect of the self is immortal, and although the body dies, the essential self continues (e.g., Wis. 2:23; 3:1–8; 8:13, 17; 9:15; 15:3; cf. 4 Macc. 9:7–9; 10:4; 18:23; Philo, *On Giants* 3.13–14; *On the Life of Abraham* 258; *Questions and Answers on Genesis* 3.11). Thus, God shows love for people by helping them make their way through the *kosmos* and by removing them from it at death. These early writers were less concerned with the space of eternity than in describing it as a condition of the self.

In sympathy with Hellenistic Judaism, the Fourth Gospel presents Jesus' resurrecting power already at work: "I *am* [present tense] the resurrection and the life." Resurrection is not a singular future event but a quality of existence characterized by life that begins now. For John, life (*zōē*) is not simply continuing physical operation but existence animated by the Spirit in which one knows such things as love, light, truth, grace, and one-ness of community.

Today's passage contributes significantly to understanding "eternal life" in John (cf. 3:15–16, 36; 4:14, 36; 5:24, 39; 6:27, 40, 47, 54, 68; 10:28; 12:25, 50; 17:2–3). Eternal life begins in the present but also continues beyond death when the essential part of the self dwells in perpetuity with God (11:25b–26). Jesus is preparing "abiding places" in heaven for the community (John 14:1–14).

This story is the climactic sign that reveals Jesus as one who reveals God. It helps readers understand why Jesus could go knowingly and willingly to death: He anticipated eternal life. John wants members of the community to believe that they too will receive such life (v. 15). Jesus' followers can endure misunderstanding and hatred from persons who share the worldview and violent practices of the *kosmos* (see, e.g., 15:18–16:4) because the disciples already experience life that they know will never end. What Jesus did for Lazarus, Jesus does for all who believe.

Palm Sunday or Passion Sunday/Year A

Matthew 21:1–11; 27:11–54

The Mount of Olives, or Mount Scopus, is mentioned several times in Jewish tradition as the place where the Messiah will appear (Josephus, *Antiquities* 20, 167–72). Zechariah 14:1–5 speaks of "a day" when "the LORD" will defend Jerusalem against "the nations," that is, Gentile armies attacking Jerusalem, and "his feet shall stand on the Mount of Olives." When Roman troops occupied Jerusalem at Passover, kept the temple under surveillance from the Fortress Antonia, and posted troops all around the temple courtyard, the intensely scriptural community of the early church would have heard the overtones of Zechariah.

"A donkey tied, and a colt with her" recalls Zech. 9:9–10: "Rejoice greatly, O daughter Zion! Shout aloud, O daughter Jerusalem! Lo, your king comes to you; triumphant and victorious is he, humble and riding on a donkey, on a colt, the foal of a donkey. . . . He shall command peace to the nations." The Messiah comes humbly and brings shalom. Rabbinic literature widely regards the humble donkey or colt as the animal of the Messiah; the donkey is not a warhorse.

Spreading "cloaks on the road" recalls the anointing of Jehu as king of Israel: "They all took their cloaks and spread them for him on the bare steps; and they blew the trumpet, and proclaimed, 'Jehu is king'" (2 Kgs. 9:13). *Hosha-na* means "save us." Jews waved branches and cried out "Hosanna!" at Sukkot, the Feast of Tabernacles. "Blessed is the one who comes in the name of the Lord" (21:9) precisely quotes Ps. 118:26.

In his trial of Jesus, Pilate asks, "Are you the king of the Jews?" Not nuanced in the varieties of apocalyptic, Pilate's question reflects the concerns of Roman government: Was Jesus an insurrectionist? Fear of revolt against Roman rule led to Pilate's execution of Jesus, on the charge put on the cross itself: King of the Jews (Roman law required the crime to be made public on the *titulus* of the cross).

In the death sentence (27:15–26), Matthew speaks of a "custom" of releasing for the crowd any prisoner whom it wanted. Outside the Gospels, we have no confirmation of this custom. In this scene, the Gospels give the strong impression of "blame shifting," of removing responsibility for the crucifixion from Pilate to the "crowds." Pilate's historical reputation for excessive cruelty is effectively covered over here. In Mark it was the chief priests' "envy" that led to Jesus' delivery to Pilate; Matthew changes Mark to make the crowd envious. A standard way in which Jews appealed to Rome for justice and relief from oppression was to stress that earlier Roman authorities had not persecuted Jews but looked favorably upon them.[8] The early church uses the same plea: Pilate did not persecute us.

Matthew tells us that the "people as a whole" say, "His blood be on us and on our children!" This has often been interpreted as a curse upon the Jewish people, condemning them to suffering for the crime of deicide. We suggest instead that preachers recall the blood of Jesus at the Last Supper, "poured out for many for the forgiveness of sins" (Matt. 26:28). Indeed, that is the gospel.

The "whole cohort" of Roman soldiers mock and abuse Jesus in the *praitōrion*, the governor's official residence, which was located either in Herod's palace or the Fortress Antonia. The two "bandits" (*lestai*), crucified with Jesus, could have been social bandits, political offenders, or both. Roman custom was for victims to be crucified naked and their clothing given to the executing soldiers; thus, Matthew says that the soldiers "divided" Jesus' clothes after the crucifixion.

Easter Day/Year A

Matthew 28:1–10

Whereas Mark 16:1 has three women visit Jesus' tomb to anoint him, in Matthew only Mary and Mary Magdalene go to "see the tomb." Jews in the ancient world sat by their loved ones' graves for three days to make certain that they had not been buried alive. The two Marys are faithfully present throughout Matthew's story of Jesus' passion. They saw Jesus die (27:56), saw him buried (27:61), and found his tomb empty on Easter Sunday (28:1). As earlier in Matthew, so here they persist in their loyalty to Jesus.

The angel instructs them to tell the disciples that Jesus has been raised and is going ahead of them to Galilee. Matthew reports that "they left the tomb quickly with fear and great joy, and ran to tell his disciples" (v. 8). Unlike the guards (v. 4) who were overcome by fear, the women were not. As they went, Jesus met them and they worshiped him (v. 9). The risen Jesus first appears to the two Marys; they are the first to worship him and the first to tell his "brothers" that they will see him in Galilee (v. 10)—the first witnesses to the risen Christ and his first missionaries.

The idea of resurrection in the scriptures of Israel refers to the restoration of the people Israel from exile and from sin, for example: "Thus says the Lord GOD: I am going to open your graves, and bring you up from your graves, O my people; and I will bring you back to the land of Israel" (Ezek. 37:12). "Come, let us return to the LORD. . . . After two days he will revive us; on the third day he will raise us up" (Hos. 6:1–2). Jesus' resurrection cannot be severed from God's promise of restoration of the people Israel.

Israel's scriptures also tell of particular individuals who were raised from the dead or who ascended into heaven or both: Enoch (Gen. 5:21–24), the widow's son brought back to life by Elijah (1 Kgs. 17:17–24), Elijah himself (2 Kgs. 2:1–13), and the son of the Shunammite woman raised from the dead by Elisha (2 Kgs. 4:8–37). Jewish belief in resurrection became more widespread after the killing of many *hasidim* by the forces of Antiochus IV Epiphanes (see Dan. 12:1–3; 2 Macc. 7).

Around the time of Jesus, the Pharisees affirmed the resurrection of the dead. The Sadducees denied it, however, and it was the "Sadducees [not the Pharisees who] came to him, who say that there is no resurrection" (Matt. 22:23; Mark 12:18; Luke 20:27). As the rabbinic tradition has it, "All Israelites have a share in the world to come," but it makes an exception for those who "say that there is no resurrection of the dead" (*m. Sanhedrin* 10:1). Another Mishnaic tract claims, "The Holy Spirit leads to the resurrection of the dead. And the resurrection of the dead shall come through Elijah of blessed memory" (*m. Sotah* 9:15).

The apostle Paul spoke of his encounter with the risen Christ this way: "But when God . . . was pleased to reveal his Son to me . . ." (Gal. 1:15–16).

He also cites appearances of Christ to various apostles, beginning with Cephas and ending, "last of all," with his appearance to Paul himself. To these earlier stories Matthew (and the other Gospel writers) add the empty tomb. The empty tomb is implied by the encounter with the risen Christ, but it does not imply that Christ is risen. The empty tomb requires an explanation, which the angel gives: "He is risen." Yet, Matthew tells us, among the followers of Jesus who later met him in Galilee, "some doubted" (28:17). The New Testament neither describes nor explains the resurrection; the resurrection explains the New Testament. It is the foretaste of the world to come, occurring in the middle of human sin and alienation.

Second Sunday of Easter/Years A, B, and C

John 20:19–31

Tension between the synagogue of Jesus' followers and the traditional synagogue underlies the motif of fear in 20:19b. The closed house reminds readers of the Johannine synagogue: a fearful community that feels trapped in a hostile setting. Ironically, John pictures traditional Jewish folk (who should live peacefully) creating an environment of nonpeace for John's community. However, not even a locked door can keep Jesus away. He appears with a quintessential Jewish blessing: peace (that is, communal well-being).

Jesus sends the disciples into the world in the same way that God sent him (20:21). In v. 22, Jesus empowers the disciples by breathing the Spirit on them (cf. Acts 2:1–21). The Spirit that empowered Jesus is now at work in the community. This Spirit is the same as Jesus' continuing presence (14:15–17, 25–31; 15:26–16:15).

The mission of the Johannine community is to reveal God's love for the *kosmos* by continuing Jesus' works (see, e.g., John 14:10–12) and teaching (e.g., John 21:15–18). On what Jesus and the disciples are sent to do, see, for example, John 3:17; 5:24; 6:38–39; 7:16; 8:16; 12:44–45; 13:20; 14:24; 15:26–27; 17:18.

Conflict with the synagogue is the backdrop of 20:23. Commentators almost all agree that some traditional synagogue excommunicated John's community (see 9:34; 12:42). In 20:22, Jesus assures the community that it does not speak or act of its own will but is prompted by the Spirit. The synagogue sometimes used the language of forgiving (*aphiēmi*) and retaining (*krateō*) sins to speak of those who can remain in the community (forgiven) and those who are banned (retained). Although members of the Johannine community have been ousted from the synagogue, v. 23 assures them that the Spirit welcomes them into the synagogue of Jesus' followers.

John introduces Thomas as an example of a person whose doubt could put his standing in the Johannine synagogue in question (20:24–29). Although Thomas hears that Jesus is alive, he does not believe. To believe in the Fourth Gospel is to acknowledge that God is revealed through Jesus. Nonbelievers are excluded from the circle of God's love (John 3:18; 5:38; 6:64–65; 8:44–47). Thomas insists on seeing Jesus before believing, and on touching Jesus' wounded hands and side (20:24–25).

A few days later, Jesus comes and stands among the community members in a house whose doors are shut and again wishes them peace (v. 26). With the living Jesus before him, Thomas believes without touching Jesus' wounded body. Thomas thus receives the Jewish gift of peace by believing that God is revealed through Jesus.

Christians have usually understood Thomas's confession, "My Lord and my God!" to indicate that John regards Jesus as God (vs. 28). However, with other Hellenistic writers, the Fourth Gospel regularly speaks of Jesus as "Lord" to mean a respected ruler. Further, as we saw in connection with John 1:1–18 (Christmas Day/Years A, B, and C), Philo spoke of the *logos* (the word) as *theos* (of divine origin) without claiming that the word is God (cf. Philo, *Questions and Answers on Genesis* 2.62). Thomas believes in this sense.

The crescendo of this narrative is 20:29. Not only does the Spirit continue to make Jesus present in the community, but it can reveal Jesus so powerfully as to overcome questions, even those as profound as Thomas's. Thus, members of the Johannine community have not seen Jesus and yet have "life in his name" (20:30–31).

Third Sunday of Easter/Year A

Luke 24:13–35

The Emmaus road story challenges all simple ideas of Jesus' resurrection. Jesus appears directly to two disciples, walks a considerable distance with them, discusses Scripture with them, and all this time they do not recognize him. Nothing is obvious about the resurrection. Only after the three of them break bread together, following their discussion of Scripture, are their eyes opened and they are enabled to recognize him.

In John's Gospel, Mary Magdalene "saw Jesus standing there, but she did not know that it was Jesus. . . . Supposing him to be the gardener, she said to him, 'Sir, if you have carried him away, tell me where you have laid him'" (John 20:14–15). Luke and John indicate that something more complex than what is apparent is going on.

Luke's Emmaus road account is a recognition story. Somewhere between Jerusalem and an unknown location, two disciples and Jesus are in conversation (*homileō*) with each other. The verb signals that Luke wants us to understand that this was not a short and snappy chat but an extensive dialogue. They discuss "the things about Jesus of Nazareth," whom they had hoped "was the one to redeem Israel" (Luke 24:19, 21). They recount how "some women of our group astounded us" with reports that Jesus was alive. Nonetheless, two further things have to happen before these disciples can "see" that Jesus is with them: He explains to them "the things about himself in all the scriptures" (v. 27) and they break bread together, as they had often done in the past. Luke uses the expression *klasei tou artou*, "breaking bread," to refer to the ritual meal of the community, one in which it had long participated with Jesus and in which it would participate in the future.

"Then [and only then] their eyes were opened" (v. 31). Luke shows us, compressed into the story of one afternoon, how the community came to understand the risen Jesus. Its direct experience of the empty tomb left it perplexed, unseeing. Even an encounter with the risen Jesus could lead nowhere. In addition to these there must be the scriptures of Israel, the pored-over scriptures, to provide the context within which Jesus Christ takes shape—the scriptures of Israel and the people Israel.

They could interpret their experience only by turning to "all the scriptures." Without them, they would have had no metaphors or symbols with which to make sense of their experience. Had they no sense of the presence of Christ, the scriptures would not have helped them understand it. Had they no scriptures, their sense of his presence would have remained vague and inarticulate.

They also knew his living presence in the ongoing practice of breaking bread together. He was "made known to them in the breaking of the bread" (v. 35). The communal practices of poring over Scripture and breaking bread are the context in which the church becomes aware of Jesus' presence with it. Also, they become aware of his presence in the lives of strangers whom they meet in walking the way of life through the ups and down of history.

The women hurried from the tomb to witness to the apostles. The apostles went toward the tomb and returned, amazed, but not believing. The two men walk toward Emmaus, "sad-faced" as the Greek has it.

Everybody's going in different directions. The practice of telling this story constructs not only a common narrative but the community itself. The two disciples missed the significance, the ultimate significance, of the stranger who accompanied them on the way to Emmaus. Christ is present in the stranger.

Fourth Sunday of Easter/Year A

John 10:1–10

A sheepfold was a pen usually made of stone walls topped with briars. It could be in the open country or attached to a house. The wall had an opening called a "gate," and when the sheep were in the pen, a gatekeeper (10:3) guarded the gate.

Those who could enter the sheepfold by the gate had a proper relationship with the sheep, while thieves and bandits would climb over the wall to steal them (vv. 1–2). When sheep do not recognize the voice of a stranger, they will not follow (v. 5), but they come to the shepherd's voice because they know it. The shepherd would lead them out of the sheepfold and walk ahead of them to a pasture for food and water (vv. 3b–4).

Jesus speaks these words to the Pharisees (9:40), using what v. 6 calls a "figure of speech" (*paroima*), a term that occurs frequently in the Septuagint. Since the Pharisees were steeped in the Septuagint, they should have grasped the point of vv. 1–5. However, typical of the distorted picture of the Pharisees in John, they do not.

In vv. 7–10, Jesus presumes not only familiarity with sheep and shepherds but also with figurative language for the community (sheep) and its leaders (shepherds). Ezekiel 34, which contains the fullest description of this metaphor, laments that Israel is guided by false shepherds who do not care for the sheep but who use the sheep for their own own benefit; the false shepherds eat the sheep (cf. Jer. 23:1–6; Zech. 11:14–17). This raises the question, "Who are trustworthy leaders for our community?"

In 10:7–21, Jesus evokes the notion of true and false shepherds to identify himself as the gate and the good shepherd and the Pharisees as false shepherds who are thieves and bandits who steal, kill, and destroy. From John's perspective, the Pharisees had long demonstrated that they were unreliable guides (see, e.g., John 7:32, 45–48; 8:13; 11:45–57; 12:19, 42–43; 18:3). When the Pharisees learn that Jesus healed the formerly blind man, they ban him from the synagogue—that is, they excommunicate him from the sheepfold of God (9:34). In so doing, they manifest their own blindness and sin (9:39–41). Hence, in John's view, they are false shepherds, and their excommunication is a false gate keeping the now sighted man out of the synagogue. They are thieves who have stolen that person's rightful community. They kill and destroy, for they participate in Jesus' death (11:45–53; 18:3).

By contrast, Jesus is a faithful guide, and his sheepfold is a trustworthy synagogue. People who enter the sheepfold through the gate of Jesus find salvation. They are not locked out, but come and go to find pasture. According to 10:10, Jesus came to give abundant life to the sheep. For John, "life" is more than survival. It is existence animated by the Spirit so that one experiences grace, love, light, truth, freedom, unity in community, and eternal continuation of the self.

The preacher can critique the picture of the Pharisees in John 10 as a caricature that uses the Pharisees as a tool, a negative foil, to defame the leadership of another community. In a positive vein, the preacher can affirm that Jesus still offers abundant life—a welcome word to people beaten up in the *kosmos*, including Jews beaten up by John's rhetoric. Since this life comes ultimately from the God of Israel, the preacher's interpretation of it should be congruent with the life that is commended from today's synagogue. True abundant life seeks to overcome ruptures in human community, such as the separation of church and synagogue. A sermon could affirm Christian community as a reliable sheepfold. The preacher can ask, "Who are false shepherds in today's world?"

Fifth Sunday of Easter/Year A

John 14:1–6

In Jewish thinking, the heart was the center of the self. John 14:1a assumes that the disciples' hearts are troubled. This passage aims to relieve their distress.

John 13 explains why the disciples are troubled. Jesus knows in v. 1 that he will soon "depart from this world" (die on the cross) and "go to the Father" (fully enter the heavenly realm). The devil possesses Judas (vv. 2, 10–11, 18–19, 21–30). The disciples cannot now go with Jesus (vv. 36–37). Peter will deny Jesus (v. 38).

As faithful Jews, the disciples trust God. Because God abides (*menō*) in Jesus, they can believe Jesus (14:1b; cf. 1:32; 5:37–38; 6:56; 12:46; 14:10, 17; 15:4–16). God's house contains many dwelling places. This house is heaven (Ps. 2:4; Isa. 66:1; Philo, *On Dreams* 1.256). Heaven is the sphere of existence of light, truth, spirit, freedom, and eternal life. At death, the essential part of the self leaves the broken *kosmos* and enters heaven, a realm of "dwelling places" (*monai*) (see, e.g., *1 Enoch* 39:4). While *monai* refers to spaces, the reader of this time recognizes that *monai* and *menō* are related. These places are less architectural than relational: God indwells self and community.

Jesus goes to prepare dwelling places for the disciples in heaven (14:2b). He will "come again" and take the disciples to heaven so that they may be with him and God.

Thomas asks a question that foreshadows his later doubts about the resurrection (14:5; 21:24–29), and Jesus replies with one of the most famous and theologically troubling and exclusivist texts in the Fourth Gospel: John 14:6.

The word "way" (*hodos*) reverberates with Jewish associations. The Septuagint frequently uses this term to speak of the life that God desires (e.g., Exod. 18:20; Ps. 1; Jer. 33:13; Wis. 5:6). Philo, much like John, uses *hodos* to refer to the way to God or heaven (see e.g., *On the Posterity of Cain* 101, 31).

This background of "way" is evoked when Jesus says, "I am the way, the truth, and the life." Although Jesus has just said in chap. 13. that the way he is going is to his death and resurrection (cf. 14:4), John 14:6 includes the whole event of Jesus' descending and ascending. The "way" that Jesus reveals is also the truth and the life. For John, "truth" is not a metaphysical category but the revelation of God through Jesus. It is also "life," that is, existence animated by the Spirit and shaped by the aims of God. According to John, Jesus is now the way to God. "No one comes to the Father except through me" (14:6b). This statement criticizes the non-Jesus-following synagogue.

The Jewish community interpreted texts according to two axioms: constitutive and prophetic.[9] This text constitutes (builds up, affirms) the synagogue of Jesus' followers by its interpretation of the trustworthiness of the path to God through Jesus. Yet no amount of theological juggling in the name of particularism, a "hidden Christ," or sensitivity to John's pastoral situation, can excise the exclusivism of v. 6. However, one of John's own insights prophetically critiques this exclusivism. If God's love for the *kosmos* (3:16a) is truly unconditional, then the divine love cannot be limited to Jesus' followers. Such a broad interpretation is consistent with the best insights of the First Testament that portray the God of Israel showing love and compassion for all, even Gentiles and enemies (e.g., 1 Kgs. 8:41–43; 2 Kgs. 5:1–19; Isa. 45:22–24).

Sixth Sunday of Easter/Year A

John 14:15–21

Today's reading summarizes the distinctive Johannine interpretation of the work of the Holy Spirit. In 14:16, the NRSV translates John's special designation for the Spirit as "Advocate" (*paraklētos*). This combines two meanings of the word, one from the Hellenistic world meaning one who functions as an advocate or helper in the legal arena, and the other and less technical meaning for one who speaks on behalf of (or represents) another.

While the Fourth Gospel does not make extensive use of legal imagery, God judges the *kosmos*, condemning those who do not follow Jesus while giving eternal life to those who do (John 3:18–19; 5:22–30; 7:51; 8:12–20, 50; 9:39; 12:44–50; 16:4b–11). The Spirit as Advocate guides the community in the way (14:6) that avoids condemnation and leads to life (15:26–27).

The Spirit continues the work of Jesus in the community after Jesus is gone. Like Jesus, the Spirit communicates truth and abides in the community (15:17). The Advocate will be a kind of rabbi, continuing to teach the Johannine synagogue Jesus' teachings after Jesus' departure, including things to come (15:26; 16:12–15). The Advocate will expose the sin of the *kosmos* and the condemnation of the ruler of this world (16:7–11). Because the Spirit prompts Jesus to indwell the congregation, the community will continue Jesus' works, and, indeed, will even magnify them (14:12–13). The Advocate will empower the community's witness in the face of hatred (15:26–27).

The orphan is a powerful symbol of abandonment and vulnerability in Judaism. John 14:18 implies that the community feels orphaned. The congregation may feel this way because (1) Jesus is going away or (2) many members of the congregation have been excommunicated from the synagogue and feel cut off from their fundamental community in the same way that orphans are cut off from their families.

Jewish covenantal thought intends care for orphans (see, e.g., Exod. 22:21; Deut. 24:17). When Jesus says, "I am coming to you. In a little while the world will no longer see me, but you will see me," the context prompts the reader to recognize that after his death and resurrection, Jesus will be manifest in the community by means of the Advocate. Jesus thus exhibits a fundamental attitude of Judaism by providing his presence for the disciples. Furthermore, the people are no longer orphaned, for the

Spirit brings them into a new community that replaces the synagogue that cast them out (John 17:11, 22).

Jesus' words, "Because I live, you also will live," have particular promise against the backdrop of the orphan imagery. Orphans often existed from day to day. By contrast, those who know God through Jesus experience life, that is, vitality energized by the presence of Jesus that manifests light, truth, grace, and freedom.

When people are alive in the Spirit, they keep Jesus' commandments (14:15, 21). "This is my commandment, that you love one another as I have loved you" (15:12). In John, love is the self-giving of one for the good of another. The descent of Jesus from heaven (including his death) defines love for John (15:13–17). Emphasis on love as the center of the life of the community is unmistakably Jewish (see, e.g., Lev. 19:18, 34; Deut. 10:12–12:1; Sir. 27:17; 40:20; Philo, *On the Virtues* 51ff.).

Ascension of the Lord/Years A, B, and C

Luke 24:44–53

Many ancient Jewish narratives end a story about a major figure with that person blessing and commissioning the community. Deuteronomy, for instance, ends with Moses' sermon (Deut. 32–33), and the *Testaments of the Twelve Patriarchs* (written in the Hellenistic era) is presented as the final guidance of the leaders of the twelve tribes of Israel to the generations living at the transition of the old and new ages.

Luke 24:44–53 follows this pattern. In vv. 44–48, Luke portrays the ministry of Jesus (and hence of the early church) in continuity with the traditions of Israel represented by Moses, the prophets, and the psalms. Not only is Jesus identified as a rabbinical interpreter of these scriptures, but these scriptures help the disciples interpret the significance of Jesus. The core of the Gospel of Luke is that the final manifestation of the reign of God is underway through Jesus. The preacher may want to underscore a Lukan point: the scriptures of Judaism, the First Testament, are essential to the Christian community. Without them, we cannot understand Jesus Christ or the reign of God.

Verses 46–49 presuppose Jewish associations. Many Jewish people in the first century believed that a period of suffering (the tribulation) would precede the final manifestation of the reign of God. Luke interprets the death and resurrection of Jesus in this way. The death of Jesus is not salvific but prefigures the tribulation, while the resurrection demonstrates that the apocalyptic completion of God's purposes is near. The Messiah (Christ) is God's primary agent in this transformation.

Jesus commissions the disciples to announce repentance and forgiveness of sins to all nations. The "nations" are likely Gentiles. Many Jewish texts anticipated that God would gather Gentiles into the divine reign (e.g., Isa. 60:1–7; *1 Enoch* 10:18–22). This ingathering is underway in the church. To become a part of the eschatological community, Gentiles take the Jewish step of repentance, that is, they turn away from idolatry and injustice and turn toward the God of Israel and covenantal community. Luke follows a Jewish tradition in saying that the completion of God's purposes will begin in Jerusalem and flow to other places (see, e.g., *Leviticus Rabbah* 24). Jesus promises to send the Holy Spirit (the power from on high) to strengthen the community for witness (Luke 24:49).

The passage climaxes with the ascension of Jesus to the right hand of God (see Acts 7:56; cf. Acts 1:6–11). In a priestly gesture, Jesus raises his hands to bless the disciples.

The ascension has three significant dimensions. (1) It assures the community that Jesus' commission is trustworthy. The right hand of God is a place of power. An ancient saying held that "the right hand of God is everywhere." When the community hears that Jesus is at that right hand, they know that his liberating power is everywhere. (2) Luke–Acts states repeatedly that Jesus will return in an apocalyptic cataclysm. This narrative lets the listeners know where Jesus is located until that time. (3) The story implicitly contrasts the dominion of Caesar with that of Jesus. Caesar rules the empire with oppressive force, but Jesus rules from the liberating presence of the one who is sovereign over all creation. This affirmation is key to a community whose leading missionary, Paul, comes into conflict with the imperial authorities (Acts 20–28).

The Jewish character of this passage is reinforced when, after Jesus is carried into heaven, the disciples return to the temple. There they join in the archetypal Jewish activity of blessing God. The elements of this story thus combine to bestow a Jewish blessing on the early mission of the church.

Seventh Sunday of Easter/Year A

John 17:1–11

John follows the pattern of other narratives of Jewish leaders who pray at the end of their lives (e.g., Deut. 31–33; *Jubilees* 1:19–21; 10:1–6; *2 Baruch*

54; 2 Esd. 8:19–36). Such a prayer is a "last will and testament" that summarizes key themes. Jesus also prays in the Jewish model with open eyes turned toward heaven (17:1a).

In the first part of the petition (vv. 1–8), Jesus prays that his "hour" will glorify God. In John's Gospel, "the hour" is not one thing but the series of events comprised of the death, resurrection, and appearances of Jesus as one moment of revelation.

"Glory" (*doxa*) and "glorification" echo the First Testament notion of glory as visible manifestation of power. To behold God's glory is to behold God's power and will (see, e.g., Exod. 16:10; 24:7; Wis. 9:10; 2 Macc. 2:8). When the Jewish tradition speaks of God glorifying people, it refers to God manifesting the divine will and power through them (see, e.g., Isa. 55:5; Wis. 18:8; 19:8; Sir. 45:3; 47:6). In John 17:1b, Jesus prays for the events of the hour to reveal God's liberating presence in the *kosmos*.

The purpose of the glorification or revelation of God through Jesus is eternal life (v. 2). The Hellenistic Jewish community often referred to "the only true God" (see, e.g., Philo, *On the Special Laws* 1.322; 3 Macc. 6:18). In defining eternal life as knowing God, John draws on the Jewish motif that to "know" God is to follow the way of God (v. 3; cf. Ps. 9:10; 25:4; Isa. 45:3) that can lead to immortality (see, e.g., Wis. 15:3; Philo, *That God Is Unchangeable* 143). John adapts this thought: Jesus is the way to eternal life—animation by God.

Jesus' "hour" reveals God's divine presence and power. Jesus prays (vv. 4–5) that in the next phase of existence, he will be in the immediate presence of God even as he was before God created the world (John 1:1–2).

In vv. 6–11, Jesus prays for the disciples, whom he will leave in the *kosmos*. He has performed an essential Jewish act by making the name of God (identity, character, purpose) known (v. 6; cf. Exod. 3:13–22; Isa. 52:6; John 8:24). John 17:6 is both pastoral and polemical: Although the followers of Jesus have been banned from the traditional synagogue, they are truly Jewish, for they know the divine name.

Jesus assures the synagogue of his followers that everything he has told them comes from God (John 17:7–8; cf. 17:2). The congregation does not have to be a part of a traditional synagogue to receive reliable teaching. Their instruction is from God.

In vv. 9–11, Jesus prays not for the *kosmos* but for God to "protect" (*tē-reō*) the disciples while they remain in the *kosmos* where they are harassed (15:18–16:4; 16:16–33). To "protect" does not mean to keep from all harm but to preserve the disciples as a colony of heaven though resident in the *kosmos* (cf. Wis. 10:5).

Although the disciples will scatter—that is, be harassed (16:32; cf. Zech. 13:7)—Jesus prays that they will recognize they are one as are Jesus and God. By "one" John means that they are related intimately with one another and share unity of purpose. Even when they are alone (e.g., when hated), the community is with them.

This passage, like many others in this Gospel, claims that the synagogue of Jesus' followers belongs to the tradition of Judaism. The preacher can encourage today's congregation to accept that claim while discouraging the congregation from simultaneously thinking that the church is superior to Judaism.

Day of Pentecost/Year A

John 7:37–39

This brief incident takes place at the conclusion of the Feast of Booths, or Sukkoth (see Lev. 23:34–36; Deut. 16:13, 16; cf. Neh. 8:14–18). While the Feast of Booths originated as a festival to give thanksgiving for the harvest, it evolved to commemorate the providence of God during the wandering in the wilderness when the Israelites dwelled in tents.

Three dimensions of this feast and its history are important for today's lection. First, by the time of John, the temple was destroyed, and Jews were reconceiving the celebration and meaning of this feast and many other aspects of Jewish life. Second, John 1:14 echoes this feast (especially the providence of God in the wilderness) by saying that the Word "dwelled [Greek: *skēnoō*, "pitched a tent"] among us." Jesus, the *logos*, mediates divine providence to the Johannine community. Third, according to Zech. 14:16–19, God will bring about an eschatological Feast of Booths that celebrates salvation of both Jewish and Gentile peoples. The Feast of Booths came to include a dramatic pouring out of water near the conclusion of the festival (*m. Sukkah* 4:9–10). While this rite originated as a petition for rain for fertility, it developed into a broader statement of salvation. The Babylonian Talmud explains its significance by citing Isa. 12:3: "Therefore with joy shall ye draw water from the wells of salvation" (*b. Sukkah* 48b). The ritual promises salvation.

During the climactic water ritual, Jesus cries out the words of John 7:37b–38. The reference to "thirst" (addressed to the Jewish crowd at the Feast of Booths) reminds the reader that John sometimes uses water in negative association with Jewish people. At the wedding in Cana, the water for the Jewish rites of purification was inferior to the wine of Jesus

(2:1–11). The water from Jacob's well (a Jewish source) cannot satisfy the Samaritan woman as can the living water (Holy Spirit) of Jesus (4:5–26). The water that Jesus gives satisfies thirst in a way that water from the Jewish community does not.

The Greek of v. 38 can be punctuated and translated two ways: one indicating that Jesus is the source of the living water, and the other indicating that the living water flows out of the believer. The theological worldview of the Fourth Gospel commends the first alternative. Rudolph Schnackenburg captures the spirit of Jesus' words in a simple but elegant translation: "If anyone believes in me, for [that one]—as the Scripture says—rivers of living water will flow from his [i.e., Jesus'] heart."[10] The water to which Jesus refers is the Spirit (v. 39; cf. Sixth Sunday of Easter). Jesus communicates the Spirit to the synagogue of his followers (John 20:19–23).

The passage that is cited as scripture in v. 38 is not found in any one text in Jewish literature but echoes passages that use water imagery to speak of the promises of God, salvation, or the Spirit (e.g., Isa. 44:2–3; Zech. 14:8; 16–18; Ezek. 47:1–13; *Genesis Rabbah* 70.8).

John 7:37–39 intimates that Jesus makes the theological realities celebrated through the Feast of Booths available to the synagogue of his followers apart from the temple or a traditional synagogue. The Fourth Gospel may have intended this perspective as a polemic against the synagogue (John 9:34; 12:42). However, the preacher can celebrate the positive symbolism of this text for today's church without casting such aspersion. Through the Spirit, the living Jesus makes salvation a reality in the *kosmos*.

First Sunday after Pentecost/Year A

Trinity Sunday

Matthew 28:16–20

This passage, in spite of its brevity, speaks of four matters: the appearance of Jesus to the eleven disciples, the self-disclosure of Jesus' authority, a two-part charge to the disciples, and a promise that Jesus will always be with his followers.

1. The appearance (vv. 16 and 17): The eleven disciples, having followed Jesus to the mountain in Galilee, "worshiped him." Whereas Mark ends leaving the reader wondering whether the disciples ever received the

message to follow Jesus to Galilee, Matthew assures the reader that Jesus and his disciples remained faithful to each other.

It is a mark of Matthew's honesty that he reports the mixed reaction of the disciples to Jesus. "They worshiped him," says Matthew, "but some doubted" or hesitated. As in some of the other appearance stories, not even the actual presence of the living Jesus resolves all difficulties. Unlike Luke's Emmaus road story, Matthew simply mentions the disciples' doubt or nonrecognition of Jesus and lets the matter drop, as if he and his community are accustomed to such doubt and mature enough to abide it.

2. The disclosure of Jesus' authority (v. 18): "All authority in heaven and on earth has been given to me." In the temptation story (Matt. 4:1–11), read on the first Sunday in Lent, Jesus denies himself comfort, safety, and power for the sake of the rule of God. In the Great Commission, Jesus receives as a gift from God what he rejected as temptation from the tempter. The scene is reminiscent of Dan. 7:13–14: "I saw one like a human being. . . . To him was given dominion and glory and kingship, that all peoples, nations, and languages should serve him." It also recalls the edict of Cyrus, king of Persia: "The LORD, the God of heaven, has given me all the kingdoms of the earth, and he has charged me to build him a house at Jerusalem, which is in Judah" (2 Chr. 36:23). Resurrection and return from exile are related in Jewish literature (Ezek. 37), and Jesus' resurrection takes place when the people Israel are in exile in the land of Israel.

3. The two-part charge to the disciples (vv. 19–20a): "Make disciples of all nations, baptizing them . . . and teaching them to obey everything that I have commanded you." Matthew's Greek says to make disciples *panta ta ethnē*, "of all the Gentiles." The promise to Abraham and Sarah that their descendants would be a blessing to the Gentiles is actualized as Gentiles are brought into faithful relationship with the God of Israel.

Making Gentiles into disciples involves more than baptizing them; it entails "teaching them to obey everything that I have commanded you." This line points to all of Jesus' teachings in Matthew, beginning with the Sermon on the Mount and continuing through the parable of the judgment of the nations: Matthew's *mitzvoth*. Matthew's Jesus constantly emphasizes keeping all the law, from the least to the weightiest. Doing deeds of loving-kindness is more important than saying "Lord, Lord." Sermons should place as much emphasis on teaching as on evangelism.

Prior to this point in Matthew, Jesus has done all the teaching. Now we are all to be teachers of faith.

4. The promise (v. 20): "And remember, I am with you always, to the end of the age." Matthew's Jesus is God's wisdom incarnate, and as such

he speaks here. As symbol of God he is always with us because God is always with us, as the all-present one, the *Shekhinah*, who is present wherever two or three are gathered with the Torah between them (*m. Avot* 3:2).

Proper 4 [9]/Year A

Matthew 7:21–29

This reading from the lectionary is identical with the reading for the Ninth Sunday after the Epiphany/Year A. Please go to the commentary for that Sunday.

Proper 5 [10]/Year A

Matthew 9:9–13, 18–26

Gospel statements about tax collectors put us in a quandary. We will describe tax collectors, then describe the quandary.

Jesus saw Matthew "sitting at the tax booth." After Matthew responded to Jesus' call, "many tax collectors and sinners" joined Jesus and the disciples at dinner. The tax booth assessed tolls on fish caught in the Sea of Galilee. Herod Antipas sold the rights to collect these taxes on fish to the highest bidder. The fishing was done by families who, in turn, bought the rights to fish and borrowed money from these brokers (*telōnai*, translated as "tax collectors" or "publicans"), and then paid them. Indebted to them, fisher families did not get wealthy. In turn, the brokers themselves were contracted to chief tax collectors who were clients of Herod Antipas. In this system, money flowed upward to the rich and the royalty at the expense of the poor, who got poorer.

Rich and powerful patrons were regarded both as thieves and benefactors. Josephus says of Herod the Great: "He had indeed reduced the entire country to helpless poverty after taking it over in as flourishing a condition as few ever knew. . . . In addition to the collecting of the tribute that was imposed on everyone each year, lavish extra contributions had to be made to him and his household . . . because there was no immunity from outrage unless bribes were paid" (*Antiquities* 17.306–8). Herod's brokers were also his clients and benefited from their role in the system.

Tax collectors were regarded as corrupt and disloyal collaborators with Rome. Jesus is depicted as "reclining at table" with them and with "sinners." The meaning of "sinners" is elusive, partly because we are all sinners. This group may have included various people whose very work brought them into disrepute, such as prostitutes and tax collectors. That "sinners" means "unclean" or "impure" is not at all clear. Tax collectors, for example, are not mentioned in the purity codes and, since the temple tithes were taxes, tax collectors were not by definition "impure."

Jesus responds to the Pharisees' question about eating with such people by saying "Those who are well have no need of a physician." Jesus' ministry is addressed to the "lost sheep" of the house of Israel (Matt. 10:6; 15:24), including tax collectors. They need a physician, and Jesus "calls" them as he had Matthew. According to Luke 5:32, Jesus calls them "to repentance," to transformation. Matthew does not say this.

Instead, he gives us (later) the parable of "weeds among the wheat" (13:24–30). This parable signals that Matthew's community was made up of sinners as well as saints, wheat and weeds, tax collectors who remained tax collectors. They will have to learn to live together until God sorts things out later. The church is not made up of perfect people. It is made up of folks like us. It lives by grace.

The two miracle stories in which Jesus restores life to a daughter of a ruler of the synagogue and heals the woman suffering from hemorrhages attest to the ministry of Jesus in other ways. His was a ministry of inclusion of the marginalized and healing of the sick. We note that the ruler of the synagogue had faith in Jesus, that he trusted him. The woman with the hemorrhages is healed by touching the "fringe" (*kraspedon*) of Jesus' cloak, the *zitzit* worn by pious Jews. Some Jews believed that the fringes of a *hasid* (holy man) had healing power (*b. Ta'anith* 23b). Healing stories in the Gospels turn upon the faith of the person seeking healing; they are not stories about magic.

Proper 6 [11]/Year A

Matthew 9:35–10:8

The first paragraph tells us that Jesus taught "in their synagogues," proclaimed the gospel, and healed diseases. That Jesus taught in many synagogues indicates that he was welcomed into them. He "had compassion" on the crowds, because they were "like sheep without a shepherd." The metaphor of the people Israel as "sheep without a shepherd" is drawn from the Scriptures (e.g., Ezek. 4:5–15, Zech. 10:2). The prophets used such language to criticize kings; it is so used here and elsewhere in the Gospels.

"The harvest is plentiful, but the laborers are few" calls to mind Rabbi Tarfon's statement: "The day is short, the work formidable, the workers lazy, the wages high, the employer impatient" (*m. Avot* 2:15, Neusner, *Torah from Our Sages*).

In the second paragraph, Jesus calls and authorizes the apostles. This is the one time that Matthew calls them "apostles." More commonly referred to as "the twelve," the lists of their names vary, and John refers to more than twelve. "The twelve" call to mind the twelve tribes of Israel and symbolize the restoration of the people Israel. ("Jewish restoration theology" is a term that some use in place of "apocalyptic" to designate more clearly what the Jesus movement was about.)[11] Of all these names, the meaning of Judas Iscariot remains a puzzle. Some take it to refer to a village, Keriot Hezron, south of Hebron. If so, Judas would be the only Judean among the Galilean apostles. Alternatively, "Iscariot" could be derived from *sikarios*, a member of the *sicarii*, the assassins who did their deadly work against those who colluded with Rome. The name could be entirely symbolic, a way of naming the Judean assassin who from the outset is known to be the one who will betray Jesus.

The third paragraph describes the mission on which Jesus sends the Twelve. Most striking is the first instruction: "Go nowhere among the Gentiles, and enter no town of the Samaritans, but go rather to the lost sheep of the house of Israel" (10:5). The travel narratives of the Gospels never depict Jesus as going to any of the significant Gentile (Roman) towns—Tiberias, Sepphoris, Beth Shean, and so forth. The mission to "all the Gentiles" (*panta ta ethnē*) in Matthew is the work of the risen Jesus (Matt. 28:19). Strikingly, it is the risen Jesus who calls Paul to a mission to the Gentiles (Gal. 1:15–16).

That Jesus sent his followers only to Jews explains why, later, leaders of the church in Jerusalem went only to Jews (Gal. 2:9). The apostles are to do what Jesus did—proclaim the good news, heal the sick, and to receive no payment. Rabbi Zadok would say, "Do not make Torah a spade with which to dig" (*m. Avot* 4, 5, Neusner, *Torah from Our Sages*). They are to travel light (not a bad idea for today's church). These are criteria to help determine if missionaries are genuine: Do they do what Jesus did? Do they want money? Are they distracted by possessions and status?

The purpose of this mission was not to find converts for Christianity. Matthew does not speak of the church as an alternative to the synagogue. Rather, he disagrees with fellow Jews over the best future for the people

Israel. For Matthew, this future is eventually in the Gentile mission. The mission proclaims the good news of the divine realm (10:7).

Verses 16–18 deal with conflict between the missionaries of Matthew and the synagogue. Matthew's instructions on handling this conflict are to move on to the next place and be both shrewd and innocent.

Proper 7 [12]/Year A

Matthew 10:24–39

Verses 24–25 of this passage concentrate on the relationship between a disciple (*mathētēs*) and a teacher. Matthew's Gospel, as its name suggests, is about discipleship. In this context, the disciple of Jesus is not to expect any destiny better than that of Jesus.

By the time Matthew was writing his Gospel, his community and its mission were facing hardships and rejection (at least from Matthew's perspective; we do not have the views of those who were encountered by Matthew's mission). Immediately prior to this passage, Matthew alerted his community about how to respond to persecution. He had Jesus promise them that the Son of Man will come before they have "gone through all the towns of Israel" (10:23). This remark should be taken as a word of comfort to an afflicted community, not as a literal and therefore false promise.

Matthew proceeds pastorally, advising his community not to fear. Jesus teaches his disciples to proclaim publicly what he tells them when they are together. There is "nothing secret that will not become known" (10:26). This echoes Gamaliel: "Do not say anything which cannot be heard, for in the end it will be heard" (*m. Avot* 2, 4, Neusner, *Torah from Our Sages*).

We are not to fear human beings (those who "kill the body but cannot kill the soul"). Instead, we are to fear God who, alone, "can destroy both body and soul in hell" (10:28). The downside of being told to fear God, because God can do us in, is that our fear can lead to various unfortunate responses. One is to undercut the very trust in and reliance upon God that we understand faith to be. Another is to promote the notion that we should appease God in order to prevent God's destruction from befalling us. We are being told to stand in awe of the one whose love for us is unconditional and who will not kill us.

This is precisely what Matthew says with his parable of the sparrows, all of whom are valued by God: God values the sparrow and God values you even more. God is the one who loves all others, including the human others, and because of God's care and keeping of us our lives are ultimately important and cherished. "Perfect love casts out fear" (1 John 4:18).

Then Matthew returns to the language of judgment: Whoever acknowledges Jesus before others, he will acknowledge to his Father in heaven, and whoever denies him, he will deny (10:32). Our negative acts also are of ultimate importance and matter to God. The tone of threat, however, is at odds with what Matthew has just said about God's valuing of us.

Clearly, one result of the disciples' witness was familial friction. Family members were set against each other: "One's foes will be members of one's own household" (10:36). Those brought into the Matthean community found not only warmth and inclusion but discord and contention with their closest relatives. Jesus is constituting a new family, or a new kind of family, in response to the homelessness and family breakdown that resulted from a depressed economy. He will continue to teach about his "true family" (see, e.g., 12:46–50).

In the concluding verses, Jesus teaches his followers that human relationships are less important than love for him. Note here how Matthew differs from Luke in these remarks. In Luke, Jesus says, "Whoever comes to me and does not hate father and mother, wife and children . . . cannot be my disciple" (14:26). Matthew's Jesus says that we are to love him "more than" our parents or children. We are to have an ultimate relation to the one who is ultimate and to love other people appropriately but not as God.

Proper 8 [13]/Year A

Matthew 10:40–42

These few verses conclude Jesus' teaching to his disciples about the mission on which he is sending them that began in 10:5; today's reading is in that context. Whereas earlier Matthew had talked of the dangers of the mission ("I am sending you out like sheep into the midst of wolves," 10:16), here he has Jesus speak of the welcome that the apostles are to receive: "Whoever welcomes you welcomes me, and whoever welcomes me welcomes the one who sent me."

Notice two points about this text. First, it reflects the hospitality that has characterized Jewish piety since the story of Abraham and Sarah at the oaks of Mamre, where they welcomed into their tent three strangers (Gen. 18:1–8). Jewish legend has it that their tent was open on all sides, welcoming all strangers. In Second Temple Judaism this sense of hospitality was strongly developed and applied particularly to wandering teachers, as this passage applies it to apostles who teach the good news of the kingdom on their mission.

We see this emphasis on hospitality in numerous sources: "He who shows hospitality to the wise [*talmid hakham*], it is as if he brought the first fruits of his produce to God" (*Leviticus Rabbah* 34.8). "He who greets the learned is as if he greeted God" (*Mekilta*, Exodus 18:12). "He who gives a piece of bread to a righteous man, it is as though he has fulfilled the whole Torah" (*Genesis Rabbah* 58.12). Were we to recast the words of Jesus in the light of these quotations, they might read: "Whoever welcomes you welcomes me, and whoever welcomes me welcomes the *Shekhinah* [i.e., the presence of God]."

The second point has to do with all those, lay and clergy, who perform the apostolic function of bearing witness to the grace of God in Jesus Christ. Whoever welcomes these apostles welcomes Christ, and whoever welcomes Christ welcomes the *Shekhinah*, the God of Israel. The living Christ lives in his body, the church, which embodies him as it bodies forth his message of the rule of God.

Matthew refers to those sent out on the mission for the rule of God as "little ones": "Whoever gives even a cup of cold water to one of these little ones in the name of a disciple—truly I tell you, none of these will lose their reward." From the very beginning of his Gospel, Matthew has had a special concern for the "little ones" (*micrōn*). In his genealogy and story of the nativity (1:1–25), Matthew highlights the roles played by Tamar, Rahab, Ruth, Uriah (Bathsheba), and Joseph. They are all "little people," far removed from positions of power and privilege; two were Gentiles, and three or four were at least suspicious with regard to sexual morality. But what they had in common is that they all acted responsibly (Uriah did when David did not, for example), as Joseph acted responsibly in relationship to Mary in the nativity story. They acted in ways not blessed by the social conventions of their time, as did Jesus, and in order to serve God's purposes, as the apostles are sent out to do. They are among God's little ones through whom righteousness is exemplified and who call the powerful to account.

The message of the Gospel was spread by apostles and prophets (*Didache* 11–13). The heart of the mission is the union between Jesus and those whom he sends out; to receive them is to receive him. While the contexts into which today's apostles go have changed drastically, the connection with Jesus is constant.

Proper 9 [14]/Year A

Matthew 11:16–19, 25–30

This reading picks up in midstream, after a paragraph omitted by the lectionary in which Jesus makes remarkable statements about John the Baptist, calling John "a prophet" and "more than a prophet" (11:9). John is greater than any of those "born of women," yet the "least in the kingdom . . . is greater" (v. 11). For all his greatness, John's ministry merely pointed to the coming reign of God—which is present in the ministry of Jesus. Because of its presence, the least in the reign of God are greater than John.

Now Jesus says, "We played the flute for you, and you did not dance; we wailed, and you did not mourn" (v. 17). That is, you responded neither to the wailing of John who pointed out judgment to come, nor to Jesus' wedding dance played on the flute.

Today's reading begins with the difference between Jesus and John: John "came neither eating nor drinking," whereas the Son of Man "came eating and drinking" (v. 18). John's lifestyle is described as severe; opponents of the rule of God dismiss him as mad ("He has a demon"). Jesus, on the contrary, is known for the festive character of his ministry, which involved free and open eating. In a subsistence economy where many folk were hungry much of the time, the good news was acted out around the table. Jesus is charged by his opponents ("they," according to Matthew) with being "a glutton and a drunkard, a friend of tax collectors and sinners" (v. 19).

A complicating factor here is that the text does not want us to believe the first two accusations—that John had a demon and that Jesus was a glutton and a drunkard. Does it want us to believe the third—that Jesus was a friend of tax collectors and sinners? Each is an accusation put in the mouths of opponents.

The first part of the reading ends, "Yet wisdom is vindicated by her deeds" (v. 19), "her" indicating that Jesus refers to Woman Wisdom. This points to vv. 28–30, which end not just with a wisdom teaching but with Jesus as the very embodiment of wisdom (Hebrew: *hokmah*, Greek: *sophia*), as one who is vindicated by his deeds, one who seeks the lost, one who laments over Jerusalem as a mother over her children, as one who says "take my yoke upon you, and learn from me." "Put your feet into her fetters, and neck into her collar. Bend your shoulders and carry her. . . . Come to her with all your soul, and keep her ways with all your might. . . . For at last you will find the rest she gives" (Sir. 6:24–28). This is Matthew's high Christology—Jesus as the embodiment of wisdom.

In between these wisdom referents, Jesus thanks God that "these things" have been revealed to "infants" and hidden from "the wise and intelligent." His ministry went to the poor in spirit, the hungry, and those who mourn, not to the well-to-do and comfortable (of whom there were not many in any case). The point is subversive. The "wisdom" that he taught was a wisdom "from below," the wisdom of a kingdom or realm of nobodies. Jesus is not opposed to wisdom and intelligence, but he subverts conventional understandings of them.

Jesus' statement that "no one knows the Father except the Son and anyone to whom the Son chooses to reveal him" is a form of the "priestly" axiom of Scripture, as if to say, "I love you so much that you are the apple of my eye; only you do I love." He says this to reassure the community of God's love for it. The other axiom, the prophetic, points out that God loves everybody else in exactly the same way. God loves them too, and demands that we do the same.

Proper 10 [15]/Year A

Matthew 13:1–9, 18–23

Today's reading is in two parts: the parable of the Sower and its interpretation by Matthew. Somewhere along the western shore of the Sea of Galilee, Jesus "got into a boat and sat there . . . and he told them many things in parables," beginning with the parable of the Sower. Seven or eight parables follow, making up Jesus' third long discourse in Matthew. He sat when he taught, as authoritative Jewish leaders did. Sitting in the boat allowed his voice to carry well over the water, and the surrounding hillside provided a natural amphitheater and good acoustics.

Teaching in parables was part of the wisdom tradition; Jesus takes on the role of wisdom by so teaching. The Hebrew term for parable, *mashal*, could refer to a metaphor, simile, allegory, or riddle. Matthew's later interpretation treats this parable as an allegory. While the *mashal* was the story, the *nimshal* provided the interpretation and application. In rabbinic parables a *mashal* could be retold, differently, and different *nimshalim* could be substituted for or added to an earlier version. Both of these processes happen from Gospel to Gospel. There is no necessary connection between the body of the story and its interpretation.

Matthew uses the parable of the Sower to deal with a problem for followers of Jesus: Not all Jews accepted their version of appropriate Jewish faith or their view of how Judaism should reshape itself in the late first century after the destruction of the temple. How could they explain the plurality of reactions to the good news of the rule of God? Why do some accept wholeheartedly, some for a short time only, and some not at all? The parable of the Sower is an attempt to answer this question.

As such, it has parallels in some other Jewish sources at the time. *Second Ezra* 8:41, for example, reads, "As the farmer sows over the ground many seeds, and plants a multitude of plants, but in the season not all that have been planted take root, so also those who have sowed in the world, not all shall be saved." *Second Ezra* distinguishes between the eternal power of the Torah and the transient nature of people to whom it is given but who sin in rejecting it. Both Jews who were and who were not followers of Jesus had the problem of explaining why not all seeds generated a significant harvest.

Contemporary scholars generally agree that the interpretation of the parable comes not from Jesus but from the later church. That some seed falls on "rocky" ground (v. 20) reflects the biblical understanding that God sometimes "hardens" the heart (Rom. 12:25). The importance of this understanding of the reasons for rejection is that it places the responsibility for it on God. God "hardens" the hearts of some for God's own reasons, which are not always clear to us. Hence, the rejection is a mystery. Some seeds fall on good soil, and this explains those who hear and understand the word.

Those who do (or think they do) hear and understand the word should understand themselves as recipients of God's gracious gift, one they have been enabled by God to receive. The unconditional gift of God's love, graciously given, should be gratefully received, gratitude being the proper response to grace.

Proper 11 [16]/Year A

Matthew 13:24–30, 36–43

The parable of Weeds among the Wheat and its interpretation are unique to Matthew's Gospel. That weeds and wheat growing in the same field are hard to distinguish from one another is a comment on Matthew's mixed community of saints and sinners. The weeds (*zizania*, "darnel") are too much like wheat to be easily separated from it, which is why such separation is God's business, not ours. For the rabbis, darnel was a symbol of fornication, a meaning imaginatively derived from its root word.

The presence of the weeds is explained in the saying "an enemy has done this" (v. 28). Nonetheless, the parable counsels followers of Jesus not to take upon themselves the responsibility for separating the wheat from the weeds. Instead, "let both of them grow together until the harvest" (v. 30). "The harvest" is a biblical symbol for the final judgment (Jer. 51:33, Hos. 6:11; 2 Baruch 70:2, Rev. 14:15–16). At that time, the "reapers" will collect and burn the weeds and store the wheat safely in the house-holder's barn.

The parable explains two things: the mixed response to Jesus' ministry of the rule of God in Jesus' lifetime and the mixed community of Matthew's time (the weeds and wheat, after all, grow in the same field). Followers of Jesus should respond to this situation with serenity and for-bearance for the time being. The reason for our patience, however, is less that we ought to be ready to forgive than it is the assurance that, in the end, the weeds, the work of an enemy, will get what is coming to them. Matthew is apocalyptic, and tends strongly to divide the world into win-ners and losers.

In v. 36 the disciples ask Jesus to explain the parable of the weeds to them. Jesus is often depicted as teaching in public in parables and inter-preting their meaning in private to his disciples (see, e.g., Mark 4:33–34). That is how Matthew here describes Jesus' teaching. Whether or not the parable of the Wheat and Weeds goes back to Jesus, the explanation strikes most scholars as Matthew's own allegory. In the allegory the sower is the Son of Man, the field is the world, the children of the kingdom are the "good seed," the weeds are the "children of the evil one," the enemy becomes the devil, and angels do the reaping. The evil-doing children of the "evil one" will be thrown into the furnace of fire where they will weep and gnash their teeth, while the righteous will "shine like the sun in the kingdom of their Father" (v. 43).

The parable is all neatly wrapped up in one apocalyptic package. One disturbing feature of the explanation, however, is the role of the "evil one" *(diabolos)*. John 8:44 uses the same term to speak of "the Jews": "You are from your father the devil." The point is not that Matthew and John both demonize "the Jews." It is that Matthew's identification of his commu-nity's external opponents (Jews who do not follow Jesus) and internal sin-ners with "the devil" is a step on a trajectory that can be seen in fuller form in John and later in the Christian tradition.

Visions such as Matthew's, argues Elaine Pagels, "have been incorpo-rated into Christian tradition and have served, among other things, to confirm for Christians their own identification with God and to demonize their opponents—first other Jews, then pagans, and later dissident Christians called heretics."[12] Matthew's vision here also contributes to the view that part of the joy of being in heaven consists in our awareness of the suffering of those in hell, a repulsive view of ultimate salvation.

Proper 12 [17]/Year A

Matthew 13:31–33, 44–52

In this reading, Jesus tells five parables of the "kingdom of heaven" to "the crowd." The first is the parable of the Mustard Seed which, in spite of its small size, grows into "the greatest of shrubs and becomes a tree, so that the birds of the air come and make nests in its branches" (v. 32). The kingdom of heaven is like that—it grows, slowly and in ways that the occupying imperial power cannot see, to a great size. This is a parable of God's promise and our hope. It serves to empower the people to whom it is told, to awaken their faith in tough times. It draws on the Israelite heritage of Jesus and his listeners. In Ezekiel, God promised to plant a sprig on "the mountain height of Israel" that would "become a noble cedar. Under it every kind of bird will live; in the shade of its branches will nest winged creatures of every kind" (Ezek. 17:22–23; see also Ps. 104:12 and Dan. 4:10–12, 20–27). "Every kind of bird" is metaphorical speech meaning "all the Gentiles." This part of the parable is welcoming, hospitable; Matthew's Jesus will later commission his disciples to go to "all the Gentiles" (*panta ta ethnē*).

Next is the parable of Leaven. The rule of God is like yeast that a woman mixed with flour "until all of it was leavened." Here yeast is a creative, life-enhancing power. Like the mustard seed parable, here too the contrast is between the small and the large. The woman uses so much flour that, with the yeast, there would be enough bread to feed more than one hundred people. God's rule grows like that.

Verse 44 is the parable comparing the kingdom of heaven to a "treasure hidden in a field," a treasure for which a person "sells all that he has and buys that field." Social and economic conditions in Palestine made clear why someone would bury a treasure in a field—to hide it from the Roman authorities and tax collectors. Taxes of as much as 33 percent on grain and 50 percent on fruit, plus head taxes, taxes on trade and market exchanges, and temple taxes in kind (sacrificial goods) and money (the half-shekel) added up to an exorbitant burden on farmers and fishermen. Josephus reports that Herod the Great "reduced the entire country to helpless poverty" by his heavy taxation (*Antiquities* 17.306). So people hid what they could. Jesus' hearers would have understood how a treasure came to be hidden in a field. The kingdom is like that—of great value, enough to elicit one's wholehearted devotion, and the Roman authorities cannot see it because it is hidden from them.

God's rule is also compared to a "pearl of great value" and to a fishing net that "caught fish of every kind," so many that the fishermen had to separate the good fish from the bad (vv. 45–48). Like the parable of the Wheat and the Weeds, this parable stresses that, later, God in God's wisdom will deal with the bad fish caught up in the kingdom's net; that is not our task. The kingdom is an actual social movement of mutual solidarity—feeding, freeing people from self-blame, and exorcising the demons that they had introjected into themselves from their social situation. This movement and the people in it are the pearl of great value. Each person in it is loved by God, is the apple of God's eye. The problem with which they have to deal is that everybody else is also the apple of God's eye. We are to love them as we love ourselves.

The reading ends with the comment that "every scribe who has been trained for the kingdom of heaven is like the master of a household who brings out of his treasure what is new and what is old" (v. 52). Scribes were scholars of the Scriptures and writers (which is what "scribe" means—in Latin it is *scribo*, "to write"). The scribes who wrote Matthew brought out of their treasure—the literature of the Israel of God—the ideas and images with which to convey the ministry of Jesus.

Proper 13 [18]/Year A

Matthew 14:13–21

The NRSV calls the setting of the story a "deserted place," but the Greek, *erēmos*, is better translated "wilderness." The semi-arid wilderness sometimes symbolizes chaos. However, the wilderness is also a place in which God demonstrates great care for Israel.

The account of the feeding of the five thousand reminds the reader that God provided manna for the Israelites in the wilderness (Exod. 16:13–35; cf. Num. 11:7–9, 31–32), that God fed the prophet Elijah, a widow, and her son (1 Kgs. 17:8–16), and that God fed a hundred people with only twenty loaves of barley and a few fresh ears of grain (2 Kgs. 4:42–44). Matthew understands his congregation as being in a situation similar to these wilderness times. He uses this story in part to help the church recognize that just as God's providence turned the wilderness into a place of abundance in the days of Moses and the great prophets, God continues faithfully to provide for the church amid chaos.

Apocalyptic Judaism anticipated an eschatological banquet after the apocalyptic cataclysm when God would end the old age (and all forms of distortion and evil) and establish the divine reign in its fullness (see, e.g., Isa. 25:6–8; 65:13–14; 2 Esd. 8:52–54; *2 Baruch* 29:8). The feeding of the five thousand is such a meal—demonstrating that even now God is turning the old age into the new.

At the eschatological banquet, manna-like bread was expected. *Second Baruch* also anticipates that God will feed the people with Behemoth and Leviathan, who dwell in the sea and are among the great Jewish symbols of chaos (*2 Baruch* 29:3–7). The God of Israel transforms elements of chaos into instruments of sustenance and blessing.

Jesus lifts his eyes to heaven in the manner of Jewish prayer. The expression that he "blessed" the loaves calls to mind Jewish custom. The following prayer, perhaps extant in the first century c.e., captures the spirit of Jewish prayer: "Blessed art thou, O Lord our God, [Sovereign] of the Universe, who brings forth bread from the earth" (*b. Berakhot* 35a). This practice of blessing God (and wider practices of prayer) in Judaism is so important that the first tractate in the Mishnah and the Talmud is called *Berakhot* (blessing). It helps the community recognize the divine presence and activity, and to bless God accordingly.

When the narrative says that Jesus *took, blessed, broke,* and *gave,* it interprets the Last Supper (Matt. 26:26) from the perspective of the feeding of the five thousand. The Last Supper is the paradigm for the church's participation in the Lord's Supper. The congregation is to understand the Lord's Supper as a prefiguration of the eschatological banquet. When the church in the present eats the loaf and drinks the cup, it celebrates the eschatological consummation of the world, although that consummation is still underway. The sacred meal is also one of God's provisions (manna) for the community that is living in a wilderness time.

By feeding the multitude, Jesus embodies the ancient Jewish concern for the welfare of all in the community. Hunger violates the purposes of God for human life. When Jesus commands the disciples to give the hungry crowd something to eat, the reader recognizes that the church is to continue this Jewish value. After everyone has eaten, the disciples collect twelve baskets of leftovers. This detail assures the Matthean community that the providential power to carry out Jesus' command is present. The church can do what Jesus says—feed hungry people—in the confidence that sufficient resources are available even in times of scarcity (cf. Matt. 25:34–40).

Proper 14 [19]/Year A

Matthew 14:22–33

In his ministry, Jesus confronted his followers with the promise and command of the God of Israel. That in encountering him his followers encounter the God of Israel is made clear in this story of his walking on the water. Central to the story is Jesus' statement of reassurance to his followers: "Take heart, it is I; do not be afraid" (v. 27). Matthew draws the name of the God of Israel, "it is I," from the Scriptures. "See now that I, even I, am he" (Deut. 32:39) and "I am who I am" (Exod. 3:14) are two instances of God's "name" in Scripture. Jesus' use of "it is I" indicates his special relationship to God as the one in, through, and by means of whom God is made known.

The story of Jesus walking on water is an epiphany, indicating who Jesus is—one who discloses God to us and one who, in walking on water, does what God does. The Scriptures contain many cases of God's walking on the water in relation to the exodus from Egypt and to the parting of the waters: "Your way was through the sea, your path, through the mighty waters. . . . You led your people like a flock by the hand of Moses and Aaron" (Ps. 77:19–20). "You trampled the sea with your horses, churning the mighty waters" (Hab. 3:15). Of those who "went down to the sea in ships" when a mighty storm blew up, the psalmist says:

> Their courage melted away in their calamity;
> they reeled and staggered like drunkards,
>   and were at their wits' end.
> Then they cried to the LORD in their trouble,
>   and he brought them out of their distress;
> he made the storm be still,
>   and the waves of the sea were hushed.
>   (Ps. 107:26–29)

Water is a symbol of chaos, death, life, and new life. In Jewish literature of the time, depictions of drowning and rescue were widely used. They are present in the *Thanksgiving Hymns* of Qumran and also the *Testament of Naphtali*, which describes the "ship of Jacob" in peril from a storm (6:1–10). When the storm ended, the ship landed safely by the shore and "Jacob, our father, approached, and we all rejoiced with one accord." These images were metaphorical ways of talking about persecution and the response of faithful people to persecution. Drowning accentuates the perils of persecution; the activity of God to save those in distress shows that we can trust God.

The image of a boat on a stormy sea is also an ancient image of the church and is used today by the World Council of Churches as its logo. Hence, this text is also a word of reassurance to the church in its troubles. We are the disciples in the boat—of "little faith," but some faith—and it will suffice.

The major emphasis of the text is on the identity of Jesus and of his disciples. Whatever we say about Jesus also says something about us—if he is the Master, we are his disciples; if he is the Lord, we are his servants. Here he is the one through whom God works, and we are those, like Peter, of "little faith." Yet we are saved by his grace, not by our faith (although through faith). That we have our weaknesses in no way cancels the unconditional, unfathomable character of God's gracious love.

The lectionary drops the short following paragraph in which the people of Gennesaret "brought all who were sick to him, and begged him that they might touch even the fringe of his cloak" (vv. 35–36). The "fringe" refers to the tassels that pious Jews wore to remind themselves of God's *mitzvoth* (Deut. 12:12).

Proper 15 [20]/Year A

Matthew 15:21–28

This story is about the faith of the Canaanite woman. In using the term "Canaanite," Matthew reflects early rabbinic sources where "Canaanite" is a common term for a Gentile (*m. Qiddushin* 1:3). By the time of Jesus, there were no longer any Canaanites. The emphasis is on the fact that the woman is a Gentile; the story has to do with relations between Jews and Gentiles. Tyre and Sidon customarily referred to the Gentile region northwest of Judea and Galilee.

The two key points in the passage concern demonic possession and what it meant and the attitude of the Matthean community to Gentiles.

Demons appear earlier in Second Temple literature in *1 Enoch* 37–71 in which, on the one hand, we have God, God's people, God's heavenly entourage, and the angels as agents of God's judgment. On the other hand, there are the chief demon Azazel, his angels (demons), and the kings and the mighty who "would have their counterparts among the Roman generals, governors, triumvirs, and monarchs whose activities in Judea are well documented in the sources."[13]

Roman imperialism meant that the occupied people were inwardly possessed by the same schizoid conditions of demonic control by which they were objectively possessed. There was therefore much demonic possession at Jesus' time, and this is why his role as an exorcist was so important and prominent. Demonic control implies the presence of a power greater than oneself introjected into oneself, an evil power whose control one is under. In Mark, tellingly, the Gerasene demoniac's demon is named "Legion," a name inseparable from the Roman legions. Exorcism was the ritual psychic liberation of an individual from Roman domination; it freed up energies for participating in the movement of the kingdom and removed the person from the psychic control of the death-dealing ways of the empire.

Possession is not reducible to such things as imperial occupation. But neither is it unrelated to oppressive government, extreme poverty, and the trauma that is an aftermath of the killings involved in military conquest.

The woman was a Gentile, however, and Jesus' initial response was to say, "I was sent only to the lost sheep of the house of Israel" (v. 24). After Jesus says, "It is not fair to take the children's food and throw it to the [Gentile] dogs," she responds, "Yes, Lord, yet even the dogs eat the crumbs that fall from their masters' table" (vv. 26–27). Jesus relents, saying, "Woman, great is your faith!" (v. 28).

This Gentile woman does what Jews have done since the time of Abraham: argue with God over matters of justice. Abraham, Moses, Isaac, and Job are prime examples. Jesus speaks of a nagging widow and an unjust judge, a widow who gets justice for herself in spite of the judge's indifference, and he says to pray like that (Luke 18:1–8). It is inauthentic to pray and not to work for justice for the neighbor or for oneself.

Jesus makes an exclusionary statement: "I was sent only to the lost sheep of the house of Israel" (v. 24). Matthew depicts Jesus' ministry as devoted solely to the people Israel, and only in the Great Commission does the risen Jesus tell his followers to go to "all the Gentiles" (*panta ta ethnē*; Matt. 28:19–20). Jesus' ministry, prior to the resurrection, is described as devoted solely to the people Israel and its restoration. Today's story represents a development in the history of the later Matthean community in which it opens itself to Gentiles.

Proper 16 [21]/Year A

Matthew 16:13–20

Matthew agrees with Mark 8:27 that Peter made his confession of Jesus in "the district of Caesarea Philippi." The place is important. It was first called *Panias* because it contained a sanctuary to the god Pan; when Herod the Great built there a temple to Augustus Caesar, he called it the *Augusteion.* After Herod's death, Philip elaborated the temple complex, dedicating it to the god Augustus and to himself and naming it Caesarea Philippi to distinguish it from Caesarea Maratima where Herod the Great had erected large statues to Augustus and the goddess Roma. Augustus was called "God" and "Savior," and his birth was said to have "signaled the beginning of good news [*euangelion*] for the world" (temple steles to Augustus).

That this is where the "good confession" takes place speaks volumes about notions of kingdom and rule, power, and discipleship. When the king claims to be God, to proclaim the kingdom of God is to deny that the king is God. Kingdom and rule are not like those of Caesar but egalitarian ("whoever would be greatest among you must be servant of all"), power is not that of coercive military might but that of love, and discipleship is not abject slavery but heartfelt service to the needs of the neighbor.

In answer to Jesus' question, "Who do people say that the Son of Man is?" the disciples offered the names of John the Baptist, Elijah, and Jeremiah. In Judaism, Elijah was (and is) a harbinger of the days of the Messiah: "Lo, I will send you the prophet Elijah before the great and terrible day of the LORD comes" (Mal. 4:5). The Baptist plays an Elijah role in the Gospels. Matthew adds Jeremiah to Mark's list, reflecting his interest in Jeremiah (see Matt. 2:17; 27:9; and allusions to Jeremiah in 7:15–23; 11:28–30; and 23:37–39).

But to Jesus' second question, "Who do you say that I am?" Peter responds, "You are the Messiah, the Son of the living God" (v. 16). "Messiah" (*mashiach* in Hebrew) meant "anointed one" in Judaism, whether anointed king, prophet, priest, or teacher. There was no agreed upon understanding of the term. Nor did the Messiah necessarily have to use force and violence to bring in the days of the Messiah: "[T]heir king shall be the Lord Messiah. (For) he will not rely on horse and rider and bow, nor will he collect gold and silver for war" (*Psalms of Solomon* 17:32–33). Some forms of eschatology did not include a Messiah figure. Matthew modifies Messiah with "Son of the living God" to make clear that, as the people Israel is God's child, so is this child of Israel.

Jesus blesses Peter, names or renames him "Peter," and says, "on this rock I will build my church" (v. 18). Cephas and Peter (*petros*) both mean "rock"; perhaps each is a nickname. Isaiah said, "Look to the rock from which you were hewn. . . . Look to Abraham your father and to Sarah who bore you" (51:1–2). Jesus says he will give to Peter the "keys of the kingdom" to bind and loose, a theme from Isaiah where God says of Eliakim,

"I will place on his shoulder the key of the house of David; he shall open, and no one shall shut; he shall shut and no one shall open" (22:22).

But in response to Jesus' declaration that he would suffer, Peter responds, "God forbid it, Lord!" and receives a rebuke from Jesus: "Get behind me, Satan!" (vv. 22–23). Peter had missed the contrast with Augustus's kind of power and rule. My followers, says Jesus, will "deny themselves and take up their cross and follow me" (v. 24). It shall not be among you as it is among the Gentiles; among you those who would be first of all must be least of all. Lose your life this way and you will find it.

Proper 17 [22]/Year A

Matthew 16:21–28

In our comments on Proper 16, we discussed in part today's reading because it is part of the same literary unit. Because the lectionary breaks up what belongs together, we deal further with it here.

Verses 21–23 relate Jesus' statement that he must "go to Jerusalem and undergo great suffering at the hands of the elders and chief priests and scribes, and be killed, and on the third day be raised"; Peter's rebuke, "God forbid it, Lord! This must never happen to you"; and Jesus' retort, "Get behind me, Satan! You are a stumbling block." This is the first passion prediction in Matthew. That Jesus did indeed think he would be killed makes a lot of sense; after all, he had the example of John the Baptist and was likely aware of what had happened to every leader of a "kingdom of God" movement.

"Chief priests" as a term rarely appears in rabbinic literature (*m. Ketubbot* 13:1–2). "Elders" is absent from the Mishnah. "Scribes" were scholarly writers and, as we have seen, there were scribes in Matthew's community (indeed, the New Testament was written by scribes). The scribes referred to here are in Jerusalem. They are not "all the scribes," but scribes retained by the aristocratic chief priests. Strikingly, Pharisees are not mentioned; in fact, they are almost totally absent from the passion narratives in all the Gospels. Nor is the Roman governor mentioned, which is doubly odd because only Rome had the authority to crucify, a penalty it imposed on rebels, insurrectionists, and bandits. Bandits were perceived as a threat to the emperor because many an emperor had begun his career as a bandit, as had David (1 Sam. 22:1–2).

Peter moves quickly from being the "rock" on which the church is founded to being a "stumbling block to" Jesus and associated with Satan.

Here Matthew probably has his eye on those who deny the suffering and death of Jesus, those who would later be called "gnostics" or "Docetists" because they claimed that Jesus only "seemed" (*dokeō*) to suffer and die. Peter serves as a negative example of a disciple, one not to be emulated. He also shows how any faithful person can also sin and err, as Peter does in his misunderstanding of Jesus' messiahship.

Jesus adds that on the third day he will be raised (v. 21), a theme found in Hosea: "Come, let us return to the LORD; for it is he who has torn, and he will heal us; he has struck down, and he will bind us up. After two days he will revive us; on the third day he will raise us up" (Hos. 6:1–2). And Jonah was said to have been "in the belly of the fish three days and three nights" (Jonah 1:17).

Jesus says to his disciples that "those who want to save their life will lose it, and those who lose their life for my sake will find it" (v. 25). This does not mean that those who "lose themselves in love" for Jesus will not undergo physical death. Even Jesus did that. It means that the only way to have one's life in any ultimate sense is to accept that it is a loving gift of God's grace and to spend it in the love of God and neighbor. To do that is to live and to live, ultimately, in God's love. To be so wrapped up in concern for one's own physical, economic, and psychological safety that one is unable to love God with all one's self or one's neighbor as one's self is already to be dead. First Timothy speaks of a "widow who lives for pleasure" as being "dead even while she lives" (5:6), contrasting her with "the real widow" who "set her hope on God" (5:5).

Proper 18 [23]/Year A

Matthew 18:15–20

Today's reading, except for its opening verse, which appears in Luke 17:3–4, is Matthew's manual of church discipline. It is highly unlikely that it goes back to Jesus. In the opening verse, Jesus says, "If another member of the church sins against you, go and point out the fault when the two of you are alone." The point of the reading is as old as Lev. 19:17: "You shall not hate in your heart anyone of your kin: you shall reprove your neighbor, or you will incur guilt yourself." The term translated "reprove" by the NRSV has also been translated as "reason with." This is the other side of what Jesus said in the Sermon on the Mount: "So when you are offering your gift at the altar, if you remember that your brother or sister has something against you, leave your gift there before the altar and go;

first be reconciled to your brother or sister, and then come and offer your gift" (5:23–24).

In both cases, the principle is the same: Work out your relationship with your neighbor face-to-face. When it is time to worship, do not presume to ask God to forgive your sins against your brother and sister unless you are willing to seek their forgiveness first. If you have something against your neighbor, do the same: Go to the neighbor and work it out honestly and straightforwardly. When we consider how destructive it is for a congregation when members engage in "triangulating," never dealing with issues in an above-the-board way, this is remarkably candid and helpful advice.

In case, however, the brother or sister is deaf to your entreaties, "take one or two others along with you, so that every word may be confirmed by the evidence of two or three witnesses" (v. 16). Israelite tradition required that no one could be judged guilty on the basis of one witness alone (Num. 25:30; Deut. 17:6). Nor, in rabbinic literature, could a husband render accusations against his wife without two witnesses (*m. Sotah* 1:1). Notice that this command from Jesus still deals with the matter at hand in a face-to-face relationship but now enlarges the group within which it is dealt with. This is not unlike having a wise friend involved as a mediator.

"If the member refuses to listen to them, tell it to the church" (v. 17). Again, the issue is kept within the community. Conflict can be dealt with openly or repressed. Congregations do not, as a rule, like to deal with conflict, and pastors often avoid it like the plague, to their own distress. But when repressed it is never gone, just invisible, and it simmers silently away in the hearts and minds of people to express itself in unhealthy and unhelpful ways. Any pastor or congregant, for example, who ever received an anonymous letter from some other angry member of the congregation knows what this means. When that happens between members, it is frequently taken as an invitation to leave the congregation, and frequently accepted.

If even this fails, Matthew's recommendation is excommunication: "Let such a one be to you as a Gentile and a tax collector" (v. 17). Later, however (v. 22), Jesus says that we are to forgive our brother as many as "seventy times seven" times. Reconciliation within the community remains the norm.

The passage ends with Jesus saying, "Where two or three are gathered in my name, I am there among them" (v. 20). Similarly, in the Mishnah, Rabbi Hananiah ben Teradion says that "if two sit together and words of the Torah [are spoken] between them, the Divine Presence rests between them" (*Avot* 3:2). Jesus abides within the community called in his name.

Proper 19 [24]/Year A

Matthew 18:21–35

The parable of the Unforgiving Servant is introduced by Peter's question, "Lord, if another member of the church sins against me, how often should I forgive? As many as seven times?" Jesus answers, "Not seven times, but, I tell you, seventy-seven times." Two points are of note here. First, Peter asks about a sin against himself ("against me"), not about a sin against the community, the topic of the prior conversation. Second, the Greek for "seventy-seven" (*hebdomekontakis hepta*) can also be translated as "seven times seventy-seven," or 539. In either case, Jesus' point is clear: There are no restrictions to forgiveness.

The parable is about a king settling accounts with his slaves, in particular one who owed him ten thousand talents. A talent was valued at somewhere between six and ten thousand denarii. One denarius was the equivalent of a day's pay. Ten thousand talents, therefore, would constitute a debt that had gone through the ceiling. The "slave" in question would have been an important government official, not, for example, a tenant farmer.

Because he could not pay, "his lord ordered him to be sold, together with his wife and children and all his possessions, and payment to be made" (v. 25). While passages in the Scriptures allow for the selling of children into slavery (e.g., Isa. 50:1), this was contrary to the oral Torah (early rabbinic law) at the time of Jesus. Nor could wives be taken away for any reason. Debts could be repaid only through return of property (*m. Bava Batra* 10:8). The parable, hence, seems to be about Gentiles. Some commentators say otherwise and elicit rabbinic passages to support their position, but those passages have to do with theft, not debt (Josephus, *Antiquities* 16, 1.1).

The slave begged for patience and, remarkably, the king "forgave him the debt" (v. 27). Considering the enormity of the debt, his forgiveness is hard to fathom, but that is precisely the point about God's love for us: It is unfathomable.

But then the slave refused to exercise the very patience for which he had prayed when it came to dealing with a fellow slave who owed him the minor sum of one hundred denarii. He "threw him into prison until he would pay the debt" (v. 30), after seizing him by the throat. In Roman law, creditors were allowed to haul debtors forcibly before the authorities (*manus iniectio*).

When the king heard of this, he berated the unforgiving servant: "Should you not have had mercy on your fellow slave, as I had mercy on you?" (v. 33). Here, of course, is the point. We who have been so unfathomably and freely loved should in turn love God with all our selves and our neighbors as ourselves, which means, in part, that we treat them as we would want them to treat us. Matthew's version of the Lord's Prayer is in play here: "Forgive us our debts, as we also have forgiven our debtors" (6:12).

While the parable seems to be told about Gentiles, Jewish peasant farmers in Galilee were all too familiar with unpayable debt piled up from low yielding kinds of agriculture, incredibly high taxation, and loans made necessary by these factors. Jesus' hearers would have readily understood both the parable and the cancellation of debts promised in the jubilee year legislation of the Torah (Lev. 25:10ff.).

The parable ends with the angry "lord" handing over the unforgiving servant "to be tortured until he would pay his entire debt" (v. 34). How torture was to get blood out of a turnip is not clear. Torture, also, while common in the Mediterranean, was not acceptable in Jewish law— another indication that the parable is about Gentiles.

Proper 20 [25]/Year A

Matthew 20:1–16

Matthew's parable of the Laborers in the Vineyard would have struck an immediate chord in the hearts of its hearers. The landowner goes into the marketplace to hire laborers "early," "about nine o'clock," "about noon," "about three o'clock," and "about five o'clock." Each time, he finds workers "standing idle in the marketplace." These are people thrown out of work by the economic conditions brought about by Roman occupation. The scene resembles that around the day-labor office in the inner city or the street corner where migrant workers assemble hoping to be picked up for a day's work. In this context Jesus tells a parable of a generous employer.

It is also a parable that Jesus' Jewish hearers would have readily understood. Judaism has about 1,100 parables, many of which are vineyard parables featuring an *abba*, a beloved father, and an *amon*, a beloved son. Often they have to do with varieties and qualities of work in the vineyard and rates of pay.[14] Their ears would have been attuned to the movement of this parable and surprised by its ending.

The vineyard itself is a symbol of the people Israel: "For the vineyard of the LORD of hosts is the house of Israel, and the people of Judah are his pleasant planting," says Isa. 5:7, as he enters upon prophetic self-criticism of the vineyard.

The landowner pays the laborers a denarius for a day's work, and he gives them their pay at the end of the day (v. 8). This was in keeping with the Torah's instructions on paying laborers: "You shall not keep for yourself the wages of a laborer until morning" (Lev. 19:13). The reason is, simply, that they are poor and need the money. One of the primary functions of the law in Israel is the protection of the poor, the vulnerable, and the marginalized. Indeed, Torah is the voice of the vulnerable.

Every Jewish parable has a *mashal*, a story, and a *nimshal*, the interpretation and application of the story. Matthew's *nimshal* says that "the last will be first, and the first will be last" (v. 16). This *nimshal* hardly seems appropriate to the body of the story, in which there is no reversal except in the order in which the wages were paid. Otherwise, the laborers are all treated equally, some fairly and some more than fairly but equally.

One Jewish parable tells of Moses and Samuel both being "equal before the Omnipresent," although Moses served God for a hundred years and Samuel for fifty-two; they are compared to two laborers, one of whom worked a whole day and the other only one hour, yet each received one dinar for his work. "Sweet is the sleep of the laborer," says the Palestinian Talmud, *Berakhot* (2.8.5c.) "whether he has eaten little or much."

The landowner is the major character in Matthew's parables; the laborers are the "straight men." A better name for the parable would be "the Prodigal Employer" or "the Full-Employment Employer." Any of these titles brings out the character of the story more adequately and also relates it to contemporary issues.

The parable has a double reference—one to the situation at Jesus' time in which he carried out his mission of feeding the hungry, healing the sick, and freeing up the possessed, and the other to God and the unfathomable generosity of God's grace toward all the laborers in the vineyard of God's realm. The parable is pertinent to Jesus' commitment to the most marginalized people in his society (under Roman occupation all Jews were marginalized, some more than others) and to God's gracious gift of the kingdom.

Proper 21 [26]/Year A

Matthew 21:23–32

At the beginning of chapter 21 Jesus enters Jerusalem, where the rest of Matthew's story plays out. In today's reading, the chief priests and elders come to Jesus and ask, "By what authority are you doing these things, and who gave you this authority?" (v. 23). These groups will constitute Jesus' primary antagonists throughout the passion narrative. In Mark's earlier story, the Pharisees disappear completely after chapter 12; Matthew retains them but they have a lesser role than the chief priests and elders.

"Chief priests" refers to the priestly aristocracy that lived in opulence in Jerusalem, not to the many groups of priests from around the countryside who rotated into and out of Jerusalem to serve in the temple. The chief priests were in collaboration with the Roman governing power and under its control (for example, the high priest's vestments were kept under lock and key by the Roman governor, and he had to ask for them before entering the Holy of Holies once a year on the Day of Atonement). Chief priests and elders had a vested interest in the status quo; they would or could not affirm a challenge to it. They are not, by the way, "the Jews." They are compromised leaders.

Jesus responds to their question with one of his own: "I will also ask you one question; if you tell me the answer, then I will also tell you by what authority I do these things" (v. 24). This is a typically rabbinic response. A famous story is of the student who asked a rabbi, "Why do rabbis always answer a question with a question?" The rabbi pondered a moment and said, "So what's wrong with a question?"

Jesus' question then is, "Did the baptism of John come from heaven, or was it of human origin?" (v. 25). He springs a trap for those who tried to trap him, thus standing the situation on its head. The assumption is that John's authority was from God; Jesus' commitment to the movement of God's rule seems to have been closely tied to that of John, with the difference that whereas John thought of it as coming, Jesus proclaimed it as already present, as a gift. We can live now in the power of the future.

Jesus then tells the parable of the Two Sons, one of whom refused to work in a vineyard but later changed his mind and did, and the other who said he would but did not. The question (again) is, "Which of the two did the will of his father?" (v. 31). They answer, "The first." Jesus then comments that the tax collectors and prostitutes will enter the kingdom of

God "ahead of you" (v. 31). The tax collectors and prostitutes "believed" John, whereas the chief priests and elders did not.

To appreciate what is going on here we must note that while the chief priests and elders were in league with Rome, so were tax collectors and prostitutes. Tax collectors not only cheated and robbed those from whom they collected taxes (if they collected more than they owed their patrons, they pocketed the difference) but supported the occupying power in doing so. Prostitutes serviced the army (Tiberias was notorious as an "R and R" facility for soldiers stationed on the frontier). Yet they will enter the kingdom of heaven because they responded to Jesus (at least some of them did; some, doubtless, did not). Yet the chief priests and elders are guilty of the same collaboration with the brutal occupying power.

We should notice that Jesus does not say that the chief priests and elders will not enter God's realm. He says that tax collectors and prostitutes will enter it "ahead of you," not "instead of you." If tax collectors and prostitutes can be forgiven and repent, cannot also chief priests and elders?

Proper 22 [27]/Year A

Matthew 21:33–46

Matthew's parable of the Wicked Tenant Farmers has long been allegorized in the history of the church as describing the murderous lengths to which Jews would go to resist God. Murdering "the Son," allegorized to be Jesus, was the last straw. As a result, God abandoned Israel and gave the covenant to Gentile Christians. John Chrysostom made all these points in his exegesis of the parable, concluding that "for the crucifixion, their crime, they were to endure extreme punishment: the calling of the Gentiles and the casting out of the Jews."[15]

This parable can be found in these other places: Mark 12:1–12; Luke 20:9–19; and the *Gospel of Thomas* 65–66. Thomas provides the shortest version and the only one in which the vineyard is not, in the end, given to "others" or, as Matthew has it in the NRSV, "to a people that produces the fruits of the kingdom" (v. 43). Whether *Thomas*'s version was reworked, progressively, by Mark, Luke, and Matthew we cannot say. It is, however, a simpler version totally lacking any context in the life of Jesus.

Whether the parable, in any of its forms, alludes to Jesus' crucifixion is questionable. Jacob Neusner's thoroughgoing study of texts referring to "the Messiah" in early Judaism turned up no instance in which the Messiah is spoken of as "heir" or as "inheriting."[16] Hence, whether the hearers of the parable would have associated it with Jesus is also questionable.[17] And how could the parable have meant to allegorize Jesus with no mention of his resurrection? Moreover, Matthew even drops Mark's references to the son as the last sent, as the only son, and as the "beloved" son.

Two more critical points: The parable probably does not go back to Jesus, unless we are ready to explain Jesus' quoting of the Septuagint, the Greek Bible (vv. 33, 42). Nor does Matthew's revised *nimshal*, in which the vineyard is given to another "people" instead of to "others" (i.e., "other tenant farmers") necessarily mean "the Gentiles" or "the Christians." An *ethnos* could refer, simply, to another "group."

Simply put, the parable follows the same transitions found in the parable of the vineyard in Isa. 5: God's high hopes for Israel, his vineyard; God's utter disappointment at Israel's sins; and the future destruction of the vineyard. So the parable of the Wicked Tenant Farmers is best read as prophetic self-criticism, not as unprophetic criticism of "them" ("the Jews") and uncritical extending of all God's promises to us. And it should also be read in the light of God's unfathomable grace and ongoing faithfulness and mercy to sinners.

We Christians have been tending our corner of the vineyard for two millennia. Our record is spotty at best, shameful and horribly so at worst. The parable's criticism is directed at Israel's leadership, those who tend the vineyard that, in turn, is the people Israel. God does not throw out the vineyard—just the tenants.

As Matthew tells it, when the chief priests and the Pharisees heard this parable, "they realized that he was speaking about them" (v. 45). And Matthew is the only Gospel that includes the Pharisees in the story (in Mark "the chief priests and the scribes" of 11:18 are the "they" of 12:12, and in Luke the same two groups try at that time to arrest Jesus [20:19]). Matthew's expansion of the story should not trip up the preacher.

Proper 23 [28]/Year A

Matthew 22:1–14

In his parable of the Wedding Feast, Matthew elaborates considerably upon the parallel story in Luke 14:16–24. The differences are numerous: In Luke, this is a parable; in Matthew, it is a parable of the rule of God. In Luke, a man gives a banquet; in Matthew, a king gives a marriage feast for his son. In Luke, the man sends out one servant to invite people; in Matthew, the king sends his servants. When Luke's servant reports that all those invited excused themselves from attending, the man sends him back out to invite the poor, the maimed, the blind, and the lame; in Matthew, the king sends out his troops and destroys the murderers of his servants and burns their city. Finally, Matthew adds a story about the guest with no wedding garment who is, consequently, tied up and thrown into the outer darkness where people weep and gnash their teeth. Then to his *mashal* (story), Matthew adds a *nimshal* (interpretation) to the effect that many are called but few are chosen.

Such extensive differences exemplify why some scholars conclude that Matthew reworks the sayings source that he has in common with Luke more drastically than Luke does. Matthew's changes do not always make sense, however. For example, the man without the "wedding robe" (v. 11) was among those invited from the streets at the last minute. Were the rest of the guests going about their ordinary business wearing wedding robes? Should we, today, wear gowns or tuxedoes in the unlikely event that we might be summoned to a celebration? If not, should we be bound, cast out, and condemned to weep and gnash our teeth? Is this what the rule of God is like? If so, should we desire it?

In his revision of this story, Matthew seems to be working out his reaction to the destruction of Jerusalem by the Roman army. In that event, Caesar's general did indeed send his army, murder the inhabitants in huge numbers, and burn the temple and city. To Matthew, this seems to have happened because those same inhabitants did not attend the banquet. How shall we interpret Matthew's revised version of the parable of the banquet?

First, in both Jewish and Christian writings, the kingdom of God was often compared to a banquet (see Woman Wisdom's banquet in Prov. 9). In one such Jewish parable, invitations go out ahead of time, yet some people appear properly dressed while others show up dirty from working on farms. These latter were called "foolish ones." The king wanted to make them stand while everybody else drank and feasted, but the rabbi said, "Let both sit down, but let the clean servants eat and drink" (*b. Shabbat* 153a).

In Matthew, the Jewish leaders not only refused to attend the banquet but committed violence against those who invited them to it. Hence, the invitation was extended to the people in the streets, the marginalized. Yet there is a warning even here: Being admitted to the kingdom is not tantamount to being allowed to stay in it. Getting in is easy; staying in has its requirements. We are allowed in by grace; we are allowed to stay in by doing the will of God, that is, by feeding the hungry, giving water to the thirsty, and visiting the sick and those in prison, as the parable of the Last Judgment will make clear.

Proper 24 [29]/Year A

Matthew 22:15–22

This story concerns two things: taxes and coins. The tax in question is the so-called tribute to Caesar, the *kensos Kaisari* (v. 17). Roman rule under Herod Antipas in Galilee and Roman governors in Judea brought several layers of rulers and their respective requirements of taxes or tribute on top of tithes and offerings. The massive building projects and gifts to Caesar's family and foreign cities added to the load carried by peasant farmers and artisans. When the tribute to Caesar was introduced in 6 B.C.E., Judas the Galilean led a rebellion against it (Josephus, *Jewish Wars* 10.1). Subsequently, it was collected in Judea (where our story takes place at the temple) but not in Galilee.

Coins were the mass medium of the ancient world. They carried the emperor's image and a message regarding his divine status and role. A coin to Caesar said, "Hail, Lord of the Earth, Invincible, Power, Glory, Honor, Blessed, Great, Worthy Art Thou to inherit the kingdom."[18] Julius Caesar's coin shows his spirit ascending into heaven to take its place among the gods. Augustus Caesar's coin refers to him as "son of God" (*divi filius*), and Tiberius Caesar's coin praises him as "supreme bridge builder" (*pontifex maximus*), high priest of the empire. Tiberius's coin was the one most commonly used in Judea at the time of Jesus.

The tribute to Caesar was a *kensos*, a census or poll tax, and had to be paid in Roman coin with Caesar's image and slogan on it. "The Pharisees" and "Herodians" try to lay a trap for Jesus by asking whether it is lawful to pay the tribute to Caesar. What the Herodians are doing in Judea when they are supporters of the Galilean Herod Antipas, who had no authority in Judea, is puzzling in Matthew and Mark (neither Pharisees nor Herodians appear in this story in Luke 20:20–26). Also, Matthew heightens the conflict with Pharisees in his account by accusing them of malice (v. 18) and referring to them as "hypocrites" (an epithet that Matthew uses thirteen times compared to three in the rest of the New Testament).

Not to pay the tribute to Caesar would have been to engage in open rebellion against the empire. Clearly the aristocratic priestly families in Jerusalem and the Herodians would have supported the tax because they lived off the various taxes, tithes, and tributes collected from the people.

Later rabbinic attitudes toward taxes were that Jews ought to pay them except in conditions where the "tax farmer" (tax collector in the Gospels) made arbitrary and excessive demands on people or enriched himself in the process. Yet on several occasions Jews had been willing to die rather than endure the image of Caesar in the temple (Josephus, *Jewish Wars* 10.1).

But to carry Caesar's coins in one's pocket is already an instance of accommodation to imperial rule, if not collaboration with it. Hence Jesus' sharp question: "Whose head is this and whose title?" (v. 20). His follow-up remark, "Give therefore to the emperor the things that are the emperor's, and to God the things that are God's" (v. 21), is in the Pharisaic/rabbinic tradition. "Rabbi Eleazar of Bartota says: 'Give Him [God] what is His, for you and yours are His'" (*m. Avot* 3.7, Neusner, *Torah from Our Sages*).

Jesus' answer may not be altogether as clear as it is often taken to be. What things properly belong to Caesar? If a foreign power ruled over our country, what would we think properly belonged to that foreign power? Our taxes? Is Jesus settling a discussion or setting us off on a path to thinking? He is usually presented in commentary on this story as posing no threat to Roman rule. Why then did Romans execute him?

Proper 25 [30]/Year A

Matthew 22:34–46

This reading consists of two paragraphs, the first dealing with the greatest commandment and the second with the meaning of Jesus' messiahship.

There are numerous instances in Second Temple Jewish literature of teachers simplifying the numerous commandments of Scripture to a handful. Here are some. "A heathen came to Shammai, and said to him, 'Accept me as a proselyte on the condition that you teach me the whole Law while I stand on one foot.' Then Shammai drove him away with the measuring rod which he held in his hand. Then he went to Hillel, who received him as a proselyte and said to him, 'What is hateful to you do not to your fellow: that is the whole Law; all the rest is explanation; go and learn" (*m. Shabbat* 31a). (Shammai and Hillel were older contemporaries of Jesus.)

The *Testament of Daniel* says, "Love the Lord in your whole life and one another with a sincere heart" (5:3). Philo of Alexandria said, "There are . . . two fundamental teachings to which the numerous individual . . . teachings are subordinated: in reference to God the commandment of honoring God and piety, in reference to humanity that of the love of humanity and justice."[19] Earlier, Mic. 6:8 had reduced the commandments to three,

Isaiah 56:1 to two, and Hab. 2:4 to one: "The righteous shall live by faith." Amos 5:4 also reduced the commandments to one: "Seek me and live." Jesus' teaching here is remarkably close to that of the liberal Pharisees.

As to vv. 41–46, there was no agreed-upon understanding of "messiah" at the time of Jesus or at any later time.[20] Indeed, that point is assumed by this passage. If everybody agreed on the meaning of the title "messiah," why was there a need to discuss it? Many kinds of messiahs were hoped for among Jews—priestly messiahs, prophetic messiahs, royal messiahs, teaching messiahs—and some forms of Jewish hope did without a messianic figure. If there was one thing they had in common it would have been the hope that the peace and justice of the world would be perfectly restored, that swords would be beaten into plowshares and spears into pruning hooks, that war and oppression would end and economic justice would be the case everywhere.

The argument that Matthew has Jesus make with the Pharisees (the source in Mark 12:35 does not name the audience) is exegetical. It turns on the interpretation of Ps. 110:1: "The LORD says to my lord, 'Sit at my right hand until I make your enemies your footstool.'" Psalm 110 itself is an enthronement psalm. It would have been recited on the occasion of crowning a new king or lord. The term "lord" meant "boss" and had a wide range of meaning.

The early church used Ps. 110:1 to back up the claim that Jesus had ascended to God's right hand. In a sense then, it is the risen and ascended Jesus who is speaking in this paragraph (indeed, the early church heard all Jesus' sayings as the sayings of the risen Jesus). The point being made here is that to claim that the Messiah is "son of David," while true so far as it goes, is an insufficient understanding of the messiahship of Jesus. To claim that Jesus is Messiah in one sense is too much (war, for example, has not vanished from the earth) and too little (he is the one in, through, and by means of whom we are laid bare before the God of Israel, the creator and redeemer of heaven and earth).

Proper 26 [31]/Year A

Matthew 23:1–12

Understanding this passage (and Matthew as a whole) requires that we recognize that Matthew was in conversation with and opposition to the Pharisaic academy that moved from Jerusalem to Javneh (on the coast) after the destruction of the temple in 70 C.E. He is encouraging his community to stay faithful to its understanding of how the people Israel should move forward after 70 and not to follow the leaders of the synagogue across the street. This is a heated, but intra-Jewish, discussion.

This passage introduces Matthew's diatribe (23:1–36) against the scribes and Pharisees. The comparatively brief parallels in Mark 12:37b–40 and Luke 20:45–47 are spoken about the scribes but not the Pharisees. Matthew, however, ratchets up the rhetoric against the Pharisees. This kind of name-calling was used by numerous groups in the ancient Mediterranean. A question to ask of it is whether it is coherent with Jesus' commandment to love even the enemy (Matt. 5:44; Luke 6:27). The reason to ask such a question is to keep before ourselves the responsibility to preach the gospel, not the ancient language of vilification.

The polemic opens with Jesus saying "to the crowds and to his disciples" that "the scribes and the Pharisees sit on Moses' seat; therefore, do whatever they teach you and follow it" (v. 2). Jesus is saying that the scribes and Pharisees teach with authority and are to be followed—a remarkable point. Moses' seat was a distinctive seat in ancient synagogues. One such seat is in the Israel Museum in Jerusalem; sculpted from basalt, it was found in the second-century synagogue in Capernaum, down the block from "Peter's house," a first-century house in which a congregation of Jesus followers met.

"They do not practice what they teach" (v. 3). The gap between preaching and practice is a problem for all of us and is not a useful way to differentiate between "us" and "them." In fact, Pharisaic/rabbinic Judaism repeatedly insists on the requirement of rendering our behavior coherent with our teaching.

When Matthew says that the scribes and Pharisees "do all their deeds to be seen by others" (v. 5), he is echoing Pharisaic/rabbinic teaching: "He that makes worldly use of the crown [of Torah] shall perish" (*m. Avot* 1:13). And, "A man must not say, 'I will study so as to be called a wise man, or Rabbi, or an elder, or to have a seat in the Academy,' but he must study out of love, and the honor will come of itself" (*y. Shevu'ot* 4:2, 35b).

Pharisees and scribes put heavy burdens on the shoulder of others, Jesus says (v. 4). The Pharisees did apply the laws of priestly purity to their own everyday lives, but they were not in any position to require other people to carry out these practices.[21] Indeed, rabbinic Judaism itself did not have anything like this capacity for several centuries. Whether those who did adopt a Pharisaic way of life found it burdensome is a question to which we have no answer. The typical Jewish attitude toward the law, however, is one of joy and delight in it (Ps. 119).

"They make their phylacteries broad and their fringes long" (v. 5). Perhaps it was the straps holding the phylacteries that Matthew thinks were broad; a phylactery was a cube. How does one broaden a cube? Matthew tells us also that Jesus himself wore fringes (9:20; 14:36; see Mark 6:56 and Luke 8:44).

After a few verses criticizing scribes and Pharisees for pretentiousness, Jesus concludes, "The greatest among you will be your servant. All who exalt themselves will be humbled, and all who humble themselves will be exalted" (v. 12). A precise rabbinic parallel is, "He who humbles himself God will exalt, he who exalts himself God will humble" (*b. Sanhedrin* 17a).

In v. 23, beyond this reading, Jesus distinguishes the "weightier matters of the law," namely, "justice and mercy and faith," from the lighter and says, "It is these you ought to have practiced without neglecting the others." That is, practice all the commandments, with priority on the weightier ones. The prophets and the rabbis made exactly the same point.

Proper 27 [32]/Year A

Matthew 25:1–13

Matthew's parable of the Ten Bridesmaids (as the NRSV calls them) is an apocalyptic story encouraging members of Matthew's community to hold fast to their faith in the return of the Son of Man and not be dismayed over its delay.

The term "bridesmaids" is inappropriate because these ten maidens are waiting upon the groom, not the bride. The ten maidens took with them oil-fed lamps. The wise (*phronimoi*) maidens also took along additional vessels (*aggeiois*), or flasks, of oil. When the bridegroom was delayed, they all fell asleep. At midnight, when he arrived, the foolish maidens discovered that they were running out of oil for their lamps. Having to go out and try to purchase more oil, they missed the bridegroom's arrival and were not allowed into the marriage feast. The bridegroom said to them, "Truly, I tell you, I do not know you." The story concludes, "Keep awake therefore, for you know neither the day nor the hour" (v. 13).

Understanding the story requires some knowledge of marriage customs at the time. Marriages were arranged between families. The era of romantic love when a couple meets, falls in love, and decides to marry is in the distant future. In Jesus' time, "individuals" did not get "engaged" to one another. Instead, a couple were "betrothed" to each other, their families promising each other that they would marry at a later date (a year or several years in the future). During the betrothal period the terms of the relationship were negotiated between the families.

When the second stage of the marriage took place, the bride was transferred to the house of the groom, specifically to the house of the groom's father. Here a marriage feast was celebrated (remember the king who gave a wedding banquet for his son in 22:2). This feast could last up to seven days. It was this feast to which the foolish maidens were denied entrance because of the bridegroom's delay.

The bridegroom's delay would have been due to the final stages of negotiating the marriage contract between the two families. Three things had to be agreed upon: dowry, bridewealth, and indirect dowry. This was a complex prenuptial agreement that made clear what wealth went from which family to which, that underwrote the new couple financially, and that protected the bride's future well-being in the event of a possible divorce or the early death of her husband (a common occurrence). Bridewealth was goods and services given by the groom's family to the bride's family. Indirect dowry was wealth given by the groom's family to the bride or roundabout through her relatives. Dowries went the other way, thus giving each family a vested interest in the well-being of the new couple. All this made divorce quite expensive for the groom.

Negotiations about all this would take time and account for the delay. The bridegroom does come, however, and the point is christological. God was identified as the bridegroom of the people Israel (see, e.g., Isa. 54:5, Hos. 2:16), and in the early church Jesus is referred to as the bridegroom (Eph. 5:21–33; John 3:29; Matt. 9:15). Jesus will return and bring the rule (kingdom) of God. The wise followers of Jesus will be alert and will be prepared.

The more at ease we find ourselves with the current state of the world, with its almost constant warfare and the hunger of two-thirds of its population, the sillier it seems to hope and work for the coming of the kingdom of God. The more pained we are by the state of the world, the more realistic does it seem to hope and work for that time.

Proper 28 [33]/Year A

Matthew 25:14–30

There is a rabbinic parable somewhat like Matthew's parable of the Talents: "A king has two servants, one who fears and loves the king, one who only fears him. The king goes away and . . . leaves his palace and estate to these servants to deal with. The one who only fears the king does nothing, and the gardens and grounds become waste and desolate; the one who loves the king plants trees and flowers and fruit. Then the king returns; he is pleased with the one servant and angry with the other" (*Yalqut Shimoni*, Deuteronomy 837, Lachs, *A Rabbinic Commentary on the New Testament*). The interpretation is that the servant who fears the king will enjoy this world; the one who both loves and fears the king will enjoy both this world and the world to come.

In Matthew's parable, the fearful servant said to the king, "I went and hid your talent in the ground" (v. 25). We have already seen the parable about the man who bought a field and discovered a treasure buried in it. Since a talent was worth a great deal, the pay of an ordinary worker for about fifteen years, holding one for a king who would return was an enormous responsibility. Burying money in the ground was looked upon as the best way to ensure against its being stolen (*m. Bava Batra* 4:7–9).

The master said to the trustworthy slaves, "You have been trustworthy in a few things, I will put you in charge of many things; enter into the joy of your master" (vv. 21, 23). This theme occurs often in rabbinic literature: "God does not give greatness to a man till he has proved him in a small matter, only then does He promote him to a great post. . . . He tested David with sheep . . . and God said, 'You were found faithful with the sheep, I will give you My sheep that you should feed them,' and so with Moses, who fed his father-in-law's sheep. To him God said the same" (*Tanhuma Shemot* 14).

The statement to the fearful slave that "you ought to have invested my money with the bankers [*trapezitēs*]" (v. 27) would have been understood by Matthew's hearers. Such banks, depositories for big-time investors, the state, or the temple, were in the urban centers of Jerusalem, Caesarea Maritima, Tiberias, and Sepphoris.

Matthew's conclusion, that the "worthless slave" should be tossed "into the outer darkness, where there will be weeping and gnashing of teeth" (v. 30) actually is a lighter punishment than Luke's ending to the parallel parable: "But as for these enemies of mine . . . bring them here and slaughter them in my presence" (Luke 19:27).

Matthew's parable was addressed to the situation in which waiting for the coming of the Son of Man, the second coming of Jesus, was becoming difficult due to its long delay. The king in the parable left on a journey and only "after a long time" (v. 19) did he return to settle accounts with his servants. Matthew has urged constant watchfulness in several parables—the Two Servants, the Ten Maidens, and now the Talents. The question is: Who will be able to participate in the master's joy?

The other question is: How do we wait? Matthew answers that we wait not by burying the treasures of our faith but by investing them in the mission of the kingdom of God. Waiting is not a passive activity. The enterprising and active followers of Jesus who spread the good news will enter their master's joy. For Matthew there is a time limit to this activity, but the function of the time limit should be to energize our activity. It is like a basketball game played with urgency while the clock is ticking because there is only so much time in which decisions can be made.

Proper 29 [34]/Year A

Matthew 25:31–46

The parable of the Last Judgment, unique to Matthew, is rich in themes found in the Jewish tradition: feeding the hungry, giving drink to the thirsty, welcoming the stranger. The *mitzvah* "do not oppress the stranger," "remember that you were slaves in Egypt," we "know the heart of the stranger," is a foundational principle of biblical faith. Repeated in some form thirty-six times in Scripture, it is the most frequently occurring commandment or expression of Jewish spirituality.

All the actions cited by Jesus are deeds of loving-kindness (*gemilut hasadim*). They are at the heart of Judaism: Said Simeon the Righteous, "On three things does the world stand: on the Torah, and on the Temple service, and on deeds of loving kindness" (*m. Avot* 1:2). "He who receives his fellow man kindly, it is as if he has received the Shekhinah" (*Genesis Rabbah* 48.9). "He who visits the sick will be saved from Gehinom" (*b. Nedarim* 40a).

The midrash on Ps. 118:19 reads, "In the future world man will be asked: 'What was your occupation?' If he replies, 'I fed the hungry,' then they will reply, 'This is the gate of the Lord. He who feeds the hungry, let him enter.' So with giving drink to the thirsty, clothing the naked, with those who look after orphans, and those generally who do deeds of loving kindness. All these are gates of the Lord, and those who do such deeds will enter them" (*Midrash Psalms* 243b).

Visiting those in prison does not appear on Jewish lists of deeds of loving-kindness. Jews did not build prisons.

Matthew's parable has to do with Gentiles. Although the NRSV says that "all the nations" (v. 32) will appear before the Son of Man for judgment, the better translation would be "all the Gentiles." The Greek term is *panta ta ethnē*. Matthew consistently uses *ethnē* to refer to Gentiles (4:15; 6:32; 10:5; 12:18; 20:19; 21:43; 24:7). And they will be judged on how they treated "one of the least of these who are members of my family" (v. 40), one of these *adelphoi*, "brothers," of mine. This is the way Matthew characteristically refers to the disciples whom Jesus sends out on the mission of the kingdom. As you treated these missionaries of mine, so you treated me: "Whoever welcomes you welcomes me, and whoever welcomes me welcomes the one who sent me" (10:40).

Jesus is in the line of Jewish thinking which claims that "every nation which has not known Israel and which has not trodden down the seed of Jacob will live" (*2 Baruch* 72:4–6). Jesus' missionary disciples, like the people Israel, are to be a light to the Gentiles. How Gentiles receive them is important.

The parable is usually given a universal interpretation: However you treat anybody is how you treat Jesus. Such an interpretation is not at odds with the more particular one that Matthew intends. In either case, Gentiles are rewarded for the deeds of loving-kindness that they do on behalf of strangers and those in need.

In the Christian tradition, Martin Luther gave the most profound christological interpretation to this parable. The poor, the hungry, the naked, and the prisoner present to us the needs of Christ; they are "little Christs" to us. In responding to the concrete needs of the neighbor, we too are "little Christs," presenting the love of Christ to them. Christ is incarnate in the stranger.

Year B

First Sunday of Advent/Year B

Mark 13:24–37

The Gospel of Mark is apocalyptic. Although the roots of apocalypticism are as old as Isa. 56–66 and Zech. 9–14, this movement came to full expression from 300 B.C.E. to 200 C.E. (see, e.g., Dan. 7–12, *1 Enoch*, *2 Baruch*) as many Jews perceived a contradiction between the divine promises of blessing and their repeated experience of oppression and evil. How would God keep the divine promises? they asked.

According to the apocalyptic theologians, God created the world good, but Satan (the snake) persuaded the first human pair to seek knowledge that belonged to God. Consequently, God cursed the world. This old age was marked by the influence of Satan and the demons, sin, poverty, social oppression, sickness, violence, and death.

To keep God's promises, God would end the present and initiate a new world (divine realm) that manifests divine aims: the rule of God, forgiveness, freedom, abundance, and eternal life. To bring the new age, God would send warriors from heaven to destroy evil and to instantiate the divine realm. This interruption would be preceded by a time of suffering, called the tribulation, when evil intensified the struggle against God.

For Mark, Jesus Christ is the means whereby the God of Israel keeps the divine promise to re-create. God's invasion of the old world began with the baptism of Jesus and came to penultimate manifestation at the crucifixion (a tribulation event) and resurrection (a demonstration of the presence of the divine realm). Mark 13:3–23 interprets historical conditions in Mark's day as the tribulation (the suffering of 13:24; cf. Proper 28/Year B).

Mark 13:24–37 is the climax of the apocalypse. In vv. 24–25, at one level, the creation of the world in Gen. 1 is reversed. The downfall of the heavenly bodies shows that the structures that support the present order will be dismantled so that a new world (the divine reign) can be created (see, e.g., Isa. 13:10; Ezek. 32:7–8; Joel 2:10). At another level, vv. 24–25 are a caustic political comment. The Romans worshiped astral bodies. The destruction of the heavenly powers shows the condemnation of Rome and its gods.

For Mark, Jesus is the apocalyptic Son of Man, a figure from heaven whom God sends into the world to destroy Satan and to establish the divine realm. Since the resurrection, Jesus has been at the right hand of God in heaven (Mark 14:62). Per Daniel 7:13–14, Jesus as Son of Man will come from heaven to complete redemption. Jesus will send angels to gather the elect (those who witness to the divine realm) from throughout the cosmos. The reference to the "four winds" and "the ends of the earth to the ends of heaven" (13:27) refers particularly to those who carry the gospel to Gentiles (13:10).

Christians sometimes say that Jesus Christ "fulfilled" God's purposes for the world. However, today's passage reminds us that Christians are at one with the Jewish community in recognizing that God's hopes for the world are unfulfilled. The authors of this book do not think that history is moving toward an apocalyptic moment as described in Mark 13:24–27. Nonetheless, in league with the deepest hopes of Judaism, this passage asserts God's unrelenting desire for the world to become a realm of love, peace, and justice. Indeed, the focus of today's text is not upon Jesus Christ per se but upon the intention of the God of Israel to regenerate the world. Instead of expecting a singular moment of transformation, we believe with many in the Jewish world that God is constantly present in history urging human communities to turn away from oppression and to live in love, peace, and justice. Given this shared perspective, the time is ripe for synagogue and church to work together to increase such qualities of life throughout the world.

Second Sunday of Advent/Year B

Mark 1:1–8

The opening lines of some documents in antiquity identified the contents. Mark 1:1 indicates that the following narrative (Mark 1:2 through 16:8) is the *beginning* of the gospel. Here the word "gospel" (*euangelion*) refers to the central message of the community. For Mark, the gospel is the news that God is ending the present, broken age and will replace it with a refurbished world (the realm of God).

Jesus is the Christ (anointed one), that is, God's agent in displacing Satan and the oppressive powers of the old age. The ministry of Jesus demonstrates that the power of the divine realm is at work. The gospel story will finish only after the gospel has been preached among Gentiles (Mark 13:10), Jesus has returned (13:24–27), and the realm of God is fully in place (cf. First Sunday of Advent/Year B).

In 1:2–8, Mark uses John the Baptist to alert the reader to the apocalyptic nature of the ministry of Jesus. In vv. 2–3, Mark attributes to Isaiah a conflation of Exod. 23:20; Mal. 3:1; and Isa. 40:3 to interpret John. John is a prophet similar to the one described in Mal. 3:1–5 who announces that God's judgment is coming and will be followed by redemption. Isaiah was especially popular among apocalyptists because they used the Babylonian oppressors and the exile to interpret Rome (latter-day idolatrous and unjust Babylon) and their situation of exile as they awaited the apocalypse. Isaiah 40:30 reinforces the theme from Malachi: John prepared the community for the eschatological invasion of the present, broken world by Jesus.

Apocalyptically oriented Jewish groups sometimes initiated people into their communities by baptism, as in John's immersion of repentance for the forgiveness of sins (1:4–5; cf. Third Sunday of Advent/Year C). In apocalyptic thinking, sin is a power in the old age that keeps human beings and elements of nature in bondage to repressive forces. Repentance is the dynamic action of turning away from disobedience and injustice, and toward God, obedience, justice, and living in covenant in the divine realm. The word for "forgiveness" (*aphesis*) often means "release." Those who are baptized by John turn away from complicity with the sin of the present age in anticipation of release from bondage in the coming realm of God.

John is dressed in the manner of Elijah (1:6; 2 Kgs. 1:8). Apocalyptic theologians expected Elijah to return before the apocalypse in a role similar to John's (Mal. 4:5–6; Sir. 48:10). According to Mark 9:9–13, John fulfilled the function of the returning Elijah. Mark uses John's fate to reveal the character of the Herods of the world and to prepare the community for similar rejection (13:9–23; cf. Proper 10/Year B).

John's dress is also reminiscent of that of Adam and Eve when evicted from Eden (Gen. 3:21). Apocalypticism thought of the end-time as similar to the beginning. John leads the community to the gate of the new Eden, but Jesus must lead them into it (1:7–8). In 1:7, power is a fundamental issue: God, acting through Jesus, has more power than John, Caesar, Herod, the Jewish leaders, Satan, the demons, or other entities. While John prepares people for the new age with repentance and immersion, Jesus will baptize them with the Holy Spirit. The Spirit continues to manifest the divine realm after Jesus returns to heaven. Furthermore, the Spirit will sustain the community when their testimony to the divine realm brings them into conflict with those who do not believe that God is using Jesus to finalize the divine reign (13:11).

Third Sunday of Advent/Year B

John 1:6–8, 19–28

Today's lectionary texts present the Gospel of John's understanding of John the Baptist in his role of one who was "sent from God" "to testify to the light" (vv. 7, 8), a point that the Gospel makes twice in the opening three verses. This repetition indicates John's fondness for parallelism, a feature of Hebrew poetry that he uses extensively in the Prologue to the Gospel (1:1–18). In the Fourth Gospel, John the Baptist loses many of the features attributed to him in the Synoptic Gospels. The Fourth Gospel does not mention, for example, that he baptizes Jesus. Instead, John's theological function of bearing witness to Jesus, "the one who is coming after me" (v. 27), takes precedence over all other functions.

John 1:1–18 is an ancient wisdom, christological hymn, that is, a hymn that sings of Jesus' preexistence, his coming into the world, his suffering, and his exaltation. Other such hymns are Col. 1:15–20; Phil. 2:6–11; and Heb. 1:2b–4. Today's passages about John the Baptist intrude into the grand philosophical and poetic language of the Prologue to present a narrative account of the role and importance of John the Baptist. In providing this narrative, the Gospel does two important things. First, it tells us that John "was a man sent from God" (v. 6). Other than Jesus, no other person in the Fourth Gospel is said to have been "sent from God." John did not show up by happenstance, but served God's purpose of providing a witness to the light so that others might come to believe in the life-giving presence of that light as it shone in Jesus. Second, John anchors the philosophical language of the opening sentences, which is rooted in the creation story and engages the philosophical concept of Logos, in the history and land of the people Israel (he came to his own place or home and his own people, v. 11).

Tension between the witness to Jesus as the light and "the Jews" is introduced in the very beginning of the narrative. In vv. 19–28, we find the first conflict with "the Jews" in John's Gospel. John uses the expression "the Jews" sixty-four times (in contrast to Luke's four and Matthew's five). Conflict with some Jews lies in the background of John's community, conflict that occurred after the time of Jesus. Three times the Gospel claims that Jesus followers have been expelled from the synagogue (9:22; 12:42; 16:2). Whether this took place because of an action by the Pharisaic academy at Javneh or was a local matter is unclear (and subject to much scholarly dispute).

John does not use "the Jews" to mean "all Jews." In today's reading, for example, John says that "the Jews sent priests and Levites" (v. 19) to question the Baptist but later says these same priests and Levites "had been sent by the Pharisees" (v. 24). This shows us that when we read the term "the Jews" in John we have to see it in its literary context; here it means "the Pharisees." John frequently uses "the Jews" and "the Pharisees" synonomously (e.g., 9:13, 18, 40).

When the Fourth Gospel uses the term "the Jews" to indicate opposition to Jesus, it does so to name the people on the wrong side of a christological debate, namely, those who do not accept (a) that Jesus is the Messiah and (b) the Fourth Gospel's understanding of what his messiahship means. The conflict here is between two sides of a late first-century argument, not a conflict that tells us anything about Jesus' (or the Baptist's) relations with Jews about the year 30.

Fourth Sunday of Advent/Year B

Luke 1:26–38

As we point out on the Second, Third, and Fourth Sundays of Advent/Year C, Luke 1–2 establishes the Jewish background of Jesus and, hence, of the Lukan community. This motif permeates today's lection.

In Luke 1:26, the presence of the angel Gabriel confirms that the event of Jesus is a part of the movement toward the eschaton, the realm of God (Dan. 8:16 and 9:21). The unimpressive circumstances of Jesus' birth testify to the continuity of these events with Judaism, for Judaism began under unimpressive circumstances (Abraham and Sarah) and involved unusual births (e.g., Isaac). Even at its most powerful, Israel was a minor force. To think of the God of Israel acting in such a birth is consistent with Jewish perception of the time.

Mary and Joseph are betrothed, that is, arrangements are made for their marriage (per Deut. 22:23). The Greek "Mary" translates the Hebrew "Miriam," the sister of Moses, who helped lead the Israelites from slavery to freedom (Exod. 15:20). Mary, similarly, helps the community journey from the old age toward the new. Luke stresses that Mary is a virgin to show that the Holy Spirit is responsible for Jesus.

The expressions "greeting" (*chaire*) and "favored one" (*kecharitōmenos*) are related to the Greek for "grace" (*charis*), and indicate that God acts through Mary to express grace, that is, to express the divine sovereignty and realm (cf. Zeph. 3:14–15; Joel 2:21; Zech. 9:9; Sir. 18:17). Continuing "the Lord is with you," the angel uses a phrase that communicates that God is acting for redemption (cf. Fourth Sunday of Advent/Year A).

At Mary's perplexed response (1:29), the angel speaks one of the most powerful assurances in Judaism: "Do not be afraid" (cf. Proper 14/Year C). Jesus will be Son of the Most High, a synonym for Son of God (1:35), a leader whom God chooses to help the life of the community embody covenantal qualities (see, e.g., Exod. 4:22; Ps. 2:7; 89:26–27; Jer. 31:20; Sir. 36:11; 2 Esd. 6:58). By saying that God will give Jesus the throne of David and that Jesus will rule over Jacob (1:32–33), Luke means that God will keep the promises to David (2 Sam. 7:13–14) and to the ancestors through the manifestation of the divine realm by Jesus. In Luke's mind, a direct connection runs from Israel through Jesus to the early Lukan community and into the realm of God, when all of God's people—Jewish and Gentile—will live together in peace in the dominion that has no end (1:33b). Luke never suggests that Jewish identity disappears in the divine realm.

Mary questions how these things can be since she is a virgin (1:34). That the Holy Spirit will come upon her calls to mind Isa. 32:15, which sings of the spirit coming upon the community as part of the restoration of justice, peace, and abundance. When God overshadows Mary (cf. Luke 9:34), God fills her as God filled the temple (Exod. 40:35; cf. Ps. 91:4) while also protecting her as God protects the head of a warrior in battle (Ps. 140:7). Jesus will be holy, that is, set aside to witness to God's purposes.

Mary's response to the angel models the way Luke would like people to respond to the news of the manifestation of God's realm through Jesus (1:38). She has repented of her doubt and trustingly seeks to serve the realm. Indeed, her response, "Here am I," reminds the reader of similar responses by Moses, Isaiah, and other leaders in Israel. By making Mary a model believer, Luke signals that in the divine realm the situation of women will be fully restored.

Christmas Day/Year B

Luke 2:1–20

Please see Christmas Day/Year C for the commentary on this reading.

John 1:1–14

Please see Christmas Day/Years A, B, and C for the commentary on this reading.

First Sunday after Christmas Day/Year B

Luke 2:22–40

This reading demonstrates the fidelity of Joseph and Mary to Judaism. It uses two Jewish prophets to interpret the ministry of Jesus (and the early church), especially the Gentile mission, as expressions of Judaism. After the birth of Jesus, the parents do all that the law requires to establish a Jewish identity—circumcision, purification, presentation to God, and offering of sacrifice (2:21–24). This lection gives the preacher an opportunity to acquaint the congregation with these aspects of Jewish life. The passage directly names Torah five times; each reference assumes Torah's positive character and normativity (vv. 22, 23, 24, 27, 39).

For males, circumcision was a sign that God had graciously received the child into the covenantal community and that the parents would raise the child in covenantal faithfulness (2:21; cf. Gen. 17:9–27; Lev. 12:2–3; *Jubilees* 15:25–27). Women engaged in purification after childbirth (Lev. 12:2–5). The reference to presentation in 2:22–23 cites Exod. 13:2 and echoes the consecration of the firstborn to God to witness to God's holiness and desire for covenantal living (Exod. 13:1–2, 11–16; 22:29–30; Num. 3:13; 8:17–18; 1 Sam. 1:22–24). The mother's purification included sacrifice of sheep (or turtledoves for the less affluent; Lev. 12:6–8).

Simeon, a prophet, is righteous and devout (Luke 2:25). He is looking forward to the consolation of Israel, that is, the fulfillment of God's promises to Israel—promises not only for Israel to be blessed but also for Gentiles to be blessed through Israel. Such consolation means the end of Roman repression and other forms of evil, and the manifestation of the realm of God. The Spirit has inspired Simeon to recognize that God is soon to send a messiah to begin the transformation and now leads Simeon to recognize Jesus in that role (2:26–28).

In vv. 29–32, Simeon interprets Jesus in language that sounds Septuagintal, thereby giving these words authority akin to Scripture's. Simeon can see that God is keeping the divine promises ("your word") through Jesus to bring about salvation (i.e., the divine realm) publicly and for the benefit of all (v. 31). This event will be glory for Israel (for it demonstrates the truth of Israel's witness) and includes the ingathering of the Gentiles (v. 32). The child is destined for "the falling and the rising of many in Israel," meaning that Jews will disagree on whether Jesus and the Gentile mission are divine vehicles. The conflict will eventuate in Jesus' crucifixion, which will pierce Mary's soul (vv. 34–35).

Luke often testifies to the restoration of gender egalitarianism in God's realm by pairing male and female characters in similar roles. While Anna is not as fully developed a character as Simeon, she is a prophetess with recognized Jewish credentials (through the tribe of Asher; Deut. 33:24–25) who interprets Jesus as means of redemption (2:36–38).

When Luke later presents Jesus and the disciples in conflict with Jews in the Gospel and Acts, Jesus and the church are not rejecting Judaism per se but rather disagreeing with other Jews over the degree to which Judaism could be adapted for Gentiles in view of the coming eschaton. In the heat of disagreement, the church caricatured Judaism and soon turned its disagreement into an ideology of supersessionism. By showing the Jewishness of Jesus' origins, Luke uses today's passage to suggest that the claims of the church derive from Jewish soil. Today's preacher can help today's congregation appreciate the Jewish spirit at the heart of Christianity and repent of the Christian caricature and rejection of Judaism.

Second Sunday after Christmas Day/Year B

John 1:1–18

Please see the Second Sunday after Christmas Day/Years A, B, and C for the commentary on this reading.

Epiphany of the Lord/Year B

Matthew 2:1–12

Please see the Epiphany of the Lord/Years A, B, and C for the commentary on this reading.

First Sunday after the Epiphany/Year B

Baptism of the Lord

Mark 1:4–11

On the Second Sunday of Advent/Year B, we took up Mark 1:4–8, with its presentation of the eschatological baptism of John as preparing the community for the apocalypse. By echoing 1:4–8, the baptism of Jesus indicates that the ministry of Jesus is apocalyptic.

Jesus comes from Galilee. In Mark, Galilee (home to both Jewish and Gentile peoples) is a place of positive revelation, in contrast to Jerusalem. Jesus begins his witness to God's rule there, and will appear there after the resurrection (and perhaps at the apocalypse; Mark 14:28; 16:7). The leaders of Jerusalem, by contrast, kill Jesus.

The Jordan River is a significant symbol. Fresh water in a semi-arid land, the Jordan makes fertility possible and represents vitality and life. Since the Israelites crossed the Jordan as they entered the promised land, it signifies crossing from one way of life (wandering) to another (settlement). Similarly, Jesus' ministry leads the community from the old world to the realm of God with its eternal vitality.

After Jesus is immersed, the heavens tear apart as they will at the apocalypse. The NRSV accurately captures the forceful quality of the Greek *schidzō*—a ripping, as at Mark 15:38 (cf. Zech. 14:4; Isa. 36:22; 37:1; 48:21). The Spirit descends like a dove on Jesus. Mark typically mentions the Spirit in connection with eschatological confrontation and conflict (e.g., 1:12; 3:29; 13:11), thus suggesting that it here intimates the presence of the Spirit with the community through such times. These themes are multiplied through the reference to the dove. In Gen. 8:8, a dove returns to the ark after the flood to show that the destruction (judgment) by the waters of chaos is ended and that the new era of renewal is at hand. In Gen. 1:1–2, the Spirit hovers bird-like (see Deut. 32:11) over primeval chaos, preserving the chaos from destruction. Several rabbis refer to the dove as a symbol of such hovering (*b. Berakhot* 3b; *b. Hagigah* 15a; *Genesis Rabbah* 42.4).

Immersion represents Jesus' death (Mark 10:38–39). The leaders in Jerusalem will kill Jesus to prevent the coming of God's realm through him. Mark views this suffering as part of the tribulation that precedes the apocalypse. Similarly, the baptism of Jesus' followers symbolically initiates them into a community that is not only awaiting the apocalypse but, like the servant community of Isaiah, will suffer when it comes into conflict with the powers of the present age as a result of its witness (see, e.g., Mark 13:1–24; Proper 28/Year B). The story of the baptism of Jesus, however, assures the community that the Spirit is constantly with them and makes it possible for them to endure (13:11). The baptism of Jesus is thus a model for what happens through the immersion of the followers.

In the commentary for the First Sunday after the Epiphany/Year C, we say more about the voice from heaven that also speaks in Mark 1:11. This voice identifies the baptism as the occasion on which Jesus is, for Mark, identified as God's agent (like the king of Israel in Ps. 2:7) to bring about justice in community. However, this mission, as in Isa. 42:1–9, prompts resistance that leads Jesus and those who follow him to suffer.

By presenting Galilee as a place of positive revelation (anticipating Jerusalem as a place of negative response to Jesus), Mark lays the groundwork for criticism of Jewish leaders from the beginning of the Gospel. However, a contemporary preacher can call attention to Markan contributions to Christian baptism without defaming Judaism. Indeed, baptism should remind the church to put to death its tendencies to make life a chaos for Jewish people.

Second Sunday after the Epiphany/Year B

John 1:43–51

The subject of John 1:19–51 is the first four days of Jesus' ministry in John, which follow the Prologue to the Gospel. Our text begins on day four, "the next day," when Jesus decides to go to Galilee. On this day, Jesus begins to disclose his glory (*doxa*) to the disciples. In Galilee, Jesus "found Philip and said to him, 'Follow me.'" Like Peter and Andrew, Philip is from Bethsaida in Galilee; he follows Jesus simply because he was called.

Christology is at the heart of John's Gospel, as the Prologue announces: "The Word became flesh and lived among us, and we have seen his glory, the glory as of a father's only son, full of grace and truth" (1:14). That the disciples do not understand who Jesus is (the Word made flesh) or where he is from (the Father) or who they are in relation to him begins to be made clear in today's reading.

Philip illustrates this. He finds Nathanael and says to him, "We have found him about whom Moses in the law and also the prophets wrote" (v. 45). But Philip had not found Jesus—Jesus had found Philip (v. 43). And while it is true that Moses and the prophets wrote about Jesus, from John's perspective it is not the whole truth, for Jesus is "the father's only son, full of grace and truth." To try to understand or assess Jesus in terms of the Torah and the prophets is insufficient and, by itself, will lead only to rejection in John.

Philip compounds his misunderstanding by identifying Jesus as "son of Joseph from Nazareth" (v. 45), occasioning the counterquestion, "Can anything good come out of Nazareth?" (v. 46). Jesus was from Nazareth but, more importantly for John, he was sent from God; his true origins are "in the beginning" when the Word was with God.

Then Jesus sees Nathanael and says of him, "Here is truly an Israelite in whom there is no deceit!" (v. 47). Nathanael wants to know how Jesus got to know him, and Jesus tells him, "I saw you under the fig tree" (v. 48). Although Philip had invited Nathanael to see Jesus (v. 46), it was Jesus who saw Nathanael, not vice versa, just as Jesus found Philip, not vice versa. In awe of Jesus' unusual knowledge, Nathanael proclaims him as "the Son of God . . . the King of the Jews" (v. 49).

In rabbinic fashion, Jesus questions Nathanael and his miracle-based faith: "Do you believe because I told you that I saw you under the fig tree? You will see greater things than these" (v. 50). John tells stories of signs and then invites us to move beyond them; they are not ends in themselves. What will Nathanael see?

He will see "heaven opened and the angels of God ascending and descending upon the Son of Man" (v. 51). As the gate of heaven opened for Jacob with the angels of God ascending and descending upon a ladder, for John the angels ascend and descend upon Jesus. Jacob had said, "Surely the LORD is in this place—and I did not know it! . . . How awesome is this place!" (Gen. 28:16–17). So Nathanael will ultimately move beyond interpreting Jesus in terms of what he already knows and beyond miracles to knowledge of Jesus as the revealer of God.

Jesus' disciples' faith in him is shaped by their Jewish understandings, views that Jesus constantly corrects, as this passage illustrates. This will be a major theme of John—misunderstanding on the part of Jesus' disciples and, even more, of Jews who are not Jesus' disciples. John's Jesus is shaped entirely by John's Christology.

Third Sunday after the Epiphany/Year B

Mark 1:14–20

John was arrested (Mark 1:14a) and killed because he condemned Herod for violating Torah by marrying Herodias after destroying her marriage to his brother Philip (6:14–29). Herod represents power in the present, broken world.

The content of the Gospel, defined in 1:15, presumes the Jewish apocalyptic worldview summarized on the First Sunday of Advent/Year B. "The time" is the apocalypse. This moment is "fulfilled," that is, God has decided to effect the cosmic transformation when all things manifest the divine purposes in all ways and at all times.

Although scholars debate whether "has come near" (*eggidzō*) means "has arrived" or "is drawing near," Mark clearly means the latter. While the future divine realm is now present through the ministry of Jesus, God's rule will not be universal until the apocalypse (13:24–27). In preparation for that, people repent (Second Sunday of Advent/Year B) and believe the gospel, that is, trust that God is bringing the divine realm through Jesus.

The designation "disciple" (1:16–20) translates *mathētēs*, which means "learner," calling to mind the relationship between a rabbi and a follower. Disciples learned the content of the rabbi's teaching, the pattern of rabbinic thinking, and often lived with (or near) the rabbi to absorb the rabbi's approach to life.

The call of Jesus' first disciples echoes Elisha's call by Elijah (1 Kgs. 19:19–21), who left parents and livelihood to learn from Elijah how to witness to God's sovereignty and will for covenantal faithfulness and justice.

These early disciples are in the fishing business, a solid occupation providing a way of life which would have been middle class in their time. James and John are sufficiently prosperous to have hired hands. These economic matters are key: The call to witness to the realm of God takes priority over present sufficiency. The disciples, like Elisha, trust God to provide for their daily needs as they follow Jesus and learn to witness.

Fishing involved two steps that metaphorically describe eschatological discipleship. First, workers pulled a net through the water from a boat or dragged a net from the shore to gather fish, then they sorted the catch into the usable and unusable. These images are informed by Jer. 16:16–18, where God sends persons to gather the community for judgment prior to the restoration of Israel, and Ezek. 47:10–12, which describes, in the regenerated world, people fishing in the Dead Sea (cf. 1QH 5:7). The disciples of Jesus gather people for the realm of God and the great separation (judgment) that takes place at the apocalypse. The word "followed" is a nearly technical expression for discipleship in Mark.

Apostleship, as explained in Mark 3:13–15, involves: (1) being with Jesus to absorb this apocalyptic rabbi's teaching and lifestyle, (2) announcing the coming of the divine realm through Jesus, and (3) exorcizing demons.

As Mark unfolds, the reader becomes aware that the Twelve in this narrative are not models to be fully emulated. They repeatedly misunderstand Jesus (see, e.g., 4:10–12; 5:36–37; 8:14–17; 9:33–37; 10:35–45); they abandon Jesus in the garden (14:50); and Peter denies Jesus (14:66–72). The literary-theological purpose of this portrait of the disciples is to press readers to ask whether they are as misperceptive and unfaithful as the disciples. Mark's negative portrayal of the Twelve reflects the Jewish practice of self-criticism that intends to strengthen the criticized. Despite their failures, the risen Jesus redeems the disciples (16:7), recalling the faithfulness of God to Israel when Israel wandered.

Fourth Sunday after the Epiphany/Year B

Mark 1:21–28

This text is a Markan paradigm of the ministry of Jesus. It also caricatures Jewish leaders and institutions who are not part of Mark's community and asserts the superiority of Jesus. In those days, local synagogue leaders customarily invited visiting rabbis to speak (1:21). While Mark does not report the content of Jesus' teaching, we assume that Jesus is explaining the realm of God (1:14–15). The exorcism embodies this realm, that is, it liberates a person from psychic oppression.

Mark 1:22 is a polemic against the scribes.[22] The crowd is astounded at Jesus' teaching because Jesus "taught them as one having authority, and not as the scribes." Authority (*exousia*) in Mark refers to the power of the divine realm over demons (e.g., Mark 2:10; 3:15; 6:7; cf. 11:28–34). In Judaism, scribes were recognized interpreters of tradition, but Mark implies that the scribes do not recognize God's realm. This initial picture of the scribes is just the first element of Mark's systematic program to discredit Jewish leaders.

A person with an unclean spirit appears in the synagogue (1:23). The term "unclean spirit" is a Jewish expression for a demon (see, e.g., *Testament of Benjamin* 5:2; *b. Hagigah* 3b; *b. Sotah* 3a; 1QM 13:5). People in antiquity believed that demons were beings, Satan's assistants, who moved into a person, group, object, or element of nature, and controlled significant aspects of that person or thing. On the First Sunday of Advent/Year B, we explain that Satan and the demons emerged in Jewish literature from 300 B.C.E. through 200 C.E. to explain the massive experience of evil.

Today we might say that the literary figures of the demons are objectifications of evil.

The demoniac's appearance in the synagogue implies that synagogues (and other Jewish institutions) are haunts of demons. Mark thus lays the foundation for eventually claiming that many Jewish leaders and institutions are possessed by demons (Palm Sunday or Passion Sunday/Year B).

The demoniac recognizes that Jesus can destroy the demon because Jesus is the Holy One of God, the agent of God who will restore the earth to holiness, that is, to the qualities of the divine realm (1:24). Jesus speaks to the demon in the language of a first-century exorcist. The word "rebuked" (from *epitimaō*) is a technical term for demon exorcism and recurs in Mark to interpret other important events (e.g., 3:12; 4:39; 8:30, 32–33; 9:25; 10:13, 48). The description of the demoniac convulsing and crying out is typical of exorcism narratives to show that the demon has left the person.

Verse 27 describes Jesus presenting "a new teaching" authenticated by exorcisms. In fact, Jesus' teaching as Mark presents it is a form of Jewish apocalypticism adapted to suggest that Jesus is God's agent in bringing the apocalypse. The first-century world contained many exorcists.

This story is a miniature of the ministries of Jesus and the church (liberating people from the demons as signs of the realm of God) and even of the apocalypse. The liberation of the demoniac is a miniature and proof of the coming liberation of the cosmos. Further, the mention of the exorcism in the context of teaching communicates that teaching casts out demons. The idea of teaching as exorcism is a striking idea for ministry today. Yet the preacher must point out that Mark presents false pictures of the scribes (and other Jewish leaders) as nonauthoritative, and of synagogues as possessed. Indeed, if we are to speak of demons in this context, then we must say for centuries the church has been possessed by the demonic ideologies of anti-Judaism and anti-Semitism. Fortunately, God can cast out this demon.

Fifth Sunday after the Epiphany/Year B

Mark 1:29–39

Today's lection demonstrates that the realm of God, announced in 1:14–15, is indeed beginning to be manifest through Jesus' ministry. Mark interprets the miracles in these stories as signs of the divine reign. At the same time, these texts help set the stage for a claim by Mark: The coming of the realm of God through Jesus includes not only the glory of the miracles and Jesus' triumphant return from heaven but also the suffering of Jesus and the disciples because of their witness (Mark 8:31–38). While the miracles are impressive, they are only part of the story of the transition from old age to new.

Mark 1:29–31 takes place on the Sabbath. Jesus and his followers go from the synagogue to the house of the brothers Simon and Andrew to observe the Sabbath. In the early part of the Gospel, Mark portrays Jesus as a faithful Jewish person so that, later, when the Markan Jesus criticizes aspects of Jewish practice, the reader understands Jesus to do so from the perspective of a rabbi prophetically criticizing comrades in community.

Simon's mother-in-law has a fever (on Simon's marital status, see 1 Cor. 9:5). While she is sick in bed, her life is limited by confinement and pain, and she is not able to contribute to maintaining the household. Jesus heals her in a manner often characteristic of Jewish healers when he takes her by the hand. (At other times, Jesus heals simply by speaking a word—even from afar.) When Mark says Jesus "lifted her," the word is *egeirō*; it is also used for "raised up" in reference to the resurrection. While Jesus does not raise Simon's mother-in-law with a resurrection body, her healing is characteristic of restored life in the realm of God.

In Mark 3:31–35, Jesus redefines the family not as blood kin but as "whoever does the will of God" (cf. Proper 5/Year B). Mark 1:29–31 shows that the family constituted by doing God's will and the biological family need not be exclusive. One's physical kin can also be those who do the will of God.

Jesus' wider followers also observe Jewish custom as they wait until sundown (the end of Sabbath) before bringing the possessed and sick to Jesus (vv. 32–34; cf. Lev. 23:32; Neh. 13:19). By using the double expression, "that evening, at sundown," Mark goes out of the way to make sure the reader recognizes the Sabbath fidelity of those who come to Jesus.

Mark engages in hyperbole by describing "the whole city" gathering at Jesus' door, perhaps Gentiles as well. This report of popular support encourages readers to identify with the Jesus movement. Verse 34 reports that Jesus would not permit the demons to speak. On the Sixth Sunday after the Epiphany/Year B, we take up the enigmatic issue of Jesus' commands in the Gospel of Mark not to testify to the presence of the realm of God.

Verses 35–39, with their picture of the crowds seeking Jesus, reinforce the sense that Jesus was positively received in Galilee. Verse 35 presents Jesus as joining the great Jewish tradition of morning prayer to fit one for mission during the day (see, e.g., Ps. 5:4; 88:14; 119:147; *m. Berakhot* 4:3). Although Mark presents Jesus as a Jewish figure, Mark contributes to the separation of Judaism and Mark's community in v. 39 by referring to the congregations where Jesus preached and healed as "their" synagogues.

Sixth Sunday after the Epiphany/Year B

Mark 1:40–45

In the ancient world, the word "leprosy" seldom applied to Hansen's disease, as we think of it today, but to a range of ailments in which the skin developed scales, inflammation, and/or lesions, often turned white, and was sometimes contagious. Persons with such diseases wore distinctive dress, let their hair go disheveled, covered their upper lips, and cried, "Unclean, unclean," so that other persons would not touch them and thereby become unclean (Lev. 13:45–46; cf. Num. 12:12; *b. Niddah* 64b). Although such restrictions can seem dehumanizing and socially isolating, they were part of standard Jewish protocol (Lev. 13–14) for providing the ill with a healing environment, for protecting the community, and for reintegrating the persons into social interaction. Typically, the ill were quarantined while the disease ran its course, then engaged in rites of purification and received a priestly pronouncement to welcome them back into society. By asking Jesus for cleansing, the leper requests Jesus to do in a short time what would ordinarily take a week through the temple ritual.

Commentators debate whether 1:41 should follow ancient manuscripts that read "moved with pity [better: with compassion]" (*splanchnistheis*), or those that read "moved by anger" (*orgistheis*). The former is preferable both because it resonates with the way God responds with compassion for Israel, and because Mark later develops similar themes (e.g., 6:34). The God of Israel acts compassionately for the leper through Jesus.

After the healing, Jesus directed the leper not to tell anyone about the healing but to follow Jewish procedure by going to the priest and to make an offering to thank God for the healing (1:43–44). The leper, however, ignored these Jewish practices. On the one hand, Mark wrote when the priestly ministry had ended because of the destruction of the temple, and this story assures the Markan community that lepers (and others whom they represent) can be restored without benefit of priestly presence. On the other hand, the leper's disregard is an implicit rejection of a Jewish practice. Mark authorizes the disregard of other Jewish customs as well (e.g., 2:18–22; 2:23–3:6; esp. 7:1–23). The leper's testimony is so effective that towns could no longer hold the crowds coming to see Jesus (1:45). Mark wants readers to think that abandoning Jewish practice need not threaten the size of the community; in fact, he shows that turning away from Jewish custom increased the number of people who identified with Jesus' demonstration of God's rule.

Christians often wonder why Jesus commanded the leper and some others not to tell anyone about certain miracles (cf. 1:34; 3:12; 7:36; 8:26; 8:30; 9:9, 30). Apocalyptic thinkers thought God had a specific time and plan to make public the news that the world was in its last days and that the apocalypse was imminent. While Jesus was authorized to make such an announcement, the time had not come for it to go forth more broadly. The leper disobeys by testifying freely, and the news of the presence of the divine reign is so compelling that it cannot be contained. This helps explain why the news about Jesus traveled so widely during Jesus' lifetime.

The pastor can help today's congregation recognize that while the church developed other ways of dealing with persons with skin diseases (and analogous conditions), such developments do not warrant disrespecting Jewish practices. Indeed, a pastor can help today's congregation recognize the wisdom that benefits both the sick (providing healing) and the community (preserving its overall health) in ancient Jewish patterns.

Seventh Sunday after the Epiphany/Year B

Mark 2:1–12

Although Christians sometimes use this pericope as occasion to ponder the relationship of healing and sin, that theme is not central to the text. Mark uses the story to heighten criticism of the scribes and other Jewish leaders and to establish Jesus' authority.

Four friends bring a paralytic to Jesus for healing. When they cannot reach Jesus through the door, they dig a hole through the thatch and mud roof and lower the mat containing the paralytic (2:3–4). The role of the friends in this story calls attention to the importance that community can have in regeneration. The paralyzed man can get to Jesus only with the help of his friends. Jesus acts in behalf of the paralytic only after seeing his friends' trust that the realm of God was coming to expression through Jesus' ministry (i.e., "their faith"). The story does not explicitly say that the paralytic had faith.

Jesus announces the forgiveness of the paralytic's sins. While Jesus' statement may presume an ancient, though not universal, viewpoint that some sicknesses resulted from sin, speculation about the relationship between sin and illness is incidental here. Instead, Mark uses Jesus' pronouncement to show the spiritual imperceptivity of the scribes. The expression "Your sins are forgiven" (v. 5) is a circumlocution. Jewish people often used this way of speaking to indicate that God is the subject of the action. The reader knows immediately that God has forgiven the sins of the paralytic.

Historical scribes (recognized teachers in Judaism whose name derived from the close attention they gave to Scripture) would know the theological implication of "Your sins are forgiven." Mark, however, portrays the scribes as "questioning" (*dialogizomai*), an expression that has a contentious overtone (see, e.g., Mark 8:16–17; 9:33; 11:31). They misunderstand their tradition, for they mistakenly think Jesus has forgiven the sin of the paralytic (2:6–7) and committed blasphemy (an act that deserved death in an earlier generation—Lev. 24:15–16). Mark's misrepresentation of the scribes' understanding subverts their authority in Mark's day.

Jesus responds to the scribes in typical rabbinic fashion by asking them a question that pushes them toward a conclusion: Which is easier—to announce that God forgives sin, or to heal (2:8–9)?

By healing the paralytic, Jesus provides visible demonstration that sin is forgiven in the realm of God as interpreted by Jesus (v. 10). Mark signals the connection with the divine realm by speaking of Jesus as "Son of Man." This expression, from Dan. 7:13–14, refers to a figure whom God will send from heaven as cosmic judge and redeemer, and whose ministry finally establishes the realm of God. The Son of Man does not forgive sin; only God does that. But God has given the Son of Man authority to effect the divine realm, which includes forgiveness of sin.

The story ends ironically. The paralytic joins the crowd glorifying God; the scribes are paralyzed by their inability to recognize the presence of God's realm.

A contemporary minister can help the congregation recognize that the narrative confirmed to the Markan community that God forgives the sin of persons who were in that community (especially Gentiles). However, the text makes its point by falsifying the theological perspective and authority of the scribes. The preacher can help Christians realize that God releases people from the paralyzing power of sin through Judaism as well as through Christianity. God can even forgive the church of the sin of anti-Judaism.

Eighth Sunday after the Epiphany/Year B

Mark 2:13–22

In Mark 2:13–14, Jesus calls Levi to leave a tax booth along the road where he collected usage taxes (tolls, customs) for Rome. Tax collectors often gouged their fellow Jews for the taxes plus even more money, and the people often regarded tax collectors as quislings. Jesus calls Levi to follow, that is, to become a disciple. Presumably Levi repents (1:15) and abandons his old age entanglements (as in 1:16–20). If so, this means he stops supporting Rome and fleecing people. If Levi repents and follows Jewish restitution practices, he would repay the gouged people fourfold (Exod. 22:1; Lev. 6:5; Num. 6:5–7) or twofold (*m. Ketubbot* 3:9; *m. Bava Qamma* 7:1–5). If he does not repent and make restitution, his is the epitome of cheap grace.

In Mark 2:15, Jesus reclines with tax collectors and sinners, persons who flagrantly disobeyed Torah. Jews reclined at formal dinners for conversation about important issues, and Mark implies that Jesus is conversing with tax collectors and sinners about repentance and joining the movement toward the realm of God. Some scholars think that Jesus' meals with such folk prefigure the eschatological banquet.

In v. 16, Mark pictures Pharisees questioning Jesus. Jesus' reply (v. 17) circulated independently in the tradition before Mark (see *2 Clement* 2:4; *Barnabas* 5:9; Justin Martyr, *Apology* 1.15.8) and likely meant, "Those who are well (such as Pharisees and other Jews who will be a part of the realm of God) have no need of a physician (being invited into the divine realm by Jesus), but those who are sick (the unfaithful, such as tax collectors and sinners)." In one sense, Mark uses this saying to justify the mission of Jesus and the church. In another, the statement is ironic: Mark wants us to think that by questioning Jesus, the Pharisees are theologically sick.

Although fasting had multiple meanings in Judaism, many people in Mark's time, including John the Baptist and some Pharisees, fasted in preparation for the apocalypse (Matt. 11:19; Luke 7:34; *b. Sanhedrin* 97b–98a). This passage explains that the church resumed fasting after the ascension, even though Jesus and the earliest disciples did not fast. (On early Christian fasting, see *Didache* 8:1.)

In that time, cloth shrank when it was washed. Putting an unshrunk patch on a shrunk garment would only cause the patch to tear away. New wine was placed in a new wineskin so that as the wine fermented, the skin would expand (vv. 21–22). An old wineskin was stretched; filling it with new wine would cause it to explode. Mark presents the scribes and Pharisees as old wineskins who cannot expand to receive the new wine of the realm of God. The new wine needs a new community to contain its effervescence.

Preachers can urge their congregations today to seek and welcome contemporary analogues of tax collectors, sinners, and others who have need of a physician, figuratively speaking. Pastors can challenge tax collectors and sinners to repent of their socially destructive ways and make restitution. Recovering the spiritual discipline of fasting would deepen many congregations. However, Mark's attitude toward Jewish leaders is itself spoiled wine that should be put out of the church lest it continue to sour and sicken Christian attitudes and behavior toward Judaism. The time is ripe for the church to pour the new wine of a refreshed view of Judaism into the new wineskin of revitalized relationships with the synagogue based on the recognition of God's love for all and God's will for justice for all.

Ninth Sunday after the Epiphany/Year B

Mark 2:23–3:6

Both passages in today's reading are conflict stories in three parts: (1) Jesus, and sometimes the disciples, say or do something; (2) Jewish leaders object that Jesus violates an aspect of Judaism; (3) Jesus replies with an authoritative saying that puts down the opponents and that justifies Jesus' actions and the disciples' and the church's departures from Judaism. As part of Mark's justification of the widening gulf between Mark's community and the traditional synagogue, Mark further uses the conflict stories to caricature Pharisees and other Jewish leaders as incompetent and unfaithful. Mark climaxes 1:21–3:6 by indicting the Jewish leaders for Jesus' death (3:6).

Driven by the imminent apocalypse to proclaim the reign of God (1:38), Jesus and the disciples were traveling a road that passed through grainfields (2:23). Hungry, they plucked grain, prompting Pharisees to declare the behavior unlawful because they worked on the Sabbath (2:24; cf. Exod. 20:8–11; 34:21).

Mark draws an analogy between this event and 1 Sam. 21:1–6. When Saul plotted to kill David to eliminate David's threat to the throne, David fled (1 Sam. 20:30–34). While fleeing, David requested bread from the chief priest at Nob. The only bread available was the bread of the Presence—bread set on the altar, especially on the Sabbath, to demonstrate God's presence and to be eaten by the priests (Exod. 25:30; Lev. 24:7; 1 Chr. 9:32). Because of the urgent situation, the priest gave the bread to David.

As David's situation prompted the priest to abrogate the usual custom, so the nearness of the apocalypse fuels Mark's urgency to set aside Sabbath practice in order to announce the coming of the realm of God. Some in the Pharisaic movement voiced sentiments similar to those of Jesus in v. 27 (*2 Baruch* 14:18, *Mekilta Exodus* 31:13–14; cf. *b. Yoma* 85b; *b. Eruvin* 43a). However, apocalyptic and polemical exigency drive vv. 27–28, and Jesus can adjust Sabbath practice for the greatest benefit. While the Sabbath was a gift for the old age, a greater benefit than weekly rest impends: the final manifestation of the divine realm. These motifs invoke the apocalyptic notion of the divine realm as an eschatological Sabbath (Gen. 2:1–4). Mark vilifies the Pharisees to rationalize the church revising and even abandoning Jewish Sabbath customs.

A similar perspective operates in Mark 3:1–6. The healing of the man with the withered hand demonstrates how the Sabbath can benefit humankind under the aegis of Jesus' demonstration of the realm of God (cf. 1:21–28). Unfortunately, both this text and the previous one overlook similar urges already in Jewish literature that legitimized, on the Sabbath, both the effort to heal and to save life (e.g., *m. Yoma* 8:6; *m. Betzah* 5:2, 31:3; *b. Shabbat* 117b, 128b), and resistance to tyrants (1 Macc. 2:41). Even more unfortunately, Mark adds a devastating irony to the conflict story. When Jesus asks the Jewish leaders whether the Sabbath is a day to do good or to do harm, they make it a day of plotting the ultimate harm: the death of Jesus (3:6).

The end of the age has not come and does not appear imminent. The driving force in Mark's rationale for abandoning Sabbath observance has thus disappeared. Recognizing the wisdom in Jewish practice, Christians have sometimes observed a form of Sabbath rest on Sunday. However, Christians in North America have given up Sabbath practice at a very time when the frenetic world desperately needs God's gift of rest. The great benefit and witness for today would be for the church to *join* the synagogue in recovering Sabbath practice as a sign of the great renewal God seeks for all.

Last Sunday after the Epiphany/Year B

Transfiguration of the Lord

Mark 9:2–9

The Markan context is key to interpreting today's reading. In 1:14–15, Jesus announced that the definitive realization of the realm of God was at

hand. From 1:16 to 8:26, Mark demonstrated the prolepsis of that dominion through Jesus. In 8:27–31, Mark reveals that Jesus will be crucified by
powers in the world that resist the coming of the divine rule. Likewise, in
8:34–38, Mark prepares the disciples to suffer when people colluding with
evil attempt to stamp out their witness to the coming of God's realm. In
9:1, however, Mark ventures that the community can endure such suffering because it will be short term: The divine realm will come in the generation of Mark's listeners.

Mark says that the transfiguration took place "six days" after the events
described in 8:27–9:1, recalling Exodus 24:16 when God spoke to Moses
out of a cloud. The sixth day is not the seventh. In Judaism, the number
seven was sometimes associated with the eschatological world. The revelation on this mountain is for folk who still live in the old world. The
mountain is a traditional Jewish symbol of a place of contact with the heavenly world.

The English "transfigured" renders the Greek *metamorphoō*, from
which we get "metamorphosis." Jesus' body changes from material of the
old age that decays and dies to the body of the realm of God that neither
decays nor dies but lives forever. The clothing of the transfigured Jesus (v.
3) is the garb of angels and other heavenly figures (Mark 16:5; Dan. 7:9;
1 Enoch 104:2; Rev. 3:5; 4:4; 7:9). On the resurrection body, see 1 Cor.
15:35–49; Dan. 12:3; 2 Esd. 7:97; *2 Baruch* 51:3–12; *1 Enoch* 38:4; 104:2).
Readers behold Jesus in the present as he will be after the apocalypse in
the complete manifestation of the realm of God.

Christian commentators sometimes think that Mark presents Jesus as
superseding Moses and Elijah, as well as Judaism itself. Despite Mark's
persistent criticism of Jewish leaders, nothing in the text supports this
idea. Moses and Elijah suggest that Mark wants us to understand Jesus as
an heir of Judaism. Elijah did not die but was translated to heaven (2 Kgs.
2:9–12) and was expected to return with the divine realm (Mal. 4:4–5;
2 Esd. 6:26; cf. Mark 9:9–13); some Jews expected Moses similarly
(*Deuteronomy Rabbah* 3.17 on 10:1). Moses and Elijah were often joined
not only as archetypal representatives of Judaism but of the world to come
(*Pesiqta Rabbati* 4.2).

The "dwellings" of vv. 5–6 are booths (*skēnē*) and recollect the Feast of
Booths, which commemorates God dwelling, or "tenting," with the
Israelites during the wilderness wandering (Lev. 23:39–43). This feast also
became a prototype for the eschatological world (Zech. 14:16–19; Neh.
8:14–17; cf. *Testament of Abraham* 20). Nothing comes of Peter's sugges-

tion to "make three dwellings," indicating that while the transfiguration is a prolepsis of the divine realm, that realm is not fully present.

The cloud is a traditional and dramatic Jewish symbol of the divine presence (see, e.g., Exod. 16:10; 19:9; 24:16; Num. 14:10; Ezek. 1:4) and is associated with the coming world (Dan. 7:13; 2 Esd. 13:3; 2 Macc. 2:8). The redeemer will come on a cloud, a conveyance under divine direction (Mark 13:26; 14:62).

The divine voice from the cloud initially repeats the message at the baptism (Mark 1:9–10; cf. Deut. 18:15). The heavenly voice adds "Listen to him," impressing the reader with the fact that *God* authorized the teaching of Mark 8:27–9:1 that Jesus and the disciples will suffer. This addition is Mark's pastoral attempt to prepare the community for its own suffering (Mark 13:9–13).

Ash Wednesday/Year B

Matthew 6:1–6, 16–21

In this Ash Wednesday lection, Jesus instructs his disciples on a variety of topics all under one theme: "Beware of practicing your piety before others in order to be seen by them; for then you have no reward from your Father in heaven" (v. 1). The behavior that Jesus recommends is contrasted three times with that of "the hypocrites" (vv. 2, 5, 16) and once with that of "the Gentiles" (v. 7). "The hypocrites" here are stand-ins for the Pharisees, Matthew's target of invective throughout his Gospel. It was standard practice in the ancient world to engage in name-calling when referring to one's opponents. The *Didache*, a later Christian document, calls heretics hypocrites (8.1), and Jews would sometimes call Christians hypocrites.

With regard to giving alms (vv. 2–4), Jesus instructs his disciples not to "sound a trumpet before you, as the hypocrites do in the synagogues and in the streets," but to do their alms-giving "in secret." There is no mention in rabbinic literature of blowing a trumpet when giving alms (*zedaqah*), but there are numerous statements that the poor should be helped secretly: "He who gives *zedaqah* in secret is greater than Moses" (*b. Bava Batra* 9b). "Rabbi Yannai once saw a man give money to a poor man publicly. He said: 'It had been better that you gave him nothing than that you should have given to him and put him to shame'" (*Hagigah* 5a). "There were two vestries in the Temple, one called the Vestry of the Secret Ones. . . . In [it] . . . the sin-fearing men used to put their gifts secretly, and the poor of gentle birth were supported from them secretly" (*m. Sheqalim* 5:6).

On prayer, Matthew contrasts Jesus' instructions with what "the hypocrites" in the synagogues do: "They love to stand and pray . . . so that they may be seen by others." Instead, pray "in secret; and your Father who sees in secret will reward you" (v. 6), and, while praying, "do not heap up empty phrases" (v. 7). Jews and many others stand to pray (in some Christian traditions, persons either stand or kneel while praying). While the synagogue was and is the place for communal prayer, rabbis urged Jews to pray anywhere when the time for prayer arrived. There is nothing essentially hypocritical about this.

Matthew's criticism here is aimed at motive: praying so as to be seen by others, parading one's piety. Doing things from the right motive (*kawwanah*) and out of love of God (*lishmah*) are constant themes of Jewish teaching. The Babylonian Talmud says, "It matters not whether you do much or little, so long as your heart is directed to heaven" (*b. Berakhot* 17a). "He who prays must direct his heart" (*t. Berakhot* 3:6). For this reason, one does not heap up empty phrases in prayer. "Do not babble in the assembly of elders, and do not repeat yourself when you pray" (Sir. 7:14).

When you fast, "do not look dismal, like the hypocrites. . . . But when you fast, put oil on your head and wash your face, so that your fasting may be seen not by others but by your Father" (vv. 16–18). We have no knowledge that the disciples and Jesus fasted, which makes the point here puzzling. Like the other teachings in today's reading, it is not found in the other Gospels. Moreover, in Mark 2:18 (as well as Matt. 9:14 and Luke 5:33) Jesus is asked, "Why do John's disciples and the disciples of the Pharisees fast, but your disciples do not fast?" However, Matthew's church may have fasted.

First Sunday in Lent/Year B

Mark 1:9–15

The Spirit (not Satan) initiated the encounter between Jesus and Satan in the wilderness (Mark 1:12a). This detail reminds the Markan community that not only did God initiate Jesus' confrontations with Satan but that the Spirit leads the church to confront Satan as a part of its testimony to the divine realm.

The term "drove" (*ekballō*) is forceful and implies muscular confrontation with Satan; elsewhere in Mark, it often refers to Jesus casting out demons (e.g., 1:34, 39, 43; 3:15). The term "immediately" occurs more than forty times in Mark and gives the narrative apocalyptic urgency. People must act quickly, for the end is near.

On the one hand, the wilderness (*erēmos*) is a place of threat. Bereft of easy sources of food and water, people perish there. The Israelites wandered in it. Demons and other evil powers lived in the wilderness (see, e.g., Tob. 8:3; 4 Macc. 18:8). On the other hand, God preserved Israel and its leaders (e.g., Moses, Elijah) in the wilderness. Some writers believed God would begin to manifest the divine realm there, perhaps to prove divine power in the teeth of evil (e.g., Isa. 35:9; 40:3; *1 Enoch* 10:4–5; 1QS 28:1).

The "forty days" bring to consciousness other periods associated with "forty" in which God maintained Jews in periods of difficulty or revelation (e.g., the flood, Gen. 7:4; Israel wandering in the wilderness, Exod. 16:35; Moses on Sinai, 34:28; Elijah in the wilderness, 1 Kgs. 19:8).

Satan appears in the Hebrew Bible as an agent who serves God (Job 1:6; Ps. 109:6; Zech. 3:1–12). However, as we develop further on the Fourth Sunday after the Epiphany, in the Hellenistic age, some Jewish writers personified Satan and the demons as a way of explaining evil in the world. Satan, who has extensive powers, tries to wrest the world away from God and to claim the honor that belongs only to God.

In apocalyptic Judaism, "temptation" or "testing" (*peirazō*) refers to the temptation to turn away from God prior to the apocalypse and to ally oneself with Satan or other rulers of the present, as in Mark 8:11; 10:2; 12:15. Those who resist temptation are strengthened for the new world (see, e.g., Dan. 12:10; *1 Enoch* 94:5; 96:2–2). Temptation is strongest during the tribulation, the time of increased suffering as the apocalypse nears (see commentary for First Sunday of Advent/Year B).

The beasts are with Jesus as with Adam and Eve in Eden (Gen. 2:18–20). After the fall, angels kept the first pair out of the garden (Gen. 3:24). Mark's combination of communion with the beasts and the angels' ministrations signals that the realm of God is at hand, for the end of that realm is like the beginning in the garden.

While many Christians no longer accept Satan as a personal being, the figures of Satan and the demons represent forces in the world—racism, sexism, ethnocentrism, addictions—that resist God's aim for all to experience love and justice. On the one hand, this narrative assures the reader that, just as God sustained Jesus, so God continues to sustain the community when its witness brings it eyeball to eyeball with evil. On the other hand, Mark elsewhere uses the vocabulary of temptation found here to suggest that Pharisees and other Jewish leaders are in league with

Satan (Mark 8:11; 10:2; 12:15). The latter claim is an example of how an ideology can function similarly to the way Satan functions in Mark: to pervert life. When the church is tempted to continue distortions of Judaism such as the one perpetrated by Mark, the text reminds us that the Spirit strengthens the church to resist that temptation.

Second Sunday in Lent/Year B

Mark 8:31–38

According to Mark 1:1–8:30, the final manifestation of the realm of God is underway through the ministry of Jesus. Mark pictures Jewish leaders resisting that message, and in 3:6, some Jewish officials plan to kill Jesus. Meanwhile, the disciples fail to grasp Jesus' ministry and their own mission. In 8:27–30, Mark confirms that Jesus is the Messiah. (We discuss Mark 8:27–38 further on Proper 19/Year B).

In 8:31, Jesus refers to himself as the Son of Man, an apocalyptic character mentioned in Daniel whom God would send from heaven to establish God's realm and to judge all peoples (Dan. 7:13–14). The phrase "must undergo great suffering" employs a form of speech (*dei* = "it is necessary") that indicates God directs circumstances that lead to the suffering of the Son of Man. In Mark, the suffering of Jesus does not have salvific power in its own right. The idea that Jesus must suffer is part of the apocalyptic worldview that held that God had determined certain events on the path to the apocalypse. Mark does not present Jesus' death as an act of atonement or vicarious sacrifice. (On the motif of ransom in Mark 10:45, see Proper 24/Year B).

Mark's references to suffering are not to general pain (e.g., illness) but to suffering resulting from resistance to the divine realm. Jesus suffers because the Jewish leaders reject his testimony to God's realm and lead Romans to crucify him.

Some Christians believe that the Jewish people expected a glorious military messiah, and that the connection between suffering and the realm of God was a new idea. However, Jewish tradition more often thinks of Judaism as an unlikely vessel through whom the ruler of the universe seeks to bless all. Abraham and Sarah, for instance, were unlikely channels for the universal sovereign. Even at the height of power, the Jewish nation was a small player. This tradition knows that faithful witness sometimes begets suffering (see, e.g., Isa. 52:13–53:12; 4 Macc. 4:15–18:5), but testifies that God is faithful to those who endure resistance (see Palm Sunday or Passion Sunday/Year C).

According to Mark 8:34–38, Jesus' messiahship shapes discipleship. Just as Jesus suffered because of testimony to the divine reign, so the disciples and, by implication, the Markan church, will suffer (take up their crosses and follow) as a result of resistance to their words and actions. An irony is at work. Those who try to save their lives (v. 35: those who avoid suffering by not witnessing faithfully) will lose their lives (v. 38: the Son of Man/cosmic judge will be ashamed of them and condemn them at the apocalypse). Those who lose their lives (who suffer for the sake of the gospel) will save them (be received into the final form of the divine reign after the apocalypse). This perspective is indebted to the Jewish point of view on suffering summarized above.

The preacher can commend enduring perspectives in this text: Witness to the divine realm can cause suffering, but God's presence with the community helps us not only endure but find meaning in suffering by recognizing it as an occasion for witness. (A pastor needs to avoid reinforcing neurotic attitudes toward suffering present in some congregations.) The preacher must challenge other aspects of the text. To think that God wills such suffering denies God's unconditional love and intent for justice for all. Since the first century, Jewish leaders have not caused Christians to suffer. Instead, Christians have caused Jews to suffer. The preacher, therefore, might help the congregation explore how Jewish faithfulness in the midst of suffering, especially suffering caused by Christians, is a vital testimony. Across the centuries Jewish communities have often lost almost everything. Yet they have gained an identity that sustains them in unbelievable agony.

Third Sunday in Lent/Year B

John 2:13–22

John places the story of the cleansing of the temple early in Jesus' ministry, whereas the other Gospels place it late. This is one of many differences between John's account and those of the Synoptics. They report that Jesus accused the money changers and sellers of making the temple into a "den of robbers" (Matt. 21:13; Mark 11:17; Luke 19:46), whereas John has Jesus say, "Stop making my Father's house a marketplace!" (2:16). In Mark and Luke, but not Matthew, "the chief priests and scribes" seek to "destroy" Jesus after the incident. John introduces his story by referring to "the Passover of the Jews" (2:13). In John, this story reinforces the theme of conflict with "the Jews."

Jerusalem at Passover was often in a fever pitch. Passover is the celebration of God's liberation of the people Israel from slavery in Egypt. But anyone walking to Jerusalem from Bethany or Bethphage, crossing the Mount of Olives and looking at the temple from across the Kidron valley, would have seen the Fortress Antonia, home to the Roman Tenth Legion, standing next to the temple and Roman soldiers posted on the parapets of the fort and on top of the wall surrounding the temple complex. Jews came to celebrate freedom from Egyptian bondage under the watchful eyes of the Roman legion. The people were in exile in the land of promise; Rome had replaced Egypt. Any demonstration at the temple would have been dealt with swiftly by the instruments of Roman rule, namely, Pilate and the army.

In the temple, Jesus "found people selling cattle, sheep, and doves, and the money changers seated at their tables" (v. 14). The latter changed Roman money bearing images of Caesar into Tyrian money that had on it no human likenesses. Jesus uses a whip to drive humans and animals out of the temple, dumps the coins on the ground, and upsets the tables of the money changers—the only time in the Gospels that Jesus resorts to violence (his usual teaching is against violence, including counterviolence).

Then he says, "Stop making my Father's house a marketplace!" (v. 16). Jews believed that God dwelt in the temple; Jesus shares that belief. The Synoptics have Jesus refer to the temple as "my house," but for John it is "my Father's house." His Christology is not Jesus-centric as is that of the Synoptics. The temple is no ordinary building, in which buying, selling, and changing money would have been permissible. Instead, the words of Zech. 14:21 pertain: "And there shall no longer be traders in the house of the Lord of hosts on that day." Jesus reclaims the temple as his Father's house. For John, this is not an attack on the temple but on turning it into a marketplace. The dilemma for us is that no organized religious activity can go on without the use of money; Sunday school materials, for example, have to be purchased.

"The Jews" ask Jesus what justifies his actions (v. 18). He responds, "Destroy this temple, and in three days I will raise it up" (v. 19). There is a shift in meaning, associated with the shift in the Greek terms for "temple." The temple should be a house of Jesus' Father (*oikon tou patros mou*), not an emporium (*oikos emporiou*). Now Jesus changes terms again: "Destroy this temple [*ton naon*], . . ." John explains that he was speaking "of the temple of his body" (v. 21), not a temple of stone, which "the Jews" supposed when they commented that it had taken forty-six years to build it (v. 20).

By the time John was written, of course, there no longer was a temple of stone. The disciples of Jesus had as their temple, instead, the presence of the living Christ. Rabbinic Jews found the presence of God in the study of Torah, in prayer in the synagogue, and in deeds of loving-kindness.

Fourth Sunday in Lent/Year B

John 3:14–21

The reading for the Fourth Sunday in Lent contains a most frequently quoted verse: "For God so loved the world that he gave his only Son, so that everyone who believes in him may not perish but may have eternal life" (v. 16). It also says that God sent his son into the world not "to condemn" it, but "that the world might be saved through him" (v. 17). Then it drops the other shoe: "Those who do not believe are condemned already, because they have not believed in the name of the only Son of God" (v. 18).

How are we to interpret this set of statements? Is everyone who does not believe in Jesus "condemned already"? What of the child of faithful Christian parents who was born severely retarded and who was never able to "believe"? Is that child condemned? Or is Jesus' love simply too weak to overcome difficulties, including those of people who died before Jesus or who were never reached with the gospel?

The Gospel of John represents the views of a community strongly inclined to sectarianism, aware of the opposition between "us" (the insiders) and "them" (the outsiders). The "enemies" of John's community include (1) "the Jews" from whose synagogues the community was expelled and toward whom hostility dominates chaps. 5–12; (2) "the world," the wider opposition of Gentiles that dominates chaps. 14–17; (3) followers of John the Baptist (1:9, 15, 30, 19–24, 35–37; 3:28–30; 10:41); (4) other Jesus followers (6:66; 8:31ff.; 14:9); (5) Jesus followers who stayed in the synagogue (12:42–43); and (6) Jesus followers in apostolic churches seen in the ongoing contrast between the "Beloved Disciple" and Peter.[23]

A community such as John's feels itself alone, alienated, and persecuted (which is not to deny that it was actually alone, alienated, and persecuted). What we find in John represents one side of a conflict with various outsiders and, possibly, some insiders who have deviated and defected from the community. Hence, we find statements to the effect that only those within this community, who understand Jesus as we do, are saved.

There is a tension and contradiction in today's reading between its grand opening statement of God's intent to save and its crushing follow-up that those who do not believe are condemned already. The Scriptures contain both exclusivist statements and utterly universal and inclusivist statements. Paul says of Jesus, for example, that "one man's act of righteousness leads to justification and life for all" (Rom. 5:18), with no hint at condemnation. When we deal with the exclusivist statements, we cannot forget the inclusivist ones where the sheer, unfathomable, and gracious love of God is proclaimed.

We propose that the exclusivist statements be taken as statements of reassurance to a beleaguered community: God loves only you; you, indeed, are the apple of God's eye. These are "priestly" statements, mediating the love of God to a particular community (or sometimes person). However, there are also prophetic statements that stress that other people are God's: "I have other sheep that do not belong to this fold" (John 10:16).

God does, indeed, love all those who believe in Jesus. That is because God is the God who loves all. And we who are loved by the one who loves all should, in turn, love all in loving the one who loves all. Saying "yes" to God's love is important; it is not, however, a condition that must be met if God is to love us.

Fifth Sunday in Lent/Year B

John 12:20–33

In John 10:16, Jesus said to his followers, "I have other sheep that do not belong to this fold. I must bring them also, and they will listen to my voice. So there will be one flock, one shepherd." In today's passage, some of these "other sheep" show up—"some Greeks" (*Hellēnes*; v. 20). These Greeks may have been Gentiles. As Gentiles in Matthew visited the newborn Jesus in Bethlehem (the "wise men" from the East), in John also they seek Jesus. They could be either Gentile "God-fearers" who had associated with the synagogue, or Greek (Hellenistic) Jews coming to Jerusalem for Passover, for 12:1 indicates that Passover is the setting for this scene.

John 12:19 has "the Pharisees" say, "You see, you can do nothing. Look, the world has gone after him!" That "some Greeks" appear asking for Jesus lets the reader know that these Pharisees were correct. The Greeks approach Philip, a disciple with a Greek name who comes from Bethsaida, which was close to the Decapolis, the Gentile "ten cities," and say to him, "Sir, we wish to see Jesus" (v. 21). He then goes to Andrew, who also has a Greek name and is from the Decapolis.

They express a desire to "see" (*idein*) Jesus. John sometimes uses this verb to denote ordinary seeing, but he also uses it to indicate accepting, affirming, and understanding Jesus as the incarnate Logos (see, e.g., 1:18; 4:45; 5:37; 6:2).

The rest of the passage is devoted to Jesus' explaining the phrase "the hour of the Son of Man." He immediately says to the Greeks, "The hour has come for the Son of Man to be glorified" (v. 23). Jesus then unpacks this by talking of his suffering and resurrection yet to come: This grain of wheat will fall into the earth and die, yet bear great fruit. So Jesus will suffer and die and be "lifted up from the earth" and "will draw all people" to himself (v. 32).

What Jesus says of himself is also true of his disciples. They must identify with him by not so clinging to their lives that they lose them but by giving up in their lives those false securities and certainties to which they cling with clenched fists: "Those who hate their life in this world will keep it for eternal life" (v. 25). With Jesus, self-giving of oneself in love is what is ultimate. Only by lovingly "letting go" of the values of "this world" can the disciples "bear fruit" and be honored by God: "Whoever serves me, the Father will honor" (v. 26).

The Jewish tradition emphasized the "sanctification of the divine name" (*Kiddush ha-Shem*). The rabbinic midrash (interpretation) on Ps. 68 says about Israel: "Why are the children of Israel called dove-like? To tell you that as a dove does not struggle when it is killed, so the children of Israel do not struggle when they are killed for the hallowing of the Name"[24] (*Midrash Psalms* 68.8). Jesus, out of his agony—"Now my soul is troubled" (v. 27)—and who is to be slaughtered by the hand of the Roman Empire, prays, "Father, glorify your name." The response comes in a voice from heaven (*bat qol*): "I have glorified it, and I will glorify it again." Jesus' death and resurrection are his glorification, but God has glorified God's name before and will now do so "again."

The tragedy is that Jesus was not the last Jew to die "to the sanctification of the divine name." One clear message of the crucifixion story should certainly be that no one would ever have to climb up on a cross again.

Palm Sunday or Passion Sunday/Year B

Mark 11:1–11; 15:1–39

In Mark 11:1–6, Jesus' foreknowledge regarding the colt indicates that he can be trusted when speaking of future events—his death and resurrection, the tribulation, and the apocalypse. Mark's colt recalls Zech. 9:9–10,

in which God's representative enters Jerusalem to end violence and establish the divine reign even among Gentiles.

Mark pictures the crowd as misunderstanding Jesus. They spread their
coats and leafy branches to greet Jesus as a conqueror (11:8; cf. 2 Kgs.
9:13), whereas Jesus is the suffering messiah (Mark 8:30–31); the leafy
branches symbolized political independence (1 Macc. 13:51; 2 Macc.
10:7). In 11:9–10, the crowd adapts Ps. 118:26 (a temple liturgy) to celebrate Jesus reestablishing the dominion of David—a golden age of self-
determination—yet by Mark's day, the temple had been destroyed. Mark
did not envision a Davidic political state but the cosmic divine realm. Jesus
supersedes David (12:35–37).

While Mark earlier had portrayed the crowds reacting positively to
Jesus, the Gospel now sets the stage for the crowd to turn against Jesus.
The preacher, while needing to criticize Mark's caricature of the crowd,
might also explore how today's listeners misappropriate the realm of God
for partisan purposes.

Mark was aware that the Romans had the power to put people to death,
but he edits the story of the crucifixion to lay major responsibility on Jewish leaders. He interprets Jewish officials as under the influence of Satan
(8:11; 10:2; 12:15). In 3:23–26, Mark claims that a house divided against
itself cannot stand, especially Satan's house.

In 14:43, Jewish leaders manipulate the crowds, as they do throughout
the trial. In 14:53–65, Mark depicts the Jewish council (who functioned
as a kind of grand jury to ascertain whether to bring cases to the Romans)
as unfaithful by violating its own procedures: holding the trial at night,
questioning witnesses privately rather than publicly, ignoring the rule that
at least two witnesses must agree, accepting false witness. For Mark, the
testimony at the trial is "a house divided."

The Gospels themselves are divided on the story of the trial of Jesus
before the council. Luke's description of it in 22:54–71 deletes many of
the features of Mark's story that are in violation of Jewish law concerning
capital trials. John's Gospel has no trial of Jesus before the council. Some
scholars find John historically more likely.[25]

In 15:8–15, Mark pictures Jewish leaders pressing the crowd to call for
Pilate to release Barabbas, a companion of murderers, and to crucify Jesus.
Mark is bitterly ironic: The priests, who are supposed to mediate life,
become advocates of death. Instead of showing compassion for the dying
Jesus, chief priests and scribes mock him (15:32).

Jesus speaks in 15:34 from Ps. 22:1. In antiquity, citing a portion of a
text recollected the whole. Psalm 22 moves from anguish to trust that God

will redeem. Jesus accepts the cross in the confidence that it is part of the coming of the divine realm.

When Jesus dies, the curtain of the temple rips apart, making the temple dysfunctional (15:38).

The preacher must help the community recognize that Mark polemically magnifies the Jewish role in Jesus' death, even creating the theme of collusion with Satan as the ultimate reason Mark disavows connection with traditional Judaism. Ironically, Christian false testimony about Judaism has been more pernicious than the falsehoods attributed to the witnesses at Jesus' trial. Preaching from a text focusing on death, a pastor can help the congregation put to death Christian false witness concerning Judaism. Otherwise, we will find that the credibility of our witness is destroyed as if it were a curtain ripped from top to bottom.

Easter Day/Year B

Mark 16:1–8

One of the purposes of the extensive description of the burial of Jesus in Mark 15:42–57 is to establish that Jesus did not just appear to die, but truly expired.

On the Third Sunday after the Epiphany/Year B, we noted that Mark portrays the disciples as slow to understand both Jesus' mission and their own. While Jesus predicted the crucifixion and resurrection (8:30; 9:31; 10:34; 14:26–28), the disciples were not prepared and fled. Peter denied Jesus. Only the women stayed with Jesus to the end (15:40–41). None of Jesus' followers, even the women, expected the resurrection, as is seen in 16:1 when women take spices to lay the body to rest in the Jewish way.

The women discovered the empty tomb on Sunday, thus authenticating Jesus' remark that the resurrection would take place after three days. The pattern of prediction-fulfillment within the narrative of Mark reinforces the reader's confidence in things that Jesus predicts but that do not fully take place in the book of Mark itself (especially the tribulation of 13:4–27 and Jesus' apocalyptic return forecast in 14:28).

Even the stone rolled back from the entrance to the tomb does not alert the women to the resurrection. When they look inside and see the youthful figure dressed in white, they are not joyful but alarmed (16:4–5). The reader, however, recognizes that this young person is a heavenly figure, for the robe is described as "white" in the same way as Jesus' transfigured clothing in 9:3 (cf. Rev. 7:9, 13).

While the risen Jesus does not appear directly in Mark (16:1–8 is an empty tomb story), the heavenly messenger leaves no doubt that God raised Jesus (v. 6), that is, Jesus now has the resurrection body of the realm of God (see Last Sunday after the Epiphany/Year B).

The young man tells the women that the risen Jesus is going ahead of them to Galilee—a place where the divine realm is revealed amidst Jewish and Gentile worlds (v. 7; cf. First Sunday after the Epiphany/Year B). Scholars debate whether the encounter with Jesus in Galilee was to be a resurrection appearance or the second coming. In any event, for Mark the resurrection of Jesus is not the climax of the story. The climax is beyond the narrative of the Gospel of Mark: the apocalyptic return of Jesus to bring about the final manifestation of the realm of God. The resurrection gives the community the certainty that the divine realm is coming so that they can endure turmoil and tribulation.

The youth instructs the women to tell the disciples and Peter to join Jesus in Galilee. While the disciples have been unfaithful to Jesus, Jesus is faithful to them.

At this crucial juncture, however, the women fail. They flee the tomb and keep silent. However, Mark's emphasis in v. 8 is on not the women (e.g., Why did *they* not do what the angel told them?) but on the reader. The women's reaction pushes the reader to ask, "What will *I* do with the message of the coming of the realm of God at the heart of Mark's Gospel? Will I be silent? Or will I take confidence in Jesus going before me (as to Galilee) and witness even among Gentiles (13:10)?"

The contemporary preacher can ask the church the same question that Mark asked the ancient community: Will the congregation keep silent regarding the divine realm, or witness to it? Mark's question has particular (if unintended) power. Will the preacher keep silent with respect to Christian misinterpretation and prejudice against Judaism? Or will the preacher urge the congregation to seek reconciliation and common mission with the Jewish community as a part of the great reunion of the human family in the realm of God?

Second Sunday of Easter/Year B

John 20:19–31

Please see the Second Sunday of Easter/Years A, B, and C for the commentary on this reading.

Third Sunday of Easter/Year B

Luke 24:36b–48

The resurrection of Jesus is not the resuscitation of a corpse but the first resurrection in the realm of God. Apocalyptists anticipated that each person would have a renewed body no longer subject to decay or death in the realm of God (1 Cor. 15:35–49). The resurrection of Jesus is the definitive revelation that God is effecting the change from the old world to the divine realm.

Each scene in Luke 24 widens the circle of witnesses to the resurrection and increases our clarity about the significance of Jesus' rising from the dead. In 24:1–12, the angel tells the women that God has raised Jesus. On the road to Emmaus, Jesus becomes known to the two travelers in the breaking of bread (24:13–35), revealing one way the risen Jesus will be present in the community. Here the resurrected Jesus appears to a larger body of disciples and commissions them for ministry after the ascension.

In Luke 24:36, Jesus stands among them. His words, "Peace be with you," are a standard Jewish greeting that wish shalom on all who hear the words; shalom is a part of the ministry of Jesus (see, e.g., Luke 1:79; 2:14, 29; 7:50; 8:48; 10:38, 42; Acts 10:36). The disciples are terrified and misperceive Jesus as a ghost, literally, "a spirit" (*pneuma*; 24:37). Some Jews in antiquity believed that after death, "some sort of residue of what had been the life of the person" abided in a netherworld, but also could sometimes roam the earth and could even be called up by the living (*b. Berakhot* 18b; 2 Esd. 7:80; 1 Sam. 28:3–19; Isa. 8:19).[26]

Jesus speaks reassuringly to the community (Luke 24:38). The opening words recall how God speaks to Israel in fearful situations (e.g., Isa. 41:10; 44:8; Jer. 1:8; 10:5; Ezek. 2:6). Luke wants the reader to recognize that just as God was trustworthy in Israel's past by going with Israel through the circumstances that prompted their fear, so they can trust God to act faithfully through Jesus and the church.

In v. 39, Jesus invites the disciples to confirm that he is a resurrection body by touching his hands and feet. Whereas the Johannine Jesus calls attention to the nail prints in his hands to show continuity between the crucified and risen Jesus (John 20:20, 25, 27), the Lukan Jesus refers to hands and feet to show he is not merely the residue of a person but a resurrected self.

Jesus further confirms that he is present in resurrected form by eating a piece of fish (vv. 41b–43). In the realm of God, people continue to eat and drink; food is present in abundance. Indeed, soon after the apocalypse, the community of the saved will celebrate God's victory and the cosmic transformation with an eschatological banquet (which sometimes includes fish: *2 Baruch* 29:3–9; cf. Isa. 25:6–8; 2 Esd. 8:53–54; *1 Enoch* 62:14; 1QSa 2:11–22; 1QS 6:4–6).

We discuss Luke 24:44–48 in connection with the Ascension of the Lord/Years A, B, and C. The meaningful unit of interpretation should span vv. 36b through 53.

The disciples had lived with Jesus for some time and heard him interpret the divine realm (including foretelling the resurrection), but they do not understand this event even when the resurrected Jesus is physically with them (vv. 37–38, 41)! They need instruction. Small wonder that today's congregation—removed not only in time and space but worldview—should also puzzle over the meaning and need clarification.

Fourth Sunday of Easter/Year B

John 10:11–18

In this passage, John's Jesus describes himself as "the good shepherd" and sharply contrasts himself with "the hired hand" who "sees the wolf coming and leaves the sheep and runs away—and the wolf snatches them and scatters them" (vv. 11–12). This is part of a highly polemical passage in which Jesus has also contrasted himself as the "gate" (i.e., sheep gate, which one can still see in stone enclosures in Israel) with "all who came before me [who] are thieves and bandits" (v. 8).

The Scriptures are rich with prophetic criticisms of rulers of Israel who were "bad shepherds" or who failed to be faithful shepherds. The expression "like sheep without a shepherd" occurs frequently in the scriptures of Israel and in the Gospels (Num. 27:17; 2 Chr. 18:16; Ezek. 34:5, 8; Zech. 10:2; 11:15–17; Matt. 9:36; Mark 6:34). Hence, the comments here attributed to Jesus are in the tradition of prophetic criticism leveled at unfaithful shepherds of Israel.

Similarly the prophetic literature of Israel said of these false shepherds that in shirking their proper responsibilities toward the people Israel they had left the people vulnerable to "wolves" (Jer. 23:1–8; Ezek. 34; Zeph. 3:3, *1 Enoch* 89:12–27). Thus, Jesus' comments in John reflect Jewish prophetic self-criticism.

Nonetheless, John's version reaches beyond prophetic self-criticism and takes on a polemical edge that has about it more of the ring of rejection of the "other" than of prophetic self-criticism. In looking back over the history of Israel, we can come up with numerous examples of faithful shepherds of the people. Moses comes readily to mind as one who goes so far as to argue God into being a faithful shepherd (Exod. 32:7–14). Polemical overreach occurs when John's Jesus says, "All who came before me are thieves and bandits." Clearly, some were not.

Yet it would be blindly optimistic to deny that there are false shepherds. The church in its two millennia of history has known plenty. Jim Jones, who proved to be a wolf to his own flock in Jonestown, Guyana, comes to mind as a notorious recent example, as do numerous clerical child abusers and sexual harassers who regularly make the headlines.

The message of John 10:11–18 is that Jesus is a shepherd whom we can trust ultimately. Indeed, the message is more than that. Since everything we say about Jesus also says something about God (and about we who make these statements), the message is, more profoundly, that God is faithful; "the Father knows me and I know the Father" (v. 15). Jesus as the one who is "sent from God" discloses God as the God of a singular promise (the promise of God's *hesed*, "steadfast love") and so can be trusted ultimately as God can be trusted ultimately. And we are those who are hence called upon to understand ourselves in any ultimate sense as loved by God and by Jesus and thus commanded, in turn, to love God with all our selves and our neighbors as ourselves. This we can do on the condition that we trust in the unconditional love of God in Jesus.

We do not have to regard all leaders of Israel as thieves and bandits in order so to trust God. Indeed, that is incompatible with forgiving seventy times seven. God works through human sin and error and can, therefore, even make use of us.

Jesus has "other sheep that do not belong to this fold" (v. 16). This group is more extensive than we imagine. Jesus loves all his sheep so much that, on his own "authority" (*exousian*), he lays down his life and takes it up again.

Fifth Sunday of Easter/Year B

John 15:1–8

Today's passage is a statement from Jesus to his disciples about what it means to "abide" (*menein*) in Jesus, a verb that occurs eight times in these eight verses. The meaning of abiding in Jesus and the consequences of doing so or not are the topics.

The reading opens with a *mashal,* "parable," of the vine and the branches, with Jesus declaring, "I am the true vine, and my Father is the vinegrower." The statement in v. 5—"I am the vine, you [disciples] are the branches"—can also be taken as a metaphor for the church, each member of which is a branch of the vine. The passage as a whole is the interpretation and application, *nimshal,* of the parable.

The vine is a metaphor for the people Israel. "I planted you as a choice vine, from the purest stock. How then did you turn degenerate and become a wild vine?" (Jer. 2:21). In a passage directly related to Jesus' claim that he is the vine and his Father the vinegrower, Isaiah says,

> On that day:
> A pleasant vineyard, sing about it!
>   I, the LORD, am its keeper;
>   every moment I water it.
> I guard it night and day
>   so that no one can harm it;
>   I have no wrath.
> If it gives me thorns and briers,
>   I will march to battle against it.
>   I will burn it up.
> Or else let it cling to me for protection,
>   let it make peace with me,
>   let it make peace with me.
> In days to come Jacob shall take root,
>   Israel shall blossom and put forth shoots,
>   and fill the whole world with fruit.
>   (Isa. 27:2–6)

Jesus' Father is the "vinegrower" who makes it possible for the vine to prosper and bear fruit. John's Christology is not Jesus-centric; it is God without whom the vine would not live and without whom the branches would receive no care.

Genuine discipleship—loving the neighbor, engaging in deeds of loving-kindness—is possible for Jesus' disciples if they "abide" in him, for if they do, they will "bear fruit" (vv. 2, 4, 5). The disciples are already cleansed (v. 3) and pruned, by having heard and believed, taken to heart, the words of Jesus.

Verses 5b–7, however, indicate that we who are Jesus' followers may not now sit back and relax just because we abide in him and have already been cleansed and pruned by his teaching. As God "removes every branch in me that bears no fruit" (v. 2), so "whoever does not abide in me is thrown away like a branch and withers; such branches are gathered, thrown into the fire, and burned" (v. 6). We can read such language as the language of threat or of prophetic warning alerting us to the imperative of the gospel. That Jesus is the vine and we are the branches is the good news; it is grace, it is in the indicative. Now comes the imperative.

If the good news were only grace, it would be cheap grace. It is also the command to love one another and to deal justly with those whom we love. It is not enough for us simply to have heard Jesus, to have been with him. We must genuinely abide in him and, if we do, he will genuinely abide in us.

Both Jesus and our neighbors are different from us, in different ways. The theme of mutual abiding, of living in a relationship of mutuality with those who are different from us, is also a fundamental biblical theme (Adam and Eve in their mutuality with and difference from one another are made in God's image). Yet such mutuality also entails action, namely, loving the neighbor.

"My Father is glorified by this, that you bear much fruit and become my disciples" (v. 8). It is God who is glorified by our bearing fruit, not Jesus.

Sixth Sunday of Easter/Year B

John 15:9–17

The theme of mutual abiding in love continues in today's reading. For John, everything begins with God: "As the Father has loved me, so I have loved you" (v. 9). God is the alpha and omega of all that Jesus is and does: "It is God the only Son, who is close to the Father's heart" (1:18). God's primordial love for Jesus is the spring from which Jesus' love for them, his followers, wells up. God and Jesus exist in a relationship of love and mutuality, as Jesus exists in a relationship of love and mutuality with his disciples and as we are to exist with one another.

God's love makes Jesus who he is. Jesus makes this love known to those who believe in him: "The Father loves the Son and has placed all things in his hand" (3:35); "The Father loves the Son and shows him all that he himself is doing" (5:20). Jesus' very name—*Joshua* in Hebrew, *Yeshua* in Greek—means "God saves" or "God is salvation." The God whose radical love is embodied in Jesus is the God whom he called "Father" or "Abba," according to Mark 14:36 (see also Rom. 8:15 and Gal. 4:6). Jesus does not save us from God. Instead, God saves us through Jesus.

Today's reading carries this good news one step further, stressing now the commandment, imperative side of the gospel. We abide in the love of God and Jesus, but this abiding must mean something, must count for something, must result in a transformed way of life.

Jesus' followers are to reiterate in their relationships with Jesus, with one another, and with the other sheep that are not of this flock the mutual love that Jesus has had with God and that he has made known to them. They are to keep his commandments: "If you keep my commandments, you will abide in my love, just as I have kept my Father's commandments and abide in his love" (v. 10).

One commandment is "that you love one another as I have loved you" (v. 12). This is not a brand-new commandment. John has stated it before: "I give you a new commandment, that you love one another. Just as I have loved you, you also should love one another" (13:34). This is standard Israelite commandment, or *mitzvah* (Lev. 19:18, 34). Its more radical form—"you shall love the stranger as yourself"—appears in various forms thirty-six times in the scriptures of Israel. Often in Scripture the adjective "new" means "renewed," as it does here; each Hebrew month began with a *new* moon but not with a *brand-new* moon.

The stress on mutuality appears in Jesus' calling his followers "friends" (*philoi*), instead of "servants" (*douloi*; vv. 14–15). Those who exist in relationships of mutuality with each other are appropriately called "friends." We are friends of the one who is friend of each and all, and we are supposed, therefore, to be a friend to each and all of those who are created in the image of God. There are no limits to God's love; it transcends the boundaries of our community and includes those "not of this flock."

Jesus' love for his friends is gracious. One of them will betray him, another will deny him. But he loves them. So it is with us; he loves us because of who he is—one loved by God—not because of how meritorious we are.

Nonetheless, and here is the second commandment, we are to "bear fruit" (v. 16), as John returns to the metaphor of the vine. We are to spread in the world that love which Jesus shares with God and with us.

Ascension of the Lord/Year B

Luke 24:44–53

Please see Ascension of the Lord/Years A, B, and C for the commentary on this reading.

Seventh Sunday of Easter/Year B

John 17:6–19

Today's text, traditionally referred to as Jesus' "high priestly prayer," is actually an excerpt from Jesus' final prayer in John 17. In vv. 1–5, Jesus asks God to glorify him so that he may glorify God. His being "raised up" on the cross and from the grave will be the glorification of both God and Jesus; this is Jesus' loving gift of himself. The context is still that of 13:1–4, where Jesus and his disciples were "at supper" together. The practice of praying at the end of a meal was and is a traditional Jewish practice in which God is blessed, again, for being the ground and end of life and well-being. Verse 3 recaps Jesus' teaching: "This is eternal life, that they may know you, the only true God, and Jesus Christ whom you have sent." Eternal life, for John, is available now in knowing God and Jesus; there is no waiting for the eschaton.

The high priestly prayer is in four parts: Verses 6–8 summarize what Jesus has done; in vv. 9–11a, Jesus prays for the disciples "in the world"; in vv. 11b–16, Jesus petitions God to be "Father" to the disciples who are weak; and in vv. 17–19, he asks God to sanctify, or make holy, the disciples.

Verses 6–8 make it clear that the disciples are disciples because of what God has done—"They were yours and you gave them to me"—not because of their own strength or merit. God has given Jesus much more than these disciples; they are a fraction of "everything you have given me." Yet they "know in truth" and "have believed that you sent me." Hence, they have eternal life and Jesus has finished "the work that you gave me to do" (v. 4).

In vv. 9–11a, Jesus prays "on behalf" of the disciples whom God has given him. It is reassuring to all disciples of Jesus, then and now, to know that he prays to God on our behalf. Central to this part of the prayer is Jesus' awareness that his disciples will remain "in the world," beset by all its burdens, difficulties, and temptations. Jesus "is glorified in" his disciples if they keep his commandments. When the lives of his followers replicate the mutual abiding in love that has characterized Jesus' relation to the Father and to them, his disciples will glorify him (v. 10).

In vv. 11b–16, Jesus asks the "holy Father" to "protect" his faithful but imperfect disciples: "Protect them in your name that you have given me, so that they may be one, as we are one" (v. 11b). This verse is often taken as clear evidence that the early church was one. The request "that they *may* be one," however, indicates that the opposite was the case. Here John breaks free of his sometimes sectarian limitations and prays for the unity of different groups of Jesus' disciples. We need to pray and work for it still. Jesus' disciples are weak, vulnerable to rejection from "the world," so he prays that God will "protect them from the evil one" (v. 15). The "evil one" (*tou ponērou*) refers to Satan, not Judas (Jesus washed Judas's feet and ate with him, knowing of his betrayal), and is so used the only other time it appears in the New Testament (2 Thess. 2:3, 8–9).

The prayer concludes (vv. 17–19) with the request that the Father sanctify Jesus' followers in the truth, the word. They are sent into the world, as Jesus was, to live lives of mutual love and thereby to make known the transforming grace of God. They are the "sent ones of the Sent One," and their mission, for its success, requires that they live lives of integrity and love, disclosing to others what has been graciously disclosed to them.

Day of Pentecost/Year B

Acts 2:1–21

Pentecost was a Jewish holy day observed fifty days after Passover (*pentēkonta* = fifty in Greek; Lev. 23:15–21; Deut. 16:9–12). Pentecost originated as a harvest festival, but by the first century C.E. had also come in some Jewish circles to celebrate the giving of the law on Sinai. Luke uses this passage to remind the reader that the earliest community of Jesus' followers, empowered by the Spirit, was thoroughly Jewish. Indeed, this first Pentecost takes place only among Jewish people. A second experience of the outpouring of the Spirit among Gentiles in Acts 10:34–44 shows that the mission of the church is to gather Gentiles into the final eschatological harvest (Luke 10:2). When Gentiles come into the church, God welcomes them alongside Jews into the eschatological covenant just as God welcomed Israel into covenant with God at Sinai.

The experience of the Spirit is not private and isolated, but takes place in and forms community. The wind is reminiscent of the one that hovered over creation (Gen. 1:1–2); this wind is a part of God's re-creation of the world. Fire in Jewish literature often represents the divine presence and judgment. Further, the tongues of fire recollect Sinai and the making of the covenant (Exod. 19:16–19). Fire also signals prophetic inspiration. To receive the Spirit is to be filled with this multivalent fire.

Acts 2:5–12 makes it clear that the "other languages" prompted by the Spirit are not glossalalia, or "unknown tongues" (speaking in ecstatic sounds that are not combined to make a conventional language), but actual languages. In the background, of course, is the separation of the human family into separate language groups as God's curse at Babel (Gen. 11:1–9). The disciples speak languages that they otherwise have not been taught such that Parthians, Medes, Elamites, and others understand the disciples' testimony to the word of God. The miracle of Pentecost is mutual understanding and community.

In Acts 2:5–12, this miracle takes place only among "devout Jews from every nation under heaven," but Luke regards it as the model for mutual understanding among Jewish and Gentile peoples after the conversion of Cornelius and the start of the Gentile mission. Many Jewish writers anticipated a great reunion of the human family in the eschaton. According to Luke, the church under the Spirit anticipates that reunion.

In Acts 2:14–21, Peter performs one of the most important tasks of preaching when he names the experience of the people in theological terms with the help of a text from Scripture (Joel 2:28–32). Luke adds the words "in the last days" to the passage from Joel to make it clear that the phenomenon of the miracle of understanding and the social roles and events described in the passage are signals that the present age is ending and the apocalypse is ahead. The Spirit will soon pour out on "all flesh," that is, also on the Gentiles. Social inequalities and divisions existing since the fall disappear as sons and daughters prophesy equally, as do young men and slaves (Acts 2:17b–18). Furthermore, the elements of creation will come apart as God uncreates the present world as a part of creating the new one (the realm of God; vv. 19–20). In the midst of the trauma and chaos of that transition all, including Gentiles, who call upon God will be saved (v. 21).

It is a tragic irony that many in the church soon not only lost sight of the Jewish character of this vision of the ingathering of the whole human family but declared that Jewish people should be excluded from the community of God. This passage passes judgment on such perverse thinking while reminding today's church that we have the opportunity to follow the leading of the Spirit into rapprochement with the Jewish people.

First Sunday after Pentecost/Year B

Trinity Sunday

John 3:1–17

Please see the Second Sunday in Lent/Year A, and the Fourth Sunday in Lent/Year B for the commentary on this reading.

Proper 4 [9]/Year B

Mark 2:23–3:6

Please see the Ninth Sunday after the Epiphany/Year B for the commentary on this reading.

Proper 5 [10]/Year B

Mark 3:20–35

Our text presumes that in the time of Mark some families broke apart, as many members remained in the established synagogue while others left to identify with the Markan community, which still understood itself as a Jewish group. Today's passage offers a rationale for persons leaving the traditional Jewish household and becoming a part of Mark's community.

In Jewish antiquity, identity was familial: to be was to be a part of a family. The household was a vibrant center of religious life, as well as a base for housing, clothing, and food. Younger people were to honor their parents, that is, to respect senior generations but also to provide for them materially (Exod. 20:12; Deut. 5:16; cf. Exod. 21:18–20; 27:16; Lev. 19:3; Deut. 21:18–21; Prov. 19:26; 28:24; Sir. 3:1–36). Administration of justice and community discipline took place within the household.

In Mark 3:19b–21, Jesus' family hears that Jesus has lost touch with reality. They come, out of family duty, to restrain Jesus. The verb "restrain" (*krateō*) means to take away forcefully. Not only does the family aim to stop Jesus' ministry, but their comment in v. 21 gives the scribes the opportunity to claim that Jesus was allied with Beelzebul (Satan), ruler of demons (v. 22). Attributing the work of Jesus to the power of the demons is the unforgivable sin (3:28–30).

When Jesus' family of origin comes, the crowd voices the traditional Jewish expectation: When the parent calls, the daughter or son heeds (vv. 31–32). The question in v. 33, however, urges the reader to reconsider the assumption. Jesus looks at those in the room and resolves the question: "Here are my mother and my brothers! Whoever does the will of God is my brother and sister and mother" (vv. 34–35). For Mark, those who do the will of God are those who embrace the manifestation of the realm of God through Jesus.

Mark uses this saying to justify persons leaving their traditional Jewish households of origin for his community. However, people coming into the church do not simply jettison their old ties but rather become a part of the eschatological family ("*Here* are my mother and my brothers"). According to Mark, families of origin, like the mother and brother of Jesus, may get in the way of the realm of God.

In 3:25 Jesus says, "If a house is divided against itself, that house will not be able to stand." While Mark's larger concern in 3:23–27 is to accuse the Jewish leadership of Mark's time of being a divided house (see the commentary for Palm Sunday or Passion Sunday/Year B), the immediate context also applies to families, for when family members are divided over whether to embrace the Markan community's testimony to the realm of God, that family cannot stay together.

To be sure, families of origin can sometimes impede a person's witness to the realm of God. Yet the preacher needs to help the congregation recognize that abandoning the family often works against the realm of God with its promise of unconditional love and justice for all; the result can be personal pain as intimate ties are rejected, social confusion as longstanding relationships disintegrate, and economic peril (especially for older parents) as family members disappear. A Jewish household in antiquity was in a position similar to today's parents who discover a son or daughter has joined a cult. A preacher should not be cavalier about such households, but sensitive to their anguish. Further, Jewish families have shown remarkable capacity to sustain identity and witness for more than three millennia. In today's world of dysfunctional relationships, the preacher may commend such families as models of tenacious love and justice characteristic of God's realm.

Proper 6 [11]/Year B

Mark 4:26–34

The disciples do not understand Jesus' teaching and ministry (4:1–10), and in response Jesus explains the purpose of the parables (4:11–13). Whereas most Christians think parables are intended to communicate a straightforward message, Mark cites Isa. 6:9–10 to explain that for people not in the circle of disciples, the parables are not to clarify but to obfuscate. The parables contain perspectives on the coming of God's realm that are to remain a "mystery," not fully understandable to the general populace, until the time is right. Meanwhile, Jesus interprets the parables for the disciples.

These themes make sense of vv. 33–34. The crowd could not get the full meaning of the parables because the time for fully revealing them had not come. Jesus explained the parables to the disciples so that when the time was right, their mystery would be unveiled (4:21–23). Since Mark discloses the allegorical interpretation (cf. 4:1–9), he evidently believed the time of unveiling had come. The Markan community had a special responsibility for alerting people to the apocalyptic moment, which included interpreting the parables. If they would not take on this responsibility, they would fall under judgment (4:24–25).

The allegorical meaning of the parable of the soils is made clear in 4:14–20. The church, like the sower, broadcasts the word, that is, the news of the manifestation of the divine realm (v. 14). The fates of the seeds describe circumstances in which people turn away from the realm: Satan deprives people of understanding the divine purposes through Jesus (4:15; 8:27–30), persecution (4:16–17; 13:9–13), and inability to disentangle oneself from the old age and its wealth (4:18–19; 10:17–27). The explanation concludes with a traditional Jewish image of the coming of the apocalypse and the realm of God as a harvest (4:20).

This part of Mark explains why many people at the time of Jesus did not grasp the parables (or Jesus' ministry). The time was not right. It explains why many people do not respond favorably to "the word." It encouraged the Markan community to sow the word even when results were discouraging and their social world was in turmoil.

The two parables in today's lesson use the motif of contrast between what is planted and what results in order to encourage the Markan community. The stories adapt similar motifs in Jewish literature to Jesus and the community announcing the coming of the realm of God (see, e.g., 2 Esd. 4:28–29, 35–39; 8:36–62; 9:31–33; cf. Isa. 55:10–11).

Mark 4:26–29 compares the coming of the divine realm to the planting and growth of seed. After a farmer plants seed, growth ensues. When the grain is ripe, the farmer comes with the sickle for the harvest. The message of Jesus and the church may seem tiny (sowing the word), but it points to the apocalypse (the eschatological harvest). By using agricultural growth imagery, Mark suggests association with Gen. 1. God created the world, and its processes of plant growth have never stopped. Just as people can count on plants to grow, so they can count on the coming of the realm.

Mark 4:30–32 compares the coming of the realm to the planting and growth of a mustard seed. The tiny seed becomes a great shrub. The birds making nests in the shade are Gentiles who are included in the divine reign (Ezek. 31:6; *1 Enoch* 90:3; *Midrash Psalms* 104:10).

In a day when many pastors and congregations are discouraged, these parables offer encouragement. Though one may not see immediate, dramatic results from preaching, organizing the youth, rehabilitating neighborhood houses, or working at Jewish-Christian dialogue, God works through them to help manifest the divine realm.

Proper 7 [12]/Year B

Mark 4:35–41

The miracle stories in Mark are mini-apocalypses. A person or group is in a situation that represents in miniature the brokenness of the old age. Through Jesus, God rescues, exorcises, heals, or provides, thus prefiguring the restoration of life in the realm of God.

The destination of Jesus and the disciples is "the other side," the east side of the Sea of Galilee—Gentile territory (v. 35). Jesus is here an eschatological Jonah taking the realm of God to the Gentile world, thus portraying preaching to Gentiles not as a Christian innovation but as a heritage of Jewish mission. The presence of the "other boats" (v. 36) makes the event public: People in addition to Jesus and the disciples are to see the calming of the storm.

The description of the storm in v. 27 evokes the threat of chaos, often represented by water symbolism (see, e.g., Gen. 1:1–2; Dan. 7:2; *2 Baruch* 53:1–12; 56:1; 58:1–16; *Testament of Naphtali* 6:1–8). On the sea, God is often in conflict with agents of chaos (see, e.g., Job 26:12; Ps. 72:8; 89:10; Isa. 27:1). The situation of the Markan church in the great tribulation is itself a chaos (Mark 13:4–19).

Jesus is asleep in the stern. He is not uncaring; Judaism sometimes uses sleep as a symbol of trust in God (e.g., Job 11:18–19; Ps. 3:5; 4:8). The disciples should share this trust, for Jesus had given them authority over demons and other disturbances of the old age (Mark 3:14–15). However, per Mark's usual presentation of the disciples, they do not recognize their powers and are afraid.

Upon awaking, Jesus rebukes the wind and silences the sea. The first-century listener would recognize God working through Jesus, for Jewish literature repeatedly asserts God's power over the sea (e.g., Job 26:11–12; Ps. 104:6–7; Isa. 51:9–10). Even more, as we saw on the Fourth Sunday after the Epiphany/Year B, the term "rebuked" (*epitimaō*) is used for demon exorcism. A form of "Be silent" (*siōpa*) appears similarly in Mark 1:25 (cf. 2 Esd. 6:41–42; *2 Enoch* 40:9; 43:1–3; 69:22). Agents of Satan who seek to keep the world in chaos cause the storm. Jesus' silencing the storm demonstrates that Jesus has the power to silence demons that beset Mark's church.

The questions of v. 40 are directed not just to the disciples in the narrative but also to the reader. In Mark, faith is trust that the realm of God is at work through Jesus and will soon be realized at the apocalypse. Given the power of Jesus, why do they continue to be afraid? Do they not have enough faith to endure to the apocalypse? Verse 41 suggests a fitting response: profound awe. The reader knows the answer to the final question. Jesus is the one through whom God brings the divine realm.

The preacher could ask how chaos pummels today's congregation and how Jesus is in the midst of the community to help them make their way through it. That aside, however, viewed from the perspective of the whole Markan narrative, this story is subtly pernicious. As we saw on Palm Sunday or Passion Sunday/Year B, Mark interprets Jewish leaders as being possessed by demons. This text asserts that Jesus has the power to rebuke such leaders, a power fully revealed when the veil in the temple is torn in two, suggesting that the destruction of the temple and the subsequent social distress were throwing Jewish leadership over to chaos (15:39). Similar attitudes among Christians throughout history have often made life a raging storm for the Jewish community. This story reminds us that just as Jesus had the power to exorcise the sea, so the risen Jesus can rebuke the demons in today's church that would make life chaos for Jewish people.

Proper 8 [13]/Year B

Mark 5:21–43

Our comments on the Second Gospel frequently call attention to Mark's hostile caricature of many Jewish leaders. Here, however, Jairus, a leader in a synagogue who probably presides over worship, seeks Jesus' help (5:22–24a).

For Jairus to beg at the feet of Jesus was a dramatic gesture in the first century when social status was important. Here, Jairus, a powerful figure, admitted inferiority and acknowledged the superiority of an itinerant healer. The message is that if Jairus could do so, anyone can.

The incident in 5:24b–30 emphasizes the healing of the woman and increases the tension in the story of Jairus's daughter. Will she die while the entourage stops for the woman? Mark does not specify the kind of hemorrhage that flowed for twelve years, though it may have been unrelieved menstruation. The woman's situation highlights the tragedy of the old age: Its physicians could not heal her and left her impoverished (5:26).

Christians frequently imply that ancient Judaism was an inferior religion because, in its view, whereas the woman had a medical problem, the bleeding made her religiously unclean and the community isolated her (see e.g., Lev. 12:1–8; 15:19–30; *m. Niddah* 7:4; Josephus, *Antiquities* 3.261). Such deprecation fails to respect practical wisdom and cultural difference. Blood carries many communicable diseases; quarantine embodied compassion for persons who might be affected but are not yet, and relieved infected persons from the burden of knowing they infected others. (Leviticus 13 speaks of diseases that can be contracted.) Furthermore, many Jews believed that blood contained the power of life (Lev. 17:10–16) and belonged in the body. Outside the body, blood was a force no longer directed toward the purpose God intended. Uncontrolled blood had the capacity to threaten order. Hence, the community developed rites to contain such uncontrolled force.

The woman courageously makes her way through the crowd to touch Jesus' garment (5:27–29), recalling the idea that power in a holy person (or that person's clothing) could be released by touch. While Christians puzzle about why Jesus asks, "Who touched me?" (vv. 30–32), the most direct explanation is that Mark wanted the healing to become public to impart to the reader the message of v. 34: Through faith, people like the woman encountered the realm of God through Jesus and were welcomed into the community awaiting the final restoration. The story also challenges the Markan community to welcome such folk.

In the meantime, Jairus's daughter dies (v. 35). When Jesus says, "Do not fear; only believe" (v. 36), the reader remembers vv. 24b–34. Mark makes a subtle dig at traditional Jewish households by picturing rituals of mourning taking place when the one who can raise the dead is on the way. The reprimand thickens when Mark pictures the mourners laughing when Jesus says that the child is sleeping. The mourners think Jesus has literal sleep in mind, and recognize neither that Jesus speaks figuratively of the dead as "sleeping" as they await resurrection (per apocalypticism), nor that Jesus can raise the girl (vv. 38–40a). When Jesus raises the daughter, the message of v. 34 is intensified: Faith that the divine realm is coming through Jesus releases people from the power of death.

The preacher can point out that the positive message of these stories does not require caricature of Judaism. Persons who are similar to Jairus and the woman with the issue of blood continue to find that faith is a channel through which restoration and resurrection take place.

Proper 9 [14]/Year B

Mark 6:1–13

The setting of 6:1–6a is a synagogue on the Sabbath. In key Markan texts thus far, this was the setting for negative encounters between Jesus and people in synagogues (1:21–28; 3:1–6; cf. 2:23–28), leading us to expect a similar turn here.

Mark's skill as a storyteller is apparent here. Initially we think that the crowd is responding positively to Jesus (v. 2). The group is "astounded" at Jesus' ministry (as in 1:22; 7:37; 11:18) and asks, "What is this wisdom that has been given to him?" The use of the passive "has been given" indicates they recognize that Jesus is teaching and performing mighty works under the aegis of a power beyond him.

However, as v. 3 unfolds, a shadow falls over the crowd's attitude. They think of Jesus not as a religious leader but as a carpenter who worked with wood, stone, or metal. In antiquity, a person's lineage and identity usually came through the father, and the designation "son of Mary" may be a slander. The mention of Jesus' siblings calls to mind an earlier incident when Jesus' family thought that Jesus was affected by a demon (3:20–21) and Jesus declared that the household in the realm of God is made up not of biological kin but of those who do the will of God (3:31–35; cf. 10:28–31). When Mark says, "And they took offense at him," the meaning is clear: The congregation of people who have known Jesus since birth thought Jesus was under the influence of Satan.

In v. 4, Jesus replies with a proverb that was well known in antiquity. The prophetic motif calls to mind the memory of Jewish people rejecting the prophets (see, e.g., 1 Kgs. 19:10; 2 Chr. 24:20–22; 36:15–16; Neh. 9:6; Jer. 26:20–23; 38:4–6; Acts 7:52; *Jubilees* 1:12; Josephus, *Antiquities* 10.3.1). This detail reinforces Jewish responsibility for Jesus' death in Mark and for the harassment of the church (13:9–13). Jesus can enact few signs of the realm of God in his hometown (vv. 5–6a). This passage is part of Mark's continuing effort to undermine the reader's confidence in Jews who do not identify with the Jesus movement.

By contrast, Mark 6:6b–13 juxtaposes the obedience of the Twelve, which results in signs of the realm of God: repentance, exorcisms, healings. While Mark often portrays the Twelve as unperceptive (cf. Third Sunday after the Epiphany/Year B), today's lection shows that when persons faltering in witness do what Jesus says, the realm of God becomes manifest. This text addresses the Markan church in its faltering witness:

If you do what Jesus says, signs of the divine realm will appear. A preacher might develop a sermon around this theme for a congregation today whose witness languishes.

As we note in connection with Proper 9/Year C, the instructions to the Twelve are typical of the instructions given to itinerant missionaries in the Hellenistic world (6:8–11). Such persons would embark on a mission with few resources, dependent upon persons along the way for support. The general population looked upon this as trusting and faithful behavior. People interpreted community provision for them as a sign of the deity's blessing on the mission. The mission of the Twelve met these criteria (vv. 12–13).

The theme of juxtaposition suggests an approach for a sermon. The preacher could juxtapose Mark's polemic against the congregation in the synagogue with the call of the preacher to tell the truth, even regarding distortions in the biblical witness. Indeed, the preacher who is truly obedient to Jesus (as are the Twelve in vv. 6b–13) will seek to exorcise the demon of distortion of Judaism from Christian witness.

Proper 10 [15]/Year B

Mark 6:14–29 and 30–42

The lectionary separates Mark's story of Herod's banquet from the immediately following story of Jesus' feeding of the five thousand. We treat them together because the stories contextualize each other (they are mirror-images) and because Mark and Matthew (14:3–21) put them together. What Herod's banquet celebrates, Jesus' feeding denies, and vice versa. Mark does not tell the story to explain the execution of John the Baptist. He tells it to highlight the contradiction between the rule of God and the rule of Caesar, between the way of life and the way of death.

Herod Antipas was the Roman puppet ruler of Galilee. He served the economic purposes of the empire and used the military to make the system work. Other than the elites in Rome, the system benefited local plantation owners, members of the royal court, military big shots, and the temple oligarchy. These are the people Herod invited to his party. The party was a Hellenistic banquet; inviting friends to one's birthday party was a Hellenistic, not a Jewish, custom. A dancing girl provides the entertainment, and John the Baptist is beheaded (executions also served as entertainment in the Roman Empire). Two points that Mark does not mention are important: (1) Royal, wealthy, and powerful guests reclined to eat, as was the custom. (2) The nobodies of the time, women and slaves, served the meal and tended to the needs of the banquet-goers. Mark depicts one kind of king, one kind of kingdom, and one kind of banquet.

Mark next tells us that Jesus "had compassion on" the crowds following him "because they were like sheep without a shepherd" (6:34). This expression taps into a rich vein in the tradition of Israel, namely, the prophetic criticism of kings who are supposed to be shepherds of the people (Ezek. 34:2) but who instead feed themselves and let the sheep go hungry: "The people wander like sheep; they suffer for lack of a shepherd" (Zech. 10:2). This reference links these two stories to each other.

In the story of Jesus' feeding of the five thousand, every element present in the story of Herod's banquet shows up in its reverse, mirror-image form. Jesus' banquet takes place in a desert, not a palace. Jesus' guests are the hungry, the destitute, and those who mourn, not the courtiers, officers, and big shots of Galilee. Jesus' apostles serve the food; they do the work done at Herod's banquet by the nobodies, women, and slaves. Jesus' guests are told to "lie down" to eat (the Greek *anaklinai* means "lie down," although the NRSV translates it "sit down"). Jesus treats the hungry and the destitute as royalty!

Overwhelmingly important points are made by Mark's (and Matthew's) joining of these two stories. The rule or kingdom of God contradicts that of Caesar and Herod, and vice versa. No one who goes up against the kingdom of Caesar will have a long career. John's life ends in this story, and the reader knows that Jesus' will also end soon. To proclaim that only God is king or that only God rules, contradicts the claim that the king is God. Followers of Jesus are to understand that: "You know that among the Gentiles those whom they recognize as their rulers lord it over them, and their great ones are tyrants over them. But it is not so among you; but whoever wishes to become great among you must be your servant, and whoever wishes to be first among you must be slave of all" (Mark 10:42–44 and par.). Jesus' banquet shows the community acting out what it preaches (in spite of the disciples' complaining). These historical parables from the early church give us clues about how to live in the oppressive present in the power of the future rule of God that is already among us. If we are to use the terms "king" and "kingdom," we should let Jesus determine their meaning, not Herod.

Proper 11 [16]/Year B

Mark 6:30–34, 53–56

Today's reading provides the setting for the feeding of the five thousand in Mark. It follows the story of Herod Antipas's birthday banquet which, in good Greco-Roman fashion, he threw for himself. The banquet was in Herod's palace; by contrast, the feeding of the five thousand occurs in "a deserted place" (vv. 31, 32, 35), reminiscent of the desert in which God fed the people Israel.

The guests at Herod's banquet were "his courtiers and officers and . . . the leaders of Galilee" (6:21). Those fed by Jesus in the desert were the "many," who had "no leisure even to eat" (v. 31). Herod's guests, in Hellenistic fashion, reclined on couches to eat and would have been served by women and other "nobodies," the powerless serving the powerful, the poor serving the rich. In stark contrast, Jesus' banquet takes place on the grass and everyday people are the guests. The disciples serve them, doing the work of the women and other "nobodies," demonstrating the point that "among the Gentiles those whom they recognize as their rulers lord it over them. . . . But it is not so among you; but whoever wishes to become great among you must be your servant" (Mark 10:42–43 and par.). Jesus' ministry was not just talk; it was words acted out in deeds, deeds interpreted by words.

Herod's banquet began with his wife's (i.e., his former sister-in-law's) "grudge against" John (v. 19) and ended with Herod's order that John be killed. In contrast, Jesus orders the crowd to be fed, and his banquet begins with "compassion" for the common people "because they were like sheep without a shepherd" (v. 34). The God of Israel was a God of compassion, *rahamim*, derived from the word for "womb"—a God of womb-like love for the people (Isa. 54:7–8). "Sheep without a shepherd" was a frequent expression among prophets who criticized kings who fed themselves while the people went hungry, precisely the situation in Jesus' time (see Ezek. 34:5, Zech. 10:2). As God is the shepherd of Israel (Zech. 11:17), so here Jesus is the shepherd devoted to restoring the people Israel in their situation of occupation and all that it brought—poverty, hunger, weeping, and mourning.

Jesus "began to teach them many things" (v. 34). Mark does not describe the content of Jesus' teaching, but the feeding of the five thousand is an acted parable from which many lessons can be learned, as has already been indicated. Eating and drinking, for example, signify attaining wisdom (Prov. 9:5).

Verses 53–56 summarize Jesus' healing ministry in Galilee. Jesus carries his ministry into the "villages or cities or farms" (v. 56). People turn out with their sick, bringing them "on mats to wherever they heard he was" (v. 55). Our reading began with the observation that "many [*polloi*] were coming and going" (v. 31), meaning that large numbers of people were following Jesus. They do so again in the summary, begging that they "might touch even the fringe [*kraspedon*] of his cloak" (v. 56), the tassels that pious Jews wore on the four corners of their shirts.

This story is a graphic description of what Jesus meant by the "kingdom of God." It was an actual, acted-out movement among the lost sheep, the destitute and the hungry among the people Israel (and the destitute were most of the people of Israel at this time). It was the mirror-image of the kingdom of Herod Antipas and was motivated by compassion—a movement whose leaders were to be servants and to provide food for the hungry and healing for the sick.

Proper 12 [17]/Year B

John 6:1–21

John 6 deals with Jesus' relationship to the Jewish festival of Passover. Verses 1–4 indicate that Jesus went to the "other side" of the Sea of Galilee, followed by a "large crowd" impressed with his healing miracles. "Jesus went up the mountain and sat down there with his disciples" (v. 3) when "the Passover, the festival of the Jews, was at hand" (v. 4). Jesus on the mountain calls to mind Moses' having gone up Sinai and points to John's conviction that the gift of Torah to the people is brought to completion by the gift of Jesus Christ. Jesus sat down, which indicates that he was an authoritative teacher in Israel; sages and rabbis customarily sat down to teach. That Passover is referred to as the feast "of the Jews" points up John's alienation from the synagogue.

Passover celebrated God's freeing of the people Israel from bondage in Egypt and proclaimed freedom from all forms of enslavement for all peoples, as it still does. It reenacted God's protection of the firstborn of the Israelites and God's feeding the frightened Israelites in the desert with the "bread of heaven." "For their hunger, you gave them bread from heaven" (Neh. 9:15; see Ezek. 16:4).

In the Synoptics, the claim about not having enough money to feed the crowd was put on the lips of the disciples. John has Jesus put it as a question to Philip: "Where are we to buy bread for these people to eat?" (v. 5) in order "to test him." Jesus' followers in John regularly fail to understand what has been disclosed to them. Andrew, again typically, fails to do so. He remarks that a boy has five loaves and two fish but asks, "What are they among so many people?" (v. 9). Yet Jesus "knew what he was going to do" (v. 6) and set about doing it.

Jesus says, "Make the people sit down" (v. 10). The Greek is *anapesein*, "to recline or lie down," not "sit." The point is important, for the rich and the royal lie down to eat. Jesus treats the crowds as royalty. They recline on "a great deal of grass" (v. 10), an echo of Ps. 23:2: "He makes me lie down in green pastures." Then Jesus took the loaves, gave thanks, and distributed them to the crowd, "as much as they wanted" (v. 11), with twelve baskets left over. The surplus points to the superabundance of God's grace (it is always God who enables Jesus to do what he does in John), a grace more than adequate to our needs. The feeding of the five thousand is modeled on Elisha's feeding of a hundred men with "twenty loaves of barley and fresh ears of grain," including the generation of leftovers: "For thus says the LORD, 'They shall eat and have some left'" (2 Kgs. 4:42–43).

The response of the people who "saw the sign" of the feeding is to say, "This is indeed the prophet who is to come into the world" (v. 14). Jesus departs, aware that they might "take him by force to make him king" (v. 15). The miracles in John are signs that point beyond themselves to a deeper faith, but those who "see" the signs often stop in amazement at the miracle. Jesus does not wish to play an authoritarian role.

Today's reading ends with the miracle on the sea (vv. 16–21). This story associates Jesus closely with the God of Israel and God's supremacy over the sea. A violent storm blows up as the disciples struggle in the darkness with the "great wind" and high waves. They see Jesus "walking on the sea" and are "terrified." Jesus says to them, "It is I; do not be afraid" (v. 20). This episode is clearer in the Greek, where Jesus says "I am" (*egō eimi*), using the name of God (Exod. 3:13–14). In this theophany, Jesus discloses who he is, correcting the people's misunderstanding.

Proper 13 [18]/Year B

John 6:24–35

In this passage, Jesus interprets who he is and what was intended in the feeding of the five thousand. The scene is set when the crowd "got into the boats and went to Capernaum looking for" him. Not all five thousand went to Capernaum. Galilean fishing boats were not large, and an armada would have been required to take five thousand people to Capernaum. The issue here is that people of partial faith are looking for Jesus.

Several questions and a request structure this passage: "Rabbi, when did you come here?" (v. 25). "What must we do to perform the works of God?" (v. 28). "What sign are you going to give us?" (v. 30). "Sir, give us this bread always" (v. 34). Jesus answers each question, clarifying what true faith entails. Questions are important; without them there are no answers. Questions are "teachable moments," and the misunderstandings they express give Jesus an opportunity to make things clear. As a good teacher, he takes advantage of these moments.

"Rabbi, when did you come here?" allows Jesus to discuss the motives of those who seek him. You seek me, he says, "not because you saw signs, but because you ate your fill of the loaves" (v. 26). The sign (miracle) was a symbol pointing beyond itself to a deeper hunger that the "Son of Man will give you" (v. 27). "Son of Man" indicates Jesus' role as making God known in the experiences of his ministry. "Will give," in the future, leads his questioners to be open to what is yet to be revealed. Jesus' followers should work for "the food that endures for eternal life" (v. 27).

"What must we do to perform the works of God?" leads Jesus to comment that the work of God is to "believe [*pisteuēte*] in him whom he has sent" (v. 29). The Greek translated "believe" means to trust, to have faith, to give one's heart to (the German word *belieben* is the immediate root of the English "believe"; it means to belove).

"What sign are you going to give us?" "Our ancestors," say the questioners, "ate the manna in the wilderness: as it is written, 'He gave them bread from heaven to eat'" (v. 31). Jesus responds that God, not Moses, gave their ancestors the bread from heaven (as "He gave them . . ." makes clear) and that God now "gives you the true bread from heaven," that is, Jesus, who came from heaven and "gives life to the world" (v. 33). That Jesus is the true bread does not imply that the manna was "false" bread; a simple affirmative statement does not allow negative implications to be drawn from it. It means, rather, that this bread gives life to "the world," not just to the people Israel.

"Sir, give us this bread always [*pantote*]." *Pantote* connotes recurrence after recurrence of giving. Once more, the questioners misunderstand and want Jesus, again and again and again, to "give us this bread." Once more using the name of God (*egō eimi*), Jesus says, "I am the bread of life" (v. 35). In John's theology, everything Jesus is and does is made possible by God and the love of God in which Jesus abides. God is the bread of life; "it is my Father who gives you the true bread from heaven" (v. 32), as Jesus had just finished saying. "Whoever comes to me will never be hungry, and whoever believes in me will never be thirsty" (v. 35). The gracious love of God, made known in Jesus Christ, never fails. This does not mean that we will never suffer from physical hunger. Jesus made it clear that he is not talking about bread of which we can eat our fill. It does mean that, whatever happens, we can trust in the unfailing presence of God's gracious love.

Proper 14 [19]/Year B

John 6:35, 41–51

Today's passage furthers Jesus' discourse on the meaning of the "bread of life." The reading opens with v. 35: "I am the bread of life. Whoever comes to me will never be hungry, and whoever believes in me will never be thirsty." In v. 38, Jesus says, "I have come down from heaven," to which "the Jews" respond, How can Jesus, whom we know to be the son of Joseph, say, "I have come down from heaven"? (v. 42). John claims that "the Jews began to complain" (v. 41), recalling the complaining ("murmuring") of the Israelites in the desert (Exod. 15:24). John again heightens the animosity and conflict in his story.

Jesus' response is to command "the Jews" not to "complain" among themselves (v. 43): "No one can come to me unless drawn by the Father who sent me; and I will raise that person up on the last day" (v. 44). The implication is that those who do not come to Jesus were not drawn by the Father to do so and their not coming to Jesus is no failure on their part. John would say, however, that such persons are "condemned" (3:18), which leaves us with a problem: Is it or is it not true that only those can come to Jesus whom the Father draws to him? Are some to be condemned because the Father did not draw them to Jesus? An attentive congregant might well think of this question; attentive preachers certainly should.

Jesus then says, "It is written in the prophets, 'And they shall *all* be taught by God'" (v. 45). Commentators typically say that whereas in Jewish faith only the people Israel were the object of God's blessing, now that blessing is intended for all people without respect for ethnic identity. This interpretation mis-describes the faith of the people Israel in whose scriptures all peoples were included in one economy of blessing: "In you [Abram] all the families of the earth shall be blessed" (Gen. 12:3). The Gentiles Melchizedek, Abimelech, Jethro, Balaam, Rahab, Ruth, Ittai the Gittite, Hiram, Naaman, and Cyrus play positive roles in the history of Israel; Ishmael is circumcised before Isaac is born and is included in the covenant with Abraham and Sarah; Jonah goes to Nineveh, a Gentile city, to bear witness; "the LORD blessed the Egyptian's house for Joseph's sake" (Gen. 39:5). God's word had always been intended for "all people."

Because only he "has seen the Father" (v. 46), Jesus for John is the only one through whom eternal life is possible and "whoever believes" in him "has eternal life" (v. 47) now. To "the Jews" Jesus remarks, "I am the bread of life. Your ancestors ate the manna in the wilderness, and they died" (vv. 48–49). Those who eat of Jesus will "not die" (v. 50). The shift in meaning here is obvious. The ancestors died physical deaths. So would and did those who believed in Jesus. They, however, have eternal life, but not so anyone who does not eat his "flesh" (v. 51).

Some, actually most of humanity, will be forever condemned because they did not eat the flesh of Jesus. Judaism claims, to the contrary, that one does not have to be a Jew to be saved; "righteous Gentiles" also have a place in "the world to come." They have only to keep the seven commandments of the Noachide covenant, six of which are negative and can be kept while taking a nap. One is positive and says that we have to live in a society that has a justice system. While Judaism regards the Torah as the greatest gift of God's unconditional love, it does not turn that gift into a condition apart from which God is not free to love other people. Should we make the mistake that Judaism avoids?

Proper 15 [20]/Year B

John 6:51–58

Passover remains the setting of this discourse on the "bread from heaven," and Jesus gives this teaching "in the synagogue at Capernaum" (v. 59). Jews are preparing to participate in Passover, to eat the paschal lamb, unleavened bread, and various foods that recall and reenact the exodus and wilderness wandering, including the manna from heaven. The discourse begins with a repetition of the last verse from last week's reading: "I am the living bread that came down from heaven" (v. 51). Whoever eats of this bread will have eternal life, a future promise, and this bread is, indeed, Jesus' very flesh.

John's Gospel was favored by gnostic groups, who had an aversion to the body. The strong emphasis in John 6 on eating Jesus' flesh may have been added to the text after it was retrieved from the gnostics because its inclusion would not have led them to be attracted to John. The emphasis on eating Jesus' flesh is anti-gnostic.

Again, "the Jews" murmur, as their rebellious ancestors did in the desert against Moses, and ask, "How can this man give us his flesh to eat?" (v. 52). Jesus responds simply by claiming that "unless you eat the flesh of the Son of Man and drink his blood, you have no life in you" (v. 53). He goes on to say that "those who eat [*trōgōn*] my flesh and drink my blood have [now] eternal life, and I will raise them up on the last day; for my flesh is true food and my blood is true drink" (vv. 54–55). *Trōgōn*, repeated in

v. 56, means to "gnaw" or "crunch" what one is eating, an utterly graphic expression. *Trogein*, the infinitive, is used only here and in 13:18: "The one who ate my bread has lifted his heel against me," referring to Judas. Most likely, John used it to resist gnostic or proto-gnostic anti-body attitudes. Jesus' response does not engage the question "How?" Rather, it uses the occasion to make a point about John's view of the Eucharist.

Then John returns to his theme of mutual indwelling: "Those who eat my flesh and drink my blood abide in me, and I in them" (v. 56). This matter of living in relationships of mutuality with those who are different from us, as we and Jesus who are different from each other can mutually indwell one another, is a beautiful metaphor. Sadly, John's sectarian tendencies lead him to draw a tight circle around those who participate in this mutual indwelling. All those outside the circle have no life in them.

In v. 57, Jesus expresses his dependence on the Father—"I live because of the Father"—giving a more theocentric cast to this passage. "Whoever eats me will live because of me" (v. 57). As Jesus depends on God for life, so Jesus' disciples depend on Jesus for eternal life. But they also, thereby, depend on God who is the ultimate giver of Jesus. God also gave and gives life to the people Israel and to all people and things that live.

God gave the manna to Israel in the wilderness. Yet Jesus sharply contrasts his bread with "that which your ancestors ate, and they died" (v. 58). God is certainly free to do a new thing in Jesus. But John creates a problem in claiming that God gave a death-dealing bread to the Israelites, for the question then is: Why should God now be trusted to give a life-giving bread? Preachers need to deal with this text and others in such a way as to affirm the trustworthiness of God in whom we are called to place our trust.

That is what John was about in this passage. It was not written so that "the Jews" could read it and feel rejected. That mutual rejection of John's community and the synagogue lies in the past. It was written to reassure members of John's community that "the one who eats this bread will live forever" (v. 58). That is the note to strike.

Proper 16 [21]/Year B

John 6:56–69

In its ongoing focus on the Eucharist, this week's lectionary text repeats the last three verses of last week's text and then moves, in vv. 60–69, to a discussion of Jesus with some disciples who say, "This teaching is difficult; who can accept it?" (v. 60).

While teaching in the synagogue, Jesus had stated that those who eat his flesh and drink his blood "abide in me and I in them." Further, since he lives "because of the Father," "whoever eats me will live because of me" (v. 57). He contrasts this "bread that came down from heaven" with "that which your ancestors ate, and they died" (v. 58).

At this point, "many of his disciples" protest his "difficult" teaching. Who are these disciples? The passage identifies them to some extent when it says, "Because of this many of his disciples turned back and no longer went about with him" (v. 66). We may conclude that because they had heard him in the synagogue, this group represents Jewish followers of Jesus in the late first century who could not accept John's Christology and, consequently, John's understanding of the Eucharist as gnawing on the actual flesh of Jesus and thereby gaining eternal life. They are sometimes called "Jewish-Christians," but this term is unhelpful for two reasons: (1) John was also a "Jewish-Christian," and (2) John never uses the term "Christian." It was only late and somewhat reluctantly that some followers of Jesus began to call themselves Christian (see 1 Pet. 4:16; as for being called "Christians" by others, see Acts 11:26).

One point to note about this is that John therefore never uses "Christians" or "Christianity" in contrast with Jews or Judaism. There has been a rift with the synagogue, but as yet there are not two separate faiths or religions. Meanwhile, the disciples who protest that Jesus' teaching is difficult find it impossible to "listen to" (*akouein*, "accept") his teaching.

Jesus asks them, "Then what if you were to see the Son of Man ascending to where he was before?" (v. 62). Here Jesus appeals to contemporary Jewish views of Moses, Enoch, Abraham, Isaiah, and Elijah and, perhaps, to Moses' "ascent" of Sinai to receive the Torah. The argument seems to be that this is precisely what will happen, although John ends with resurrection appearances but no ascension. Hence, it is precisely such expectations that John is rebutting here because they are "fleshly": "It is the spirit that gives life; the flesh [*sarx*] is useless" (v. 63).

After all Jesus' talk about "eating his flesh," this declaration that the flesh is "useless" needs to be unpacked. These statements seem to contradict each other. But John consistently speaks both of Jesus' flesh as necessary to eternal life and of human flesh as that which is all-too-human and limited in its comprehension, darkened by misunderstanding.

"Among you," says Jesus, "there are some who do not believe" (v. 64), which is why he had said, "No one can come to me unless it is granted by the Father" (v. 65). "Because of this many of his disciples turned back" (v. 66). This passage could be taken to mean that unbelief should be dealt with pastorally rather than judgmentally because it is God's doing. The other disciples, represented by Peter, respond negatively to Jesus' question "Do you also wish to go away?" (v. 67). They "believe and know" that Jesus is "the Holy One of God" (v. 69). This is the first time in John that any disciple expresses faith in Jesus for the right reason: that he is the Sent One of God.

Proper 17 [22]/Year B

Mark 7:1–8, 14–15, 21–23

The Pharisees and scribes complain that Jesus' disciples "were eating with defiled hands, that is, without washing them" (7:1–2). Some customs, such as dietary practices, are in the Bible (see, e.g., Lev. 1:32; 15:12) while others, such as handwashing, are from the "tradition of elders," the living practice of interpreting the tradition to determine its significance for new generations. The Mishnah, Talmud, and other writings develop such tradition (on washing, see *Kelim*, "Vessels," in the Mishnah and Talmud).

Christians sometimes denigrate such Jewish acts as "external," as "works" to win God's favor, or as "burdens." They were not (see Ps. 119 on exuberant joy in keeping the law). Jews viewed traditions as God's gifts to daily remind the community of Jewish identity in a world of oppression and idolatry in which they were tempted to compromise. The outward act embodied the inner commitment to live covenantally.

Individual Jews did not always live up to the best of their tradition, as indicated by the citation of Isa. 29:13 in Mark 7:6–8. The prophets modeled Jewish self-criticism to help the community correct its life. Some Christians today soften Mark's attack on Jewish practice by regarding it as such self-criticism. However, Mark does not seek to reform Jewish practice but to sanction the church's departing from aspects of it.

Mark 7:9–13 accuses the Pharisees and scribes of neglecting the commandment to take care of their parents (cf. Exod. 20:12; 21:17; Lev. 1:2; 20:9; Deut. 5:16; *m. Nedarim* 5:6; 9:1). This violation represents many others (7:13b).

In vv. 14–15, Mark states a point (reinforced in vv. 17–18) with which historical Pharisees would agree: The test of faithfulness is not simply whether one abides by group conventions (things that go in) but is the quality of one's life (things that come out). Indeed, the Pharisees condemned the evil actions cataloged in vv. 21–22.

On the basis of the preceding arguments, Mark's Jesus "declared all foods clean," making it possible for Gentiles in the Markan community to continue their own dietary habits. Jewish members, of course, could still eat in the Jewish way.

This text is illogical. Mark rejects Jewish *tradition* by complaining that the Pharisees and scribes do not follow it. However, failure of adherents to live up to a tradition does not invalidate the tradition itself. In fact, many writers in antiquity report that the Pharisees (and many other Jews) were not the hollow caricatures Mark gives us but faithful representatives of Jewish tradition (e.g., Josephus, *Jewish War* 2.119–66; *Antiquities* 18.11–25; 13.171–73, 297–98). Documents from Pharisaic hands (e.g., the Mishnah and the Talmud) are not legalistic but rather evince vitality, a gracious vision of God, a yearning for justice, and the desire for people to live faithfully.

We can understand why Mark did not regard aspects of Jewish practice as essential: He believed that the apocalypse was imminent. The Gentile mission brought an influx of Gentiles into the community for whom Jewish customs were strange. It would be natural to ask why Gentiles should learn daily identity reminders from Judaism when they would not need them long. Mark, however, could have developed a theological rationale for such a position without libeling the Pharisees and scribes.

When the apocalypse did not occur, the church was left without a tradition of daily identity markers as powerful as those of Judaism. Consequently, the church has been more susceptible than Judaism to make compromises with culture. The Christian community might well consider recovering aspects of Jewish practice.

Proper 18 [23]/Year B

Mark 7:24–37

In Mark 7:1–23, Jesus was in Galilee declaring that the church could abandon some practices of Judaism (e.g., washing, dietary customs), thus making the Markan community more accessible to Gentiles. Today's reading demonstrates this accessibility.

Jesus goes into the region of Tyre (sometimes called Phoenicia), located about twenty miles northwest of Galilee. Not only was Tyre a Gentile area but, according to Isa. 23:1–16 and Ezek. 26:1–28:19, God condemned Tyre because its population followed idols, defiled holy places, and practiced injustice and violence in trade with Israel. At the time of Mark, Tyre was still regarded as an area of exploitation and hostility (Josephus, *Against Apion* 1.13; cf. 2 Esd. 1:11), a sign of which was that many crops grown in Galilee were sold in prosperous Gentile Tyre while Galilean peasants hungered.

The effect of Mark 7:24b is to impress upon the reader the fact that Gentiles welcomed Jesus' witness to the realm of God. This reception contrasts with Jewish leaders who were habitually suspicious.

Like the woman with the issue of blood (Proper 8/Year B), the woman in this story is not identified by relationship with a male (e.g., husband, father), but comes to Jesus on her own initiative. Mark underscores the woman as a "Gentile" (*Hellēnis*). In this context, the singular "Gentile" indicates not only that she was not Jewish but that she spoke Greek and was inculturated with a Hellenistic worldview. The addendum, "of Syrophoenician origin," evokes the fractiousness between Jewish and Gentile peoples around Tyre. Mark's return to this theme (from 7:24) shows that Mark particularly wants the reader to recollect and feel the animus between these two groups.

The statement in v. 27 is polemical. The "children" are Israel (Deut. 14:1; Isa. 1:2; *m. Avot* 3:15). In antiquity, disdain for dogs led to using the word "dog" pejoratively of people (cf. Deut. 23:19; 1 Sam. 17:43; 24:14; 2 Sam. 9:8; 16:9; 2 Kgs. 8:13; Prov. 26:11; Isa. 56:10–11; Sir. 13:18; *1 Enoch* 89:42, 46–49; *b. Bava Qamma* 83a). The mention of "bread" and "being fed" calls to mind the prefiguration of the eschatological banquet (celebrating the realm of God) in Mark 6:30–44 so that we hear in Jesus' comment that the Jewish people receive the news of this realm first. Readers disinclined toward Jewish leaders hear this caricature: "Of course, Jewish people *are* self-interested in the way represented here."

In v. 28, the woman responded with a Jewish practice: debate to change the mind of a superior, much as Moses engaged God in behalf of sinful Israel (Exod. 32:11–14), a woman of Tekoa persuaded David to allow Absalom to return (2 Sam. 14:1–24), Job wrestled with God, or, in a later time, the daughter of Rabbi Meir prompted the rabbi to pray not for sinners to disappear but for sin to vanish (*b. Berakhot* 10a). The Markan Jesus immediately yields to the woman's insight (v. 29a) and exorcises the daughter without ever seeing her (vv. 29b–30).

Given animosity between the Markan community and Jewish leaders in Mark's world, this story's description of the Gentile woman bowing before the Jewish healer and engaging in theological debate sends a potent message: Gentiles who have faith and persistence similar to this woman can be healed by the God of Israel and welcomed into the divine realm.

Indeed, Gentiles who wrestle with God can come away with unexpected blessing. Mark, of course, could have made that point without telling the story to reinforce the wearying caricature of Jews that fills the Second Gospel.

As is often Mark's custom, one story (vv. 24–30) is paired with another that is similar and yet makes its own point (vv. 31–37). The second, like the first, takes place in a Gentile setting (the Decapolis), thus underscoring the ministry of Jesus as imparting to Gentiles the healing and blessing of the God of Israel. This miracle story, like most in Mark, speaks on multiple levels. Of course the miracle demonstrates that the realm of God is moving toward final manifestation through the ministry of Jesus. The reader remembers Isaiah's confidence that, in the great season of redemption, "the ears of the deaf [shall be] unstopped . . . and the tongue of the speechless [shall] sing for joy" (Isa. 35:5–6).

Another level of the meaning of the story derives from the Jewish understanding of hearing and speaking. Judaism regarded hearing as the most important sense, for the covenant (with the commandments) was mediated through speech and hearing. The center of Israel's life is the *Shema* that begins, "*Hear*, O Israel . . ." (Deut. 6:4). This Gentile's inability to hear represents a part of the Gentile condition: they do not usually hear the word of God, and hence, do not understand it, and are not fully blessed. In Judaism, speech is important because it allows one to confess the God of Israel and to interpret God's purposes in the community.

As this story opens, the Gentile's condition (neither hearing nor speaking adequately) represents fundamental Gentile problems: they neither understand nor interpret God fully. When the Gentile comes into contact with the power of God mediated through Jesus Christ, these problems disappear. (Jesus uses typical first-century healing rituals: putting fingers in the ears, spitting and touching the tongue, sighing and looking into heaven). The story implicitly promises that the resurrected Jesus continues to heal Gentiles through the church by making it possible for them to understand and interpret the divine presence. Occasional commentators reinforce this theme by calling attention to resonance between the expression that Jesus "has done everything well (*kalōs*)" and the refrain of Gen. 1 that God saw the various parts of the world and saw that they were "good (*kalon*)." Apocalyptic theologians believed that the end time would be similar to the beginning time, the world as described in Gen. 1–2. According to Mark, Jesus makes it possible for Gentiles to be a part of that great regeneration.

Proper 19 [24]/Year B

Mark 8:27–38

We discussed this passage on the Second Sunday in Lent/Year B. However its complexity and its importance in the Second Gospel call for a second consideration.

Caesarea Philippi (about twenty-five miles north of the Sea of Galilee) was named by Herod Phillip in honor of Caesar Augustus and, thus, symbolizes Roman domination and the deification of the emperor. Mark 8:27–30 reminds the community that the suffering of the Son of Man leads through the apocalypse to the cosmic realm of God and, consequently, the end of Caesar's idolatry and oppression.

In vv. 27–30, Jesus asks the disciples questions in the manner of a rabbi. Some people think that Jesus is John the Baptist come back from the dead (Mark 6:14). Others think that he is Elijah returned from heaven as the eschatological prophet immediately before the end of history (Mal. 4:4–5; Sir. 48:10). Others think that Jesus is one of the prophets because of his prophetic teaching and because prophets were remembered as miracle workers (see, e.g., 2 Kgs. 2:19–24; 4:1–5:19; cf. Mark 6:4).

In the background of v. 29 is a wide-ranging Jewish discussion of whether a messiah would come and, if so, what that figure would be called and would do. The word "messiah" (*christos*) means, woodenly, "anointed one," that is, anointed with oil for a special purpose. Christians sometimes think that "the Jewish people" singularly expected a militaristic and nationalistic messiah. However, Jewish communities were pluralistic on this issue. Some envisioned a messiah who would institute heaven's rule on earth (with care for the poor), while others emphasized a more military figure who would defeat Rome, and some expected two such figures. Some communities did not anticipate a messiah at all. Mark interprets Jesus as messiah in v. 29, but also uses several other titles for Jesus, such as Son of God and Son of Man. One of the purposes of the Second Gospel is to show how the story of Jesus provides a meaning for these various designations for the Markan community. In connection with the Second Sunday of Lent/Year B, we point out that Mark's emphasis on the suffering of the Messiah is derived from Judaism.

On the Sixth Sunday after the Epiphany/Year B, we take the command to silence to reflect the apocalyptic timetable (v. 30). God was not ready to reveal Jesus to all.

In v. 31, Jesus predicts rejection by Jewish leaders, then the cross. These are part of the tribulation prior to the apocalypse. The point of v. 32 is that Jesus has said these things plainly so that there would be no misunderstanding. Peter, however, takes Jesus aside for rebuke, to deny that Jesus must suffer. The word "rebuke" (*epitimaō*) is used of exorcism (Mark 1:25; 3:12; 4:39; 9:25), suggesting that Peter thinks Jesus is possessed by a demon. Jesus, however, rebukes Peter, thus indicating that *Peter* has a demon (v. 33), indeed, Satan—the ruler of demons. The way of suffering is the "divine thing."

The way of the Christ is also the way of the disciples. They too must suffer, sometimes on a daily basis, as the rulers of the present age (e.g., Caesar) resist the coming realm of God and cause its representatives to suffer (8:34–38). Through this passage, Mark speaks to those in the Markan community who believed that the route to the realm of God would be glorious, devoid of suffering, and would eventuate in God installing them in positions of power in the present age. These are the "human things" of v. 33 (see Mark 10:35–45). Those who are not willing to pay the consequences (suffering) as a result of their witness to the divine reign are possessed by Satan.

Proper 20 [25]/Year B

Mark 9:30–37

Mark 9:30–32 brings forward three key themes. The first (v. 31) is Mark's presentation of Jesus as keeping the message of the realm of God a secret, or a mystery. The moment had not arrived on the apocalyptic timetable for a public revelation (cf. Sixth Sunday after the Epiphany, and Proper 6, both Year B).

The second theme is the prediction of the death and resurrection that is repeated three times (9:31; 8:31; 10:23–34; cf. Second Sunday in Lent, and Proper 19, both Year B). This repetition underscores the passion and helps the reader trust the elements in the Gospel that Jesus predicted but that had not taken place by Mark's time. Readers know that Jesus died and was raised, and, hence, they can expect the tribulation and the apocalypse.

The third theme is the failure of the disciples to understand Jesus' teaching (v. 32; cf. 4:10–12, 38–40; 6:35–44, 52; 7:17–23; 8:14–21; 9:14–28; 14:50; 14:66–72). The death of Jesus shows power exercised in the old age: brute strength used violently to maintain one's own social position. Each prediction is followed by an incident in which the disciples think of power in old-world terms (8:32b–33; 9:33–41; 10:35–45).

Verses 33–34 demonstrate that the Markan disciples continued to think and act according to old-world assumptions. As they are on the way, they argue about who would be the greatest. The social order of antiquity was highly stratified; people were expected to stay "in their place." These disciples want to know their place so they can achieve maximum benefit from it. The phrase "on the way" (v. 33) is the same as "on the path" in Mark 4:14. The implication is that when the disciples speak in this old-world way about power in community, they are in league with Satan.

In v. 35, Jesus assumes the teaching position of a rabbi by sitting. The teaching of v. 35 reveals that in the realm of God, satisfaction, security, and honor result not from striving for place but from serving. Social expectation is reversed from the old eon. Jewish literature depicts Israel as a servant community that serves the purposes of God (e.g., Isa. 41:9; 42:1; 52:13–53:12). In Mark, the disciples are to serve the realm of God. The importance of this motif to Mark is underscored by its expansion in 10:43–44.

Jesus illustrates the reversal of the old-world social pyramid in the divine realm by picking up a child and speaking in v. 37. Readers today often view children through a romantic lens that needs to be set aside when reading this text. While children were valued in the ancient Near East, they had a low place in the social order (see, e.g., Exod. 21:17; Lev. 20:9; Job 12:12; Prov. 13:24; 16:31; 19:18; Sir. 25:4–6; 30:1–2). Children here represent those in the present whose lives need reconstitution. Jesus' directive is to welcome, to receive hospitably, all whom the children represent. Such hospitality points to the social reordering that will be a part of the divine realm. The community that would be great, that would achieve eternal security, is to ask, "How can our life serve the realm of God by receiving and serving the (figurative) children of the world?"

This servant action is a means of grace, for, according to 9:37b, by welcoming children, the community welcomes not only the risen Jesus but also God.

The omnipresence of these themes in Mark suggests that some in the Markan community thought of power from the vantage point of the old age. They imagined the coming of the realm of God and the Markan community itself as arenas in which to enhance their social power. The preacher might help listeners reflect on ways that congregations and clergy continue such perception, and how this passage is a corrective.

Proper 21 [26]/Year B

Mark 9:38–50

The disciples see an exorcist casting out demons in the name of Jesus. They object because the healer is not in their group (9:38). Jesus' reply in v. 39 suggests that the objectionable exorcist is not a follower of Jesus. Some exorcists in antiquity cast out demons in the name of a recognized power.

The Markan Jesus, however, forbids the disciples from hindering the exorcist on the principle that anyone who casts out a demon in Jesus' name will not "soon afterward . . . speak evil of me" (v. 39). Mark strengthens this point in v. 40 by citing a maxim widely known in antiquity (cf. Matt. 12:30 and Luke 11:33). Verse 41 presumes the semi-arid Palestine, in which to give a cup of water was an act of hospitality; here the hospitality of the realm of God is through exorcism (and other signs of the presence of the realm). The reward or wage is a place in the reign when it is fully here.

At one level, vv. 38–41 challenge the disciples (and the community) to recognize that the power of the divine realm does not operate only in sectarian circles. The preacher might help the congregation consider the degree to which they resemble the disciples by thinking and behaving territorially. At another level, Mark contrasts this unknown exorcist not only with the disciples but also with Jewish leaders who speak evil of Jesus and who are against the Markan mission. The deeper Markan logic should lead the community to recognize that authentic witness to God's love and healing for all can take place through the synagogue as surely as through an unknown exorcist.

Through a frightening series of images, vv. 42–48 stress the importance of not interfering with the ministries of unknown exorcists. The millstone is an image of judgment (see, e.g., Judg. 9:53; 2 Sam. 22:21; Rev. 18:21; *b. Qiddushin* 29b). If the disciples (and the Markan church) inhibit such exorcists, they face eternal condemnation in hell (a place of fiery punishment, 9:44, 48; cf. *1 Enoch* 10:13; 18:9–16; 48:8–10; 90:24–27; *2 Bar.* 59:5–12; 85:13) after the apocalyptic judgment.

To avoid such a fate, Mark appears to prescribe cutting off an offending hand or foot, or plucking out an eye (vv. 43–48). However, the Jewish community did not advocate self-mutilation. This language figuratively urges the community to take steps to remain faithful. Mark's admonition recalls a Jewish mother and her seven children who were tempted by a tyrant, the Gentile oppressor Antiochus IV Epiphanes, to give up their commitment to Judaism or face torture. When the seven youths refused to abandon Judaism, they were tortured. Some were dismembered (4 Macc. 8:1–14:10; cf. 2 Macc. 7:1–42). The mother commended their faithfulness and endurance and declared that they were "gathered together into the [immortal] chorus" of the ancestors. As the martyrs were disciplined in their faithfulness, so must the Markan community be.

Verses 49–50 recollect the use of salt to speak of the covenant (see, e.g., Lev. 2:13; Num. 18:19; 2 Chr. 13:5) and fire to speak of the suffering of the tribulation. The covenantal promises will come to fulfillment through the apocalypse. In the last days, the salt will lose its saltiness, that is, the fire of difficulty will tempt the disciples to unfaithfulness. How can they respond? (How can they season it?) By having salt among themselves and being at peace—that is, by remembering that God is at work to complete the divine promises. While many Christians today do not think that we are living in the last days, a preacher can still commend an aspect of Mark's deeper witness. God is always working in the community even when its witness brings it into a fire of difficulty.

Proper 22 [27]/Year B

Mark 10:2–16

When Mark says the Pharisees "test" (*peirazō*) Jesus, we remember that Satan tested or tempted Jesus in the wilderness (First Sunday in Lent/Year B). The question of the Pharisees in 10:2 is, then, a question born of Satan.

In v. 2, Mark pictures the Pharisees as theologically hostile (*peirazō* makes it clear that they are possessed). Although adultery violates Exod. 20:14 and Deut. 5:18, Judaism provided for a husband to divorce the wife (Deut. 24:1–4). Adultery was so disruptive of household and community that the penalty for it was death (Lev. 20:10; Deut. 2:22). In Jesus' time, the death penalty was seldom, if ever, enforced for adultery. Also in this time, Jews debated the grounds for divorce. Shammai held that divorce was permissible only for sexual infidelity. Hillel claimed that divorce was possible for a wide range of reasons, for example, inability to bear children, violation of religious duty, or failure to perform household tasks. Eventually in Judaism, divorce became a woman's right.

In Mark 10:5, Jesus claims that the provision for divorce was a concession to "your hardness of heart," thus suggesting that Jews were as obdurate as Pharaoh. This "hardness of heart" is the inability to learn to live with one's partner. For Mark, hardness of heart and divorce are characteristic of the old, broken age.

The Markan Jesus bypasses Deut. 24:1–4, and in 10:6–9 instead offers a position based on Gen. 1:27 and 2:24. In so doing, Mark operates out of the apocalyptic worldview that the end-times (the realm of God) will be like the beginning time (existence as it was at the time of creation, in Eden). In the prefall world, divorce was not necessary because relationships manifested fully the characteristics that God intended. Similarly, the Markan Jesus claims that the nascent presence of the realm of God creates conditions for the relationship between husbands and wives that make divorce unnecessary.

Mark 9:10–12 is stark. The man or woman who divorces is still married to the former partner. Since divorce is not allowed, a man or woman who has sex with a new spouse commits adultery. The early church soon regarded Mark's position as too difficult, as evidenced by Matthew's allowing divorce for unchastity (Matt. 5:32).

Christians today sometimes think that divorce was strictly a male prerogative in Jewish antiquity. While it was easier for a male to get a divorce, Judaism provided a legal procedure whereby the husband would be required to give the wife a bill of divorce (cf. *m. Nedarim* 11:12; *Ketubbot* 5:5; 7:2–5, 10).

The main themes of Mark 10:13–16 came to expression in 9:33–37, which we considered in connection with Proper 20/Year B.

With respect to divorce, we believe that Judaism shows greater wisdom than does Mark. Mark's prohibition is based on the assumption that the present age is quickly ending and that the prolepsis of the realm of God creates conditions in which divorce is no longer necessary. However, the apocalypse has not occurred. While some people live proleptically in marital relationships that have qualities of the new world, many do not. To be sure, divorce should never be simply a matter of convenience, and the dissolution of a once promising relationship that is beyond repair is cause for regret. Nonetheless, in the present world, people cannot always soften their hearts to learn to live together. Divorce may offer them renewed life. Fortunately, most Christian communities today live in this latter way.

Proper 23 [28]/Year B

Mark 10:17–31

Although Christians commonly speak of "the rich young ruler," this figure is not described with all three of those characteristics in any one Gospel. In Mark, we should speak simply of the "rich man" who wants to know how to inherit "eternal life," that is, to be part of the everlasting community in the realm of God (10:17). Note that the rich man asks the question in the first person singular: "What must *I* do to inherit eternal life?" Although he lives in a time and place where poverty was rife, he focuses on his own salvation.

While Jesus' initial reply, "Why do you call me good?" sometimes puzzles Christians, it derives from the Jewish notion of goodness as a covenantal quality of life as God intends. God originates and sustains this good life (see, e.g., Gen. 1:4, 10, 12, etc.; Ps. 34:8; 106:1; 107:1). Jesus thus makes a thoroughly Jewish statement, saying, in essence, "Why do you speak as if I am the source of the good life? Only God is the source of this life." The coming realm of God is the ultimate good; Jesus is its agent.

Although Jesus' love for people is a staple theme of Christian preaching, this passage is the only one in the Synoptic Gospels explicitly stating such love. Given some Christians' claim that Jesus exercised a preferential option for the poor, it is worth noting.

The rich man is not evil to the core; he has followed the commandments (10:19). But apocalyptic theologians, such as Mark, regarded the commandments as guidance for life in the old, broken age. They also regarded the accumulation of wealth as an activity that belonged to that broken age. In the broken age, people needed to accumulate resources to survive. But Mark and other apocalyptists held that in such conditions wealth could become an idol. Jesus recognizes that the rich man has followed the commandments, but tells him to adapt his behavior to the coming and present reign of God.

As we are reminded by Luke 6:29, "Blessed are you who are poor, for yours is the kingdom of God" (cf. Matt. 5:3). Apocalyptic theologians believed that God would provide abundantly for the poor in the new age, often by communal sharing. A good example is the Qumran community, whose members turned over all they had to the community as a sign of trust in God. The whole community lived from a common fund of material resources.

Jesus instructs the rich man to do something similar—to sell his wealth and put it in the service of the poor, confident that God will provide for him. He must turn away from self-centeredness and turn toward the community.

Mark expected the apocalypse to happen soon, and so believed that the state of voluntary poverty would be short (Mark 9:1). Further, a short-term impoverished witness (based on trust in God) would lead to long-term resources in the realm of God (10:28–31; cf. 2 Esd. 7:88–99).

Ironically, the rich man's loyalty to the limited wealth of this world denied him access to the unlimited resources of the next.

Mark twice says that the wealthy find it difficult to enter the realm of God (10:23–24). Some Christians soften v. 25 by postulating a tiny gate ("the eye of the needle") through which a camel could painfully enter, but no such gate existed. This saying means what it says, although God graciously makes it possible for even the wealthy to be welcomed into the divine realm (v. 27). When thinking of God opening the eye of the needle for people to enter, Mark echoes similar passages in other Jewish literature (e.g., *b. Berakhot* 55b; *b. Bava Metzi'a* 38b).

Few Christians today think the world is about to end. If we give away everything, we are likely to become a burden to the world we seek to serve. Nonetheless, we should use our resources to witness to God's love for all and God's will for justice for all. The preacher can encourage the wealthy to see that clinging to wealth can prevent them from experiencing the fullness of the good life. Living with less, in the Jewish mode of living for the sake of others, can mean living more.

Proper 24 [29]/Year B

Mark 10:35–45

When James and John ask the question in 10:35 in language similar to Herod's in 6:22, we recognize that the same dynamics of the corrupt world represented by Herod are at work among the disciples. These disciples ask for seats on the right and the left in glory—the final manifestation of the realm of God—seats belonging to vice-rulers on either side of the throne of the ruler of that realm. Behind this question is the idea that the eschatological world would have a structure of governance similar to that of the present world. James and John assume that power will be exercised (and would bring the same personal benefits and honor) in the new age as in Herod's old-world court.

The cup (vv. 38–39) represents suffering that results from judgment on the wicked (see, e.g., Ps. 11:6; 75:8; Isa. 51:17; Jer. 25:15). Jesus and the disciples suffer not because *they* are evil. Rather, they suffer at the hands of the wicked, and their pain shows that God's judgment is about to fall on the wicked at the apocalypse. As Jon Berquist points out, this judgment removes the power of evil to make way for life as God intends.[27] Similarly, Mark's use of "baptism" echoes the reference of that word to drowning or perishing. In view of John the Baptist preparing people by baptism for the realm of God, the figurative baptism (death) of Jesus and the disciples is a part of the movement through the suffering of the tribulation to the final realization of God's realm.

James and John's request disrupts the community of the disciples (v. 41) and would have perpetuated qualities of Gentile rule. Gentile rulers, without knowing God's will for people to live in covenant, "lord it over" and "have power over" the populace, that is, they brutally control or exploit people to further their own arbitrary power. Jewish writers frequently describe Gentile rulers as tyrants (e.g., Josephus, *Wars of the Jews* 4.166; *Antiquities* 1.114; 4 Macc. 1:11). Herod (though partly of Jewish legacy, he worked for the Romans) and Pilate typify Gentile rule. The disciples are not to imitate Gentiles but to initiate Gentiles into the divine realm (Mark 13:10).

In the realm of God, the disciples are to lead by serving one another. In antiquity, the servant (*diakonos*, v. 43) and the slave (*doulos*, v. 44) served the needs or purposes of another. These multivalent images further call to mind Israel as the servant of God's purposes for all people (including Gentiles) to know God's will (see, e.g., Isa. 42:1–7). According to vv. 43–44, the disciples should serve the purposes of the divine realm.

Verse 45 offers theological grounding for the transformed understanding of leadership. Jesus came to serve the divine purposes, not to exploit, and to be a ransom for many. The term "many" probably refers to all (e.g., 2 Esd. 8:3) and has in mind the great reunion of Jewish and Gentile peoples in the realm of God.

In the first century, a slave or prisoner of war was often freed by means of a *lutron* (here translated "ransom"). Such occurrences gave rise to using *lutron* (and some of its cognates, e.g., *lutrōsis*, Isa. 63:4 LXX) as shorthand for God's redemptive work. Given this background and Mark's apocalyptic worldview that sees the liberation of the world as God's aim, it seems best to understand ransom not in terms of complicated sacrificial theory but as a figure for Jesus' life and death as a part of the means whereby God frees the world from Satan, the demons, sin, and other things that distort the divine purposes. The world, now enslaved, is en route to freedom via the apocalypse.

Proper 25 [30]/Year B

Mark 10:46–52

To understand the reading for today, we need to return to Mark 1:1–8:26. Mark 1:1–8:21 teaches that the final manifestation of the realm of God is

near, and interprets miracles and other aspects of Jesus' ministry as pro-
lepses of that realm. However, an essential element of the story is missing: the suffering (including the death) of Jesus and the suffering of the
disciples.

At one level, the healing at Bethsaida is a prolepsis of the divine realm.
Blind people, such as Bartimaeus in 10:46, were often reduced to begging.
They frequently sat along the road in rags with flies eating the pus running from their eyes. Many Jewish writers anticipate that their eyes would
be opened in the realm of God (e.g., Isa. 29:18; 35:5–7). At another level,
however, blindness is sometimes used figuratively of theological imperceptivity. Those who do not understand God are blind (see, e.g., Isa. 43:8;
56:10; 59:9–10); the saved see aright (see, e.g., Isa. 52:10; 59:11, 16; *Ahiqar*
2:48; *Testament of Gad* 5:6–7). The story thus speaks figuratively of theological perception.

The anonymous blind man in Mark 8:22–26 came to sight in stages.
Initially, he could see only dimly; with the second touch he could see
clearly. Christian bewilderment over why a second touch was required
misses Mark's point. This story figuratively summarizes the limited grasp
of the disciples to this point in the Second Gospel. Like the person at
Bethsaida, they have partial awareness of the realm of God (they know it
is coming and see its signs), but their vision is hazy.

The second touch that the disciples need begins in 8:27–9:8 with the
news that the coming of the realm of God includes suffering. Mark
9:9–10:45 portrays the disciples continuing to misunderstand the coming
of the realm, thus demonstrating that the second touch is not yet complete and will be so only at the apocalypse (Mark 16:7).

Bartimaeus's healing confirms, in narrative form, that the eyes of the
disciples can be opened and that their theological insight will be restored.
Bartimaeus's cry, "Have mercy on me," is from the Greek *eleō*, often used
in the Septuagint to render the Hebrew *hesed*, God's steadfast love or
covenantal loyalty. Bartimaeus seeks not just mercy (or pity) but a sign of
hesed and to be welcomed into the covenantal community. Divine *hesed* is
one of the primary qualities of the realm of God.

When Jesus asks Bartimaeus in 10:51 much the same question that he
had asked the disciples in 10:36, the reader contrasts the disciples'
response ("Grant for us to sit") with Bartimaeus's ("Let me see again") and
hears in the beggar's response a reference to eyesight as well as to theological perception and the desire to be in the realm of God.

Verse 52 points the way for disciples, then and now, who yet fail to
understand faith, that is, continued trust in Jesus and Jesus' interpreta-

tion of the realm of God. As noted on the Third Sunday after the Epiphany/Year B, the verb "follow" (*akolutheō*) is a technical term for discipleship—living now in the power of the future divine realm and its values.

That Jesus heals Bartimaeus by word alone—and not by touch—is significant as it indicates that the risen Jesus can restore the disciples (and the church) and prepare them for other encounters "on the way." The latter phrase appeared in 4:15 to indicate that Satan seeks repeatedly to mislead those on the way of discipleship (cf. 8:27–33). The *hesed* shown to Bartimaeus can preserve the church through such difficulties and bring us into the realm of God.

Proper 26 [31]/Year B

Mark 12:28–34

In this reading about the question "Which commandment is the first of all?" Jesus is depicted as a traditional Jew. This is also one of the rare conversations in Mark between Jesus and a representative of an official Jewish group that is not a conflict story but a typical Jewish conversation between a student who brings a question and a teacher who answers it.

The first commandment, Jesus says, is: "Hear, O Israel: the Lord our God, the Lord is one; you shall love the Lord your God with all your heart, and with all your soul, and with all your mind, and with all your strength" (v. 30). This is straight from the scriptures of Israel. Second Kings says of King Josiah that he "turned to the LORD with all his heart, with all his soul, and with all his might, according to all the law of Moses" (23:25). Jesus' quote is the Shema from Deut. 6:4–5: "Hear, O Israel, the LORD is our God, the LORD alone. You shall love the LORD your God with all your heart, and with all your soul, and with all your might." "You shall love the Lord your God" is part of Jewish daily prayer and of every synagogue service. Interestingly, in the Second Testament there are remarkably few references to our love for God (seven in all). Its stress is on knowing, obeying, and believing God.

Mark adds "with all your mind" to these quotations from Scripture. For Mark's community, which contained many Gentiles, it was important to internalize the understanding that the God of Jesus Christ is the one and only God.

"The second," says Jesus, "is this, 'You shall love your neighbor as yourself.' There is no other commandment greater than these" (v. 31). This is from Lev. 19:18b: "You shall love your neighbor as yourself." Jesus' answer to the question of which commandment is first of all is to cite two commandments, putting them together, in effect, as one. Neither may be downplayed in preference to the other. Combining the two was already done in the *Testament of Dan* 5:3. To love God is to love the neighbor and vice versa. Rabbi Akiba declared love of the neighbor "the greatest principle in the Torah" (*Sifra Leviticus* 19.18). The *Sayings of the Sages* (*m. Avot*, Neusner, *Torah from Our Sages*) reports that Rabbi Akiba said, "Precious is the human being, who was created in the image [of God]" (3:14).

The scribe responds, "You are right, Teacher" (v. 32), then reiterates Jesus' teaching. The scribe and Jesus exhibit friendly attitudes toward each other. When Matthew and Luke retell this story, however, they turn the scribe into a lawyer (Luke) and a lawyer who is also a Pharisee (Matthew). In each case, they ask the question in order to "test" Jesus. In these differences we can see that the further removed the Gospels are in time from Jesus, the more they introduce hostility into the story.

It was customary in Second Temple Judaism to concentrate the commandments of Scripture into a handful to make them easier to understand and to stress that all the commandments are ways of living out the ones that are basic. Philo of Alexandria, a first-century Jew, reduced the commandments to the same two that we find in today's reading. Hillel, a Jerusalem sage and older contemporary of Jesus, reduced them to one: "What is hateful to you do not do to your fellow; that is the whole Law; all the rest is its explanation; go and learn" (*b. Shabbat* 31a). Earlier than Mark, Paul had done the same: "The one who loves another has fulfilled the law. . . . Love is the fulfilling of the law" (Rom. 13:8, 10).

Proper 27 [32]/Year B

Mark 12:38–44

Each characteristic of the scribes that Mark names in 12:38–40 caricatures them as epitomizing old-age attitudes of being self-impressed and self-serving, all in an effort to fortify their social standing, honor, and power. With the exception of priests and others in select positions of honor, men wore a relatively short garment similar to a smock, their long robes saved for worship or other special occasions. Mark, however, portrays the scribes as wearing such robes every day, even in the marketplace, out of concern for their self-image. To be greeted with respect was to be acknowledged as a social superior. The choice seats in the synagogue were reserved for recognized teachers and dignitaries such as scribes. Seating at banquets, particularly Roman banquets, reflected social standing: Those with high position had "places of honor," with other persons seated in descending order of rank.[28] Mark obviously wants the reader to think that the scribes exhibited these attitudes. They are also accused of cheating widows out of their houses and praying overly long, not as acts of devotion but to impress others. This caricature represents the antithesis of the social world of the realm of God (Mark 9:33–37; 10:41–45). Consequently, the scribes will receive the "greater condemnation."

Mark 12:41–44 illustrates the corruption of the scribes. While Christians have usually interpreted the woman in these verses as a model whose commitment is to be emulated, scholars increasingly think that Mark intends to portray the temple in the most negative light: The woman feels compelled to bankrupt herself in order to pay her temple tax. This perspective is consistent with the fact that Mark always portrays the temple and its rulers in a negative light (11:1, 15–16, 27; 13:1–3; 14:49, 58; 15:38). The woman must sell her house to get some cash on which to live. The scribes could then buy her house, further reducing her resources. According to Mark, they "devour" her house. Mark thus pictures the scribes as spurning one of the most important dimensions of Jewish life: care for widows and others who are vulnerable (see, e.g., Deut. 10:18; 14:29; 24:17–21; 26:12; 27:19; Ps. 68:5; 146:9; Jer. 49:11; Amos 2:8). The prophets announce that the community will fall when it fails to maintain its covenant with widows (see, e.g., Isa. 1:23; 10:2; Jer. 15:8; Ezek. 22:7; Mal. 3:5).

Mark views those in league with the leaders of Israel as possessed by Satan (see Palm Sunday or Passion Sunday/Year B) and represents the temple crowd as extorting this widow by taking all she has. Not surprisingly, Mark later declares the temple bankrupt (15:38). By the time Mark wrote, the temple was destroyed, thus confirming the "greater condemnation" of 12:40.

In one respect, this text raises searching questions for today's congregations. Do we use leadership in the religious community for self-service? Do our religious communities extort and abuse the very persons they are to serve?

In another respect, the preacher must criticize the text theologically. One reason that preachers are drawn to such caricatures of Jewish leaders is that we encounter Christians today who resemble them. To help

Christians avoid such distortions, preachers sometimes make an analogy between Jewish officials in the text and today's self-impressed Christians. While the pastoral concern is worthy, this tack misrepresents Judaism in antiquity, leaves the impression that the Jewish community today is also legalistic and believes in works righteousness, and feeds one of the impulses it is supposed to undercut by suggesting that Christians are superior to Jewish people in the same way that the outmoded caricature portrays scribes as thinking themselves superior to others.

Instead, the preacher can name the caricature as a misrepresentation of Jewish life. The preacher can use the norms of the gospel (God's unconditional love for all and God's will for justice for all) to help wooden, legalistic, works-righteous Christians recognize their distortion, and to call the attention of the community to resources for renewal in the gospel itself.

Proper 28 [33]/Year B

Mark 13:1–8

By Mark's time, the temple had been destroyed (13:2). Mark 13 interprets the fall of the temple and subsequent social turmoil as the tribulation preceding the apocalypse (vv. 3–4; cf. First Sunday of Advent/Year B). Mark's pastoral purpose is to encourage the community to endure suffering (v. 13b) while continuing in witness (vv. 33–37).

Most scholars think that vv. 5–13, 21–22, allude to events taking place in Mark's world. Verses 5–6 and 21–22 suggest that the community is struggling to identify God's agent(s) in the movement toward apocalypse. The wars and rumors of wars in vv. 6–7a refer to the Roman military campaign in Palestine and to the effect of the continuing Roman presence. Mark, with other apocalyptic writers, believed that nature itself will be disturbed as the apocalypse draws near (v. 7b), and that the cosmic cataclysm will include destruction of the present creation so that it can be replaced by the new world of the realm of God (13:24–25). Mark uses a feminine image, traditional in apocalyptic, to say that these things happening in the Markan world are "but the beginning of the birth pangs," the tribulation and suffering that will climax in the apocalypse.

According to vv. 9–13, members of Mark's community face punishment from Jewish authorities (councils—probably local Jewish courts—and synagogues) as well as from governors and monarchs appointed by Rome. Romans may have heard the announcement of the kingship of God as a threat to Caesar. The reference to "beaten in synagogues" (v. 9) refers to the discipline that the synagogue could administer by lashing. It is not clear whether such discipline actually took place, or if it did, why. In v. 10, Mark summarizes the mission of the community as inviting Gentiles ("all nations") into the divine realm. Perhaps Mark's community was receiving Gentiles into the eschatological community without conversion to Judaism. On Jewish families breaking apart in response to the Markan mission, see Proper 5/Year B, and Proper 15/Year C.

Mark advises the community to flee Jerusalem for refuge in the mountains when the Romans defame the temple (v. 14). Some scholars think that Mark uses "mountains" metaphorically for God sustaining the community as God sustained some of Israel's leaders in the mountains (vv. 14–16), but even there, circumstances will be difficult (vv. 17–20). Although it will be tempted to follow false messiahs, the community can distinguish them from Jesus because Jesus will return apocalyptically (On 13:24–27, see First Sunday of Advent/Year B.)

Such intense suffering signals that the great transformation is near just as changes in the fig tree signal the coming of summer (vv. 28–31). While unable to calculate the time of the end, the community can be aware of its relative nearness and prepare for it by doing what Jesus has commanded. That is what it means to "Watch!" (vv. 32–37).

While today's preacher may not believe that the world is going to end soon, this text reminds us to interpret the signs of our times in a way that is as theologically serious as Mark's attempt was in the first century. One such sign is in the growing rapprochement between the church and the synagogue. We do not know whether Jewish leaders harassed Mark's community as described in vv. 9–13. We do know that in relatively few years, Christians turned many Jews over to councils, beat them, and worse. Instead of lamenting how the ancient Jewish community persecuted our ancestors, today's church is better advised to respond to the signs of rapprochement by seeking opportunities for *mutual* witness.

Proper 29 [34]/Year B

John 18:33–37

In John's passion narrative, these four verses provide John's account of Jesus' appearance before Pontius Pilate, the Roman procurator, in John's long story of Jesus and Pilate (18:28–19:16). John's account of the suffering and crucifixion of Jesus differs from that of the other Gospels in significant ways. Whereas they have their own versions of Jesus' trial before

the council, or Sanhedrin, John has no such account (the council is mentioned once in 11:47–53, but Jesus is not put on trial before it). In Mark,
the earliest Gospel, Jesus is crucified by the Roman soldiers (15:16–20).
In John, Pilate hands Jesus over to "the Jews" to be crucified (19:12–16).
Whereas John may be historically more accurate on the lack of a trial
before the council, Mark is more accurate on who did the crucifying,
because crucifixion was a form of execution that Rome reserved to itself.

Jesus' appearance before Pilate takes place in "the headquarters," or
praetorium. The headquarters of the Praetorian Guards and the Roman
Tenth Legion was the Fortress Antonia, adjacent to the temple, where the
Tenth Legion stayed while Pilate was in Rome. Here Pilate asks Jesus the
question, "Are you the King of the Jews?" (v. 33). All four Gospels say that
Pilate asked this question (Matt. 27:11; Mark 15:2; Luke 23:3).

Jesus' answer in John, however, differs from that of the Synoptics. It is
not now "You have said so," but a counterquestion: "Do you ask this on
your own, or did others tell you about me?" (18:34). Pilate's reply is a
rebuff: "I am not a Jew, am I? Your own nation and the chief priests have
handed you over to me. What have you done?" (v. 35). Notably, the Pharisees' last appearance in John was in 18:3. Thereafter, they drop out of the
story and are not involved in the crucifixion. The significance of Pilate's
"I am not a Jew" statement is that he is impatient with Jewish discussions
of messiah. What he wants to know is whether Jesus is a king, that is, a
threat to Roman kingship and rule.

Jesus responds by talking not about himself but by talking about his
kingdom and its nature: "My kingdom is not from this world" (v. 36). The
NRSV translation improves upon the RSV's "My kingship is not *of* this
world." Jesus' kingdom is from God, not from the world. But it is very
much of and in the world, and its aim is to bring about a world different
from the world that we know, a world of rule by might, by armies, by
oppression and exploitation. It is a rule characterized, instead, by a mutual
abiding in love. It is not *from* this world, but it would *transform* this world.
Jesus repeats the point later: "As it is, my kingdom is not from here" (v.
36). The term "kingdom" has inescapable references to place, people, and
God; they do not disappear in John. In John, Jesus had spoken of the kingdom (*basileia*) only once before—to Nicodemus (3:3–5).

This is consistent with Jesus' teaching of God's gracious gift to him of
everything that he has throughout the Gospel—it all comes "from" God,
as does he. In this passage, remarkably, Jesus graciously offers his teaching of the truth to Pilate. It is, however, lost on Pilate, sailing completely
over his head. Pilate neither understood nor had any patience with the

tender forces that work gently and in love. Philo of Alexandria, contemporary with Jesus, described Pilate as known for "a vindictive and furious temper." Philo speaks derisively of "the briberies, the insults, the robberies, the outrages and . . . executions without trial constantly repeated, the ceaseless and supremely grievous cruelty" characteristic of Pilate's reign (Philo, *On the Embassy to Gaius* 302–3).

Jesus' kingdom is a radical alternative to Pilate's.

Year C

First Sunday of Advent/Year C

Luke 21:25–36

The Gospel of Mark anticipates an imminent apocalypse. By contrast, the Gospel of Luke and the book of Acts anticipate that the church will live in the present world through a protracted delay in the apocalypse (e.g., Luke 21:9). God has poured out the Holy Spirit to empower the church through the delay (Acts 2:14–29). However, today's reading reminds us that Luke does expect an apocalypse (see also Luke 10:1–23; 12:1–13:9; 16:19–31; 17:20–37; 20:27–40; Acts 1:10–11; 2:17–21; 10:42: 12:49–56; 17:29–31).

Luke 21:5–24 uses stock apocalyptic language to describe social conditions as history draws to a close. Some of the events Jesus predicts have taken place by Luke's time (e.g., the destruction of the temple, vv. 20–22).

Luke 21:25–28 is the climax of the apocalypse. Sun, moon, stars, and other "powers of the heavens will be shaken," that is, destroyed (cf. the First Sunday of Advent/Year B). Luke highlights distress among the nations who are confused by the roaring of the sea and the waves; these nations are the Gentiles. Jewish authors sometimes use the sea, a symbol for chaos, to depict the life of the Gentile world. This remark is a subtle commentary not only on Gentile life generally but on Roman imperial rule: Rome is an agency of chaos and must be replaced for God's realm to be fully manifest.

Jesus is the "Son of Man" whose return is described in the language of Dan. 7:13–14. He comes to redeem and judge.

In vv. 29–31 Jesus compares the situation of the Lukan congregation in history to a person who observes a fig tree beginning to sprout. The fig tree is unusual in that its fruit begins to appear before the leaves. By the time the leaves begin to show, the listeners know, summer is soon to arrive. Jewish authors used figs to speak figuratively of eras of peace akin to the realm of God (e.g. Jer. 24; 1 Kgs. 4:25; Isa. 36:16; Hag. 2:19) and to seasons of judgment and restoration (Jer. 5:17; 8:13; Hos. 2:12; Joel 1:7; Amos 4:9). Listeners would know that the apocalypse, with its peace and judgment, was imminent when they saw signs of cosmic and social collapse. The delay in the apocalyptic transformation is evidently not a long one (vv. 32–33).

In vv. 34–36, Luke offers advice on how to live in preparation for the apocalypse. According to Jewish teaching, inebriation causes community members to lose control of themselves and to be unable to serve God fully (e.g., Tob. 4:5; Sir. 28:8) and so the congregation is to avoid dissipation (bouts of drinking) and drunkenness. Jesus' followers are also to avoid "the worries of this life," an expression Luke uses to refer to accumulating wealth for oneself (e.g., Luke 8:14; 10:41; 12:13–21, 22, 25, 26, 45); people can avoid the worries of this life by using their material resources to support the community, especially the poor (see, e.g., 3:10–14; 16:27–31; 19:1–10; Acts 2:44–47; 4:32–37).

With other Jewish theologians, Luke believed the apocalypse would affect "all who live on the face of the whole earth" (v. 35), but prayer would enable the community to withstand the apocalypse and face the judgment of the Son of Man. To Luke, prayer is opening oneself to the working of the realm of God through Jesus (e.g., 11:1–4; 22:40–46).

This passage is part of a first-century C.E. Jewish discussion. Many Jews expected an apocalypse to end the current age and to launch the divine realm. Luke believed that God would bring about this transformation through the return of Jesus. To Luke, belief in the second coming of Jesus expresses faith that the God of Israel will bring about the divine realm throughout the earth.

Second Sunday of Advent/Year C

Luke 1:68–79

Although the lectionary appoints Luke 1:68–79 for liturgical use, it is a key text for preaching. The actual Gospel lection for this Sunday is Luke 3:1–6, which we discuss in conjunction with Luke 3:7–18 (next week).

The first chapter of the Gospel of Luke interprets the God of Israel acting through John the Baptist, who baptized Jesus. This picture portrays a leading figure in Judaism, a priest, as authorizing the ministry of John, and, hence, the ministry of Jesus and the church. It presents that mission in unbroken continuity with Judaism.

Luke 1:68–79 (sometimes called the "benedictus" from the Latin for "blessing") has the feel of the Septuagint, thus suggesting that the story of John, Jesus, and the church continues the narrative of Israel (see, e.g., 1 Sam. 25:32; 1 Kgs. 1:48; Ps. 41:13; 72:18; 106:4). Luke models this text on the Jewish *berakah*, a prayer of blessing that begins by blessing God, then summarizing God's gracious acts that prompt the blessing. Both the Mishnah and the Talmud indicate that *berakah* is at the core of Judaism by beginning with tractates (booklets) called *Berakhot*.

The first part of the *berakah* (vv. 68–73) asserts that God, who has been faithful throughout Israel's history, is now demonstrating that faithfulness again. The term "looked favorably upon" (*episkeptomai*, v. 68) refers to a gracious divine visitation that brings salvation (see, e.g., Gen. 21:1; Exod. 3:16; 4:31; Sir. 46:14). The means of redemption is a "mighty savior" whom God will send from the house of God's servant David (v. 69). The translation "mighty savior" obscures the overt Jewish overtones in the Greek that would be more literally rendered "horn of salvation"—an idiom for God acting in providence for Israel (2 Sam. 22:3; Ps. 18:2).

Through the prophets, God has promised salvation (vv. 70–71). By Luke's time, many Jews believed that "salvation" would result from an apocalypse and would consist of the reign of God instantiated in every situation (see First Sunday of Advent/Year C). Listeners are to understand that the new age revealed through Jesus Christ (and attested by the church) is the means whereby God shows mercy to the ancestors and remembers the covenant (v. 72). In the Septuagint, *eleos* ("mercy") often translates the Hebrew *hesed*—steadfast love, trustworthiness, and covenantal loyalty.

Luke makes a significant move in vv. 73–75 by recalling God's promise of mercy and covenant to Abraham and Sarah, a promise that God was to bless all peoples (including Gentiles) through them and their descendants (Gen. 12:1–3; 15:1–21; 17:1–27; cf. Luke 1:55; Acts 3:25). For Luke, the church (particularly the Gentile mission) demonstrates that God keeps divine promises.

The role of John the Baptist in the manifestation of salvation is explained in 1:76–79. In v. 76, Luke echoes Mal. 3:1 to describe John's role as eschatological prophet, that is, one who announces that God is drawing the present epoch to a close and that people need to prepare for the apocalypse and life in the realm of God. That is what it means to "give knowledge of salvation." In 3:1–18, Luke highlights John's role as calling people to repentance and immersion as proper responses to the knowledge of salvation.

The close of the *berakah*, vv. 78–79, underscores that the divine work through John and Jesus is an expression of "the tender mercy" (*eleos*) of the God of Israel. The "dawn from on high" that will dispel darkness (Ps. 107:10) and supply light is the revelation of salvation through Jesus from birth (Luke 2:8–20) through apocalyptic return (21:25–28).

Third Sunday of Advent/Year C

Luke 3:1–18

The references to the emperor, Pilate, Herod, and Lysanias in Luke 3:1–2 do more than date the ministry of John the Baptist. They tell us that Jewish life took place under a repressive Roman regime that was so pervasive that even high priests, such as Annas and Caiaphas, were coopted by it. John announces that God is working toward a better world order (the divine realm) than the one represented by Rome.

John is an eschatological prophet whose central theme is to call people to repent in preparation for the final manifestation of the realm of God that will follow an apocalypse. Through baptism (which is related to Jewish water rites of initiation and cleansing), John gathers the repentant into a community awaiting the eschaton (v. 3). Sin is a power of the old age. To "forgive" (*aphiēmi*) is to "release," and John's baptism assures baptisands that they are released from sin and freed for life in the new world.

From the perspective of apocalyptic theologians, Isa. 40:3–5 anticipates the apocalyptic transformation, which embraces Gentiles ("all flesh").

In vv. 7–9, the targets of John's criticism are Jews. When John calls them "a brood of vipers," he means they are associated with the snake of Gen. 3:1–7 (whom some apocalyptists took to be Satan). As prophet, John advises the crowd to flee the wrath to come by "bearing fruits worthy of repentance," that is, to turn away from sin and toward God in a life that embodies divine aims. Repentance is urgent: The ax is at the root of the tree, that is, the apocalyptic separation is already underway.

John's admonition to the crowd not to presume that they are children of Abraham and Sarah evokes the Jewish premise that those with whom

God graciously cuts covenant must live covenantally. God can even raise Gentiles to be children of Abraham and Sarah.

The crowd models how readers should respond to the call to repent by asking, "What then should we do?" (3:10). The crowd lives in covenant by providing for the needs of *all* in the community. People should share coats and food; in antiquity a coat was not only for dress but was also for warmth at night. Tax collectors are not to gouge people but are to collect only the amount of money prescribed. Soldiers (likely Jewish mercenaries) are not to abuse their power by extortion, threat, or false accusation.

Today's Christian is often impatient with the fact that Luke (through John) allows the crowd to accommodate itself to the Roman occupation, to poverty and other evils, and does not incite the audience to stringent resistance or revolution. However, the undertones of this passage imply that God is on the verge of effecting cosmic systemic change through the apocalypse. In the meantime, the community is to live without being engulfed by the false values of the present and by witnessing to the divine will by keeping covenant with one another.

While John is a significant prophet, the divine realm does not come through him (vv. 15–18). Jesus baptizes with the Holy Spirit and with fire (v. 16; cf. Acts 2:1–21) and is the eschatological judge (v. 17). For Luke, the Spirit brings the realm of God to expression after Jesus' ascension. This passage prompts listeners to recognize that Christian baptism welcomes people into an eschatological community in which (through the Spirit) they live in the power of the divine realm. Repentance is the first step toward becoming a part of this group.

Fourth Sunday of Advent/Year C

Luke 1:39–55

In Luke 1, Elizabeth and Mary welcome angels who announce the pregnancies of Elizabeth and Mary. The women welcome these messages from heaven, whereas Zechariah and Joseph earlier resist. Luke thus presages a theme in the Gospel and Acts: God is restoring women (after Gen. 3, women had limited life options and were subordinate to men) to egalitarianism more like in Gen. 1–2. Christians sometimes interpret this change for women as liberation from Jewish restriction. However, Judaism is the *source* for the hope of liberation. Many Jewish people expected the end time to be similar to the beginning time of Gen. 1–2.

In Luke 1:39–45, the women act out the restoration by meeting without males. Elizabeth—and the activity in her womb—teaches the relationship of Jesus and John.

Mary's song, vv. 46b–55, is similar to the song of Hannah in 1 Sam. 2:1–10. Both songs sound like psalms. Hannah gave thanks for a change in her circumstance, from barrenness to pregnancy, the redemption of the lowly and oppressed. Mary similarly magnifies God because through her pregnancy the world is changing from old age to new, the realm of God. Mary's song echoes many psalms that celebrate victories of God. Such similarities indicate that the story of Jesus carries forward the story of Israel.

This peasant woman foreshadows leading themes in Luke and Acts. Mary models trust and witness by accepting Jesus' birth (1:38) and by celebrating the eschatological work of God, barely underway in her womb, as if that work is complete. Today's readers are also to do these things.

In vv. 46b–50, Mary speaks not only of her own experience but as a representative of God's redemptive presence. What God does for Mary, God will do for all like her. Mary's song begins like a *berakah* (see Second Sunday of Advent/Year C): with thanks for God's redemption (vv. 46–47). The ministry of Jesus exemplifies that work.

As in the First Testament, God acts benevolently for those in "an afflicted state" (a better rendering of "lowly," *tapeinos*). Future generations call Mary blessed because she was part of birthing the eschatological world (v. 48). God is the "Mighty One" who does "great [redemptive] things," an expression that implicitly contrasts God with the repressive but limited Caesar (v. 49). God's mercy is God's covenant faithfulness. Caesar may rule now, but God's trustworthiness has been proven for generations (v. 50).

In the eschatological world, God's strength restores divine purposes in the world (v. 51; see also Luke 7:1–9; 13:10–17; Acts 3:1–10; 19:1–22). In the process, God "scatters the proud," condemning the arrogant as in Luke 5:21–22; 6:8; 13:14; 14:1; and 18:9. However, condemnation is not the last word, for Luke invites the powerful to repent and join the movement toward the divine realm (e.g., Luke 3:10–14; 19:1–10; Acts 3:17–26; 26:24–32) to avoid condemnation.

God breaks the power of oppressive persons and systems while lifting the afflicted (v. 52). God exhibits fidelity by providing for the hungry while the rich become hungry because they ignored their responsibility to the poor (v. 53; see also Luke 12:13–21; Acts 5:1–11). God intends for members of the community to share their material resources with one another so that all are blessed (see, e.g., Luke 8:1–3; 16:19–31; Acts 2:42–47; 4:32–37).

Through Jesus, God continues to be faithful (show mercy) to Israel (v. 54). The mention of Abraham and Sarah (v. 55) reminds the reader that God's promise to them includes a promise to bless Gentiles (Gen. 12:1–3), a pledge that God fulfills in Acts.

Christmas Day/Year C

Luke 2:1–20

Jesus was born at the time of a registration decreed by the Roman emperor Augustus and enforced by Quirinius the Roman governor of Syria, the Roman province that included Palestine. Luke thus calls attention to Roman oppression and its idolatrous, exploitative, violent, and repressive ways. To wit: the registration was not simply to take a census but to determine the population base from which to extract backbreaking taxes.

By placing these details at the beginning of the Gospel, Luke invites listeners to contrast the realm of Augustus with the realm of God as manifest through Jesus and the church. The realm of God embodies fundamental Jewish values: trust in the one true and living God, justice, abundance for all, peace, and community as life in covenant. To be sure, occasional Romans have insight or facilitate the mission of the early community (Luke 7:1–10; 23:4, 14, 22; Acts 21:27–36; 22:22–29; 23:23–35). However, the fact that Rome put both Jesus and Paul to death epitomizes the fact that Rome is fundamentally unjust.

Verses 8–20 continue the motif of contrast. The Romans (along with many other Gentiles) believed that the birth of a new ruler, a "savior," was a divine gift. They described such births in dramatic terms: setting, characters, a public announcement. The birth of Jesus redefines the notion of "savior." The birth takes place in circumstances that appear to be much less than they are. Mary and Joseph are ordinary Jews. The birthplace may be a place for feeding animals or a guest room. While an angel choir announces the birth from heaven, the first people to receive the news are shepherds, not royals.

The birth of Jesus—especially the quality of appearing to be less than it is—is a hermeneutical key for interpreting the manifestation of the realm of God in the stories of Jesus and the early church. Roman glitz leads not to salvation but to destruction. The peasant savior promises abundance, justice, and peace. In this respect, the story of Jesus continues that of Israel, a people who appear to be less than they are. Abram and Sarai looked like a homeless couple, but were agents of God to bless the whole human family. God called politically insignificant Israel to be a light to the nations.

Jesus' birth is for "all people." With many other Jewish folk, Luke believed that Gentiles would come to the God of Israel in the last days, and that Jews and Gentiles would be reunited in the eschatological world. Luke sees God acting in this way through Jesus Christ.

People in antiquity often viewed shepherds with suspicion. They were thought to be untrustworthy, antisocial, and irreligious (see, e.g., Gen. 30:25–43). To be sure, God is sometimes positively described as a shepherd, but the reputation of shepherds prompted Rabbi Jose bar Hanina (ca. 270 C.E.) to puzzle why God would be called a shepherd (*Midrash Psalms* 23:1.2). When the angel takes the news of the savior's birth first to the shepherds, we cannot miss the point: The realm of God reaches out to the shepherds of the world, the disreputable. This emphasis is not new. From early days, Judaism contained the provision for such people to repent and be restored to community. Luke reiterates this theme throughout the Gospel and the Acts (e.g., Luke 3:3, 8; 5:32; 13:3, 5; 15:7, 10; 16:50; 17:3–4; 24:47; Acts 2:38; 3:19; 5:31; 8:22; 11:18; 17:30; 20:21; 26:20).

For commentary on John 1:1–14, please see Christmas Day/Years A, B, and C.

First Sunday after Christmas Day/Year C

Luke 2:41–52

Ancient narratives of significant figures recount youthful incidents that demonstrate the person's insightfulness from earliest days, to show that the remarkable adult life of the figure was, then, not an aberration but the fulfillment of divine promise (e.g., Philo, *On the Life of Moses* 1.21; Josephus, *Antiquities* 2.230; Plutarch, *Alexander* 5; Philostratus, *Apollonius of Tyana* 1.7). Today's text functions similarly in Luke and Acts.

In Luke 2:41, Mary and Joseph are again presented as steadfast Jews; they have been to Jerusalem to celebrate the Passover. Jewish communities regarded ages twelve or thirteen as the end of childhood and the transition toward adult responsibility. (*m. Avot* 5:1, *Berakhot* 24a; *b. Yoma* 82a). Because of huge crowds in Jerusalem and the fact that families often traveled in groups (sharing responsibility for children), Mary and Joseph could easily have lost track of young Jesus (2:43–45).

When they find him, he is sitting with the teachers in the temple—one of the most powerful symbols of Judaism. Sitting was the posture of both teachers and students. Jesus fully participates in the rabbinical conversation, as he is "listening to them and asking them questions" (v. 46). Rabbinical instruction involved both teachers and students advancing ideas and raising questions and counterquestions. The people gathered around Jesus are amazed at his understanding (v. 47), and the crowd's response (including the teachers at the temple) authenticates Jesus as a genuine and recognized interpreter of the traditions of Israel.

Jesus' parents' lack of understanding (vv. 48, 50) points to a theme in Luke–Acts: People close to Jesus do not always grasp his mission. For members of Luke's community who experienced family tension and rejection when they identified with the Jesus movement, this motif is pastoral encouragement. God has created a new household for them (the church).

The familiar "Did you not know that I must be in my Father's house?" could be rendered " . . . must be about my Father's affairs" (v. 49). Both translations make sense. The rendering "house" indicates that Jesus' ministry is legitimated by the temple, while "affairs" calls attention to Jesus manifesting the realm of God ("my father's affairs").

Jesus acts as a Jewish son. The reader would know that God, not Joseph, is Jesus' true father, and that at about age twelve, a son began to take up his father's business. The pericope highlights Jesus' Jewishness in vv. 51 and 52. Although his parents do not fully understand him, he is still obedient (v. 51). The references to growing in wisdom, and in divine and human favor (Greek: *charis* = grace) are Jewish qualities echoed in 1 Sam. 2:21, 26; Prov. 3:5; Sir. 45:1; Josephus, *Antiquities* 2.9,6; 228–231; *m. Avot* 3:1.

Later in the Gospel of Luke and book of Acts, Jesus and the church are in conflict with and criticize some Jewish leaders. However, Luke did not intend to reject Judaism and to establish a new religion, but to enter into a widespread discussion within Judaism in the last third of the first century c.e. regarding how to understand Judaism (and its future) in the wake of the destruction of the temple. Luke's view in this conversation is that the traditions of Judaism point toward the Gentile mission and the apocalyptic return of Jesus for the final manifestation of the realm of God. Today's passage shows that Jesus was raised as an observant Jewish youth and was recognized early as an interpreter of Judaism.

Second Sunday after Christmas Day/Year C

John 1:1–18

Please see the Second Sunday after Christmas/Year A for the commentary on this reading.

Epiphany of the Lord/Year C

Matthew 2:1–12

Please see the Epiphany of the Lord/Years A, B, and C for the commentary on this reading.

First Sunday after the Epiphany/Year C

Baptism of the Lord

Luke 3:15–17, 21–22

The baptism practiced by John and the early Christian communities was derived from Jewish water rites. The Jewish *miqveh* was a cleansing bath (Lev. 11:36); a woman would, for example, immerse in a *miqveh* after childbirth and a male after an emission. Judaism immersed Gentiles for conversion. At Qumran, members immersed as part of becoming a community for the eschatological world. The water does not itself purify or convert; God uses the water to impress purification or welcome on the heart.

According to Luke, John's baptism communicated forgiveness of sin and set people apart as a community for the new world (Third Sunday of Advent/Year C). After Jesus was immersed, he prayed. Prayer is the opening of self or community to the realm of God (see, e.g., Luke 5:16; 6:12; 9:18, 28–29; 11:1; 22:39–44; 23:46; Acts 1:14; 3:1; 6:4; 10:31; 14:23; 22:17; 28:80).

When Jesus was in prayer, God opened the heavens. For Luke, this opening connects this event with heaven's opening at the apocalypse (Isa. 64:1) and bespeaks divine blessing and guidance (e.g., Luke 2:13; 24:51; Acts 1:9–11; 7:55; 10:9–11). This detail tells the reader that the ministry of Jesus is under God's blessing and guidance.

The Holy Spirit descended upon Jesus "in bodily form like a dove." While commentators debate the origin of the symbolic use of the dove, the meaning is clear: The dove represents the Spirit. Perhaps this detail invokes Joel 2:28–32 (the Spirit pouring out in the eschatological age). The reference to bodily form confirms that the Spirit actually enters Jesus. Jesus can thus later give the Spirit as he promised since he is filled with it (Luke 24:49; Acts 1:7; 2:1–21; 10:34–44).

God speaks in 3:22b to interpret the significance of this event. Jews in antiquity valued hearing more than engaging the other senses. Because

God speaks here, the community recognizes 3:22b as unambiguously defining the meaning of the baptism (cf. Exod.19:3; 20:22; Deut. 4:12, 36).

God draws from Ps. 2:7: "You are my son." The second psalm was sung in Israel on the day a monarch was enthroned. God adopts the ruler by speaking these words so that the monarch is then viewed as God's son, that is, heir and representative. Similarly, these words over Jesus indicate that from the baptism onward, Jesus is invested with power to rule as God's representative. Luke–Acts explains the purpose and means of Jesus' sovereignty: to bring about the final manifestation of the divine realm.

The words "my beloved in whom I am well pleased" allude to Isa. 42:1, which describes the servant of Israel witnessing to God's faithfulness and justice. Others resist that witness and cause the servant to suffer. Luke thus shows that Jesus will bring about justice (especially after the apocalypse) by following the path of suffering love.

In Luke–Acts, the baptism of Jesus is a paradigm for the baptism of believers. God assures them of forgiveness of sin. Although heaven does not open over every baptisand, God welcomes them into the community anticipating the eschatological age. Baptism calls the community to witness to God's restoring work and promises that all who are baptized receive the Spirit. At the same time, the baptized life is sometimes one that suffers in its witness to the divine will to restore the world. But baptism promises that even in suffering, the community remembers that God is working through them even as through Jesus.

Second Sunday after the Epiphany/Year C

John 2:1–11

Some traditional interpretations of the story of the wedding at Cana are anti-Jewish. We see this in the claim that the "water jars for the Jewish rites of purification" are empty but that Jesus fills them with the new wine of the eschaton.[29] Preachers should resist falling into this trap. John's Gospel reflects one side of an unhappy split with a synagogue. But John's very unhappiness over this split reflects his deep desire to be part of the synagogue. Like several first-century Jewish groups (Matthew is another), John thought he had the right understanding for how the people Israel should respond to its new situation. Each such group had strained relationships with its rival groups.

Stone vessels were regarded as ritually pure, and their use "flourished in Galilee and Judea from the time of Herod the Great through the first century."[30] Purity or identity practices were a way for Jews to defy Roman rule and keep alive the witness of faith. Jesus defied Roman rule by leading a movement which made it clear that the king (Caesar) was not God, no matter what he claimed. Had Jesus wanted to demonstrate his anti-Judaism, he could have smashed the stone jars or, at least, not used them. But in using them to make wine, he makes it clear, instead, that his wine is pure.

Setting that aside, then, let us turn to the story. It is a wonderful account in which numerous Johannine themes come to expression: the "hour" (2:4), a "sign" (2:11), water (2:7), and the disclosure of Jesus' "glory" (*doxa*). Preachers can have a field day with this.

Jesus' mother starts the action of the story when she says to Jesus, "They have no wine" (2:3). Jesus distances himself from her with the rebuff, "Woman, what concern is that to you and to me?" (v. 4). Mark also reports tension between Jesus and his family (3:31–34). For John, this points out that, like the disciples, Mary does not, at least yet, comprehend Jesus and what he is about. Yet her response is unexpected. She simply says to the servants, "Do whatever he tells you" (2:5). Throughout the rest of the story, they do precisely that.

Here is the major theme of the story: The appropriate, faithful response to Jesus is to put one's trust in his words. Mary and the servants, although uncomprehending, do this. Mary is the first person in John's story to be justified through her faith.

The stone jars were large; each held about twenty-five gallons. Hence, Jesus' miracle created about 150 gallons of wine and this after the guests had already polished off all the wine that the steward had provided for the occasion. The point is not that Jesus encouraged excessive drinking but that the grace of God is superabundant, that it does more for us than we can ask or think.

The "hour" is another major theme of the story. Jesus first tells his mother that it had not yet come. She gives no sign of understanding but instructs the servants to do what he says. Toward the end of the story the steward mistakenly thinks it has come: "You have kept the good wine *until now*" (v. 10). But it requires the entire Gospel story to arrive at the hour of Jesus' glorification in the raising up on the cross.

Meanwhile, in this sign Jesus "revealed his glory; and his disciples believed in him" (v. 11). Their faith, into which they will be growing for a good while, is like Mary's: They believed in him although they did not yet understand. So it is with us.

Third Sunday after the Epiphany/Year C

Luke 4:14–21

The lectionary violates the integrity of Luke 4:14–30 by dividing the passage; Luke 4:21–30 is next week. The preacher may want to read the comments for both Sundays for one sermon that honors Luke's literary intent in 4:14–30.

That Jesus is under the Spirit (v. 14) vouches that Jesus' ministry follows divine guidance. Hence, Jesus' followers in Acts will be similarly empowered.

By mentioning Galilee, Luke employs theological geography, making a theological point through a geographical reference (v. 14). Galilee was a Jewish territory in which Jesus' purpose was made public, but it was not part of the Jewish power structure in Jerusalem that later crucified Jesus. Gentiles comprised perhaps half the population of Galilee, and Jews and Gentiles had friendly relations there. Although Jesus has relatively few encounters with Gentiles in Luke, the beginning of his ministry in a Gentile-friendly context points the way to the Gentile mission in Acts. The positive response to Jesus in multiple synagogues in Galilee reminds us that many Jews embraced Jesus' news of the realm of God, even though some in Nazareth, Jerusalem, and elsewhere did not (v. 15).

By adding "as was his custom" to the report that Jesus went to synagogue on the Sabbath, Luke underlines that Jesus was observant (v. 16). His ministry and that of the church do not break with Judaism but grow out of it.

In those days, a visiting rabbi would often be invited to read from a sacred text and to teach. The leader stood to read and sat to teach (vv. 16, 20). In keeping with that custom, Jesus rises to read.

The text that Jesus reads (vv. 17–19) interweaves Isa. 61:1–2 and 58:6, which, along with their context in Isa. 56–66, are key to Jewish restoration theology. That theology held that God intends to restore the now-broken world to the Edenic condition of Gen. 1–2, and this blossomed into the expectation of an apocalypse by which God would effect the restoration (the divine realm).

In vv. 18–19, much like a minister preaching from a text, Luke uses the passage from Isaiah as the text to interpret Jesus and the early Christian community as indicating that God's great restoration is underway. Each element in the text anticipates events or themes in Luke–Acts: First, good news to the poor comes as persons of means share resources with the community to provide for all (e.g., Luke 14:13, 21; 16:20; Acts 2:44–47; 4:32–39; 6:1–6). While it is hard to distinguish between the "captives" and the "oppressed," they include all who are repressed—whether by demons, political forces, or other restraints. The term translated "release" (*aphesis*) is elsewhere rendered "forgive" as in "forgiveness of sin." Luke regards sin as restraining power. Apostolic witnesses are among the imprisoned who are released (Acts 5:17–21; 12:6–11; 16:23–29). When depicting the recovery of sight to the blind, Luke refers not only to the physically sightless, but in keeping with Jewish tradition (e.g., Isa. 42:18–19; 43:8; 56:10, 19) uses the healing of blindness as a figure for the healing of spiritual imperceptivity (e.g., Luke 6:39; 14:12–24; Acts 9:1–19; 22:1–21; 26:2–23, esp. v. 18). Finally, the "year of the Lord's favor" refers to the jubilee, when debts would be forgiven, slaves would be freed, and land would be restored to its original owners (Lev. 25:8–12; cf. Deut. 15:1–7). With other Jewish authors (e.g., 11QMelch; *Psalms of Solomon* 11), Luke here uses the jubilee to image the coming eschatological world.

Fourth Sunday after the Epiphany/Year C

Luke 4:21–30

As noted on the Third Sunday after the Epiphany/Year C, today's reading should be Luke 4:14–30. A pastor may want to preach one sermon on the whole text.

Verse 21 begins Luke's homiletical interpretation of Jesus' ministry based on Isa. 61:1–2 and 58:6. Through Jesus, God is restoring the fractured world to the purposes God intended in Gen. 1–2. While the fulfillment will not be completed until the apocalypse, Luke emphasizes that the process is underway today (cf. Luke 19:9; 23:43).

The congregation initially speaks well of Jesus' one-sentence sermon and responds with the awe with which people often greet divine visitations and miracles (v. 22; cf. Luke 1:63; 2:18, 33, 47; 4:36; 5:9; 8:25; 9:43; 11:14; Acts 4:13; 9:21; 12:16). However, they soon react negatively. They also misidentify Jesus as "Joseph's son," for while he has grown up in Joseph's house, he is not Joseph's son (cf. Luke 1:35; 2:49). Luke thus implicitly communicates the Jewish idea that an emotion, even awe, is not sufficient for religious response. One must understand.

In antiquity, the proverb in v. 23a was a challenge to prove one's integrity. However, in v. 23b Luke reinforces the imperceptiveness of the congregation. They think that Jesus' ministry is defined by miracle working and do not have a sufficient grasp of the embrace or effect of the realm of God or the suffering that accompanies it.

Verse 24 announces a theme that permeates Luke–Acts: Jesus and the church are often in tension with leaders of Judaism. The passage explains why a group deriving from a Jewish figure and containing many Jewish people is in conflict with other Jewish people: They disagree regarding how Gentiles can become part of the eschatological community.

While relationships between Jewish and Gentile peoples were sometimes strained, Jewish people did not live in continuous antipathy with Gentiles. The core of the Jewish mission was to show Gentiles the way to blessing (see, e.g., Gen. 12:1–3; Isa. 42:6–7). Jews disagreed, however, over whether Gentiles must convert to Judaism to be full participants in the realm of God. Luke claims that, in view of the nearness of the apocalypse, Gentiles can enter the eschatological community by adopting core Jewish values as interpreted by Jesus and the church (Acts 15:23–29).

In 4:25–27, Luke uses two examples to introduce a key theological idea that explains why Jesus' followers welcome Gentiles into the church: the providence of God for Gentiles *as Gentiles.* Verses 25–26 recall 1 Kgs. 17:1–16, and Luke recounts that God sent Elijah, one of the most respected figures in Jewish history, to provide for a Gentile widow in Zarephath, a town in the Gentile land of Sidon. Verse 27 uses 2 Kgs. 5:1–14 to show that through the great prophet Elisha, God cleansed Naaman, who not only was a Gentile but a general in the army of Syria, an occasional enemy of Israel.

From Luke's perspective, the congregation does not understand its own tradition when it rages against Jesus and prepares to throw him over the cliff. At just that moment, however, God intervenes, as at the Red Sea, by making a way for Jesus through the crowd.

This passage offers a pastoral paradigm for the ministries of Jesus and the early apostolic community. These ministries witness to the manifestation of the divine realm, including welcoming Gentiles as Gentiles. They meet resistance. Nonetheless, when they encounter resistance, the Spirit that guides Jesus and the community will effect providence akin to leading Jesus through the hostile crowd to safety.

Fifth Sunday after the Epiphany/Year C

Luke 5:1–11

This story is a call narrative, a story in which God calls someone to service, similar to Exod. 3:1–22; Judg. 6:11–26; Isa. 6:1–13; and Jer. 1:4–13. A call narrative authenticates that the person is called and directed by God for a particular mission. This story prepares the reader to remember, after the ascension when the church is left in the world without Jesus, that Jesus had called the apostles for the special mission of representing authoritative interpretation and legitimating key decisions of the church (see, e.g., Acts 6:1–6; 15:1–29).

Jesus, by Gennesaret (the Sea of Galilee), sits in a boat to teach (Luke 5:1–3). This small narrative detail makes an important point: The event that follows is itself teaching. Jesus tells Peter to "put out into the deep water and let down your nets" (v. 4). Although they had been fishing all night (when fishing often took place), they had caught nothing.

The term "deep water" translates the Greek *bathos*, that is translated "deep" in Gen. 1:2. The deep was a fierce, untamed, dark, primal sea that existed before God began to speak into existence and bring into covenantal relationship the elements of creation. In Jewish mythology, the sea often represents chaos. Jewish writers sometimes describe Gentile existence as chaos (e.g., Ps. 66:6; Isa. 5:30; 27:1), as does Luke in Acts 4:24–26.

Peter and his companions do as Jesus says. When they let down their nets, they catch so many fish that the nets begin to break, and they signal other boats to help them. Indeed, the catch is so great the boats are in danger of sinking (vv. 4–7). This image calls to mind Jesus' comparison of the coming of the eschatological world to netting a catch (e.g., Matt. 13:47–50).

Peter, aware of the distance between his own sin and the awesome power in Jesus, tries to send Jesus away. Jesus, however, accepts Peter, with James and John, as the first apostles. This action assures all readers that they are accepted in God's grace.

On the Fourth Sunday after the Epiphany/Year B, we discuss "catching people" as a way of speaking about discipleship, the middle-class backgrounds of the disciples, and the itinerant life of Jesus and the disciples as first-century signs of faithfulness. Although apostles leave "everything" and follow Jesus, they continue to experience the providence demonstrated when they put their nets into the deep. God provides for them through the community and even through the intervention of Roman officials—agents of chaos itself (see, e.g., Luke 8:1–3; Acts 2:42–47; 23:23–35).

This event patterns the reader to count on what Jesus says. More specifically, it models the work of the early Lukan community in Acts: They are to let down their nets into the deep, the chaos of the world. When they do so, God transforms the things found in chaos into elements of the divine realm. For example, in Luke 9:10–17, Jesus commands the apostles to feed five thousand people with five loaves and two fish. When they hesitate, Jesus provides for all. Most notably, in the Gentile mission in Acts, the church lets down the nets into the Gentile chaos and brings them in full. This mission takes place at Jesus' direct command (Acts 24:47), and is a part of the great eschatological "catch." Although it sometimes feels as though the "boat" of the early church is about to sink because of conflicts regarding its catch with Jewish leaders, with Rome, and in its own fellowship, God's providence keeps it afloat.

Sixth Sunday after the Epiphany/Year C

Luke 6:17–26

In Luke 6:12–16, Jesus prays on a mountain. In Luke–Acts, prayer reveals aspects of the realm of God. As Moses addressed the community on a plain (Deut. 1:1), Jesus descends to a "level place" to interpret the divine realm (Luke 6:17). Jesus is a prophet who interprets the eschatological world much as Moses interpreted Torah (Deut. 18:15–22). He does not contradict Jewish teaching but prophetically interprets it in view of the coming apocalypse.

The large crowd has come in response to the signs of the divine realm in Jesus' ministry. However, they require deeper instruction into the nature of the great restoration.

While the terms "blessed" and "woe" occur in the First Testament in reference to the present situation of the community (blessed = enjoying the favor of God; woe = divine condemnation), by Luke's time these terms often were used in an eschatological setting. The blessed are welcomed into the realm of God whereas the woeful are condemned. Christians sometimes interpret these blessings and the woes as polar opposites—as if God categorically loves the poor and despises the rich, for example. In their larger context in Luke–Acts, however, the beatitudes and woes are not so much final judgments as invitations to join the forward movement of the realm (and avoid condemnation).

The economically destitute are blessed because God provides for them in the final manifestation of the divine reign (v. 20). They include Jesus, the Twelve (Luke 5:11), and some in the church for whom God provides through sharing resources (Luke 8:1–3; Acts 2:42–47). The rich enjoy consolation now, but Luke wants them to share with others and join the realm (v. 24; see also Luke 18:18–30; 19:1–10; Acts 2:42–47; 4:32–5:11; 6:1–6).

Because of widespread poverty, hunger was pervasive in Luke's world (v. 21). In the eschatological world, God will feed the hungry as, the reader recognizes, God already feeds through the community (see, e.g., Luke 9:10–17; 10:7–8; 11:3; Acts 6:1–6). The "breaking of bread" (Luke's name for the Lord's Supper, Luke 24:35; Acts 2:42) prefigures the eschatological banquet and the fact that divine provision is already taking place through the church. Verse 24 reminds the hearer that those who are full now will be hungry in the age to come if they keep their food to themselves, and Luke urges the sated to share with the hungry now so that they all can share the eschatological banquet (e.g., Luke 16:19–31).

People weep because of personal sorrow (Luke 7:13; 8:52; Acts 9:39) and because covenantal life is thwarted by repression (v. 21; see also Isa. 61:2; Luke 7:32; 19:41; 23:28). They will rejoice when the world is restored. Those who laugh now (v. 25) echo those in the wisdom literature who laugh at God's ways and are judged (see, e.g., Sir. 21:20; 27:13). Luke urges the foolish to repent (e.g., Luke 11:40; 12:13–21; 13:1–9).

Verses 22–23 presume that faithful people will be reviled for their witness. Conflict with leaders of Judaism and Rome is to be expected, for their Jewish ancestors persecuted prophets (cf. Luke 11:47–50; 13:34; Acts 7:52). By contrast (v. 26), the faithful are to be suspicious of those who are accorded accolades now because such people may be false prophets (see, e.g., Isa. 30:10–11; Jer. 5:31; 23:16–17). Some Jewish and Roman leaders are honored now but are false prophets (see, e.g., Luke 14:7–24).

These beatitudes and woes are in the present tense because the processes eventuating in the final manifestation of the divine realm are underway. People respond in the present as if that realm were already here.

Seventh Sunday after the Epiphany/Year C

Luke 6:27–38

Jesus here contrasts two ways of life: one based on the values of the broken old age (hate, violence, injustice, poverty), and the other embodying the realm of God (love, peace, justice, abundance). Jesus' teachings do not, however, invalidate the teachings of Judaism, but show how to put Jewish insights into practice every day to witness to the new world. The Spirit empowers Jesus and his followers to act out new age values.

Verses 27–31 address fractured relationships: enemies, hate, cursing, abuse, striking the cheek, taking another's coat, begging, taking another's goods. Responding in kind multiplies brokenness, says Jesus. Instead, his followers are to take actions that testify to God's aim to restore relationships and thereby follow the Jewish hope of turning enemies into friends in God's reign (see, e.g., *Testament of Benjamin* 4:3; *Testament of Joseph* 18:2).

Jesus recalls Exod. 23:4–5 and Prov. 25:21–22 when advising his followers to love their enemies and do good to those who hate them (v. 27). In Judaism, a curse invoked malevolence; Jesus' followers are to join some other Jewish people in responding with a blessing—wishing God's abundance—upon those who curse them, and praying for those who persecute them (see, e.g., *Genesis Apocryphon* 20:28; Luke 23:34; Acts 7:60). Jesus advocates similar responses to other situations in which one is treated as an enemy or threat (v. 29). Jesus follows Judaism in encouraging almsgiving to supply the needs of those who are poor enough to beg (v. 30).

Variations of v. 31 were well known in Judaism (e.g., Lev. 19:18; Tob. 4:15; *Epistle of Aristeas* 207; *Testament of Naphtali* 1:6; *b. Shabbat* 31a). For Luke, this verse is not just a statement of reciprocal relationship, but it invites those who yearn for the realm of God to live as if all are already within that realm.

Verses 32–36 state a theological rationale for the actions advocated in vv. 27–31. People magnify the brokenness of the present when they love only those who love them while continuing to hate others, or do good only to those who do good to them while wishing (or doing) evil to others, or lending only to those from whom they hope to receive. Even sinners (persons who are enslaved to the old world) do that. To witness to the divine reign, Jesus' community should love their enemies, do good to all (even to those who wish them harm), and lend "expecting nothing [i.e., no interest] in return."

In so doing, Jesus' disciples follow the lead of God, who is "kind to the ungrateful and the wicked" and who is merciful to all (vv. 35–36). In the background is a Jewish idea that the behavior of God, especially God's universal compassion, is the norm for human behavior (e.g., Lev. 19:2; Deut. 10:18–19; 19:17–19; Sir. 18:13; *Exodus Rabbah* 26.2; *Mekilta Exodus* 15.2).

The reference to judgment in v. 37 most likely refers not to everyday discrimination but to the final judgment (cf. Luke 12:57; 19:21; 22:30; Acts 13:46; 17:31; 24:21; 26:6–8). The word "condemn" (*katadikadzō*) describes being consigned to punishment (Wis. 2:20; 11:10; 12:27). When some in the community are tempted to deny the realm to others, Jesus echoes Jewish sentiments by urging the community to respond to all in their best interests (see, e.g., *b. Shabbat* 127a).

In this apocalyptic context, v. 38 is not simply a general life principle. Those who give (i.e., who follow Jesus' admonitions) will find that God gives them "good measure." This measure is a grain basket that is running over, which symbolizes life in the new age.

Eighth Sunday after the Epiphany/Year C

Luke 6:39–49

The final sections of the Sermon on the Plain deal with the necessity of accurately perceiving the realm of God (Luke 6:39–42) and of living its values (vv. 43–49).

The parable in v. 39 recollects the Jewish use of blindness to refer to theological imperception (Third Sunday after the Epiphany/Year C) by comparing a sightless person leading a sightless person to those who are theologically imperceptive leading others who are also imperceptive. Ecclesiastes 2:14 calls such blind guides "fools." To understand the realm of God adequately, Jesus' disciples should follow the theological vision of the master teacher, Jesus, set forth in Luke–Acts (v. 40). Acts directly warns the Lukan community against some of their leaders who articulate other theological views (e.g., the Pharisees who follow Jesus in Acts 15:5), and indirectly warns them against Jewish and Roman leaders who do not support Jesus' interpretation of the reign of God.

Those who do not see the realm of God making inroads into the world through the ministries of Jesus and the church, and who criticize those who do, are like people who have a log in their own eyes but do not notice it. When they remove the logs from their own eyes, they will be able to remove the speck from their neighbor's eye (vv. 41–42). Other Jewish teachers spoke similarly (see, e.g., *b. Arakhin* 16b; *b. Horayot* 3b; *b. Bava Batra* 16b; *b. Bava Metzi'a* 59b; *b. Qiddushin* 20b). In these verses, Luke appeals to his community and others to engage in the Jewish practice of self-criticism so they can repent and then witness more fully to the divine realm.

In vv. 43–45, Luke makes use of traditional Jewish images to provide the criteria by which to gauge one's perception of, and response to, the realm of God: the fruit one bears. Jewish writers use bearing fruit as a figure for life (e.g., Isa. 3:10; Jer. 17:10; 21:14; Hos. 10:13). A tree can only bear fruit that is particular to that tree; the kind of fruit a tree bears indicates the kind of tree it is. Figs do not come from thorns, nor grapes from brambles. Jesus calls for his followers to bring forth the fruit of the realm of God (the life of 6:27–38).

Verse 45 also echoes a popular Jewish proverb (*Genesis Rabbah* 84.9; *Midrash Psalms* 9.2). In Judaism, the heart is the center of the self. The motif of "treasure" points forward to Luke 12:33–34 (and hence to Acts 2:42–47; 4:32–5:1) and recollects that in Judaism, the good treasure of the heart is putting treasure in heaven, that is, almsgiving—a symbol of providing for all in the community as in the reign of God (cf. Sir. 29:11). A person who rightly perceives and responds to the realm of God brings forth the treasure of care for others in the eschatological community.

Some in the church call Jesus "Lord, Lord" but do not bear the fruit of the reign of God or bring forth the good treasure of the heart (v. 46). Verses 47–49 draw on Ezekiel 13:1–16. They also resonate with rabbis who compare doing the good works commanded by Torah with building a solid foundation (*The Fathers according to Rabbi Nathan* 24; *m. Avot* 3:18). Verses 47–49 use the image of houses in a river flood and the consequences of digging a deep foundation (recognizing the divine realm and doing its works), or not doing so, to speak of the great judgment that follows the apocalypse. Luke is thoroughly Jewish in saying that by grace we are welcomed into the divine realm. Grace creates an identity that should body forth the fruit of the good works of care for all. The fig tree bears figs and the grapevine grapes.

Ninth Sunday after the Epiphany/Year C

Luke 7:1–10

The name "Capernaum" means "village of commmpassion (or comfort)." Whether Luke intended theological symbolism with this name, the story bespeaks compassion on the part of both the Gentile centurion and God for the slave.

The story assumes the social stratification of the Roman era. The centurion commands a hundred soldiers in the Roman army who maintained the brutal Pax Romana. While other soldiers "extort money from anyone by threats" (Luke 3:14), the centurion is a patron—a person of power at the top of the social pyramid who greatly influenced those in the lower strata of the social world. The centurion exercised benevolent patronage by building the synagogue in Capernaum and bestowing other favors on the Jewish community. Indeed, the centurion may be a "God-fearer."

The centurion acknowledges that, although he is a commander and patron, Jesus has even more authority. Jesus needs only to speak the word from afar to heal. The story thus subtly criticizes Rome and the patron-age system: neither Rome nor the social standing of the centurion could effect healing.

The story climaxes with 7:9, "Not even in Israel have I found such faith." The centurion is the first person in Luke–Acts to beseech Jesus to heal from afar. The Gentile is thereby a model for people in Luke's later time who can conclude that Jesus, though ascended (Luke 24:50–51; Acts 1:9–10; 7:55–56), can still speak the healing word. While this statement assumes that people in Israel respond faithfully to the manifestation of the realm of God through Jesus and the church, the saying unnecessarily suggests the superiority of Gentile faith while casting a polemical shadow over faith in Israel.

By acting compassionately for a Gentile, Jesus does not do something new. The reader remembers 2 Kgs. 5:1–19 where Elisha instructs the Gentile Syrian general Naaman, a leper, to bathe in the Jordan to be cleansed. The reader remembers, further, other Jewish affirmations that God seeks to be compassionate to all in the human family (e.g., Exod. 16:11; Deut. 10:17–18; 1 Kgs. 8:41–43; Ps. 47:2; Dan. 2:47; Wis. 5:18; Sir. 35:15–16). The story, then, re-presents a concern at the heart of Jewish identity, and signals that the ministry of the church is in continuity with the ministry of Israel.

The story challenges the early church to receive Gentiles such as the centurion. The text also models how Gentile patrons (and others) can respond to the manifestation of the realm of God through Jesus and the church: the authority of the patron is not only limited but is superseded by that of God. To be blessed, patrons need to exercise power in conjunction with the divine purposes, which includes acting in ways that promote the welfare of all in the community, including those below them in the social pyramid.

Unfortunately, the centurion gives no indication of repenting from colluding with the Roman empire. Indeed, by healing the slave, Jesus makes it possible for the centurion to go about his Roman business without distraction. Furthermore, the story assumes the continuation of the patronage system and the stratification of the social world. Though healed, the slave will still serve the centurion as a slave. The larger theological framework of Luke–Acts implicitly criticizes both Caesar and slavery. Yet, while the reader knows that the rule of Caesar will be replaced by the rule of God after the apocalypse, and that the realm of God means the oppressed—including slaves—will go free (Luke 4:18), the story presumes that the social world will continue as usual until the apocalyptic cataclysm. The church in the early twenty-first century needs to be more assertive in critiquing empire and calling for freedom, justice, dignity, and egalitarianism in our social world.

Last Sunday after the Epiphany/Year C

Transfiguration Sunday

Luke 9:28–36

Jesus takes Peter, John, and James with him to a mountain to pray (Luke 9:28). In Judaism, a mountain is often a place of revelation. Prayer in Luke–Acts is the opening of the self to God's rule, and when Luke mentions prayer, we are prepared for a revelation of an aspect of God's rule (as in 3:21–22).

In the midst of prayer, Jesus is transfigured (v. 29). Jewish apocalyptic writers anticipated that in the final manifestation of the reign of God, persons would have transformed bodies in the luminescent white of the heavenly world (e.g., Dan. 10:6; *1 Enoch* 62:15–16; *2 Enoch* 22:8; Luke 24:4; Acts 1:10; 1 Cor. 15:35–49; Rev. 4:4; 7:9). The change in Jesus' face and his clothes becoming dazzling white signal that Jesus is momentarily transformed into the body he will have in the complete manifestation of the reign of God. In the midst of the broken, old age, God gives the three disciples (and the reader) a preview and assurance of the age to come.

Moses and Elijah appear "in glory" and talk with him "about his departure, which he was about to accomplish at Jerusalem" (v. 31). While Christians sometimes see this text as indicating that Jesus supersedes Judaism represented by Moses and Elijah, nothing in the scene suggests supersession. To the contrary, their presence confirms Luke's insistence, since the beginning of the Gospel, that the work of God through Jesus and the church is in continuity with Judaism.

The English translation "departure" obscures a further point of continuity with Judaism. In Greek, "departure" is *exodos*. Previous Jewish writers used the exodus from Egypt as the template by which to interpret God's liberating activity in their later days (e.g., Isa. 43:1–7 describes a new exodus). Similarly, Luke uses the exodus to interpret Jesus' death and resurrection as an event whereby the God of Israel liberates the present world by moving history toward the final manifestation of the realm of God.

The three disciples see this event, and Peter wants to make three dwellings (*skēnē*)—one each for Moses, Elijah, and Jesus (vv. 32–33). The "dwellings" (sometimes rendered "tents" or "booths") allude to the Feast of Booths (Sukkoth) that commemorated God's dwelling or tenting with the people of Israel while they wandered in the wilderness after leaving Egypt and on the way to the promised land (Exod. 23:16; 34:22; Lev. 23:42–44; Deut. 16:13). Zechariah uses the Feast of Booths as an image for the eschatological world when God and the community would forever tent together. Peter believes that the eschatological Feast of Booths is at hand.

While Peter is speaking, a cloud overshadows them, a traditional Jewish way of representing the divine presence (see, e.g., Exod. 13:21; 16:10; 19:9; 24:15–18; 40:34; 1 Kgs. 8:10–11; 18:44–45; Ezek. 10:3–4; Ps. 18:11). From the cloud, God speaks the same words as at the baptism, claiming that God has adopted Jesus as the divine agent of God's rule (Ps. 2:7) and that this path will involve suffering (Isa. 42:1; cf. Second Sunday after the Epiphany/Year C).

God emphasizes this point by adding, "Listen to him!" In Luke vv. 18–27, Jesus had stated plainly that as a step on the way to the complete manifestation of the realm of God, he would be killed and that the disciples would suffer as they witnessed to the coming of that realm. While this story reinforces the idea that the path to the eschatological world includes the suffering of both Jesus and the church, it also gives the church a sign (the transfiguration itself) to reinforce its confidence in the coming of that world.

Ash Wednesday/Year C

Matthew 6:1–6, 16–21

Please see Ash Wednesday/Year A for the commentary on this reading.

First Sunday in Lent/Year C

Luke 4:1–13

"Full of the Holy Spirit" and "led by the Spirit," Jesus resists temptation. Readers thus know that when they are filled with the Spirit (Acts 2:1–21; 10:34–44), they can withstand temptation.

In many first-century Jewish circles, temptation (*peiradzō*) referred to a period when, as the apocalypse neared, Satan would intensify resistance to God and tempt people to give up on the divine restoration. The Lukan church lives in this period. On the First Sunday in Lent/Year B, we discuss the origin and meaning of the figure of Satan, as well as the symbolism of the wilderness, the forty days, and the fasting (Luke 4:1–2).

Christians sometimes take the first temptation (to turn stones to bread) as a lure to trust in material things rather than God (v. 3). However, in Judaism human welfare is directly tied to material well-being. The realm of God restores the material world. This temptation is therefore to turn to Satan for bread (i.e., things necessary for life) rather than to God.

Luke shows that sacred tradition can help create an identity that withstands temptation as Jesus replies to Satan with Deut. 8:3. The first-century listener would complete the quotation: "One does not live by bread alone, but by every word that comes from the mouth of the LORD." In Deuteronomy, Moses cautions the people to avoid the idolatry of Canaan. When the people wandered in the wilderness, the idols did not feed them. The word of God provided manna, and it creates the covenantal community that provides resources for all.

Satan next offers Jesus the opportunity to rule all the dominions of the world and to partake of their glory if he will worship Satan (vv. 7–8). Luke uses the word *oikoumenē* ("world") to refer to the Roman Empire (cf. Luke 2:1; 21:26; Acts 11:28; 17:6; 19:27; 24:5). Satan tempts the church to accept life in the empire (with its idolatry, injustice, poverty, and other forms of brokenness) as normative. In Luke v. 8, Jesus replies to the second temptation with Deut. 6:13, a passage that calls the community to reject idolatry. As a Jew, Jesus knows that the deity one worships determines the character of the worshiping community. Worship of the God who is restoring the world will lead the community itself to be restorative.

The final temptation is for Jesus to jump from the pinnacle of the temple, an act that would immediately win a wide following. In support, Satan cites Ps. 90:11–12. Luke implies, however, that simply quoting a Bible passage is not adequate. A community must have a larger theological framework within which to interpret how passages can help the community discern God's purposes. Jesus does not simply quote Deut. 6:16 against Ps. 90:11–12, but speaks out of a hermeneutic that explores how passages can help the community identify events leading to the final manifestation of the realm of God. Deuteronomy 6:16 refers to the people in the wilderness at Massah questioning whether they would reach the promised land because they lacked water (Exod. 17:1–7; Num. 20:2–13; cf. Deut. 32:50–52; Ps. 106:32–33). Many in Luke's day similarly questioned the coming of the realm of God. Deuteronomy 6:16 reminds the people that just as God provided water at Massah, so they can count upon God to bring the divine realm through the patient work of Jesus as suffering servant (Isa. 42:1; cf. Luke 3:21–22). At the end of the temptation, Satan departs from Jesus until an opportune time (Luke 22:3–6). The church, in Acts, continues to confront Satan and to draw inspiration and pastoral encouragement to resist temptation from Luke 4:1–11.

Second Sunday in Lent/Year C

Luke 13:31–35

At Luke's mention of Herod Antipas, the ruler of Galilee (13:31), Luke's early reader would have tensed. Antipas disrespected the dead by building Tiberias on tombs (Josephus, *Antiquities* 19.36–38). He committed incest by divorcing his first spouse to marry his niece Herodias (see Lev. 18:13, 16; 20:21). When the Baptist called Antipas to account, the tetrarch beheaded the prophet (Luke 3:19–20; 9:7–9). Antipas could kill Jesus.

Jesus comments theologically on Antipas (and on similar leaders in the empire) by calling him a "fox." Jewish writers used the fox to speak of people who are cunning, distrustful, and insignificant (e.g., Neh. 4:3; *m. Avot* 4:15; *m. Berakhot* 61b; *m. Bava Qamma* 117a; *b. Hagigah* 14a). Jesus is not intimidated by the Roman tetrarch, but continues to announce the realm of God and to perform its signs (Luke 13:32–33). The reference to the "third day" contrasts Antipas (who puts to death) with God (who brings life even to the dead).

Jesus must die in Jerusalem. In vv. 33b–34a, Luke voices a tradition within Judaism that interprets Jerusalem as a city that "kills the prophets" (see, e.g., 2 Chr. 24:19–22; Jer. 26:20–23; 38:4–6; Amos 7:10–17; Luke 11:49–51; Acts 7:52). Yet, for Luke, Jerusalem is more than a killing field. It is a theological symbol as a place of revelation (even more than it is a geographical designation). At Jerusalem, the complicity of Jewish and

Roman leaders in the death of Jesus dramatizes misunderstanding and rejection of the realm of God, while the resurrection (Luke 24:1–12), the coming of the Spirit (Acts 2:1–21), and the authorization of the Gentile mission (Acts 15:22–29) demonstrate God's power to bring that realm to final expression.

In 13:34b, Jesus compares his prior relationship with Jerusalem with the feminine image of a hen seeking to protect her chicks. Other Jewish writers use similar images to speak of the wings of the divine presence in the temple protecting Israel (e.g., Ps. 17:8; 57:1; 61:4; cf. Deut. 32:11).

By the time of Luke, the Romans had destroyed the temple (Luke 21:5–6). Jewish communities debated theological explanations for its destruction. In 13:35a, Luke claims that the temple ("your house") fell because Jerusalem (representing broader Judaism) did not welcome Jesus' message of the coming realm of God. Jesus echoes Jer. 22:5–6 when God had made the temple desolate. Luke 19:44 makes Luke's conclusion even more specific and pointed: "They [i.e., the Romans] will not leave within you one stone upon another; because you did not recognize the time of your visitation from God."

The preacher can help the congregation recognize the importance of making theological sense of significant events theologically, while pointing out that Luke's interpretation of the destruction of the temple is inadequate. God promised to be faithful to Israel. For God to destroy the temple because some Jews did not welcome Jesus would be for God to violate God's trustworthiness. If God is not faithful to Israel, then no one can count on God to be faithful. A better explanation of the destruction of the temple is to regard it as the deranged result of Roman idolatry, insecurity, and injustice. Its destruction warns subsequent generations to beware of attitudes and abuses of power that are similar to those of Rome. Such rulers are worse than foxes. The church and synagogue can call them to repent. Though they destroy the Baptist and even the temple, the processes leading to the divine realm continue to move forward.

Third Sunday in Lent/Year C

Luke 13:1–9

By using the phrase "at that very time," Luke ties 13:1–9 to the teaching about the apocalypse in 12:1–59. Some persons remind Jesus that Pilate slaughtered some Galileans when they were offering sacrifice (probably at the temple; 13:1). While we do not possess a record of this incident, it is consistent with Pilate's cruel ways (see, e.g., Josephus, *Antiquities* 18.55–62, 85–89; *The Jewish Wars* 2:169–77). Jesus then recalls the eighteen "who were killed when the tower of Siloam fell on them." This tower was at the intersection of the south and east walls of Jerusalem. Josephus speculates that it fell during construction ordered by Pilate to bring more water into Jerusalem (*Antiquities* 28.60; *The Jewish Wars* 2.175). However, neither Josephus nor other writers recall these eighteen unfortunate deaths.

When Jesus asks whether the dead were worse sinners than others, he answers his own question in the negative (vv. 2, 4b–5a). Christians often become preoccupied with the fact that Jesus saw no relationship between sin and tragedy and even caricature Judaism as if all Jews regarded tragedy as punishment. The sermon could help the congregation recognize that Jewish thinking on this point was diverse. Many Jewish people (e.g., the writer of the book of Job) rejected the equation, and regarded tragedy as random evil.

In 13:1–5, Luke uses the tragedies to bring out the importance of repentance. If listeners do not prepare for the apocalypse by repenting, they too will perish. The apocalypse includes a judgment condemning the unrepentant (cf. First Sunday of Advent/Year C; *1 Enoch* 98:3, 16; 99:9). John the Baptist pleaded with people to "bear fruit worthy of repentance," that is, to live covenantally (Luke 3:8; cf. 13:6–9).

In Judaism, repentance is a positive action. The Hebrew for "repent" (*shuv*) means "to turn"—walking toward destruction, taking account of the situation, and reversing direction to avoid doom and to enjoy safety (see, e.g., Sir. 17:24). People need to repent when they violate the covenant through idolatry, injustice, and other evils. A person or community demonstrates repentance by living covenantally.

Calling to repentance is fundamental to the mission of Jesus and the church (Luke 5:32; 24:47). To join the eschatological community, people must repent (Luke 3:1–17; Acts 2:38; 3:19; 5:31; 11:18; 17:30; 20:21). Repentance results in living supportively in community (3:10–14; 16:30; 17:4; Acts 8:22; 26:20). Luke particularly notes that through the church, God gives Gentiles the Jewish "repentance that leads to life" (Acts 11:18).

The parable of vv. 6–9 centers around the fate of a fig tree. Jewish writers sometimes use the fig as a metaphor for the covenantal life (e.g., 1 Kgs. 4:25; Isa. 36:16; Jer. 24:4–7; Joel 2:22; Hag. 2:19; Zech. 3:10), and the absence of fruit represents a lapse of faithfulness and leads to judgment (Jer. 5:17; 8:13; 24:8–10; 24:1–10; Hos. 2:12; Joel 1:7; 2:12).

The parable compares the situation of Luke's generation to that of the fig tree. The owner of a vineyard rightly expects to receive figs from his fig tree. After receiving no fruit for three years, the owner decides to cut down the tree. The gardener, however, asks to extend the life of the tree for one more year in the hope that the tree will bring forth fruit. Similarly, God expected people to bear fruit, that is, to repent, but not finding repentance, God decided to end the current age. However, God has graciously delayed the apocalypse so that persons in Luke's time can repent and become a part of the realm of God. Luke's message is simple: God has given you this moment to repent; if you do not, you will perish.

Fourth Sunday in Lent/Year C

Luke 15:1–3, 11b–32

In this book, we try to pay attention to what a text actually says and not simply to traditional interpretations. This effort reveals several anomalies between today's lection and its usual interpretation.

As part of his caricature of the Pharisees and scribes, Luke creates a picture of these leaders "grumbling" when Jesus eats with tax collectors and sinners (15:1–2). The word "grumble" (*diagoggydzō*) also describes the Israelites complaining in the wilderness (Exod. 16:1–8; 17:1–7; Num. 14:1–5; Deut. 1:26–33; *m. Bava Batra* 8:1–9:10). The story in 15:11b–32 responds to this grumbling with a contorted theological rationale in the form of a parable.

Normally a Jewish parent passed property to the next generation by a will that was to take effect either at the parent's death or while both parent and heir were living (Num. 27:8–11; 36:7–9; cf. Sir. 33:19–23). The firstborn heir received a double portion.

In the far country, the younger son engages in dissolute living (debauchery, dallying with prostitutes) of a sort that is associated with Gentiles in 2 Macc. 6:4. Luke reinforces the idea that the young man essentially becomes a Gentile by having him feed pigs (15:14–17; cf. Lev. 11:17; 14:8; 1 Macc. 1:47; 2 Macc. 6:18, 7:1).

Luke claims that the younger sibling repents: "He came to himself." His motivation, however, is hardly praiseworthy: He thought of returning home only when he ran out of money and was hungry. (On repentance, see Third Sunday in Lent/Year C.)

He is so desperate that he would settle for being a hired worker who receives a daily wage in the family house. However, the father has compassion (*splanchnidzō*), feels his suffering. He embraces the youth and reinstates his place in the household (robe, ring, sandals, fatted calf, celebration). The young person in the pigpen was lost, or dead. The return home is a transfer from living death to life in the realm of God (vv. 23–24). Luke intends for vv. 11b–24 to dramatize that God welcomes all who repent—even Gentiles—in the divine realm. This idea recalls the Jewish confidence that God seeks to bless Gentiles (see, e.g., Gen. 12:1–3; Isa. 60:8–16; Jonah).

Luke tells vv. 25b–32 in such a way as to chide the older brother for not joining the celebration over the younger brother's return. At this point, we come to the greatest anomaly in the story. The father gives a party to celebrate the prodigal's return, but fails to invite the elder brother, thus neglecting one of the basic principles of ancient Near Eastern hospitality. The elder brother, who obviously functions as a type for Jewish leaders, learns about the party only as he is in the fields, working his way back toward the house. He "heard music and dancing" as he neared the house. Only when the father realizes that the elder brother is unhappy does he go to him and plead for the family to be together.

The elder brother had worked faithfully for a lifetime (15:29–30). Indeed, had he not stayed home and kept the farm going (and supported his father), there would have been nothing to which the wayward younger brother could return.

The father who had two sons lavished half his holdings on the son who was unfaithful and failed to recognize faithfulness in the older brother who nevertheless continuously supported him, thus creating the conditions for a rift in the family. Finally, however, the father comes to his senses, says to the elder brother "all that is mine is yours" and invites this faithful, supportive son to the banquet.

The faithfulness of different generations of a family to each other and of the generations of Israel to each other was a bedrock principle of biblical faith (see the genealogies of Jesus in Matthew and Luke). It takes three generations to establish a tradition of faith but the faithlessness of only one to destroy it. Had all adult children acted as did the prodigal, there would have been no Israelite (or, later, Christian) tradition to pass on to the next generation.

Fifth Sunday in Lent/Year C

John 12:1–8

The story of a woman anointing Jesus is told in every Gospel (Mark 14:3–9; Matt. 26:6–13, Luke 7:36–50). Mark and Matthew, like John, place the story in Bethany in Judea, but "the woman" is unnamed; they have her anoint Jesus' head, not his feet, as Mary does in John. Also, for them the house is that of "Simon the leper," not Lazarus as in John. Luke's story takes place in Galilee, in the home of a Pharisee, and early in Jesus' ministry, rather than late. These differences show that John's story, while it is loosely similar to the version in the Synoptics, is in the service of John's Christology. We will look at it in that perspective. It is a story rich in symbolism.

Mary's anointing of Jesus takes place "six days before the Passover" (v. 1), in Bethany, the village of Lazarus. Prior to this, Martha had questioned Jesus about his delay in coming to Lazarus's aid: "Lord, if you had been here, my brother would not have died" (11:21). Now she is different; of the two women, she serves. John mentions Lazarus a second time as "one of those at the table with him" (v. 2). This double mention of Lazarus reminds us of the point of Jesus' association with his death: "for God's glory, so that the Son of God may be glorified through it" (11:4).

Mary takes "a pound of costly perfume made of pure nard," anoints Jesus' feet with it, and wipes them with her hair (v. 3). Anointing the head would have been done to an honored guest or a royal one; also the "Messiah" was to be anointed on the head with oil. Washing the feet would be a hospitable way to greet a guest in desert country such as Bethany. Anointing the feet is odd enough that Jesus explains it in verse 7: "She bought it [the perfume] so that she might keep it for the day of my burial." In John, Mary is the first person to grasp the meaning of Jesus' death. Her anointing of Jesus is a symbolic embalming. Here is part of the symbolism: Jesus' attendance at the same table with Lazarus signals that this is the day of preparation for Jesus' burial, as Lazarus had earlier been buried, and for Jesus' resurrection, as Lazarus had earlier been raised.

Another symbolic element is introduced by John when he says that "the house was filled with the fragrance of the perfume" (v. 3). Mary's act of love for Jesus fills the house with the sweet aroma. The spreading aroma symbolizes the spread of the message of the gospel throughout the Gentile world, and was so interpreted by Ignatius in his letter *To the Ephesians* 17.1. Here John is parallel to Mark's account of the anointing: "Truly, I tell you, wherever the good news is proclaimed in the whole world, what she has done will be told in remembrance of her" (Mark 14:9).

Judas, about to betray Jesus, objects that the perfume should have been sold for "three hundred denarii and the money given to the poor" (v. 5). He said this, John comments, "because he was a thief; he kept the common purse and used to steal what was put into it" (v. 6). His utter contrast with Mary shows that some women understand Jesus better than do some apostles. Jesus defends Mary, explains her action, and adds, "You always have the poor with you, but you do not always have me" (v. 8).

His comment should not be taken as downplaying the importance of meeting the needs of "the least of these." Doing that would be taking his words out of the context of John's Gospel, in which Jesus' followers are constantly reminded to "bear fruit" in doing deeds of loving-kindness. Rather, they point to a singular event: the death and glorification of Jesus.

Palm Sunday or Passion Sunday/Year C

Luke 19:28–40, 23:1–49

"Palm Sunday" is a misnomer for today. Palms or other branches are mentioned only in Mark 11:1–11; Matt. 21:1–11; and John 12:12–19. Luke's omission of these branches is significant. Branches recollect 1 Macc. 13:49–53. For three centuries Palestine had been under foreign rule. In 141 B.C.E, Jewish rebels defeated the Syrian oppressors. When the Jewish victors recaptured the temple, they waved branches. The branches became a symbol of Jewish independence. By omitting them, Luke signals that the church is not a revolutionary movement and encourages his community to live within Roman rule even while criticizing that oppression and recognizing that God will judge Rome (see Christmas Day/Year C).

Jesus rides on a colt and the crowd spreads cloaks in the road—traditional gestures associated with the arrival of a ruler (2 Kgs. 9:13; Zech. 9:9). Luke reveals the nature of Jesus' rule by saying that Jesus came from the Mount of Olives, where God would initiate the apocalyptic event ending the current broken age and would fully manifest the eschatological reign of God (Zech. 14:4–9). The community should not engage in revolt, for God will liberate them apocalyptically. The preacher needs to help the congregation wrestle with the degree to which this political strategy is right for today.

Turning to the crucifixion, the preacher needs to help the congregation recognize that the picture of the Jewish role in the death of Jesus in the Gospels is polemic. Although some Christian preachers have often called Jewish people "Christ killers," Jewish authorities did not have the power to crucify people in the first century. Only Rome could do that, a fact acknowledged by the Gospel writers. Although the Gospels portray Jewish leaders calling vehemently for Jesus' death, scholars today believe that the Gospel writers greatly exaggerated the Jewish role in the proceedings that led to Jesus' death to help explain the tension (and separation) between Luke's community and other forms of Judaism at the time of the Gospel writers after the fall of Jerusalem in 70 c.e.[31]

Luke is not as vituperative in this regard as the other Gospels. Still, the Jewish leaders violate their own laws by bringing false charges against Jesus (Luke 23:1–2, 5). Pilate declares Jesus innocent three times (23:4, 15–16, 22), thus showing more spiritual insight than the Jewish leaders. However, Pilate reveals that Rome is also corrupt by caving in when the leaders of the people make a huge cry for the release of the known insurrectionist Barabbas and the crucifixion of Jesus, the agent of the reign of God.

For Luke, Jesus' death has little saving significance. It is not a sacrifice (or other means of redemption). Rather, Jesus is a martyr executed by unjust people and systems. This has a twofold function in Luke–Acts: (1) It demonstrates the brokenness of the present age, and, consequently, the need for the reign of God to come in its fullness; and (2) it offers pastoral guidance to the church. Just as Jesus was martyred, so the Lukan community can expect resistance and even suffering in the face of witness to the reign of God (see, e.g., Acts 4:1–22; 5:17–42; 6:8–8:1, 21:27–28:31).

This way of thinking about the crucifixion derives from Judaism. Several Jewish writers in antiquity call attention to the importance of remaining steadfast in witness even in the face of conflict and execution (see, e.g., the martyrdom of Eleazar and the mother and her seven children in 2 Macc. 4:7–6:11; 6:28–29; 7:1–42; 8:5–11, 17–26; 9:1–9; cf. 4 Macc. 3:19–18:24; Isa. 52:12–53:12). Luke is one with these writers in emphasizing that God is faithful to those who suffer because of their own faithfulness.

Easter Day/Year C

Luke 24:1–12

Faith in the risen Jesus did not arise instantaneously on the morning of Easter Sunday. The Gospels display the confusion, doubt, and disbelief of Jesus' followers ("these words seemed to them an idle tale," v. 11). They also depict the disciples as remembering Jesus' words (v. 6) or studying the Scriptures and continuing to break bread together (24:32; "he had been made known to them in the breaking of the bread," 24:35). Faith in the living Christ came from the ongoing and transforming awareness of Christ's presence to the community as it explored the Scriptures and broke bread together.

Among Jews, Pharisees believed in resurrection (Acts 23:6–8). After the Maccabean war, belief in resurrection as God's way of dealing with righteous martyrs gained credence among Jews. Enoch and Elijah had been "raised" into heaven (Gen. 5:24; 2 Kgs. 2:9–12). Philo's *On the Life of Moses* describes Moses' "empty tomb" (2.291). Tales of heroes rising from the grave and ascending into heaven were told by Ovid in his *Metamorphoses* (14.805–51). Ovid describes Romulus as having made a resurrection appearance to Proclus Julius on the road outside Alba Longa. Paul argues from belief in the resurrection of the dead to belief in the resurrection of Christ (1 Cor. 15:13–14), not vice versa. Hence, Luke and the other Gospel writers tell a story that would have fallen on receptive ears among both Jews and Gentiles.

Two features distinguish Gospel accounts of the resurrection of Jesus from other resurrection stories in circulation at the time. One is that Jesus is forcefully present, not slightly. The other is that the stories of Jesus' resurrection bring a community, a *koinonia*, into existence; they do not merely concern isolated individuals. Christ is present to the church in the lively preaching of the Word, in the breaking of bread, in the sharing of love, and in the needs of "the least of these."

In Luke's story of the empty tomb, unlike Mark's, it is the women who believe and who are the eyewitnesses of the empty tomb. Returning to the tomb from having "rested" on *Shabbat* (23:56), they bring ointments to anoint Jesus' body for burial. Instead, they find the stone "rolled away" and the body missing! They are "perplexed" (*aporeō*). The empty tomb by itself does not produce faith. "Two men," later referred to as "angels" (24:23), ask, "Why do you look for the living among the dead? He is not here, but has risen" (v. 5).

At their suggestion, they recall Jesus' words that he must be "crucified, and on the third day rise again" (v. 7). These words make available the initial interpretation that forms their perception of what has happened. There is no uninterpreted experience. The women then tell "all this to the eleven and to all the rest" (v. 9). But the male disciples disbelieve their story, finding it an "idle tale." Throughout his Gospel, Luke is much concerned to tell the story of faithful women, even at the expense of making the male apostles look bad, which their attitude of male superiority here clearly does. Peter, however, runs to the tomb, looks for himself, and goes home "amazed" (v. 12), a typically Lukan expression for response to wondrous events. The important role of women followers of Jesus receives backing from Luke. These women could remember and tell the story because they had seen and believed and borne witness.

This is not the end of Luke's story. Jesus appears twice more in the Gospel: to the two disciples on the road to Emmaus and to the community where the disciples explored the Scriptures (24:44–46) and worshiped (24:52–53).

Second Sunday of Easter/Year C

John 20:19–31

This reading is John's account of resurrection appearances that take place prior to the formal conclusion of his Gospel in 20:30–31: "Now Jesus did many other signs in the presence of his disciples, which are not written in this book. But these are written so that you may come to believe. . . ." Mary had faithfully related to the disciples what Jesus had said to her, and they were now gathered in a house.

John reports that the doors were locked "for fear of the Jews" (v. 19). Whatever fear of conflict with Jews may have overshadowed John's community in the late first century is read back into the story of Jesus. Verse 19 should not be taken literally. What is important here is that the community of faith always comes together in times that produce anxiety. The terrors of history are our frequent companions.

Even the preaching and teaching of the gospel and the assurance of Jesus' resurrection, of which Mary, Peter, and the "other disciple" were aware, did not dispel the disciples' fear. To all the disciples Jesus then appears and declares his peace: "Peace be with you" (v. 19). This is said to "the disciples," not to "the twelve" or to a list of named apostles. These disciples represent all of Jesus' disciples. The appropriate way to hear Jesus' "Peace be with you" is to hear it as addressed in the present tense to each of us now. Our fears have no more been dispelled than were theirs, but the risen Jesus with his peace is present to us through the Spirit, which still brings his message of peace. It is indeed a peace which passes understanding (Phil. 4:7).

Recognizing him from the wounds in his hands and side, the disciples are filled with joy (v. 20), and Jesus repeats his blessing of peace (v. 21). Jesus enables us to live lives of joy in the midst of conflict, suffering, and fear. But at precisely this point, Jesus reminds his disciples (them and us) that his peace is not something that we are to sit back and enjoy. Throughout John's Gospel he has told his disciples that they are the sent ones of the Sent One, and now he repeats this as well: "As the Father has sent me, so I send you" (v. 21). Then he breathes on them, as the Spirit breathed upon the waters in the first verses of Genesis, and says, "Receive the Holy Spirit. If you forgive the sins of any, they are forgiven them; if you retain the sins of any, they are retained" (v. 23).

The disciples are to be in the world as Jesus was in the world, bearing the good news of God's salvation through Jesus Christ. But they will be able to undertake this mission only in the presence of the Holy Spirit. Apart from that, their fragile and ever imperfect faith will not find a way to carry through on the mission.

Thomas, however, is not there. This apostle, the patron saint of all questioners among the faithful, doubted and would not believe without evidence or reason to do so. When Jesus reappears a week later, he invites Thomas to put his hand into Jesus' side and to see Jesus' hands. Jesus does not rebuff Thomas's doubting; he answers it. As a consequence, Thomas too believes: "My Lord and my God!" (v. 28).

Then, addressing the disciples of John's own late-first-century congregation and all subsequent ones, including us, Jesus says, "Have you believed because you have seen me? Blessed are those who have not seen and yet have come to believe" (v. 29).

The sent ones of the Sent One will bring into being many other and later congregations of believers. They and we have not experienced Jesus firsthand. Yet amid our fears and anxieties and with all our questions, the Holy Spirit makes Jesus present to us and brings joy to our hearts.

Third Sunday of Easter/Year C

John 21:1–19

John 21 seems to be an addition to the original Gospel, which concludes with chapter 20's formal ending. An indication that it was added later is that it refers to the appearance of Jesus to the disciples by the Sea of Galilee as "the third time Jesus appeared to the disciples" (v. 14), although Jesus had already appeared three times—to Mary and twice to disciples in the house. Also, in spite of having been sent on a mission, the disciples are at home in Galilee going fishing just as they were when Jesus first called them.

Nonetheless, the two stories in today's reading present significant opportunities for teaching the Christian faith. The first (vv. 1–14) finds seven of the disciples at the "Sea of Tiberias" with Peter saying "I am going fishing" (v. 3). The other six go along, "but that night they caught nothing" (v. 3). Jesus appears along the lakeside, but as happens in other resurrection appearance stories, the disciples do not know that it is he (v. 4). Affectionately, he asks, "Children, you have no fish, have you?" (v. 5). He instructs them to throw the net off the right side of the boat, which they do, and they haul in 153 large fish without tearing the net (vv. 6–11).

Meanwhile, "the disciple whom Jesus loved" recognizes Jesus and says to Peter, "It is the Lord!" (v. 7). Peter pulls on some clothes, jumps into the water, and swims to the shore. The Beloved Disciple, the important authority figure for John's community, recognizes Jesus; he who had believed without seeing Jesus (20:8), now sees Jesus, whereas Peter, who had believed because he saw Jesus, does not this time recognize him.

Meals of bread and fish are hugely important in all the Gospels. In Christian visual art, meals of bread and fish are portrayed long before symbolic meals of bread and wine are. As the Emmaus disciples became aware of Jesus' presence in the "breaking of bread," so here, over breakfast, all the disciples "knew it was the Lord" (v. 12). In eucharistic language, Jesus "took the bread and gave it to them" (v. 13), reflecting the community's experience of the living presence of Jesus at the Lord's Supper as the host of the meal.

The next story (vv. 15–19) is a conversation between Jesus and Simon Peter. Jesus, three times, asks Peter, "Do you love me more than these?" (vv. 15, 16, 17). Peter had denied Jesus three times (18:15–18, 25–27); Jesus now, in turn, asks for three confessions of Peter's love. Denying Jesus is serious, and Jesus seems to be asking, How certain are you of your relationship to me now?

The faith of all followers of Jesus is fragile—an important theme in John. But in John's Gospel, Jesus does not reject those who deny or even betray him. Yet Peter is called to a pastoral responsibility: three times Jesus says to him, in response, "Feed my lambs," "Tend my sheep," "Feed my sheep" (vv. 15, 16, 17). Before giving Peter responsibility for the flock, Jesus tests Peter's relationship to him. As God tested Abraham and Jesus, so here Jesus tests Peter—as we should examine the depth of our own relationship to God. When Peter was younger he went wherever he wished (v. 18), even into denial of Jesus. But the mission on which he is sent by the Sent One will lead Peter, as it did Jesus, to lay down his life for the sheep: Someone "will take you where you do not wish to go" (v. 18). Peter's commitment to be a good shepherd of the flock will also lead to the glorification of God.

Fourth Sunday of Easter/Year C

John 10:22–30

The context of this reading is in Jerusalem at the Feast of the Dedication, a new festival begun as a celebration of the cleansing of the temple in 164 B.C.E. at the end of Judas Maccabeus's successful revolt against Antiochus IV Epiphanes. Antiochus tried to stamp out Judaism by ending its ritual practices, including temple worship and circumcision. First Maccabees 1:60–61 says, "According to the decree, they put to death the women who had their children circumcised, and their families and those who circumcised them; and they hung the infants from their mothers' necks." Some Jews abandoned Judaism under the murderous pressure of Antiochus's army, but the Maccabeans successfully resisted. Today this festival is known as Hanukkah and is celebrated for its contribution to religious freedom. Because it commemorates a military victory, it is a minor, noncanonical observance. Had Antiochus succeeded in bringing an end to Jewish faith and practice, there would be no church today.

According to John, "the Jews" asked Jesus, "How long will you keep us in suspense? If you are the Messiah, tell us plainly" (v. 24). There were various forms of messianic expectation prevalent among Jews, but no agreed-upon understanding of what the Messiah would be like. Some expectations were pacifist—the teaching, prophetic or priestly messiah; some apocalyptic expectations were nonmessianic. The belief that the Messiah would be a human being (not God incarnate) was common to all forms of messianic expectation, as was the belief that the Messiah would usher in an age in which there would be no more war, occupation, oppression, or economic injustice: "They shall beat their swords into plowshares, and their spears into pruning hooks; nation shall not lift up sword against nation, neither shall they learn war any more" (Isa. 2:4).

Jews do not see that this has yet happened. Christians tend not to notice that all forms of eschatological or apocalyptic expectation involve such down-to-earth matters as peace, justice, and economic sufficiency for all. Consequently, when Jews and Christians debate whether Jesus is the Messiah, they talk past one another. For Christians, Jesus is the one through whom we have come to know God and God's loving grace.

That is what Jesus talks about in his response to the question put to him. His remark "The Father and I are one" (v. 30) makes this clear. "Whoever has seen me has seen the Father" (14:9). Jesus nowhere claims to have brought in universal peace and justice, nor does he claim to be the Messiah. He speaks of himself as the Son of Man often, but not as the Messiah. In this passage, he does not directly respond to the request to "tell us plainly" if he is the Messiah.

Instead, he says that his questioners "do not belong to my sheep," a sign of which is that they "do not believe." But his sheep hear his voice (v. 27). He gives them eternal life and "no one will snatch them out of my hand"

(v. 28); they are forever safe. In John, "eternal life" is available now, in the present, through faith in Jesus. Expectation of a new era of human history when all is changed and war will have given way to peace has all but disappeared.

Some Jews, Jesus' sheep, believed Jesus and followed him. Some Jews did not. We should be grateful that some did. Otherwise, we Gentile Christians would never have been faced with the promise and command of the gospel. We should be able to understand that some did not. They did not see that the world had been redeemed.

Fifth Sunday of Easter/Year C

John 13:31–35

Today's reading is part of a longer passage that begins at v. 21. To understand the meaning of the "new commandment" that Jesus gives his disciples in v. 34, this larger literary context must be taken into account. Immediately following the footwashing (vv. 12–20), the disciples are at supper with Jesus around the table. Jesus announces that "one of you will betray me" (v. 21). The Beloved Disciple asks Jesus, "Lord, who is it?" (v. 25). Jesus answers, "It is the one to whom I give this piece of bread when I have dipped it in the dish" (v. 26). And he gave the bread to Judas, son of Simon Iscariot (v. 26). At this point, Satan enters into Judas and Jesus says to him, "Do quickly what you are going to do" (v. 27); Jesus remains in control of events, as he does throughout John.

Jesus' giving of the piece of bread to Judas is an act of love. It is a gesture of love to the one whom he knows will betray him to the Roman authorities. "Love one another as I have loved you" is to be understood in the context of this incredible gesture, in two senses. First, Jesus loved the one who was now becoming his worst enemy. Second, Jesus loved his disciples to the extent of giving his life for them. This is not just some general piece of folk wisdom, with the meaning of love left vague and undefined or open to being filled with whatever passes for "love" in the culture. It is love as Jesus loved; love of the enemy, love to the point of giving one's life for the beloved.

Jesus' disciples (and that includes us) always have and always will manage to lack faith, to be unaware of Jesus and the meaning of being his disciples, to fail Jesus and to betray him. Notice that no one at the supper understands (v. 28). Jesus loves precisely such a motley bunch as us. Notice also that Jesus is fully aware of Judas's intentions; he knows what Judas is "going to do." Jesus had already said that "the one who ate my bread has lifted his heel against me" (v. 18). But within the context of a meal with the characteristics of the Eucharist or Lord's Supper, Jesus loves even Judas, clearly the most reviled figure in the Gospel narrative. Jesus' love, a love that extends even to the epitome of the malevolent disciple, reveals a singular God with a singular love. This is what it means to love.

Jesus' "hour" of glorification has come: "Now the Son of Man has been glorified, and God has been glorified in him" (v. 31). Jesus' glorification is his crucifixion, and the process for that has been set in motion with Judas's departure. But John's is not a Jesus-centric Gospel; it is a theocentric Gospel. It is God who has been glorified; it is the *doxa tou theou*, the glory of God, that is revealed in a love that is so radical that it is willing to give up its life for the love of the neighbor and the glory of God.

Jesus' unreserved love for his friends—his ignorant, fragile, weak, and failing friends—is given voice in his address to them as "little children" (v. 33). He explains to them that where he is going, they cannot follow. They will look for him but will not find him; they do not understand. But as Jesus loves even the most reprehensible of them, Judas, so Jesus loves also them (and us) in the midst of their and our failures, misunderstandings, ignorance, and even, sometimes, betrayals.

His "new" commandment is the kind of love that he himself exemplifies for them: "For I have set you an example, that you also should do as I have done to you" (13:15).

As Judas betrayed Jesus, so Peter (vv. 36–38) will deny him three times. Under pressure, we are all ready to deny Jesus. Yet Jesus loves Peter and calls Peter, and us as well, to love as Jesus has loved him, to the extent of giving up his life for his friends.

Sixth Sunday of Easter/Year C

John 5:1–9

John 5:1–18 is a controversy story in which Jesus and "the Jews" are at odds over the Sabbath, a story that ends with the claim, "For this reason the Jews were seeking all the more to kill him" (v. 18). The lectionary cuts off the healing miracle at the pool of Beth-zatha from the controversy to which it leads. While probably done from the best of motives, the effect is to take the first half of the story out of its literary context.

Sabbath is a major theme of the Scriptures, but the term is not well understood by most Christians.[32] Sabbath (*Shabbat*) reminds us of God's intent for all creation, that as God rested after the sixth day of creation (Gen. 2:2), so should we and all those whom we employ. Even farm animals were to be given a rest on *Shabbat*; even the land itself was, every seventh year, off-limits to human purposes (Lev. 26:34). At the same time, *Shabbat* is, like the Eucharist, a foretaste of things to come, an eschatological sign in the midst of time of a future free from toil. One thing is banned on *Shabbat*: work.

While keeping *Shabbat* is a commandment, other commandments override it. "Danger to life annuls the Sabbath, for we are to live by doing God's commandments, and not to die by them" (*b. Shabbat* 1:32a). The rabbis derived this principle from Lev. 18:5: "You shall keep my statutes and ordinances; by doing so one shall live." The following kinds of business may be conducted on the Sabbath: planning good deeds, arranging alms for the poor, business dealing with public health or saving life, public affairs, arranging the marriage or education of one's children, or teaching them a handicraft; "the Scripture forbids 'thy business,' but God's business is permitted" (*b. Shabbat* 1:50a).

Today's reading is framed by Jewish ritual concerns. It occurs in Jerusalem during "a festival of the Jews" (v. 1) and ends on the note "Now that day was a sabbath" (v. 9), setting up the ensuing controversy. The understanding of *Shabbat* is critical to the story. The standard commentary take on the story is that Jesus and "the Jews" differ over the proper way to worship God on *Shabbat*. The difficulty with this understanding is twofold: First, Jesus was a Jew. Second, Jesus does nothing that can be construed as "work"; he simply speaks to the paralyzed man. The alleged offense is that the man was carrying his mat (v. 12), and Jesus' apparent offense is that he told him to do so. The Mishnah lists thirty-nine classes of work that may not be done on the Sabbath (*Shabbat* 7:2). The purpose of doing so was to clarify the meaning of "work."

The historical-critical point to remember about this story is that it arises from the conflict-laden situation of John's late-first-century community. A mutual hostility was apparently generated between two Jewish communities over many things, including the proper way to worship God on *Shabbat*—but not over whether God should be worshiped on *Shabbat*.

Certainly both Jews and Christians should be able to agree that the deed of loving-kindness involved in healing the paralyzed is God's business and should be done on *Shabbat*. After all, as Rabbi Joshua ben Levi said, "On Sabbath, a man should always walk with an easy and leisurely gait, but to do a good act, a man should always run, even on Sabbath" (*Midrash Tanhuma, Bereshit* 2).

That more people are in the mall on Sundays than in church should give preachers pause before they denigrate the Sabbath.

Ascension of the Lord/Year C

Luke 24:44–53

Please see the Ascension of the Lord/Years A, B, and C for the commentary on this passage.

Seventh Sunday of Easter/Year C

John 17:20–26

Today's reading ends Jesus' concluding prayer. (Commentary on 17:6–19 is found in the Seventh Sunday of Easter, Year B.) As Jesus earlier prayed, "I have made your name known to those whom you gave me from the world" (v. 6), so here he prays "on behalf of these, but also on behalf of those who will believe in me through their word" (v. 20). Reversing our customary expectations—we typically pray to God in the name of Jesus—here, Jesus prays to God for us. This is Jesus in his pastoral or priestly role.

Jesus and God mutually abide in one another: "You, Father, are in me and I am in you." Jesus prays that this mutuality and difference may characterize his disciples in their relationships with each other and with God and Jesus: "May they also be in us" (v. 21). He continues: "The glory that you have given me I have given them, so that they may be one, as we are one, I in them and you in me, that they may become completely one" (vv. 22–23).

The prayer has both a present and a future reference. It is a prayer, first, that the disciples whom God gave to Jesus may be one and, second, that those who "will believe" may be one and these present and future disciples may "become" one. Unity is never a fixed reality to be taken for granted as accomplished. Rather, it is an ongoing gift from God, who makes it possible for us, and an ongoing demand if we are, indeed, to carry out our mission of bringing "the world" to the knowledge that "you have sent me and have loved them even as you have loved me" (v. 23). This one-ness remains an imperative task that lies before the churches.

As Jesus has made God known to those of us who come to know God in, through and by means of Jesus, so Jesus hands over to us what had been his mission of making God known to the ensuing generations of people who come to know, trust, and place their ultimate confidence in God through the witness of the church.

The Johannine themes of glory (13:31–32) and love (13:1), which are heavily stressed in the Gospel, return to prominence in this prayer. Jesus says that he has given to his followers "the glory that you have given me" (v. 22), and he concludes his prayer with the claim that he will make God's name known "so that the love with which you have loved me may be in them, and I in them" (v. 26). If indeed love, in the sense of genuine unity and not merely as some vague feeling, is in Jesus' disciples, then Jesus is in them (or in us, to bring the point home). The corollary is that if such oneness is not in us, then Jesus is not in us, with the proviso, lest that comment be harsh, that Jesus nonetheless loves his fragile and faltering disciples.

The God of Israel was made known to the Israel of God through the glory of God, the *kabod YHWH*. The same glory of God is made known to Jesus' followers through the mutual abiding in love between the Father and Jesus and between the Father and Jesus and Jesus' followers, all of them, then and now. Not only that, but this oneness has been made *visible* in and through the gift of Jesus, the Sent One of God (17:3; 3:16) and is to be made visible in the oneness that characterizes the life of the sent ones of the Sent One. Jesus here prays that this oneness, this mutual indwelling, will in fact be the case. It is both a gift ("I have given them," v. 22) and an as yet to be realized actuality (so that this love "may be in them," v. 26). In working for unity, we are not asked to accomplish anything other than what has already been given to us. It should not be as difficult as we make it.

Day of Pentecost/Year C

John 14:8–17

Chapter 14 focuses on Jesus' imminent departure from his disciples. Jesus engages in a tender conversation with his anxious disciples, who dread his going and do not understand its meaning. Twice Jesus says to them, "Do not let your hearts be troubled"; the second time he adds, "and do not let them be afraid" (vv. 1, 27). Verses 1–7 focus on Thomas's fears and lack of understanding: "Lord, we do not know where you are going. How can we know the way?" (v. 5). Jesus' answer, "I am the way" (v. 6), is a reassuring word spoken to a perturbed disciple. Thomas's early, naive faith has been rattled. His question and Jesus' answer constitute a quest for reassurance (the earlier assurance having been shaken) and a reassuring reply.

That is the context in which today's passage is set. Jesus has just said that "no one comes to the Father except through me" (v. 6) in his attempt to reassure Thomas. This statement is a doxology—you should praise God for having been given reliable access to God's grace. It should not be turned into a hammer with which to beat non-Christians. But Philip now says, "Lord, show us the Father, and we will be satisfied" (v. 8). The first attempt at reassuring the disciples, fearful over Jesus' impending absence as he goes to his "father's house" (v. 2), has not succeeded in calming their nerves. Philip remains unsatisfied and asks to see the Father.

It is understandable that the disciples are disquieted by Jesus' impending absence. A crisis that hangs over the entire New Testament is not only that Jesus has gone away but that his promised return has not yet taken place. Ever since the church has lived in the "in-between" time, and John's community seems to have lived in that time more intensely than most others. The church today continues to live in the in-between time. John's message to us is pastoral, as Jesus' words to Thomas and Philip and the early community were pastoral: Do not let your hearts be troubled, neither let them be afraid.

Jesus' reassuring words to Philip are "Whoever has seen me has seen the Father" (v. 9). As God dwelt in the midst of the people Israel (Exod. 25:8), so God dwells now in their midst in one member of the people Israel—Jesus. Just as God once acted out of utter grace to covenant with a physical people—which was the only way that God could make an unreservedly gracious covenant—and so sank a carnal anchor in the world, so here God is incarnate in Jesus.

John's Christology is not Jesus-centric, however; it is theocentric: "The words that I say to you I do not speak on my own; but the Father who dwells in me does his works" (v. 10). Jesus and his Father "abide" (*menein*) in one another, and Jesus is going to his Father's house, where there are many "dwelling places" (*monai*), that is, "abiding places." Trust me, says Jesus. "Believe me [*pisteuete*] that I am in the Father and the Father is in me" (v. 11). This does not mean merely "Think it," but "Trust me" when I tell you.

Those who do place their ultimate reliance on Jesus will, Jesus says, "do the works that I do and, in fact, will do greater works than these, because I am going to the Father" (v. 12). Their weak, faltering faith, evident in their questions, can become a kind of trust that empowers them to do even greater works, greater in that they will do them even though Jesus is absent.

As a final (in this reading) reassurance, Jesus promises them and us "another Advocate," the "Spirit of truth," who will abide with and in us.

Meanwhile, we can pray to Jesus (vv. 13–14), and he will be present when we gather in worship.

First Sunday after Pentecost/Year C

Trinity Sunday

John 16:12–15

Last Sunday's reading dealt with Jesus' farewell conversation with his followers. This week's reading is a discussion of the work of the Advocate, whom Jesus promises will come after he departs. The disciples continue to be disconsolate and fearful. They still have difficulty knowing that they face the same future as Jesus, that, like him, they too will suffer: "An hour is coming when those who kill you will think that by doing so they are offering worship to God" (16:2). Jesus tells them these things and, as a result, their hearts are filled with sorrow (v. 6).

Unless he departs, Jesus tells the disciples, "the Advocate will not come to you; but if I go, I will send him to you" (v. 7). The work of the Advocate will be to "prove the world wrong about sin and righteousness and judgment: about sin, because they do not believe in me; about righteousness, because I am going to the Father and you will see me no longer; about judgment, because the ruler of this world has been condemned" (vv. 8–11). Again, Jesus reassures the disciples that they are not wrong.

The Advocate will make utterly clear the *sin* of those who do not believe in Jesus, the *sham righteousness* of those who try (and fail) to comprehend Jesus on the terms of "the world," and the *counterfeit judgment* that seeks Jesus' crucifixion without realizing that his crucifixion is also his glorification, his crowning moment, his being "lifted up" on the cross. These claims set the context for today's reading.

The Advocate, now called the Spirit of truth, will guide Jesus' followers "into all the truth" (v. 13). Much ink has been spilled and many controversies waged in the history of the church over the meaning of these words. Do they mean that every new truth or every so-called new truth for which anyone makes a claim is that into which the Spirit is leading us? By what criteria do we determine if a "new truth" is actually true? Or do they mean, as seems likely from the entire Gospel of John, that the weak, partly faithful, and confused disciples (that includes us) will increasingly be led into fuller understandings of the truth that Jesus has already been making known to us but that we only dimly comprehend and only partly trust? For John, it is clearly the latter.

God is the primordial ground of the revelation communicated by Jesus and the Spirit of truth. The Spirit "will not speak on his own, but will speak whatever he hears" (v. 13). Just as everything that Jesus had was given to him by the Father (5:19), so everything the Spirit says he will "take [from Jesus] . . . and declare it to you" (v. 14).

In chap. 14, Jesus urged his followers not to let their hearts be troubled or afraid, and he gave them his peace: "Peace I leave with you; my peace I give to you" (14:27). His followers in today's reading (and today's church) still need to hear his words of comfort and peace. Indeed, the Spirit is sometimes called the "comforter," from the Latin *cum* (with) and *fortis* (strength). The Spirit will fortify Jesus' disciples to face the difficulties and suffering that all too often come as a consequence of speaking the truth. Just as a pregnant woman's labor brings pain but the birth of her child brings joy, so the suffering of Jesus' followers will ultimately turn into rejoicing (vv. 20–22). In the apprehensions inherent in this "in-between time," we have an Advocate.

Proper 4 [9]/Year C

Luke 7:1–10

Please see the Ninth Sunday after the Epiphany/Year C for the commentary on this reading.

Proper 5 [10]/Year C

Luke 7:11–17

Nain is a village located in the region of Galilee, about a day's walk (twenty-five miles) from Capernaum. At the town gate, Jesus encounters a large funeral procession leaving the town to entomb a corpse. At that time, bodies were not buried inside villages.

The corpse is that of the only son of a widow. In those days, a woman's social identity and economic security were typically tied to the male who was responsible for her—father, husband, husband's brothers, or son. Because the son is the only male the narrator mentions, we assume that he was the only male left to take care of her. Left alone, she faced poverty and social isolation. That is why the Jewish tradition calls upon the community to provide for widows and others on the margins of life (e.g., Lev. 22:13; Deut. 10:18; 14:14–19, 29; 24:17–22; 25:5–10; 26:12; 27:19; Ps. 68:5; 94:1–7; 146:7; Isa. 1:16–17, 21–25; 10:2; Jer. 49:1).

When Jesus saw the widow, he had compassion for her. Compassion (*splanchnidzomai*) implies feeling another's pain deeply (Prov. 26:22; 2 Macc. 9:5–6; Sir. 30:7; *Testament of Zebulun* 7:2). This reference recalls the compassion that God has for Israel and that the people of Israel are to have for one another (*Testament of Zebulun* 8:1, 3). Several apocalyptic theologians expected that the new age would be one of compassion for all (*Testament of Zebulun* 8:2; 9:7–8)

The procession stops. Jesus approaches the bier and calls to the son to rise. He rises and speaks in the presence of all, thus confirming that his resurrection is real. The resurrection provides economic and social security for the woman's future.

Commentators universally point out that Luke 7:11–17 calls to mind very similar circumstances in 1 Kgs. 17:8–24 when Elijah raises the son of the widow of Zarephath (cf. Luke 4:25–26). It is also similar to Elisha reviving a Shunnamite widow's son in 2 Kgs. 4:18–37. Through these prophets God does, indeed, care for widows in accord with the divine promises vocalized by Moses in Deut. 10:18 and other passages. According to Deut. 18:15–22, Moses too is a prophet. Readers remember that while typical Israelites do not raise the dead, they are to join God in caring for widows in the manner prescribed in Jewish literature.

By raising the widow's son at Nain, then, Jesus does not do something new, but reaffirms the intention of God to provide for widows. Jesus' action also reaffirms the Jewish practice of providing for widows, and the passage implies that the members of the church are to care for widows (and others on the margins of life) in the same way as the Jewish people.

This theme is reinforced throughout Luke–Acts. In Luke 18:1–8, justice for a widow is key to a parable. In Luke 20:47, religious leaders are criticized for "devouring widows' houses." In Acts 6:1–7, the Twelve act in this vein by creating the office of deacon to ensure that both Hebrew and Gentile widows receive a fair distribution of food. In Acts 9:36–43, Peter comforts the community of the friends of Dorcas (many of whom were widows) by raising Dorcas from the dead.

Acting in behalf of widows brings the prophetic concern (Moses, Elijah, Elisha) to life. Moreover, in the sermon at Nazareth, Jesus interpreted such actions as witnessing to the presence and character of the realm of God (Luke 4:18–27). The actions of the community are a practical means whereby God provides for widows.

Proper 6 [11]/Year C

Luke 7:36–8:3

Because the story of the woman who anoints Jesus' feet is nuanced differently in all four Gospels, it is important to focus on this story in each Gospel.

The text is set at a meal in the house of Simon, a Pharisee. In Mark, Simon is a leper, whereas in Luke, he is a Pharisee. Luke makes this change in order to criticize Pharisees. In Mark, the unnamed woman is not a "sinner." Luke designates her thus to create circumstances for a controversy with Simon regarding forgiveness (Luke 7:37). In the first century, the term "sinner" implied flagrant disobedience. Christians often assume that this woman was sexually immoral because hair loose from the head was sometimes a sign of a prostitute (Num. 5:18 LXX; *m. Sotah* 1:5).

In Luke, the woman anoints Jesus' feet to express love for the God of Israel (7:38–39). The expression "have been forgiven" (7:47) is a divine passive, a verb form indicating that God (not Jesus) has forgiven her. The woman's action expresses eschatological joy similar to that of others in Luke–Acts (see, e.g., Luke 2:10; 6:23; 8:13; 10:17; 15:7, 10; 24:41, 52; Acts 8:8; 13:52; 14:17; 15:3).

When Simon does not recognize that the woman has been forgiven and resists her presence in the community (7:39), Jesus responds with a rabbinic practice of telling a story from which to draw a point. A creditor forgave two debts: one of five hundred denarii (a denarius was a day's wage) and another of fifty denarii; the one whose debt is forgiven more loves more (7:40–43). According to Luke's Jesus, the woman had greater debt and loves more than the Pharisee who had a smaller debt and loves less. The text communicates that the Pharisees have an inadequate understanding and practice of forgiveness.

Luke misrepresents the theology of forgiveness prevalent among the Pharisees (and other Jewish groups) in the first century. A scholar explains that for Judaism in antiquity, "Mercy is the attribute which best expresses [God's] nature, and it is shown to all . . . creatures."[33] For example, 2 Esdras says, "I know, O Lord, that the Most High is now called merciful, because [God] has mercy on those who have not yet come into the world; and gracious, because he is gracious to those who turn in repentance to his law; and patient, because he shows patience toward those who have sinned, since they are his own creatures; . . . and abundant in compassion, because he makes his compassions abound more and more to those now living and

to those who are gone and to those yet to come" (7:132–36). Comment-
ing on Exod. 15:13 ("Thou didst lead them in mercy"), the rabbis say,
"Thou hast wrought grace [*hesed*] for us, for we had no works, as it is said,
'I will mention the lovingkindnesses of the Lord' (Isa. 63:7) and again, 'I
will sing of the mercies of the Lord forever' (Psalm 89:1). And from the
beginning the world was built upon grace" (*Mekilta* 9, Montefiore and
Loewe, *A Rabbinic Anthology*). Human beings are to emulate God by
accepting those whom God forgives (*Sifre Deuteronomy* 1).

Luke caricatures Simon in this story to undercut the credibility of the
Pharisees (and other Jewish leaders) of Luke's own day and thereby to help
justify the increasing separation between the church of Luke's time and
other Jewish communities. The preacher needs to challenge this misrepresentation as historically mistaken and theologically inappropriate. Indeed,
by misrepresenting Simon (and other Jewish communities), both Luke and
Christians who promulgate Luke's distorted picture place themselves in the
position of needing the divine mercy at the heart of Pharisaism.

Proper 7 [12]/Year C

Luke 8:26–39

In Luke 4:18–19, Jesus proclaims that as the realm of God becomes manifest, the captives and oppressed are released. Today's passage confirms
this claim and offers a biting commentary on Rome.

Demons appear in Jewish literature to help explain intense evil in the
world. People in the Hellenistic era believed that demons were personal
beings—Satan's assistants—who inhabited individuals, communities, and
physical objects. Demons limited the capacity of individuals or groups to
be what God fully intended by directing aspects of self or community
toward brokenness, chaos, violence, or evil.

Jesus and the disciples cross the Sea of Galilee to the country of the
Gerasenes, a Gentile area in which Alexander the Great established Greek
cities as a part of his hellenizing campaign in the Mediterranean world.
The Romans maintained a significant presence among the Gerasenes to
remind the population of Caesar's power.

When the boat reaches shore, two signs immediately appear that Jesus
is in Gentile territory: a naked person possessed by demons that lived
in tombs, and swine on the hillside. The demoniac periodically would
break his bonds and run; tombs were much like caves, with bodies laid out
within. Contact with corpses in the tombs would make the demoniac

unclean (see, e.g., Num. 19:11–16; Ezek. 39:11–15). Even more importantly, according to Isa. 65:1–7, Gentile existence is like dwelling in tombs, and Ps. 67:6 (LXX) figuratively speaks of the Gentiles as being bound by chains.

As part of commanding the unclean spirit to leave the demoniac, Jesus asks its name. In antiquity, to know the name of an entity was to have a measure of power over it. The word "legion" designated a unit of about six thousand Roman soldiers. The appearance of the term here is an acid political judgment: The Roman government, a powerful force in Gentile existence, is under the control of demonic forces. Indeed, Caesarism is here metaphorically described as a demoniac violently out of control. However, the realm of God is stronger than that of Rome, for Jesus casts out Legion.

The Jewish community regarded pigs as unclean (see, e.g., Lev. 11:17; Deut. 14:8). Even more significant for interpreting today's lection is the fact that Jewish literature sometimes used swine as a figure for destructiveness. Psalm 80:13, for instance, compares an enemy who ravages Israel with a wild boar from the forest. The Romans are such a force. This figurative interpretation is strengthened when the demons beg to enter the pigs and Jesus sends them to the "abyss," an underworld region where agents of chaos are consigned (Rev. 20:3).

The former demoniac sits "at the feet of Jesus, clothed and in his right mind." To sit at the feet is to await instruction as a disciple. To be in one's right mind is to be able to know and serve the God of Israel and to participate fully in covenantal community. The former demoniac demonstrates that Gentiles, including Roman leaders, can be restored when they come into the sphere of the God of Israel through Jesus Christ and the church.

Although the former demoniac wants to leave his home and travel with Jesus, the Savior sends the exorcised person back with the commission to witness by declaring "how much God has done for you," a phraseology reminiscent of Septuagintal ways of describing God's activity in behalf of Israel. Not only is God acting among Gentiles for liberation as God has always acted in Israel, but God will liberate the people from Rome just as God liberated the slaves from Pharaoh.

Proper 8 [13]/Year C

Luke 9:51–62

The narrative of Jesus' travel from Galilee to Jerusalem (9:51–19:27) uses theological-geographical symbolism to represent discipleship as a journey from discovery in Galilee (the final manifestation of the realm of God is underway) through confrontation with powers that resist the realm (Roman-Jewish political complex) to decisive demonstration of the presence of the realm (Jerusalem). Along the way, Jesus instructs the disciples in faithful witness. Acts interprets discipleship as a journey by calling it "the Way" (Acts 9:2; 18:25–26; 19:9, 23; 22:4; 24:14, 22). As long as the community lives before the return of Jesus, it is always "on the way" toward the realm of God. Luke 9:51–19:27 instructs the church for this way and models life on it.

The expression "when the days drew near" has a Septuagintal ring and implies that God has decided that the time has come for the dramatic disclosure of the divine realm at Jerusalem (9:51). The notion of Jesus being "taken up" reminds the reader of 2 Kgs. 2:11 and that God is faithful to Jesus (and to those who follow Jesus) even as God was faithful to Elijah (and those who followed him, e.g., Elisha).

The description of Jesus setting "his face to go to Jerusalem" echoes Isa. 50:7 and Ezek. 21:1–2. God called these prophets to announce condemnation because of disobedience (especially idolatry and injustice), to invite repentance, and to disclose God's promise of restoration. Though they suffered because of their witness, God vindicated them. The mission of Jesus and the church follow this prophetic tradition.

A Samaritan village did not receive Jesus because he was going to Jerusalem (9:52–56). This detail explains why Jesus did not minister to Samaritans, though he commands the church to do so (Acts 1:8). Although the Gospel of Luke refers positively to Samaritans (Luke 10:33; 17:16), God's timetable calls for that work not to take place until Acts 8:4–25. Consequently, the disciples have no reason to call fire down from heaven (2 Kgs. 1:10).

Someone along the road wants to follow Jesus (Luke 9:57). Verse 58 contrasts Jesus' homelessness with foxes and birds, which do have homes, to stress the tenuous character of Jesus' existence, which is the model for the disciples. As noted further at Proper 9/Year C, many ancient people regarded the itinerant life of a religious leader as a sign of faithfulness. Itinerants trusted in their deities to provide "daily bread."

Another potential follower wanted to act out one of the most important responsibilities in the ancient Near East: to respect the dead by giving them a proper burial (v. 59). While scholars debate the precise meaning of Jesus' reply (v. 60), it is best to take it as Semitic hyperbole intended to impress the reader with the idea that commitment to the realm of God is so urgent that it takes priority over all other responsibilities and commitments. The divine realm will have no dead.

We find the same point in Jesus' reply to the next person who wanted to follow Jesus but who first wanted to honor one of the fundamental tenets of Judaism by showing respect to the family by bidding them farewell (vv. 61–62). Pushing the plow (witnessing) to the realm of God takes priority over present familial relationships. The realm of God will reconstitute all relationships in the great reunion of the human family.

As the book of Acts makes clear, all who follow Jesus must recognize the relativity of all relationships and responsibilities in this broken age. They must commit themselves to witness to the divine realm, be prepared for harassment (and even persecution), and trust God to make provision for them during tenuous times of witness.

Proper 9 [14]/Year C

Luke 10:1–11, 16–20

Luke sometimes authorizes an aspect of the life of faith by showing that it originates in or echoes a practice of Israel, was demonstrated (and adapted) by Jesus, was carried out by the Twelve, and hence should be taken up by the early church. Today's passage depicts traveling witnesses to the realm of God in this pattern: the seventy elders of Moses to Jesus through the Twelve to a wider circle as pattern for the church in Acts.

When Moses is overburdened by leading the people in the wilderness, God pours a measure of the spirit into seventy elders from the twelve tribes to act in Moses' behalf (Num. 11:16–25; cf. Exod. 24:1, 9). Similarly, Jesus chose twelve apostles and sent them on a mission to witness to the realm of God (Luke 9:1–6). A larger mission expands to seventy. In Judaism, two witnesses are required for veracity, so the missionaries go in pairs. In Acts, this pattern is adapted in the early church.

Jesus empowers the seventy with words and power similar to his own to announce and work the signs of the divine realm. Those who reject the testimony of the seventy reject not only the missionaries but also Jesus and God (10:16).

Jewish literature frequently refers to the realm of God as a "harvest" (e.g., Isa. 27:12; *2 Baruch* 70:2; 2 Esd. 4:26–29). The seventy are to announce the final manifestation of this realm (10:9). The witnesses travel like lambs in the midst of wolves because many people resist the divine realm (v. 3). In the manner of 2 Kgs. 4:29, they give no customary greetings along the road because their mission is urgent. When they visit a house and its inhabitants share in the peace that comes from embracing the divine realm, the peace will abide, but if the residents resist the realm, they will be left in the turmoil of the old age. The missionaries will depart feeling the peace that comes from knowing they are doing their part to witness to the realm (vv. 5–6).

The seventy carry no purse (for money) or bag (for provisions; v. 4). The missionaries are to trust local residents to provide them with housing and food (v. 7). Traveling religious and philosophical leaders often lived in this itinerant fashion. Many people in the ancient world believed that local provision for such travelers was a sign of divine approval. Itinerants were faithful as they trusted each new day for bread.

When a town refuses to affirm the divine realm through the ministry of Jesus, the witnesses are to wipe the dust of that community from themselves (vv. 10–11). To carry earth from one place to another was to transport the sphere of authority represented by the earth (2 Kgs. 5:17). By shaking off the dust, the witnesses leave behind the old-age influences of such towns. As prophets, they announce that such settlements will meet a fate worse than Sodom at the last judgment (v. 11; cf. Gen. 19:24–28).

True to Jesus' word, the missionaries embody the divine realm by subduing demons (v. 17). They have authority over snakes and scorpions (symbols of evil: Ps. 58:3–4; Sir. 21:2) and over Satan's emissaries (v. 18). While Satan still exercises power, that ability is temporary, for Satan has been cast out of heaven, the source of ultimate power, and will be destroyed at the apocalypse (v. 18; cf. Isa. 14:11).

The travelers (and the church) are not to take undue joy from casting out demons in the tormented and temporary present. The deeper joy is that their names are written in heaven (v. 20). Luke refers to a book that God inscribes with the names of the faithful to assure readers that they will be included with the faithful of Israel in the new world (e.g., Exod. 32:32–33; Ps. 69:28; Dan. 12:1; *1 Enoch* 47:3).

Proper 10 [15]/Year C

Luke 10:25–37

Luke introduces the parable of the Good Samaritan as a commentary, a *midrash*, on the commandment to love God and the neighbor (vv. 25–28). Rabbinic parables, mostly later than the time of Luke, were often used to interpret Scripture or make clear how people are to behave.[34] Luke uses his parable to do both.

Luke changes the story about the commandments that he receives from Mark in a couple of ways. First, a lawyer asks his question "to test Jesus."

In Mark's version (12:28), a scribe approaches Jesus because he notices that Jesus answers questions well, and he asks which commandment is "first of all." Some interpreters claim that Luke understands the question to be intentionally hostile. If so, Luke imports the hostility into a story from which it was missing. It was the nature of teachers in Israel (as in seminaries and universities today) to question each other. We should all be open to question and willing to question. There is nothing wrong with questions; without them there are no answers.

Second, although Jesus' answer quotes Deut. 6:5 and Lev. 19:18 (see Mark 12:29–30), Luke nonetheless differs from Mark here too. In Mark, Jesus answers the question by quoting the Shema: "The first is, 'Hear, O Israel: the Lord our God, the Lord is one; you shall love the Lord. . . .'" Luke drops the Shema. For Jews, the first commandment begins "I am the LORD your God, who brought you out of the land of Egypt, out of the house of slavery; you shall have no other gods before me" (Exod. 20:2–3). The first word is one of grace, of what God has done for Israel. The rest are Israel's loving response to God's gracious love. Law is rooted in grace; grace is lived out in law (*torah*, "way of life").

Josephus tells us that organized gangs of bandits made travel dangerous (*Jewish War* 2, 228–30). Peasants who heard this story might well have thought of the man as rich and having something worth stealing, wealth gotten at the expense of their poverty. They may have thought him unusually foolish to be traveling alone on a bandit-infested road. In any case, he was mugged, robbed, and left for dead. Two ordained people, a priest and a Levite, scurry past, leaving plenty of leeway between themselves and the man in the ditch. That the ordained do not practice the commandment to love their neighbors as themselves should give preachers pause.

This parable is a layperson's joke on the clergy. The contrasting term to "priest and Levite" would have been "Israelite" or *am ha-aretz*, "person of the land." Luke turns the man who comes to the aid of the victim into a Samaritan, giving the parable a different twist (Luke was interested in the mission to the Samaritans, e.g., Acts 8:25). We should turn it into the "parable of the good Jew" or "the good layperson."

The parable is intentionally provocative. It is not syrupy. Bandits leave a victim for dead. The ordained cannot be bothered. A hated Samaritan in this danger zone of a bandit-infested road risks his own well-being to minister to human need. But the parable has been standard fare in the church for so long that to recover its provocativeness we free it from its frequent anti-Jewish interpretation. The tacit assumption that all goodness must come from outside the people Israel is dismissible ideology.

Proper 11 [16]/Year C

Luke 10:38–42

Genesis 1–2 pictures women and men in mutuality and partnership. Only after the fall are women subordinated to men (Gen. 3:14–19). By the time of Luke, movement toward egalitarianism had emerged in the Hellenistic world, including Judaism. But Mediterranean society was conflicted over whether the roles of women should be restricted, or open to new possibilities. The restoration of women to mutuality with men is an aspect of the realm of God, a theme in Luke–Acts, and figures into today's passage.

On the one hand, Christians sometimes caricature first-century Judaism as only oppressive of women. To be sure, Jewish sources contain some statements in this vein, for example, "May the words of the Torah be burned if they should be handed over to a woman" (*y. Sotah* 10a). However, Judaism was pluralistic on this issue. Jewish literature can celebrate women's creativity, power, and expanded possibilities (e.g., Prov. 31:10–31; *Genesis Rabbah* 47 on 17:15; *Exodus Rabbah* 21 on 14:15). The Rabbis lift up Beruria as a quick-witted woman respected as an interpreter of Torah—for example, when her husband, Rabbi Meir, prayed that lawless people should die, she admonished him to seek their repentance (*b. Berakhot* 10a).

On the other hand, while Luke–Acts shows impulses toward liberation, this material does not portray women as fully self-determining. For instance, Luke holds up Elizabeth and Mary as model believers, pictures the women who come from the tomb as the first preachers of the resurrection, and shows women in leadership in Acts (e.g., Dorcas has a house church in her home). However, Luke does not place a woman in the Twelve or as elder or deacon. Luke's women are more than the handmaids of men, but seldom bold leaders.

Mary and Martha are Lukan women. Luke mentions them in their own right without reference to males. Evidently they owned their own home and determined who entered it. When Martha "welcomed" Jesus, she extended formal hospitality to him: a meal, water for light bathing, conversation, possibly lodging.

When Mary sits, she assumes the posture of a disciple at the feet of a rabbi receiving instruction in the ways of God (e.g., *m. Avot* 1:4). The phrase "what he was saying" ("his word") echoes Jesus speaking the "word of God" (Luke 8:11) and underscores the fact that Mary receives full instruction in the realm of God.

Martha maintains a traditional role. The Greek word that Jesus uses to describe Martha, *merimnaō*, is the same word Luke's Jesus uses elsewhere to speak of the anxiety of the present age that will disappear in the divine realm (e.g., Luke 8:14; 12:11, 22, 25–26; 21:34).

In deference to male authority, Martha attempts to get Jesus to send Mary to the kitchen to reinforce traditional women's roles (and thereby, from the narrator's point of view, to prolong old-age anxiety). However, Jesus says that Mary has chosen "the better part" or "better portion," an expression that often occurs in Jewish literature to bespeak a share in the promised land (e.g., Num. 18:20) or an inheritance (Wis. 2:9; Sir. 14:9) and that here refers to a place in the realm of God that "will not be taken away."

Luke thus depicts Mary in line with the progressive view that was increasingly common in ancient Judaism. Luke assures such women that in the church they need not fear a return to repression but can enjoy a measure of liberation. While a fuller measure of liberation is needed, impulses toward it are already in place.

Proper 12 [17]/Year C

Luke 11:1–13

This teaching on prayer is infused with Jewish perspectives. Other references to prayer in Luke–Acts are to be understood from the perspective of this passage: For Luke, prayer is openness to, and confidence in, the coming of the realm of God.

Many Christians in the previous generation believed that the Aramaic "Abba" ("Daddy") lay behind the word "Father," and introduced a level of familiarity with God unknown in Judaism (11:3). Recent scholarship, however, shows that some first-century Jews related to God with the intimacy of "Abba" (e.g., Hanina ben Dosa, Honius). The Lukan Jesus does not supersede Judaism on this point, but prays as do other Jews.

In Judaism, the speaking of the name of God evinces awareness of the divine presence (v. 2). To hallow (make holy) God's name is to recognize the sovereignty of God and to live in response to God's unconditional love and call for justice. The community is to pray for the complete manifestation of the divine realm.

The central element is the petition for "daily bread" (v. 3). In Judaism, bread is a multivalent symbol for all things necessary for existence (from physical things to meaning in life). Jesus and his followers are itinerant missionaries who need bread afresh every day. Readers who recognize that

God responds to this petition by providing for the itinerants are assured that God will provide for later generations.

Most scholars think that Luke 11:4a changes Matthew's "debts" (Matt. 6:12) to "sins." As we point out at Proper 5/Year A, Matthew uses the term "debt" to include actual economic debt and other forms of indebtedness (marks of the old age). Indebtedness is a form of slavery. To "forgive" (*aphiēmi*) is to "release"; in the divine realm God effects an eschatological jubilee by releasing people from economic and figurative indebtedness. Members of the community witness to the realm of God by releasing others from indebtedness. By retaining the language of indebtedness (11:4b), Luke interprets such phenomena as sin (from which the community is liberated in the divine realm). The expression "as we ourselves forgive" assumes that the community will put this part of the reign of God into practice by releasing community members. To pray this petition is to commit oneself to releasing captives from debt (4:18).

The "trial" in the final petition refers to the great tribulation shortly before the apocalypse (11:4c). The petition asks God to spare the community from passing through that time.

In vv. 5–8, Luke uses a rabbinic mode of arguing from the lesser to the greater. If a tired householder will get up in the middle of the night to provide hospitality (bread for a meal) for a late-arriving guest, how much more can the community count on God (who is loving and just) to complete the manifestation of the divine realm.

The petitions of vv. 9–10 refer not to asking in general but to seeking in behalf of the divine realm. The community can knock in confidence that God, like a good human parent, will not give a child a snake or a scorpion (things that hurt) when the child asks for a fish or an egg (things that support life).

In the final line of the passage, Luke changes Matthew's "your [God] in heaven [will] give good things to those who ask" to read that God will "give the Holy Spirit to those who ask." For Luke, the Spirit is an agent who continues to empower the community to witness to the divine realm in the world, even after the ascension. Even in the midst of adversity, the Spirit is present in the community.

Proper 13 [18]/Year C

Luke 12:13–21

This text exemplifies a fundamental Jewish perspective on blessing and material things. In this view, the human being does not simply *have* a body but *is* a body; the self is not divided into physical and nonphysical aspects, but is a whole. God intends for people to live in abundance, security, and community, and to be free from fear, threat of nonsurvival, and personal and social chaos. In covenantal community, members share material goods with one another so that all are relieved from anxiety about where to get daily bread, and all are free to participate fully in covenantal life and witness. In Judaism, optimum blessing is a community that provides abundantly for all.

Such sharing is a double benefit. (1) By it, God provides for the poor, the widow, the orphan, and others on the margins of existence. (2) Covenantal sharing expresses pastoral care for those who have goods, for it relieves them from the dangers of making wealth an idol. The covenantal view of material resources discourages the wealthy from hoarding and greed—attitudes that create chaos and injustice in community. The attempt to create personal security by hoarding actually brings about insecurity and destruction.

In this set of values concerning wealth and community, an unknown person asks Jesus to tell a sibling how to divide the family inheritance (Luke 12:13). When questions about the division of a family inheritance arose, Torah provided guidelines for just disposition (so that the inheritance would provide fairly for all), and counseled disputants to take their questions to a community leader (e.g., Num. 27:1–11; 36:7–9; Deut. 21:15–17; cf. *m. Bava Batra* 8:1–9:10). While Jesus does not interpret inheritance laws (12:14), he takes the occasion of this request to warn the listeners (a great crowd, 12:1) against greed (v. 15). Life consists not in accumulating possessions but in covenantal relationship with God and community that includes sharing one's goods so that all can be blessed.

The parable of the foolish barn builder illustrates the destructive effects of greed. A wealthy person's land produced so abundantly that storage space ran short. In such circumstances, a faithful Jewish person would immediately share the overflow with the community, as did the reapers who left grain in the fields for persons who had no incomes (see, e.g., Lev. 19:9; 23:22; Deut. 24:19; Ruth 2:2).

The rich farmer, however, tears down serviceable barns and builds larger ones to hoard the crops and other things (12:18). In v. 19, the barn builder voices an attitude that was widespread in Judaism as the epitome of the life that is self-serving and self-destructive (e.g., Judg. 19:4–9; Eccl. 2:24; Isa. 22:13; Tob. 7:10; Sir. 11:19; *1 Enoch* 97:8–9). The bitter irony is that the means by which the barn builder has tried to "lay up for many years" (hoarding) causes the builder's destruction.

The epithet "fool" is a biting word for a person who pays no attention to the divine ways and whose life is consequently cursed. The phrase "this very night" refers to the apocalypse and the great judgment that follows when God will condemn the barn builder because the fool has stored up treasure for selfish use but has not been "rich toward God." In Judaism and in Luke–Acts, one is rich toward God by using one's resources as means of blessing for all in the community.

This text does not simply condemn the rich, but encourages members of the community to use their resources in the service of all (Acts 2:42–47; 4:32–37) and, thereby, to avoid the fate of this barn builder (cf. Acts 5:1–11).

Proper 14 [19]/Year C

Luke 12:32–40

Luke 12:1–13:8 is designed to help the community discern some dynamics, dangers, and consequences of living faithfully as the old age winds through the tribulation toward the apocalypse and the final restoration (see First Sunday of Advent/Year C; Luke 12:1–8, 49–59). Much of this teaching presumes that the community is fearful. Luke assures the community of God's support during the transition of the ages. Indeed, since God provides food and drink for ravens, lilies, and Gentiles, Luke's community can count on divine sustenance during the anxious and painful tribulation (12:22–31). Today's text encourages the congregation to live faithfully as it awaits the great transformation.

The expression "Do not be afraid" was spoken in Israel by God and others during uncertainty to strengthen the community to endure difficulty. The motif "little flock" is a standard Jewish designation that bespeaks the vulnerability of the covenantal community (12:32; cf. Jer. 13:17; Ezek. 34:1–31; Zech. 10:3). God will strengthen the church even as God strengthened Moses, the exiles, and others in adversity. The community need not fear because God will *give* it the divine realm. This expression resonates with Dan. 7:13–14 and reminds the readers that this realm is not the result of anxious human effort (12:13–31) but of divine grace.

Jesus' followers convert their possessions into alms because God will provision the coming era of regeneration (vv. 33–34). In calling the disciples to almsgiving, Luke draws a fundamental continuity between the church and Judaism. Almsgiving is essential to Jewish identity, for it is a means whereby the providence of God becomes an everyday reality for the needy. The willingness to part with one's possessions for others is quintessential Jewish testimony to confidence in the coming realm (Tob. 4:5–11; Sir. 29:11–12; 35:1–2; *1 Enoch* 38:2; *2 Enoch* 50:5). Acts 2:42–27 and 4:32–5:11 picture the disciples selling their goods as other members of the community have need.

Verses 35–40 admonish listeners to remain faithful as they await the complete arrival of the divine reign. Although the specific requirements for faithfulness are spelled out more broadly in Luke–Acts, the fact that these verses immediately follow a call to almsgiving suggests that sharing of possessions is fundamental.

Verses 35–40 employ events from everyday Jewish life to image faithful waiting. People wore their flowing robes loosely when at home but tied them more tightly to be "dressed for action" when they left—as for a wedding celebration. Jewish literature sometimes uses this expression for "ready to serve" (e.g., 1 Kgs. 18:46; 2 Kgs. 4:29). The lit lamps connote watchfulness (see, e.g., Exod. 27:20; Lev. 24:2) and the Christian community joining Israel as "light of the world" (Isa. 42:6).

Jewish literature of the later Hellenistic age often uses a householder's return home to speak of God's final full appearance (with the divine realm) in the world, as in vv. 36–38. Household servants were expected to have the place completely ready for use whenever the householder returned. For instance, they were to have the lamps lit and be awake to unbar the door, a task that could only be done from inside.

The disciples are to serve (i.e., witness) through the long night of awaiting Jesus' return (v. 38). If they do so, they will be a part of a remarkable thing: The householder will serve them a meal (v. 37). Likely this reference is to the eschatological banquet that celebrates the complete instantiation of the divine realm.

Proper 15 [20]/Year C

Luke 12:49–56

As noted previously, Luke 12:1–13:9 prepares Jesus' followers for the difficulties and opportunities of living through the transition from the old age through the apocalypse to the complete manifestation of the reign of God. Today's lection claims that growing tension between the traditional synagogue and Jesus' followers is a part of the tribulation.

Verse 49 uses the traditional Jewish language of judgment as fire (see, e.g., 2 Kgs. 1:10; Isa. 66:15–16; Amos 1:4; *1 Enoch* 91:9; 100:1–2, 9; Luke

3:9). Jesus brings judgment—the separation of the faithful from the unfaithful. The final judgment will not take place until after Jesus' baptism, that is, after his death and resurrection (v. 50). In the meantime, the witness to the coming of the realm of God by Jesus and the disciples offers people the opportunity to repent and to become a part of the community of the new age.

We need to understand the saying that Jesus came not to bring peace but division against the background of the preceding comments as well as events taking place in the Lukan community (v. 51). The division to which Luke refers is the separation of the final judgment; the message that the realm of God is now coming to completion through Jesus will prompt people to respond with either repentance or disdain. That separation is already preliminarily taking place, as the next verses make clear.

Some traditional Jewish households ostracized family members who identified with Jesus and the eschatological message (vv. 52–53). In the economy of the time, family cohesion was essential to the survival of all members of the family, particularly the more vulnerable—the elderly, widows, and children. Also, Jewish identity was rooted in the family—a Jewish person is a person in relationship with others. Religious practice centered in the household. Judaism stressed the importance of children honoring their parents and parents educating their children (see, e.g., Exod. 20:12; Lev. 19:3; 20:9; Deut. 5:16; 21:18–21; 27:16; Prov. 19:26; 28:24; Sir. 3:1–16), and such honor included taking care of parents in old age. Thus, when the parent-child relationship ruptured, the care of the senior adult was jeopardized.

Luke uses vv. 52–53 to justify why some families were going against a core value of Judaism by breaking apart when some members came into the church. By placing these words in Jesus' mouth, Luke justifies this breach of covenantal life.

By placing vv. 54–56 near the end of the long discourse in Luke 12, Luke claims that such matters as those mentioned in this speech are signs that the tribulation is underway and the apocalypse is near. These events include harassment and suffering at the hands of both Roman and synagogue authorities (vv. 4–11), unmitigated greed (vv. 13–21), anxiety (vv. 22–31), slothfulness in mission (vv. 32–48), and family breakup.

In 12:1–13:9, Luke uses motifs from Judaism to comfort the Christian community as it lives through tension with and moves toward separation from the traditional synagogue. The preacher today needs to help the congregation recognize that such thinking is theologically inappropriate and works against the rapprochement now taking place between many churches and synagogues. The preacher particularly needs to caution the congregation that the realm of God does not prompt people to abandon care for others, as might result from today's lesson if children leave the household and no longer honor their parents in the full-bodied Jewish sense. Instead of painting Judaism negatively, the preacher can help the congregation recognize that divine providence supports both church and synagogue when their witnesses to the divine realm bring them into conflict with others.

Proper 16 [21]/Year C

Luke 13:10–17

While the picture of Jesus teaching in a synagogue on the Sabbath (Luke 13:10) affirms that Jesus practiced the Jewish faith, the reader may be suspicious. In Luke–Acts synagogues often are the stages for conflict between Jesus (or the disciples) and Jewish leaders. Such controversies represent disputes between the synagogue and the early church.

Christians sometimes think of Sabbath regulations as legalistic. But from a Jewish perspective, the Sabbath is a divine gift of rest from ceaseless toil, a day of joy that remembers Eden and is a foretaste of the "days of the Messiah." It is also a day that builds up the Jewish community and maintains its identity and witness.

Luke highlights the restoration of women as part of the realm of God. As a further measure of inclusivity, Luke pairs women and men (as in 13:10–17/14:1–6; cf. Elizabeth and Zechariah, Anna and Simeon).

In today's passage, a woman unable to stand up straight for eighteen years appears (v. 11). Her condition limits her activity, and may cause her pain. According to v. 16, the woman's illness results from being bound by Satan. This language suggests that her illness is a form of demonic possession. It has made her a captive in the sense of Luke 4:18–19. When Jesus lays hands on her, she is immediately restored and stands, in Jewish fashion, to praise God (vv. 12–13). This story is good news to all figuratively bent-over women: The divine realm liberates them to stand up straight.

A Jewish leader is indignant that the healing takes place (v. 15) because he interprets healing as work (Exod. 20:9–10; Deut. 5:13–14). However, as Jesus argues, Judaism provided for Sabbath actions to care for one's animals.

Jesus argues from the lesser to the greater in vv. 15–16. Torah directs owners to untie their animals and lead them to water on the Sabbath (*m. Shabbat* 5:1–4; 15:1–2; *m. Eruvin* 2:1–4; *b. Shabbat* 113a; *b. Eruvin*

20b–21a). If people water their animals on the Sabbath, how much more can the woman be unbound!

Christians sometimes think Jesus was almost the first to use the title "daughter of Abraham" as a parallel to "son of Abraham" to mean a full member of the covenantal community. Jewish writers, however, spoke of women in this way (*b. Gittin* 80a; *b. Ketubbot* 72b; *b. Sukkah* 49b; *b. Pesahim* 110b; *b. Sanhedrin* 49b). The Lukan Jesus thus does not depart from Judaism on this point, but speaks in solidarity.

The passage closes with Luke reporting that Jesus shamed the Jewish leaders. The crowd, by contrast, rejoices at this event and Jesus' other words and actions (v. 17).

Luke uses the opposition between Jesus and the synagogue leaders in this text (and in other controversy stories) to explain why the church abandoned certain aspects of Jewish life, such as Sabbath observance: Jesus authorized such changes in the face of arbitrary Jewish legalism. The Gospel writers sometimes caricature Torah and synagogue as legalistic. But the Jewish community understood Torah as God's gracious gift and guide for life, and Jewish leaders sensitively discussed how best to interpret it. Although the Gospel writers misrepresented Judaism in order to justify the church's new and different traditions, today's preacher can point out, without polemic, that the earliest churches believed they were living in the last days and were focused on the Gentile mission. While the church insisted that Gentile converts adopt the spirit of Judaism (Acts 15:28–29), some Jewish identity markers (e.g., Sabbath observance) did not seem as necessary since history would end soon. The preacher can raise the question of whether the church today has enough identity markers to maintain its identity in an idolatrous time.

Proper 17 [22]/Year C

Luke 14:1, 7–14

The setting for this reading is a *Shabbat* dinner to which Jesus had been invited by "a leader of the Pharisees" (v. 1). It follows immediately upon a story (13:31–35) in which "some Pharisees" befriended Jesus and warned him that Herod Antipas intended to kill him. Extending hospitality to Jesus, as some Pharisees did, is in keeping with the deepest values of Jewish faith, which took Abraham and Sarah's hospitality to the three visitors to their tent at the oaks of Mamre as a model for how strangers and wanderers are to be treated (Gen. 18:1–8). As a wandering teacher in Israel,

Jesus regularly depended on the hospitality of strangers to him, a stranger in their communities.

Luke introduces a note of suspicion into his story, however, when he comments that the Pharisees "were watching [*paratereō*] him closely" (v. 1) in the sense of "keeping a close eye on him." Luke's late-first-century hostility to Pharisees surfaces here, in sharp contrast to the earliest writer of the Second Testament, Paul, who never has a negative thing to say about Pharisees.

Then, says Luke, Jesus told a parable to the Pharisees (v. 7). The parable is instigated by the fact that Jesus noticed that "the guests chose the places of honor" at the dinner. Like the Pharisees, he too is observing closely. Luke has Jesus tell the parable against the Pharisees. It should not be preached as an attack on Pharisees, however, but rather against the tendency in all of us to seek the places of honor.

The parable is in actuality a wisdom teaching; it has no story, *mashal*, that would classify it as a parable. The wisdom teaching is, simply, that when invited to a banquet we should "go and sit down at the lowest place" (v. 10), and then, if the host so decides, we may be invited to "move up higher" where we can be "honored in the presence of all" (v. 10). The alternative, to sit at the place of honor and then be publicly disgraced by being asked to give up our place and have to take the lowest place, is to be avoided (vv. 8–9).

This is straight out of the wisdom tradition of Israel: "Do not put yourself forward in the king's presence or stand in the place of the great; for it is better to be told, 'Come up here,' than to be put lower in the presence of a noble" (Prov. 25:6–7). The only thing different about Luke's understanding of Jesus' teaching is that it buys into the honor/shame nature of Hellenistic society. Don't be disgraced (v. 9), but move up to be honored (v. 10) in the eyes of all. The question seems not to be whether to seek the places of honor but how to do so. If that were all that this passage amounted to, it would be unfortunate.

Happily, it is not. Jesus makes a sharp linguistic turn and starts speaking the language of the kingdom of God (although such language seems merely to follow rather than to follow from the "parable"). "Those who humble themselves will be exalted" (v. 11), he says, recalling the kingdom motif that the servant of all is first of all.

He follows this with the teaching that when we give a dinner, we should not invite the well-to-do who can reciprocate but, instead, "the poor, the crippled, the lame, and the blind" (v. 13). (Ironically, Jesus as a wandering teacher was himself the guest of a Pharisee whose hospitality he could not reciprocate.) In their very inability to "repay" us, we will find blessing (v. 14). This is in keeping with the practice described in the feeding of the five thousand where the disciples did the work of the nobodies of the Roman/Hellenistic world and the poor were treated like the royalty and the wealthy. It stands in sharp contradiction to Roman and Hellenistic dining practices as vividly described in the story of Herod's banquet.

Proper 18 [23]/Year C

Luke 14:25–33

This passage is about the cost of discipleship. The gift of God's gracious love and the presence of the kingdom among us now are freely available. But they are not cheaply available, and serving God's kingdom—that is, following Jesus—has its demands. Luke goes all out to make that point clear.

Whereas Matt. 10:37–38 has Jesus say that whoever loves father or mother more than him is not worthy of him, Luke raises the ante and has Jesus say, "Whoever comes to me and does not hate [*misein*] father and mother, wife and children, brothers and sisters, yes, and even life itself, cannot be my disciple" (v. 26). This is powerful language; hatred (*misein*) is diametrically opposed to love (*agapaō*). With its strong family ethic, evident in the worship of the synagogue, rabbinic Judaism has no parallels to this language about hating the immediate members of one's family.

How are we to understand this hard saying, that we cannot be Jesus' disciples without hating our loved ones? Fortunately, the context in Luke gives us some help. Immediately preceding this reading, Jesus tells a parable of a man who invited many people to a dinner. But all of those invited made excuses: I have to see some land I bought, I have to test the oxen I just bought, I have just been married and cannot come (14:16–20). The host responded by sending out his servant and inviting instead "the poor, the crippled, the blind, and the lame" (v. 21).

The banquet is the kingdom. The excuses represent the kinds of ties that people have—to real estate, to work, and to family—ties that keep us from giving our ultimate commitment to the work of God in the world. In the light of the parable, Jesus' teaching about hating our loved ones is not recommending that we feel hatred for them. The parable, and the teaching that interprets it, is not about feelings. It is about choices, decisions. Luke's Jesus will later say, "You cannot serve God and wealth" (16:13).

Christian tradition distinguishes between having an ultimate relation to the ultimate and a proximate relation to the proximate. That is, we are to love persons as persons and God as God, not vice versa. We are to love persons as ends in themselves, not as things to use (even as excuses). Jesus is saying in Luke 14:25–27 that we cannot be like the man in the parable who skipped the banquet because he had married a wife. And we cannot be like the men who said no to the invitation because they had to see to their land and oxen. If we are to be his disciples we must "give up all [our] possessions" (v. 33).

The language is hyperbolic. We are to have a relative love for the relative and an ultimate love (with all ourselves) for God and God's kingdom. We do not start building a house that we cannot finish (v. 29) or begin a war that we cannot win (v. 31). The Rabbis asked, "Who is wise? He who can anticipate the future" (*b. Temurah* 32a). We are to assess critically whether we can finish what we start, whether we can stay the course of discipleship. Can we make the commitment to peace, justice, economic sufficiency for all, and respect for the well-being of the stranger that commitment to the kingdom and following Jesus entail? The parable in 14:15–24 shows how overcommitment to wealth, possessions, or people can result in our refusing the decision to be disciples of Jesus.

Proper 19 [24]/Year C

Luke 15:1–10

Today's reading consists of two parables about the lost and the found. Luke's setting includes "tax collectors and sinners" who came "to listen to" Jesus, and Pharisees and scribes who grumbled that Jesus welcomed sinners. Luke's using the parables as an occasion for Jesus to speak against scribes and Pharisees reflects his theological agenda, not the context in which Jesus spoke the parable.

The parable of the Lost Sheep is also in Matt. 18:12–14, where Jesus tells the parable to his disciples. In the *Gospel of Thomas* 107, it is simple and has no narrative: "The (Father's) imperial rule is like a shepherd who had a hundred sheep. One of them, the largest, went astray. He left the ninety-nine and looked for the one until he found it. After he had toiled, he said to the sheep, 'I love you more than the ninety-nine'" (Funk and Hoover, *The Five Gospels*).

Luke's parable of the Lost Sheep (vv. 3–7) describes strange behavior on the part of the shepherd who, on discovering that one sheep is lost, "leaves the ninety-nine in the wilderness" in order to "go after the one that is lost" (v. 4). This shepherd would most likely wind up with ninety-nine lost sheep. Nonetheless, the shepherd returns home, happy to have found his lost sheep, and calls together his friends and neighbors to rejoice with him. Jesus declares, "There will be more joy in heaven over one sinner who repents than over ninety-nine righteous persons who need no repentance" (v. 7). Luke is unique in interjecting the motif of repentance into this parable. This is in keeping with Luke's understanding of Jesus' mission: "I have come to call not the righteous but sinners to repentance" (5:32).

In a direct reproach to the grumbling of the scribes and Pharisees, the friends and neighbors, like the friends and neighbors of the woman who found the lost coin, rejoice over finding the lost sheep. This may be Luke's own way of grumbling about the grumblers, something of a mixed message. Matthew's point, that it is not God's will that any of the little ones perish (18:14), is more in keeping with the all-inclusive grace of God.

Luke's parable of the Lost Coin asks, What woman, upon losing a silver coin, would not light a lamp, sweep the house, and search carefully until she found it (v. 8)? There is a rabbinic parallel to this parable: "If a man loses a coin in his house he kindles many lights, and seeks till he finds it. If for something which affords only an hour's life in this world, a man kindles many lights, and searches till he finds it, how much more should you dig as for hidden treasure after the words of the Torah, which gives both life in this world and in the world-to-come?" (*Canticle Rabbah* 1.9).

Luke uses this parable to stress the theme of repentance (v. 10). Since it is only in Luke among the Gospels, we have no way to know of other and possibly earlier forms it might have taken. But, similar to the parables of the Pearl of Great Price and the Hidden Treasure, it is about the rule of God.

These two parables themselves, apart from the question of to whom and against whom Jesus speaks them in Luke, are among the most beautiful of the parables. They express the good shepherd's love for all the sheep, especially the lost ones, a traditional theme of biblical Israel, and of our special responsibility to the vulnerable and those in danger, and the rejoicing that should arise upon their being found.

Proper 20 [25]/Year C

Luke 16:1–13

The parable of the Dishonest Manager is one of the most difficult passages in Luke–Acts. Christians often work hard to interpret the wealthy owner as God and the action of the manager as a model for the community to emulate (e.g., the disciples are to be as creative, even cagey, in witness as the manager was in economic life). By contrast, we propose that Luke uses this story ironically to cast a negative light on some Pharisees (and other Jewish leaders). The dishonest manager is not a model but a foil for the Pharisees. They are as misguided as the manager.

Wealthy people in antiquity often left everyday operations of their estates in the hands of administrators who had great freedom to manage the resources. The manager in this story has squandered the owner's property (v. 1). The verb "squandered" (*diaskorpizō*) is also used to describe the actions of the prodigal in Luke 15:13.

The owner prepares to dismiss the manager and calls for an accounting of his assets, an action that calls to mind the coming day of judgment (vv. 1–2). The manager, recognizing the need for employment in the immediate future, reduces one client's bill from one hundred jugs of olive oil to fifty, and for another client changes the bill from one hundred containers of wheat to eighty (vv. 3–7). He cheats the owner and thereby violates Jewish principles of dealing honestly with one another in covenantal community.

The manager has acted "shrewdly" and is a child "of this age" (v. 8). The word "shrewd" (*phronimōs*) also is used in the Septuagint to describe the snake in Gen. 3:1, suggesting that the manager's behavior is in league with the snake who is responsible for the fall. The phrases "this age" and "children of this age" often refer to the present broken world and to those falling under judgment (e.g., CD 20:34). According to v. 9, the manager has made friends for the time after he is terminated in this age, but those who are like him, who accumulate dishonest wealth (*mammon*), face an "eternal dwelling" in condemnation like the rich person of Luke 16:19–31.

Verses 10–12 teach that those who are not faithful in managing other people's resources cannot be trusted with their own. By contrast, the faithful can be trusted. Verse 13 is stark: "You cannot serve God and wealth [*mammon*]." *Mammon* is an idol. Those who serve it—like the dishonest manager—will be excluded from the divine realm.

Verse 14 explicitly connects this theme to Jewish leaders by describing Pharisees as "lovers of money." Luke uses the dishonest manager to stereotype Jews: "You are those who justify yourselves in the sight of others; but God knows your hearts." Indeed, "what is prized by human beings"—making friends by dishonest dealings—is an "abomination" to God, and will be condemned accordingly.

Our interpretation is supported by the literary context. In 15:1–2, some Jewish leaders grumble (as when the children of Israel murmured against Moses in the wilderness) that Jesus and the disciples welcome tax collectors and sinners as part of the reign of God. The parables in Luke 15:3–24 defend this practice. The prodigal, who squandered wealth (15:13), shows that even Gentiles can repent and be welcomed into the divine realm. The older sibling is similar to some Jewish leaders who do not welcome Gentiles into the community that is witnessing to the divine realm (15:25–32). Luke 16:1–13 explains that such people understand the ways of God no better than did the dishonest manager. Indeed, whereas the prodigal squandered resources but repented, the dishonest manager squandered the owner's resources and compounded the dishonesty.

While the passage is not a blanket condemnation of Jewish leaders, it does warn readers against leaders who are lovers of money, as are those in 16:14. The preacher needs to note and critique Luke's use of the Pharisees to symbolize lovers of money as inaccurate while recognizing that the kind of love of money represented in this story does destroy persons and communities.

Proper 21 [26]/Year C

Luke 16:19–31

This is the justly famous parable of a rich man, who is unnamed, and Lazarus, "a poor [*ptōchos*] man." Lazarus was not just poor; he was destitute, hence the use of *ptōchos* to describe him. "Covered with sores," he lay at the rich man's gate and ate the scraps from his table. Only the dogs cared for him—they licked his sores (v. 21). The rich man, in contrast, wore "purple and fine linen" (v. 19), the dress of royalty and the wealthy (Judg. 8:26; Sir. 45:10, Esth. 1:6) and "feasted sumptuously every day" (v. 19).

Amos 6:4–6 describes people such as this rich man well: "Alas for those who lie on beds of ivory, and lounge on their couches, and eat lambs from the flock, and calves from the stall; who sing idle songs to the sound of the harp, and like David improvise on instruments of music; who drink wine from bowls, and anoint themselves with the finest oils, but are not grieved over the ruin of Joseph!" Amos says that they "shall now be the first to go into exile" (6:7). In the parable, the rich man goes to "Hades" (v. 23), the Greek place of the dead, which Luke interprets here as a place of torment.

There the rich man "looked up and saw Abraham far away with Lazarus by his side" and in torment cried out, "Father Abraham, have mercy on me, and send Lazarus to dip the tip of his finger in water and cool my tongue; for I am in agony in these flames" (vv. 23–24). This ploy will not work. John the Baptist had said, "Do not begin to say to yourselves, 'We have Abraham as our ancestor'; for I tell you, . . . every tree therefore that does not bear good fruit is cut down and thrown into the fire" (3:8).

Abraham rejects the rich man's request, observing that he had his good things in his lifetime and "between you and us a great chasm has been fixed, so that those who might want to pass from here to you cannot do so" (v. 26). The chasm was "fixed" by the rich man in his disregard for the sufferings of Lazarus outside his gate.

This parable should be read in the light of Luke's Sermon on the Plain in 6:20–21, 24–25: "Blessed are you who are poor, for yours is the kingdom of God. Blessed are you who are hungry now, for you will be filled. Blessed are you who weep now, for you will laugh. . . . But woe to you who are rich, for you have received your consolation. Woe to you who are full now, for you will be hungry. Woe to you who are laughing now, for you will mourn and weep." The parable encapsulates these beatitudes and woes. Jesus had said that there would be a great reversal, and Lazarus and the rich man experience it.

Not even in Hades does the rich man repent. He is still arrogant, regarding Lazarus as his servant! He wants Lazarus to cool his tongue and to go to his father's house and warn his brothers (vv. 27–28). Abraham responds, "They have Moses and the prophets; they should listen to them" (v. 29). Indeed, the Torah is primarily concerned with the protection of the vulnerable, the treatment of strangers, the plight of orphans and widows, the oppression of the poor by the rich, the cruel behavior of rulers. It is the voice of the vulnerable. And the prophets constantly reiterate these themes. The rich man rejected the Torah and the prophets when he rejected Lazarus.

Strikingly, Abraham adds, "If they do not listen to Moses and the prophets, neither will they be convinced even if someone rises from the dead" (v. 31). Two points are important here. First, Luke affirms and does not reject the Torah. Second, faith in the risen Jesus includes keeping the law by loving, tending to, our vulnerable neighbors as we love ourselves. If the commandments of God and the suffering of the neighbor do not compel us to act, neither will the resurrection of someone from the dead—even Jesus.

Proper 22 [27]/Year C

Luke 17:5–10

This short reading falls into two parts. The first (vv. 5–6) compares faith to a grain of mustard seed; the second (vv. 7–10) says that slaves (servants of the reign of God) should not expect to be thanked for doing what they ought to do. Jesus' servants should give thanks, not expect thanks.

The saying about the grain of mustard seed differs from its parallel in Matt. 17:20, where faith can move a mountain; here even small faith can "say to this mulberry tree, 'Be uprooted and planted in the sea,' and it would obey you" (v. 6). The ability to cause a tree to be moved from one place to another appears in rabbinic literature: "May this carob tree be moved, and it was" (*b. Bava Metzi'a* 58b).

The story begins with the apostles demanding of Jesus, "Increase our faith!" (v. 5). He replies, "If you had faith the size of a mustard seed . . ." (v. 6). Jesus' answer suggests two things. "If you had faith" implies that the apostles do not. Second, even the least amount, if the apostles had it, would enable them to make remarkable accomplishments for the kingdom of God. The language about moving a tree (or a mountain in Matthew's version) is hyperbolic and metaphorical. This is not about making our gardening easier.

Luke 17:1–10 is about the requirements of discipleship. There are four sayings. The first saying (vv. 1–2) cautions Jesus' followers to do nothing to "cause one of these little ones to stumble." The second (vv. 3–4) requires Jesus' followers to forgive those who repent of their sins.

The third (vv. 5–6) leads us to think that those who ask for faith may well not have it. Faith is a gracious gift of God, freely offered to all of us. Like the kingdom, it is already among us. But, like the kingdom, it is also not yet actual within us. We do not have to strain to attain it. We do have to receive the gift of faith and act on it. Not to act on it is not to have it. These are minimal requirements of discipleship. We do nothing out of the ordinary when we steer clear of making someone "stumble," when we forgive, or when we have faith. Without these, we are "worthless slaves" (v. 10).

The fourth saying (vv. 7–10) uses the example of the relationship between a master and a slave to make a point about those of us who are Jesus' disciples: We should not expect to be thanked for doing nothing more than we have been commanded to do. "Do you thank the slave for doing what was commanded?" (v. 9).

The master-slave relationship that Luke's Jesus describes is more Hellenistic in nature—with masters lording it over slaves and regarding them as nothing—than Jewish. A master, says Jesus, would not invite a slave to "come . . . and take your place at table," but would say "prepare supper for me . . . and serve me . . . ; later you may eat and drink" (vv. 7–8). Jewish slaves were not to be treated this way: "When Rabbi Johanan ate meat he also gave his slave to eat, and when he drank he also gave his slave to drink" (*y. Bava Qamma* 8:5, 6c).

Early Judaism expressed the same attitude as Jesus does here. "Do not be like servants who serve the master on condition of receiving a reward, but [be] like servants who serve the master not on condition of receiving a reward" (*m. Avot* 1:3). "If you have learned much Torah, do not puff yourself up on that account, for it was for that purpose that you were created" (*m. Avot* 2:8, Neusner, *Torah from Our Sages*).

Proper 23 [28]/Year C

Luke 17:11–19

The healing of the ten lepers appears only in Luke's Gospel. The story assumes familiarity with the commandments in the Torah pertaining to leprosy that have to do with "cleanness" and "uncleanness," that is, with whether one can participate in temple worship. But in the case of leprosy more was involved. The Torah thought of leprosy as an infectious disease (Lev. 13–14) and made provisions for dealing with it. While lepers were considered to have the disease, they had to announce themselves as "unclean" and to live "outside the camp" (Lev. 13:45–46).

This has all the earmarks of a public health measure designed to prevent the spread of the disease. It is not marginalizing lepers; it is an attempt to protect others from contracting leprosy. The Torah provides, as well, for pronouncing lepers clean when the disease had run its course (Lev. 13:17) and for offering sacrifice and praise to God upon being pronounced clean and reunited with the community (Lev. 14:1–32).

The ten lepers and Jesus abide by the provisions of the Torah. The lepers keep their distance, announce themselves, and cry out to Jesus to have mercy on them (vv. 12–13). He responds simply: "Go and show yourselves to the priests." They do as he instructed them, and "as they went, they were made clean" (v. 14). This event is sometimes presented as allowing healing to take place away from the limitations of the temple, but the Torah does not claim that the temple priests can heal lepers. It simply provides ways for the priest to declare clean those who have been healed.

Then the story takes an intriguing turn. One leper, after being healed, goes back to Jesus, "praising God with a loud voice," and prostrates himself before Jesus and thanks him (vv. 15–16). Then Luke adds, "And he was a Samaritan" (v. 16). Jesus asks after the other nine lepers, "Was none of them found to return and give praise to God except this foreigner?" (v. 18). To the one he says, "Your faith has made you well" (v. 19).

This is puzzling for four reasons. First, why would Jesus have sent a Samaritan to the temple? Second, the other nine were obediently doing what Jesus had instructed them to do. Our last reading from Luke ended with the point that disciples should do what they are commanded to do. These nine lepers do what Jesus commanded them to do and are criticized for it! Third, the nine lepers were also healed. Would it not also be true that their faith made them well? Fourth, in the temple they would have given praise to God as they celebrated their healing and their being pronounced clean. So why is it claimed that only the Samaritan praised God?

Analyzing how Luke edited this story is difficult because there is no parallel to which to compare it. Luke does have a special concern for Samaritans. Among the Synoptics, only Luke has Jesus passing through Samaria (17:11) and entering a Samaritan village (9:52), which Jesus, according to Matthew, strictly prohibited (Matt. 10:5). That is part of the explanation of the enigma—Luke intentionally includes Samaritans in his story. The other part, unfortunately, is Luke's negative attitude toward Jews. Only he has Jesus say, "Not even in Israel have I found such faith" (7:9). Nor does he find it here, in the nine lepers who were healed. But they were healed and, unless healing is possible without faith (even as small as a grain of mustard seed), the nine lepers are besmirched by Luke's bias. The Samaritan's joy need not be accompanied by a backhanded slap at the Jesus-obeying, Torah-observing Jewish lepers.

Proper 24 [29]/Year C

Luke 18:1–8

Today's reading is a parable (*mashal*), the meaning (*nimshal*) of which we are told at the start: "Then Jesus told them a parable about their need to pray always [*pantote*] and not to lose heart [*enkakeō*]" (v. 1). Usually the *nimshal* follows the *mashal*, but this time Luke puts the interpretation up front so that we will hear the story as being about prayer. "Always (*pantote*)" involves determination, sticking with it.

The *mashal* features stock characters—a judge and a widow. The judge does not fear God (v. 2). "Fear" of God, biblically, has to do with being in awe of God, not with "dreading" God. This is Luke's way of telling us that the judge was not wise: "The fear of the LORD is the beginning of knowledge; fools despise wisdom and instruction" (Prov. 1:7). The faithful in Israel are said to "fear God." Luke uses "God-fearers" to refer to Gentiles drawn to the God of Israel (Acts 13:16).

In every society and economy in the world, widows are particularly at risk; the poorest people in the world today are single women and those who depend on them, namely, children and the elderly. The Torah requires that special attention be paid to widows (Deut. 10:18; 14:29; 16:11). "When you reap your harvest in your field and forget a sheaf in the field, you shall not go back to get it; it shall be left for the alien, the orphan, and the widow, so that the LORD your God may bless you in all your undertakings. When you beat your olive trees, do not strip what is left; it shall be left for the alien, the orphan, and the widow" (Deut. 24:19–20). The prophets lay heavy stress on seeing that justice is done to widows (Isa. 1:17; 10:2; Ezek. 22:7).

Sirach 35:17 may be the background of this parable. It says of God, "He will not ignore the supplication of the orphan, or the widow when she pours out her complaint."

The widow "kept coming" to the judge, even though he persistently refused to grant her request for justice (v. 3). He becomes concerned that she will "wear me out [*hupōpiazē*] by continually coming" (v. 5). Consequently, he decides to "grant her justice" (v. 5). The widow's prayer is answered because of the nerve, *chutzpah*, she showed in pressing her case with the judge.

Jesus says, "And will not God grant justice to his chosen ones who cry to him day and night? . . . I tell you, he will quickly grant justice to them" (vv. 7–8). God's "chosen ones" are the Israel of God (Isa. 42:1, Ps. 105:6) and those who have come to know the God of Israel through Jesus Christ.

Remarkably, the message of this parable is to pray like this widow does! She stands in a great biblical and Jewish tradition of prayer, one that involves having the *chutzpah* to challenge God on a matter of justice in the context of a deep covenantal trust in God. It is arguing with God, as the widow did with the judge, as Abraham, Moses, and Job argued with God, as Jacob wrestled with the angel. It is a way of praying that allows us to be honest with God—and why not, since God is the one from whom no secrets are hid.

The widow's prayer is also a matter of praying and working for justice, in this case for herself. But whether prayer is petitionary (for oneself) or intercessory (for the neighbor), it is authentic when it is involved in working for justice (the social form of love). That's the way to pray. No wonder Jesus asks, "When the Son of Man comes, will he find faith on earth?" (v. 8).

Proper 25 [30]/Year C

Luke 18:9–14

This is the second parable on prayer in Luke 18, this one about a Pharisee and a tax collector praying in the temple. Jesus tells it to "some who trusted in themselves that they were righteous and regarded others with contempt" (v. 9). The Pharisee in the parable typifies this attitude, and no doubt some Pharisees were all too self-righteous. Stereotyping Pharisees as self-righteous and scornful of others, however, misses the point of the parable and distorts the Christian message.

The parable speaks to a problem that lies deeply within each of us, the ease with which we turn the love of God into self-adulation, the pride we take in our humility. When we think about it, "I'm humble" seems impossible to say, for we would be praising ourselves for being humble. Christians have long had the problem of taking God's unconditional gift of love and turning it into a condition apart from which God is not free to love, a condition that, presumably, we have met but others have not. The parable is told against this attitude that lurks in each of us.

Luke's Pharisee thanks God that he is not like other people: "thieves, rogues, adulterers, or even like this tax collector" (v. 11). He fasts and tithes. But the tax collector, in contrast, is so overcome with his own sinfulness that he "would not even look up to heaven, but was beating his breast and saying, 'God be merciful to me, a sinner'" (v. 13)! His attitude is a total contrast to the Pharisee. He is honest, straightforward, and looks down upon no one else, and it is he, says Jesus, who "went down to his home justified rather than the other; for all who exalt themselves will be humbled, but all who humble themselves will be exalted" (v. 14).

Most Christians are surprised to learn that this story is typical Pharisaic self-criticism. For instance, Rabbi Gamaliel said, "Do not walk out on the community. And do not have confidence in yourself until the day you die. And do not judge your companion until you are in his place" (*m. Avot* 2:4). Rabbi Simeon said, "And when you pray, don't treat your praying as a matter of routine; but let it be a plea for mercy and supplication before the Omnipresent, the blessed, as it is said, *For he is gracious and full of compassion, slow to anger and full of mercy, and repents of the evil*" (*m. Avot* 2:13). Rabbi Hanina ben Dosa said, "For anyone whose fear of sin takes precedence over his wisdom, his wisdom will endure. And for anyone whose wisdom takes precedence over his fear of sin, his wisdom will not endure" (*m. Avot* 3:9, Neusner, *Torah from Our Sages*).

The Rabbis of Javneh who were contemporary with the Gospels said, "I am a creature of God and my neighbor is also his creature; my work is in the city and his is in the field; I rise early to my work and he rises early to his. As he cannot excel in my work, so I cannot excel in his work. But perhaps you say, I do great things and he does small things. We have learned that it matters not whether a man does much or little, if only he directs his heart to heaven" (*b. Berakhot* 17a).

The Rabbis joked about overly pious Pharisees who walked mincingly to show their piety and bled from the forehead from bumping into obstacles because they walked with their eyes closed to avoid temptation, bent-over Pharisees demonstrating their humility, and the boringly dutiful Pharisees who *always* did the right thing (*b. Sotah* 20ff.). Jewish humor, influenced by the prophetic tradition, is at their own expense. We should develop some Christian humor that is at our expense, tell jokes on ourselves. It would help keep us humble.

Proper 26 [31]/Year C

Luke 19:1–10

Luke's story of Jesus and the "chief tax collector" Zacchaeus is a rewrite of the Matthew-Levi story (Luke 5:27–32; Mark 2:13, 17; Matt. 9:9–13). The story takes place in Jericho, an oasis in the Judean desert, east of Jerusalem. Highly fertile land, it was known for its groves of palm and balsam (Josephus, *Antiquities* 15.4.2). There were a lot of harvested crops to be taxed, which would partly account for how a chief tax collector became "rich" (v. 2). Zacchaeus's name, *zakkai*, means "innocent" or "righteous," but tax collectors did not become rich by being innocent. Zacchaeus will live up to his name in the story, but his comment "if I have defrauded anyone of anything" (v. 8) is something of a quasi-admission that he had, in fact, done just that.

Wanting to see Jesus, Zacchaeus climbs a sycamore tree (v. 4). Jesus invites him to come down from the tree, "for I must stay at your house today" (v. 5). Zacchaeus welcomes Jesus into his house and "all who saw it began to grumble and said, 'He has gone to be the guest of one who is a sinner'" (v. 7). The grumblers are the "crowd" ("all who saw it"), not the usual grumblers in Luke—scribes, Pharisees, and lawyers—but the people. Why would they regard a rich chief tax collector as a sinner?

First, Zacchaeus is not a minor toll-collector or clerk who adds the sales tax to purchases. Zacchaeus is an *architelōnēs*, a big-time tax collector. This is the only time Luke uses this expression, letting us know he is not talking about a minor tax collector. Second, Zacchaeus collects taxes to support the Roman rule and occupation of the land of Israel. If Americans grumble about taxes, imagine how much more we would grumble if we paid them to Berlin or Moscow and how negatively we would regard chief tax collectors. Third, taxes were heavy, with demands of taxes and tributes on top of tithes and offerings and massive development projects to be supported. Fourth, tax collectors and their hired thugs would collect more taxes than they had to hand over to their superiors and, thus, would become rich. If Jesus had actually "converted" many tax collectors, he would have been a national hero.

Luke's Gospel is full of negative attitudes toward the rich: "He has . . . sent the rich away empty" (1:53); "Woe to you who are rich" (6:24); the parable of the Rich Fool (12:13–21). Prior to the Zacchaeus story was that of the rich young ruler (18:18–25) with Jesus' conclusion: "How hard it is for those who have wealth to enter the kingdom of God!"

Given this, the Zacchaeus story is startling, for it confounds our expectations. Here a rich person is not only converted but promises to repay four times what he has extorted from people, thus keeping the Torah requirements for repaying stolen property (Exod. 22:1). God's saving grace is transformative, and this oppressor has been transformed. Later, in Acts, Saul, the persecutor of the early church, will become Paul the apostle to the Gentiles. These stories stand as a corrective to the point of view that claims that God will never forgive and transform oppressors. It calls into question our all-too-ready willingness to label certain people as "evil" and beyond redemption. The old saying, God works through human sin and error, is always good to remember.

The rich young ruler "became sad" when he heard Jesus say, "Sell all that you own and distribute the money to the poor . . . ; then come, follow me" (18:22). Unlike him, Zacchaeus says he will give half his possessions to the poor (19:8). He shares freely with the poor, showing that he is a genuine disciple of Jesus.

Proper 27 [32]/Year C

Luke 20:27–38

Christians sometimes speak of Judaism in antiquity as if it were monolithic. However, today's passage illustrates that ancient Judaism was pluralistic and that Jewish communities discussed with one another how to interpret aspects of Jewish theology.

The Sadducees were a wealthy group within Judaism who were friendly with the Romans and who benefited economically from this relationship. They sought to follow the written Scriptures very closely and to minimize interpretation. Because the resurrection of the dead is not taught specifically in Jewish texts that the Sadducees regarded as authoritative, they did not accept it, as Luke 20:27 acknowledges (cf. Josephus, *Antiquities* 18.16; *Jewish Wars* 2.165).

Belief in the resurrection arose among Jews in the Hellenistic age to affirm divine power and justice. God promised blessing to the human family. However, life was cursed with oppression, violence, suffering, and death. How could the community believe in the divine promises when present experience contradicted them? Apocalyptic theologians answered that after the apocalypse, God would end present painful existence and inaugurate a world in which resurrection life would make up for current suffering. Belief in the resurrection was strongest among people who were repressed. The Sadducees, who lived in luxury, had little reason to hope for a better world.

The context of controversy stories in Luke 20:1–26 prepares us to recognize that the Sadducees' question to Jesus in vv. 27–33 is polemical. They aim to undercut Jesus' authority by asking a question that is nonsense, given the fact that they do not believe in the resurrection. Luke, instead, discredits the Sadducees.

The Sadducees presume the law of levirate marriage, which provided that if a husband died and left a widow with no children, the husband's brother would marry the widow and have children with her (Gen. 38:8–10; Deut. 25:5–76; *m. Yevamot* 1:1–4). This custom provided justice in the way of economic security for women. If a woman loses seven husbands, and the levirate provision applies each time, the Sadducees want to know whose spouse she will be in the resurrection.

Luke 20:34–36 reframes the Sadducees' question by describing life after the apocalypse, when God ends the present age and fully instantiates the divine realm. Although often antagonistic toward the Pharisees, Luke shares the hope of the resurrection with them (and with the apocalyptic writers). The Sadducees do not understand this renewed world, for in it people will have resurrection bodies that no longer decay and die (*1 Enoch* 91:10; *2 Baruch* 49–52; 1 Cor. 15:35–49). Resurrected people live forever, for they are like angels (*1 Enoch* 15:6–12; *2 Baruch* 51:10). People now marry because they need to procreate to establish security (children) for their senior years. However, that activity is no longer necessary in the world to come.

The linchpin of the argument is vv. 37–38, in which the Lukan Jesus interprets Exod. 3:6 (a text that the Sadducees regarded as sacred) as teaching that the dead are raised. At the burning bush, Moses referred to the Lord as the God of Abraham, Isaac, and Jacob. Since God is the God of the living (Luke 20:38), the three great ancestors must be alive, that is, resurrected (cf. 4 Macc. 7:19; 16:25).

On resurrection, the Lukan Jesus is not antagonistic toward Judaism, but shares a Jewish interpretation. Resurrection was a way of affirming God's ultimate will for justice. How might today's community describe our hope that justice will prevail?

Proper 28 [33]/Year C

Luke 21:5–19

The Roman army destroyed the temple in Jerusalem in 70 C.E., creating a profound theological crisis in Judaism. What is the theological significance of the destruction of the temple and of the chaotic conditions in Palestine surrounding that event? Today's lection offers a Lukan response.

Jesus speaks in the future tense, as if the events in the text will occur in the future. While the apocalyptic consummation is ahead (21:25–28), most scholars think that Luke 21:5–19 (and the parallels: Matt. 24:3–28; Mark 13:3–23) use the future tense to speak of things that were actually happening during the time of Luke. Luke interprets the events to which allusion is made in this material as part of the tribulation—the time of intense suffering expected shortly before the apocalyptic cataclysm. This passage helps the community make theological sense of things that happened and are happening.

Verses 5–6 evoke Jer. 7:1–14 asserting that God destroyed the first temple because of Israel's unfaithfulness. As in 19:41–44, Luke also sees the destruction of the second temple as God's judgment on unfaithfulness (cf. 21:20–24). Verse 7 explicitly claims that historical events are signs that signal progress toward the apocalyptic transformation. Verses 8–17 enumerate such signs. Verse 8 urges the community to avoid persons who falsely represent themselves as God's agents of cosmic renewal ("I am he") or who claim that the end is immediate ("The time is near"). Verse 9—"these things must take place first"—evokes the widespread idea in apocalypticism that God is in control of the events of the last days and has a plan whereby they take place. The mention of wars, insurrections, and the rising up of nation against nation is drawn from stock apocalyptic imagery to interpret the war of Rome against Palestine in 66–70 c.e., along with other violent outbreaks of the volatile first century, as signs of the tribulation (vv. 9–10; cf. 2 Chr. 15:6; Isa. 19:2; Dan. 11:20, 25, 44; *4 Ezra* 13:21). Elements of nature also indicate that the tribulation is underway—earthquakes, famines, plagues, and astrological signals (v. 11; see also Hag. 2:6; Zech. 14:5; *Testament of Judah* 23:3; *Sibylline Oracles* 8.175).

Verse 12 presumes conflict between the Christian community and some synagogues and Roman political authorities. Some of these conflicts—including imprisonment—occur in Acts (e.g., 4:1–22; 5:17–42; 6:8–8:1; 12:1–19; 13:4–12). As directed in v. 13, the disciples witness to the coming manifestation of the realm of God in these confrontations. Jesus repeatedly gives the disciples the words for strong defenses (vv. 14–15). As noted in connection with Proper 15/Year C, families in the Lukan congregation were breaking apart, and some members had died (v. 16; cf. Acts 6:8–8:1).

God's providence sustained the church of Luke's day through such tribulation events, even opening prison doors and revealing Jesus in glory as Stephen died (v. 18; cf. Acts 7:54–8:1). At such times, the mission of the congregation was to endure (v. 19).

Today's preacher likely does not think that we are living in the tribulation of the last days. Further, as noted in connection with previous lections, the preacher can help the congregation name anti-Jewish polemic in the predictions that synagogues will persecute Jesus' followers. Indeed, for most of history the church has persecuted Jewish people. Nevertheless, faithful witness sometimes brings Christians into conflict with forces in the culture and even with other Christians. At such times, God faithfully supports the community to endure conflict.

Proper 29 [34]/Year C

Luke 23:33–43

The lectionary places Luke's account of the crucifixion on the Sunday before the beginning of Advent. At first glance, it would seem more appropriate for Good Friday. But the lectionary wants to remind us, prior to the celebration of Advent and the one who is to come, not to let sentimentality override our understanding of Christian faith, which deals with the hard edges of human history.

The prior verse (32) mentions two "criminals" as also being "led away to be put to death with him." Luke says that "they" led Jesus and the two criminals to a place called "The Skull" where "they" crucified Jesus between the two criminals (v. 33). In Luke's literary context, the appearance before Pilate, this "they" has to be understood as Roman soldiers. In v. 36, the soldiers mock Jesus, and earlier (in 23:26) Simon of Cyrene is "seized" and made to carry Jesus' cross. Roman soldiers were well equipped and ready to do such a thing. Crucifixion was a Roman penalty, carried out by the army. We should not assume that the crowds did this. Luke's audience was familiar with Roman ways; he did not need to spell out every detail for them.

Rome applied the penalty of crucifixion quite liberally. Josephus claims that thousands were crucified by Rome in and around first-century Jerusalem, two thousand after the death of Herod the Great in 4 B.C.E., and five hundred a day after the destruction of the temple in 70 C.E. Crucifixion was a horrible death. It combined torture (extreme distress to the arms and legs) and slow asphyxiation because of an inability to breathe (Josephus, *Jewish Wars* 7.203). It was typical to crucify the victims naked and to leave them not only unburied (there were some exceptions) but hanging on the cross as a warning to all those who considered revolt or sedition against the empire. It was also common to divide and take the victim's clothes. The "shame" of crucifixion was to have no public mourning, no proper burial, no place for one's loved ones to visit.

The people, who earlier had been screaming for Barabbas to be released (23:18), now stand by "watching," apparently somewhat subdued. Their attitude is changing; Luke will later imply that they repent (23:48). It is the "leaders" and the "soldiers" who scoff at and mock Jesus (vv. 35, 36). Luke distinguishes between the people and the leaders and soldiers, a distinction to which we should pay careful attention. "The Jews" do not crucify Jesus. The soldiers and the leaders (and probably not all of the latter) do.

The target of the leaders' mockery is the messiahship of Jesus: "Let him save himself if he is the Messiah" (v. 35). For the soldiers, it is the kingship of Jesus: "If you are the King of the Jews, save yourself" (vv. 36–37). Jesus never claimed to be the Messiah or the King of the Jews. He spoke of himself as the "Son of Man" and of the kingdom of God. But Luke's leaders and soldiers misunderstand salvation, seeing it entirely in terms of the continuation of life or military "liberation" and not as the restoration of the people Israel through forgiving of sins, including the marginalized, feeding the hungry, or dying the death of a martyr, a witness, to all of these.

One final puzzle is the inscription over the cross: "This is the King of the Jews" (v. 38). Why would Pilate place such an inscription there if he had declared Jesus innocent of such charges (23:14)? Since Mark and Matthew are unaware of Pilate's proclamation of innocence, many scholars have thought that Luke's claim that Pilate made it is an apologetic to an official of the Roman Empire not to regard Christians as criminal and therefore subject to persecution.

Notes

Preface

1. Jules Isaac, *The Teaching of Contempt* (New York: Holt, Rinehart & Winston, 1964).

Introduction

1. See, e.g., Paula Fredriksen, *From Jesus to Christ* (New Haven, Conn.: Yale University Press, 1988); and Alan Segal, *Paul the Convert: The Apostolate and Apostasy of Saul the Pharisee* (New Haven, Conn.: Yale University Press, 1990).
2. See, e.g., Clark M. Williamson and Ronald J. Allen, *Interpreting Difficult Texts: Anti-Judaism and Christian Preaching* (Philadelphia: Trinity Press International, 1989); and Howard Clark Kee and Irvin J. Borowsky, eds., *Removing Anti-Judaism from the Pulpit* (New York: Continuum, 1996).
3. On the history, theology, and contents of the lectionary, see the Consultation on Common Texts, *The Revised Common Lectionary* (Nashville: Abingdon Press, 1992).
4. See Charles Y. Glock and Rodney Stark, *Christian Beliefs and Anti-Semitism* (New York: Harper & Row, 1966). On the role of clergy, see their *Wayward Shepherds: Prejudice and the Protestant Clergy* (New York: Harper & Row, 1971).
5. See E. P. Sanders, *Paul and Palestinian Judaism* (London: SCM Press, 1977).
6. Some helpful texts are Richard J. Cassidy, *Jesus, Politics, and Society: A Study of Luke's Gospel* (Maryknoll, N.Y.: Orbis Books, 1978); Richard A. Horsley, *Jesus and the Spiral of Violence* (San Francisco: Harper & Row, 1987); and Luise Schottroff and Wolfgang Stegemann, *Jesus and the Hope of the Poor* (Maryknoll, N.Y.: Orbis Books, 1986).
7. John Dominic Crossan, *Jesus: A Revolutionary Biography* (San Francisco: HarperSanFrancisco, 1994), 25.
8. Ibid.
9. N. T. Wright, *Who Was Jesus?* (Grand Rapids: Wm. B. Eerdmans Publishing Co., 1992), 95.
10. E. P. Sanders, *Judaism: Practice and Belief, 63 B.C.E.–66 C.E.* (London: SCM Press, 1992), 171.
11. Luke Timothy Johnson, "The New Testament's Anti-Jewish Slander and the Conventions of Ancient Polemic," *Journal of Biblical Literature* 108, no. 3 (1989), 419–41.

Another excellent study is George M. Smiga's *Pain and Polemic: Anti-Judaism in the Gospels* (New York: Paulist Press, 1992).

12. Sanders, *Judaism*, 431.

13. Jacob Neusner, *A Rabbi Talks with Jesus* (New York: Doubleday, 1992), 125.

14. Marcus Borg, *Meeting Jesus Again for the First Time* (San Francisco: HarperSanFrancisco, 1994), 52.

15. Friedrich Hegel, *On Christianity: Early Theological Writings* (New York: Harper & Brothers, 1961), 9; Adolf von Harnack, *What Is Christianity?* (New York: Harper & Brothers, 1957), 50–51.

16. Rosemary Ruether, *Faith and Fratricide* (New York: Seabury Press, 1974), 246.

17. Neusner, *A Rabbi Talks with Jesus*, 125; Paula Fredriksen, *Jesus of Nazareth, King of the Jews* (New York: Alfred A. Knopf, 1999), 52–54; Sanders, *Judaism*, 428–29.

18. Sanders, *Judaism*, 429.

19. See Johnson, "New Testament's Anti-Jewish Slander."

20. Our translation, with indebtedness to Jon Levenson, *Sinai and Zion* (San Francisco: Harper & Row, 1985), 77.

21. Levenson, *Sinai and Zion*, 77.

Commentary

1. See James A. Charlesworth, ed., *The Messiah: Developments in Earliest Judaism and Christianity* (Minneapolis: Fortress Press, 1992); and Jacob Neusner, *Messiah in Context* (Philadelphia: Fortress Press, 1984).

2. E.g., Anthony J. Saldarini, *Matthew's Christian-Jewish Community* (Chicago: University of Chicago Press, 1994).

3. See Jon L. Berquist, *Incarnation: Understanding Biblical Themes* (St. Louis: Chalice Press, 1999).

4. Clark Williamson, *Way of Blessing, Way of Life: A Christian Theology* (St. Louis: Chalice Press, 1999), 13–18.

5. K. C. Hanson and Douglas E. Oakman, *Palestine in the Time of Jesus* (Minneapolis: Fortress Press, 1998), 37.

6. Richard A. Horsley, *Jesus and the Spiral of Violence* (San Francisco: Harper & Row, 1987).

7. Raymond E. Brown, *The Gospel according to John*, Anchor Bible (Garden City, N.Y.: Doubleday, 1966), lxxi.

8. Paul Winter, *On the Trial of Jesus* (Berlin: de Gruyter & Co., 1961), 59.

9. James A. Sanders, *Canon and Community: A Guide to Canonical Criticism* (Philadelphia: Fortress Press, 1984), 52–60.

10. Rudolph Schnackenburg, *The Gospel according to St. John*, vol. 2 (New York: Seabury Press, 1982), 154.

11. Paula Fredriksen, *From Jesus to Christ* (New Haven, Conn.: Yale University Press, 1988), 18.

12. Elaine Pagels, *The Origin of Satan* (New York: Vintage Books, 1995), xvii.

13. George Nickelsburg, *Jewish Literature between the Bible and the Mishnah* (Philadelphia: Fortress Press, 1981), 223.

14. See Clemens Thoma and Michael Wyschogrod, eds. *Parable and Story in Judaism and Christianity* (New York: Paulist Press, 1989).

15. Chrysostom, *Homilies on the Gospel of Matthew* 68.1, cited in Thoma and Wyschogrod, eds., *Parable and Story*, 83.

16. Jacob Neusner, *Messiah in Context: Israel's History and Destiny in Formative Judaism* (Philadelphia: Fortress Press, 1984).

17. See Joachim Jeremias, *The Parables of Jesus* (London: SCM Press, 1954).

18. Bruce L. Shelley, *Church History in Plain Language* (Waco, Tex.: Word Books, 1982), 59.

19. Cited in Leonard Swidler, "The Jewishness of Jesus," *Journal of Ecumenical Studies*, 18, no. 1, 106.

20. Neusner, *Messiah in Context*, xxi. That "there was a ('the') messianic idea in Judaism is to produce a picture we cannot replicate in any single and distinctive group and its definitive system of thought and life" (xxi).

21. See E. P. Sanders, *Judaism: Practice and Belief, 63 B.C.E.–66 C.E.* (Philadelphia: Trinity Press International, 1992), 458–90.

22. Mark mentions six different "official" groups of Jews—scribes, Pharisees, elders, chief priests, Herodians, and the Council—a total of forty-five times. Each mention is disparaging.

23. Raymond E. Brown, *The Community of the Beloved Disciple* (New York: Paulist Press, 1979), 59–91.

24. *The Midrash on the Psalms*, trans. William G. Braude (New Haven, Conn.: Yale University Press, 1959), 1:542.

25. Fredriksen, *From Jesus to Christ*, 119.

26. Cf. John Nolland, *Luke 18:35–24:53*, Word Biblical Commentary (Dallas: Word Books, 1993), 1213.

27. Jon Berquist, *Ancient Wine, New Wineskins: The Lord's Supper in Old Testament Perspective* (St. Louis: Chalice Press, 1991), 57.

28. See the discussion of Roman ways of dining in Galilee and Judea in John Dominic Crossan and Jonathan L. Reed, *Excavating Jesus: Beneath the Stones, Behind the Texts* (San Francisco: HarperSanFrancisco, 2002), 103–8.

29. Massey Shepherd Jr., "The Gospel according to John," in *The Interpreter's One-Volume Commentary on the Bible*, edited by Charles Laymon (Nashville: Abingdon Press, 1971), 712.

30. Crossan and Reed, *Excavating Jesus*, 168.

31. See, e.g., Ellis Rivkin, *What Crucified Jesus?* (New York: UAHC Press, 1997).

32. See Richard H. Lowery, *Sabbath and Jubilee* (St. Louis: Chalice Press, 2000).

33. George Foot Moore, *Judaism in the First Centuries of the Christian Era: The Age of the Tannaim* (Cambridge, Mass.: Harvard University Press, 1927), 1:235.

34. See Brad H. Young, *Jesus and His Jewish Parables* (New York: Paulist Press, 1989).

Reference List of Jewish Titles
in English Translation

Ahikar, trans. J. M. Lindenberger. In *The Old Testament Pseudepigrapha*, ed. James H. Charlesworth (Garden City, N.Y.: Doubleday, 1983), vol. 2.

Babylonian Talmud. Ed. Rabbi Dr. I. Epstein (London: Soncino Press, 1938).

Canticle Rabbah, trans. Maurice Simon. In *Midrash Rabbah*, ed. H. Freedman and Maurice Simon (London: Soncino Press, 1939), vol. 9.

Charlesworth, James H., ed. *The Old Testament Pseudepigrapha: Apocalyptic Literature and Testaments* (Garden City, N.Y.: Doubleday, 1983), vol. 1.

Danby, Herbert, trans. *The Mishnah* (London: Oxford University Press, 1933).

Damascus Document in *The Dead Sea Scrolls Translated: The Qumran Texts in English*. 2d ed. Trans. Florentino Garcia Martinez (Grand Rapids: Wm. B. Eerdmans Publishing Co., 1996), 33–45.

Exodus Rabbah, trans. S. M. Lehrman. In *Midrash Rabbah*, ed. H. Freedman and Maurice Simon (London: Soncino Press, 1939), vol. 3.

Fathers According to Rabbi Nathan, The. Trans. Judah Goldin. Yale Judaica Series (New Haven, Conn.: Yale University Press, 1955), vol. 10.

Genesis Apocryphon in *The Dead Sea Scrolls*. Trans. Geza Vermes (Westerman: Limited Editions Club, 1966), 205–14. Standard abbreviation: IQapGen.

Genesis Rabbah in *Midrash Rabbah*. Ed. H. Freedman and Maurice Simon. Trans. J. Israelstam and Judah Slotkin (London: Soncino Press, 1939), vols. 1 and 2.

Gospel of Thomas, The. In *The Five Gospels*, trans. and commentary by Robert W. Funk, Roy W. Hoover, and the Jesus Seminar (New York: Macmillan Publishing Co., 1993).

Jerusalem Talmud in Jacob Neusner, *The Talmud of the Land of Israel: An Academic Commentary to the Second, Third and Fourth Divisions*. University of South Florida Academic Commentary Series (Atlanta: Scholars Press, 1988). This commentary contains a full translation.

Leviticus Rabbah in *Midrash Rabbah*. H. Freedman and Maurice Simon. Ed. and trans. (London: Soncino Press, 1939), vol. 4.

Josephus. *Against Apion*. Trans. H. St. J. Thackeray. Loeb Classical Library (Cambridge, Mass.: Harvard University Press, 1926).

————. *The Antiquities of the Jews*. Trans. H. St. J. Thackeray, Ralph Marcus, Allen Wikgren, and Louis H. Feldman. Loeb Classical Library (Cambridge, Mass.: Harvard University Press, 1926–1965), vols. 4–10.

————. *The Jewish Wars*. Trans. H. St. J. Thackeray. Loeb Classical Library (Cambridge, Mass.: Harvard University Press, 1927).

Mekilta Exodus in *Mekilta de-Rabbi Ishmael*. (Philadelphia: Jewish Publication Society, 1933).

Mekilta de-Rabbi Ishmael. English and Hebrew. Trans. and ed. Jacob Z. Lauterbach (New York: Jewish Publication Society of America, 1933–35), 3 vols.

Midrash on Psalms, The. Trans. William G. Braude. Yale Judaica Series (New Haven, Conn.: Yale University Press, 1959).

Midrash Tanhuma: Translated into English with Introduction, Indices and Brief Notes. Trans. John T. Townsend (Hoboken, N.J.: KTAV Publishing House, 1989).

Neusner, Jacob, trans. *Torah From Our Sages: Pirke Avot* (Dallas: Rossel Books, 1984).

Philo. "On Abraham." In *Philo*, trans. F. H. Coalson and G. H. Whitaker. Loeb Classical Library (Cambridge, Mass.: Harvard University Press, 1935), vol. 6.

————. "On Dreams." In *Philo*, trans. F. H. Coalson and G. H. Whitaker. Loeb Classical Library (Cambridge, Mass.: Harvard University Press, 1934), vol. 5.

————. "On Flight and Finding." In *Philo*, trans. F. H. Coalson and G. H. Whitaker. Loeb Classical Library (Cambridge, Mass.: Harvard University Press, 1934), vol. 5.

————. "On the Special Laws." In *Philo*, trans. F. H. Coalson. Loeb Classical Library (Cambridge, Mass.: Harvard University Press, 1939), vol. 7.

————. "On the Giants." In *Philo*, trans. F. H. Coalson. Loeb Classical Library (Cambridge, Mass.: Harvard University Press, 1927), vol. 2.

————. "On the Posterity and Exile of Cain." In *Philo*, trans. F. H. Coalson. Loeb Classical Library (Cambridge, Mass.: Harvard University Press, 1927), vol. 2.

————. "On the Virtues." In *Philo*, trans. F. H. Coalson. Loeb Classical Library (Cambridge, Mass.: Harvard University Press, 1939), vol. 8.

————. "Questions and Answers on Genesis." In *Philo Supplement*, trans. Ralph Marcus. Loeb Classical Library (Cambridge, Mass.: Harvard University Press, 1953).

————. "On the Unchangeableness of God." In *Philo*, trans. F. H. Coalson and G. H. Whitaker. Loeb Classical Library (Cambridge, Mass.: Harvard University Press, 1930).

————. "The Embassy to Gaius." In *Philo*, trans. F. H. Coalson. Loeb Classical Library (Cambridge, Mass.: Harvard University Press, 1962), vol. 10.

Sibylline Oracles, trans. John H. Collins. In *The Old Testament Pseudepigrapha: Apocalyptic Literature and Testaments*, ed. James H. Charlesworth (Garden City, N.Y.: Doubleday, 1983), vol. 1.

Sifra: An Analytical Translation. Trans. Jacob Neusner. Brown Judaica Series (Atlanta: Scholars Press, 1988).

Sifre Deuteronomy. Trans. Reuven Hammer. Yale Judaica Series (New Haven, Conn.: Yale University Press, 1986).

Testament of Benjamin in "Testaments of the Twelve Patriarchs," trans. H. C. Kee. In *The Old Testament Pseudepigrapha: Apocalyptic Literature and Testaments*, ed. James H. Charlesworth (Garden City, N.Y.: Doubleday, 1983), vol. 1.

Testament of Dan in "Testaments of the Twelve Patriarchs," trans. H. C. Kee. In *The Old Testament Pseudepigrapha: Apocalyptic Literature and Testaments*, ed. James H. Charlesworth (Garden City, N.Y.: Doubleday, 1983), vol. 1.

Testament of Gad in "Testaments of the Twelve Patriarchs," trans. H. C. Kee. In *The Old Testament Pseudepigrapha: Apocalyptic Literature and Testaments*, ed. James H. Charlesworth (Garden City, N.Y.: Doubleday, 1983), vol. 2.

Testament of Judah in "Testaments of the Twelve Patriarchs," trans. H. C. Kee. In *The Old Testament Pseudepigrapha: Apocalyptic Literature and Testaments*, ed. James H. Charlesworth (Garden City, N.Y.: Doubleday, 1983), vol. 1.

Testament of Naphtali in "Testaments of the Twelve Patriarchs," trans. H. C. Kee. In *The Old Testament Pseudepigrapha: Apocalyptic Literature and Testaments*, ed. James H. Charlesworth (Garden City, N.Y.: Doubleday, 1983), vol. 1.

Testament of Zebulon in "Testaments of the Twelve Patriarchs," trans. H. C. Kee. In *The Old Testament Pseudepigrapha: Apocalyptic Literature and Testaments*, ed. James H. Charlesworth (Garden City, N.Y.: Doubleday, 1983), vol. 1.

Bibliography

Berquist, Jon L. *Ancient Wine, New Wineskins: The Lord's Supper in Old Testament Perspective.* St. Louis: Chalice Press, 1991.

———. *Incarnation: Understanding Biblical Themes.* St. Louis: Chalice Press, 1999.

Borg, Marcus. *Meeting Jesus Again for the First Time.* San Francisco: HarperSanFrancisco, 1994.

Braude, William G., trans. *The Midrash on the Psalms.* New Haven, Conn.: Yale University Press, 1959.

Brown, Raymond E. *The Community of the Beloved Disciple.* New York: Paulist Press, 1979.

Cassidy, Richard J. *Jesus, Politics, and Society: A Study of Luke's Gospel.* Maryknoll, N.Y.: Orbis Books, 1978.

Charlesworth, James H., ed. *The Messiah: Developments in Earliest Judaism and Christianity.* Minneapolis: Fortress Press, 1992.

Consultation on Common Texts. *The Revised Common Lectionary.* Nashville: Abingdon Press, 1992.

Crossan, John Dominic. *Jesus: A Revolutionary Biography.* San Francisco: HarperSanFrancisco, 1994.

Crossan, John Dominic, and Jonathan L. Reed. *Excavating Jesus: Beneath the Stones, Behind the Texts.* New York: HarperSanFrancisco, 2002.

Flusser, David. "A New Sensitivity in Judaism and the Christian Message." *Encounter Today* 4, no. 4 (1969).

Fredriksen, Paula. *From Jesus to Christ.* New Haven, Conn.: Yale University Press, 1988.

———. *Jesus of Nazareth, King of the Jews.* New York: Alfred A. Knopf, 1999.

Glock, Charles Y., and Rodney Stark. *Christian Beliefs and Anti-Semitism.* New York: Harper & Row, 1966.

Hanson, K. C., and Douglas E. Oakman. *Palestine in the Time of Jesus.* Minneapolis: Fortress Press, 1998.

Harnack, Adolf von. *What Is Christianity?* New York: Harper & Brothers, 1957.

Hegel, Friedrich. *On Christianity: Early Theological Writings.* New York: Harper & Brothers, 1961.

Heschel, Abraham Joshua. *The Sabbath: Its Meaning for Modern Man*. New York: Farrar, Straus & Giroux, 1951.

Horsley, Richard A. *Jesus and Empire*. Minneapolis: Fortress Press, 2003.

———. *Jesus and the Spiral of Violence*. San Francisco: Harper & Row, 1987.

Jeremias, Joachim. *The Parables of Jesus*. London: SCM Press, 1954.

Johnson, Luke T. "The New Testament's Anti-Jewish Slander and the Conventions of Ancient Polemic." *Journal of Biblical Literature* 108, no. 3 (1989): 419–41.

Kee, Howard Clark, and Irvin J. Borowsky, eds. *Removing Anti-Judaism from the Pulpit*. New York: Continuum, 1996.

Lachs, Samuel Tobias. *A Rabbinic Commentary on the New Testament*. New York: KTAV Publishing House, 1987.

Levenson, Jon. *Sinai and Zion*. San Francisco: Harper & Row, 1985.

Lowery, Richard H. *Sabbath and Jubilee*. St. Louis: Chalice Press, 2000.

Montefiore, C. G., and H. Loewe. *A Rabbinic Anthology*. New York: Schocken Books, 1974.

Moore, George Foot. *Judaism in the First Centuries of the Christian Era: The Age of the Tannaim*. Vol. 1. Cambridge, Mass.: Harvard University Press, 1927.

Neusner, Jacob. *Messiah in Context: Israel's History and Destiny in Formative Judaism*. Philadelphia: Fortress Press, 1984.

———, trans. and ed. *Torah from Our Sages (Pirke Avot)*. Dallas: Rossel Books, 1984.

Nickelsburg, George. *Jewish Literature between the Bible and the Mishnah*. Philadelphia: Fortress Press, 1981.

Nolland, John. *Luke 18:35–24:53*. Word Biblical Commentary. Dallas: Word Books, 1993.

Pagels, Elaine. *The Origin of Satan*. New York: Vintage Books, 1995.

Rivkin, Ellis. *What Crucified Jesus?* New York: UAHC Press, 1997.

Saldarini, Anthony J. *Matthew's Christian-Jewish Community*. Chicago: University of Chicago Press, 1994.

Sanders, E. P. *Judaism: Practice and Belief, 63 B.C.E.–66 C.E.*. Philadelphia: Trinity Press International, 1992.

———. *Paul and Palestinian Judaism*. London: SCM Press, 1977.

Sanders, James A. *Canon and Community: A Guide to Canonical Criticism*. Philadelphia: Fortress Press, 1984.

Schiffman, Lawrence, trans. and ed. *Texts and Traditions: A Source Book*. New York: KTAV Publishing House, 1998.

Schnackenburg, Rudolph. *The Gospel according to St. John*. Vol. 2. Translated by Kevin Smyth. New York: Seabury Press, 1982.

Schottroff, Luise, and Wolfgang Stegemann. *Jesus and the Hope of the Poor*. Maryknoll, N.Y.: Orbis Books, 1986.

Schurer, Emil. *A History of the Jewish People in the Time of Jesus*. New York: Schocken Books, 1961.

Segal, Alan. *Paul the Convert: The Apostolate and Apostasy of Saul the Pharisee*. New Haven, Conn.: Yale University Press, 1990.

Shelley, Bruce L. *Church History in Plain Language*. Waco, Tex.: Word Books, 1982.

Shepherd, Massey, Jr. "The Gospel according to John." In *The Interpreter's One-Volume Commentary on the Bible*, edited by Charles Laymon, 707–28. Nashville: Abingdon Press, 1971.

Stark, Rodney, Bruce D. Foster, Charles Y. Glock, and Harold E. Quinley. *Wayward Shepherds: Prejudice and the Protestant Clergy*. New York: Harper & Row, 1971.

Swidler, Leonard. "The Jewishness of Jesus." *Journal of Ecumenical Studies* 18, no. 1. (1981): 104–13.

Thoma, Clemens, and Michael Wyschogrod, eds. *Parable and Story in Judaism and Christianity.* New York: Paulist Press, 1989.

Williamson, Clark M. *Way of Blessing, Way of Life: A Christian Theology.* St. Louis: Chalice Press, 1999.

Williamson, Clark M., and Ronald J. Allen. *Interpreting Difficult Texts: Anti-Judaism and Christian Preaching.* Philadelphia: Trinity Press International, 1989.

Wright, N. T. *Who Was Jesus?* Grand Rapids: Wm. B. Eerdmans Publishing Co., 1992.

Young, Brad H. *Jesus and His Jewish Parables.* New York: Paulist Press, 1989.